CLYMER™

KAWASAKI

80-350cc ROTARY VALVE · 1966-1994

The world's finest publisher of mechanical how-to manuals

INTERTEC PUBLISHING

P.O. Box 12901, Overland Park, Kansas 66282-2901

Copyright ©1995 Intertec Publishing Corporation

FIRST EDITION
First Printing November, 1971

SECOND EDITION
Revised to include 1972 models
First Printing April, 1972

THIRD EDITION
Revised to include 1973 models
First Printing September, 1973

FOURTH EDITION
Revised to include 1974 models
First Printing June, 1974

FIFTH EDITION
Revised to include 1975-1976 models
First Printing June, 1976

SIXTH EDITION
Revised by Dave Sales to include 1977 models
First Printing April, 1977

SEVENTH EDITION
Revised by Anton Vesely to include 1978-1980 models
First Printing July, 1981
Second Printing February, 1983
Third Printing October, 1983
Fourth Printing June, 1985
Fifth Printing July, 1986
Sixth Printing April, 1988
Seventh Printing May, 1990
Eighth Printing May, 1993

EIGHTH EDITION
Revised to include 1981-1994 models
First Printing September, 1995

Printed in U.S.A.

ISBN: 0-89287-651-4

Library of Congress: 95-75311

MEMBER

Technical illustrations by Robert Caldwell.

COVER: Photographed by Mark Clifford, Mark Clifford Photography, Los Angeles, California.

Chapter One
General Information

1

Chapter Two
Troubleshooting

2

Chapter Three
Periodic Maintenance

3

Chapter Four
Engine, Transmission and Clutch

4

Chapter Five
Fuel System

5

Chapter Six
Electrical System

6

Chapter Seven
Frame, Suspension and Steering

7

Index

8

Wiring Diagrams

9

CONTENTS

QUICK REFERENCE DATA VII

CHAPTER ONE
GENERAL INFORMATION 1

Service hints   Mechanic's tips
Tools   Safety first
Expendable supplies

CHAPTER TWO
TROUBLESHOOTING 14

Operating requirements   Engine noises
Starting difficulties   Piston seizure
Poor idling   Excessive vibration
Misfiring   Clutch slip or drag
Flat spots   Poor handling
Power loss   Brake problems
Overheating   Lighting problems
Backfiring   Troubleshooting guide

CHAPTER THREE
PERIODIC MAINTENANCE 19

Regular maintenance   Drive chain
Racing maintenance   Brakes
Engine tune-up   Wheels and tires
Battery service   Fork oil
Transmission   Steering head bearings
Clutch adjustment   Swinging arm
Electrical equipment

CHAPTER FOUR
ENGINE, TRANSMISSION AND CLUTCH. **39**

Rotary valve engines
Engine lubrication
Preparation for engine disassembly
Engine removal
Cylinder and cylinder head
Piston, piston pin and piston rings
Left crankcase cover
Flywheel magneto and starter-generator
Engine sprocket
Right crankcase cover

Primary drive gear
Clutch
Rotary valve
Gearshift mechanism
Crankcase
Kickstarter
Crankshaft
Transmission
Drain pump

CHAPTER FIVE
FUEL SYSTEM **134**

Carburetion operation
Carburetor overhaul
Carburetor adjustment

Carburetor components
Miscellaneous carburetor problems

CHAPTER SIX
ELECTRICAL SYSTEM **171**

Flywheel magneto
Magneto troubleshooting
Starter-generator
Starter-generator troubleshooting
Rectifier
High voltage cable
Capacitor discharge ignition system
   operation

Solid state voltage regulator
Solid state regulator/rectifier
   (1979 and later)
Charging system test (1979 and later)
Lights
Horn
Main switch
Battery

CHAPTER SEVEN
FRAME, SUSPENSION AND STEERING **197**

Handlebars
Wheels and tires
Brakes
Front forks
Steering system
Shock absorbers
Fenders

Swinging arm
Rear sprocket
Fuel and oil tank
Seat
Stands and footrests
Exhaust pipe and muffler
Drive chain

INDEX **236**

WIRING DIAGRAMS. **238**

QUICK REFERENCE DATA

BATTERY IGNITION TIMING

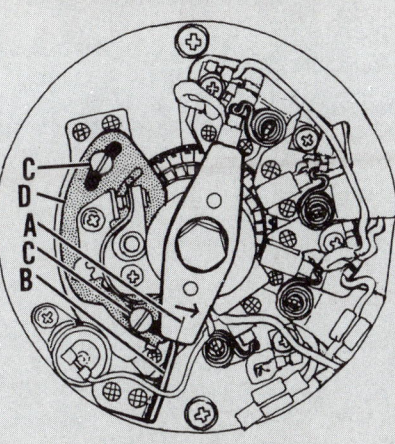

A. Timing pointer mark
B. Index pointer
C. Timing plate screws
D. Timing plate

BREAKER POINTS

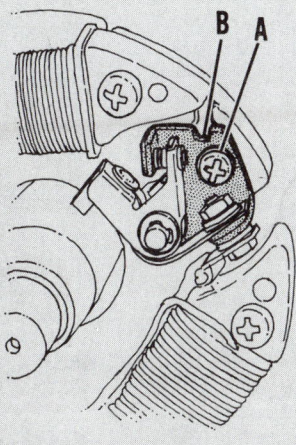

A. Point retaining screw
B. Pry slot

MAGNETO TIMING AND CDI TIMING

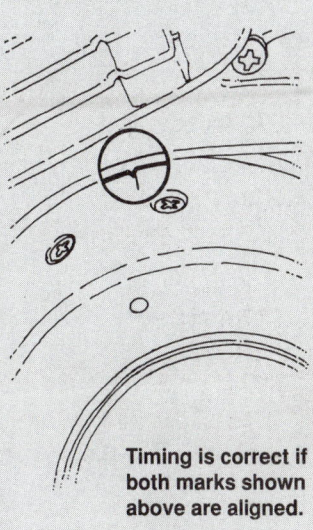

Timing is correct if both marks shown above are aligned.

ADJUSTMENTS

Clutch cable free play	See Chapter Two
Starter and throttle cable free play	0.2-0.3 in. (5.0-7.5 mm)
Drive chain free play	3/4-1 in. (20-25 mm)
Front brake cable free play	Approximately 1 in. (25 mm)
Rear brake pedal free play	3/4-1 1/4 in. (20-30 mm)

STANDARD TIGHTENING TORQUES*

Thread diameter	mkg	N·m	ft.-lbs.
5 mm	0.35-0.50	3.4-4.9	2.5-3.6 (30-43 in.-lbs.)
6 mm	0.60-0.80	5.9-7.8	4.3-5.8 (52-69 in.-lbs.)
8 mm	1.4-1.9	14-19	10.0-13.5
10 mm	2.6-3.5	25-34	19-25
12 mm	4.5-6.2	44-61	33-45
14 mm	7.4-10.0	73-98	54-72
16 mm	11.5-16.0	115-155	83-115
18 mm	17.0-23.0	165-225	125-165
20 mm	23-33	225-325	165-240

*Refer to Table 12 in Chapter 4 for specific torque values.

RECOMMENDED FUEL AND LUBRICANTS

Engine oil	A good quality 2-stroke engine oil
Transmission oil	SAE 10W/30 or 10W/40 motor oil
Front forks	SAE 5W/20 motor oil or ATF (automatic transmission fluid)
Drive chain	SAE 90 oil or special chain lubricant
Fuel	90 Research octane (regular)

IGNITION TIMING

79-100 cc models	Piston position	° BTDC	*Breaker point gap
KD80 (1975, 1976 & 1980-1987)	1.86 mm (0.073 in.)	20	**
J Series	1.58 mm (0.062 in.)	19	0.30-0.40 mm (0.012-0.016 in.)
MC1-A, MC1-B & MC1M	1.96 mm (0.077 in.)	20	**
G3SS & G3TR	1.96 mm (0.077 in.)	20	0.30-0.40 mm (0.012-0.016 in.)
D1	1.58 mm (0.062 in.)	19	0.30-0.40 mm (0.012-0.016 in.)
G4TR	1.96 mm (0.077 in.)	20	0.30-0.40 mm (0.012-0.016 in.)
G5	1.96 mm (0.077 in.)	20	0.30-0.40 mm (0.012-0.016 in.)
G31M	2.58 mm (0.099 in.)	23	0.30-0.40 mm (0.012-0.016 in.)
KD100	1.96 mm (0.077 in.)	20	**
KE100 1978 & earlier	1.96 mm (0.077 in.)	20	**
KE100 1979 & later (A8 on)	2.58 mm (0.099 in.)	23 @1,300 rpm	**
KH100 & KM100	1.96 mm (0.077 in.)	20	**
KV100	1.96 mm (0.077 in.)	20	**

115-125 cc models	Piston position	° BTDC	*Breaker point gap
C2SS & C2TR	1.78 mm (0.070 in.)	19	0.30-0.40 mm (0.012-0.016 in.)
F6	2.94 mm (0.116 in.)	23	0.30-0.40 mm (0.012-0.016 in.)
KD125	1.96 mm (0.077 in.)	20	**
KE125 1979 & earlier	2.52 mm (0.099 in.)	23 @1,300 rpm	**
KE125-A7 1980	2.52 mm (0.099 in.)	23 @1,300 rpm	**
KE125 1981 & later (A8 on)	2.52 mm (0.099 in.)	21 @1,300 rpm	**
KS125	2.52 mm (0.099 in.)	21 @1,300 rpm	**
KX125 (1974-1976)	1.91 mm (0.075 in.)	20 @6,000 rpm	Breakerless CDI

169-175 cc models	Piston position	° BTDC	*Breaker point gap
F2 & F2TR	2.09 mm (0.082 in.)	20	0.30-0.40 mm (0.012-0.016 in.)
F3	2.75 mm (0.108 in.)	23	0.30-0.40 mm (0.012-0.016 in.)
F7	2.94 mm (0.116 in.)	23 @6,000 rpm	Breakerless CDI
KD175 (1976-1979)	2.69 mm (0.102 in.)	22 @4,000 rpm	Breakerless CDI
KE175 (1976-1982)	2.69 mm (0.102 in.)	22 @4,000 rpm	Breakerless CDI

238-350 cc models	Piston position	° BTDC	*Breaker point gap
F4 & F21M	3.09 mm (0.121 in.)	23	0.30-0.40 mm (0.012-0.016 in.)
F8	2.59 mm (0.101 in.)	20	0.30-0.40 mm (0.012-0.016 in.)
F81M	2.34 mm (0.092 in.)	19	0.30-0.40 mm (0.012-0.016 in.)
F5 & F9	3.41 mm (0.134 in.)	23 @6,000 rpm	Breakerless CDI

* On all models so equipped, ignition timing is changed when breaker point gap is changed, so timing and breaker point gap should both be checked.
** On models indicated, timing is set by changing breaker point gap.

CARBURETOR ADJUSTMENTS

79-100 cc models	*Idle mixture screw	Idle speed	Float level	Fuel level
KD80 (1975, 1976 & 1980-1987)	1 1/2 turns open	**	24 mm	4 mm
J Series	1 1/2 turns open	**	18 mm	4 mm
MC1-A, MC1-B & MC1M	1 1/2 turns open	**	24 mm	4 mm
G3SS & G3TR	1 1/4-1 1/2 turns open	**	24 mm	4-4.5 mm
D1	1 3/4 turns open	**	18 mm	—
G4TR	1 1/4-1 1/2 turns open	**	24 mm	4 mm
G5	1 1/2 turns open	**	24 mm	4 mm
G31M	1 1/2 turns open	**	23 mm	—
KD100	1 1/4 turns open	**	24 mm	4 mm
KE100	1 1/2 turns open	**	24 mm	4 mm
KH100, KM100 & KV100	1 1/4 turns open	**	24 mm	4 mm

(continued)

CARBURETOR ADJUSTMENTS (continued)

115-125 cc models	*Idle mixture screw	Idle speed	Float level	Fuel level
C2SS & C2TR	1 1/2 turns open	**	18 mm	–
F6	1 3/4 turns open	**	19 mm	5 mm
KD125	1 1/2 turns open	**	24 mm	4 mm
KE125-A3, A4 & A5 (1976-1978)	1 1/2 turns open	**	19 mm	4 mm
KE125-A6 -A12 (1979-1985)	1 1/4 turns open	**	19 mm	4 mm
KS125	1 1/2 turns open	**	19 mm	4 mm
KX125 (1974-1976)	1 1/2 turns open	**	19 mm	4 mm

169-175 cc models	*Idle mixture screw	Idle speed	Float level	Fuel level
F2 & F2TR	1 3/4 turns open	**	22-24 mm	–
F3	1 3/4 turns open	**	24-26 mm	–
F7	1 1/2 turns open	**	18 mm	5 mm
KD175 (1976-1979)	1 1/4 turns open	**	18 mm	3.5 mm
KE175 (1976-1982)	1 1/4 turns open	**	18 mm	3.5 mm

238-350 cc models	*Idle mixture screw	Idle speed	Float level	Fuel level
F4	1 1/4 turns open	**	24-26 mm	–
F21M	1 1/4 turns open	**	24-26 mm	–
F8	1 3/4 turns open	**	28 mm	7 mm
F81M	1 1/4 turns open	**	28 mm	7 mm
F5	1 3/4 turns open	**	18 mm	5.5 mm
F9	1 1/2 turns open	**	18 mm	5.5 mm

* Idle mixture (pilot screw) settings are approximate and should be set for optimum running.
** Engine idle speed should be adjusted as slow as possible while maintaining smooth running without stalling.

SPARK PLUG APPLICATION AND GAP*

79-100 cc models	NGK	ND	Gap
KD80 (1975, 1976 & 1980-1987)	B7HS	W22FS	0.6-0.7 mm (0.024-0.028 in.)
J Series	B6H	W17F	0.6-0.7 mm (0.024-0.028 in.)
MC1-A, MC1-B & MC1M	B7HS	W25FN	0.6-0.7 mm (0.024-0.028 in.)
G3SS	B8HS	W24FS	0.6-0.7 mm (0.024-0.028 in.)
G3TR	B7HS	W25FS	0.6-0.7 mm (0.024-0.028 in.)
D1	B7H	W22F	0.6-0.7 mm (0.024-0.028 in.)
G4TR	B7HS	W25FN	0.6-0.7 mm (0.024-0.028 in.)
G5	B8HS	W24FS	0.6-0.7 mm (0.024-0.028 in.)
G31M	B8HN	W25FN	0.6-0.7 mm (0.024-0.028 in.)
KD100	B7HS	W22FS	0.6-0.7 mm (0.024-0.028 in.)
KE100 1978 & earlier	B8HS	W24FS	0.6-0.7 mm (0.024-0.028 in.)
KE100 1979 & later (A8 on)	B8ES	W24ES	0.7-0.8 mm (0.028-0.032 in.)
KH100	B8HS	W24FS	0.6-0.7 mm (0.024-0.028 in.)
KM100	B7HS	W22FS	0.6-0.7 mm (0.024-0.028 in.)
KV100	B7HS	W22FS	0.6-0.7 mm (0.024-0.028 in.)

115-125 cc models	NGK	ND	Gap
C2SS & C2TR	B7HS	W22FS	0.6-0.7 mm (0.024-0.028 in.)
F6	B8HS	W24FS	0.6-0.7 mm (0.024-0.028 in.)
KD125	B8HS	W24FS	0.6-0.7 mm (0.024-0.028 in.)
KE125 1979 & earlier	B8HS	W24FS	0.6-0.7 mm (0.024-0.028 in.)
KE125-A7 1980	B9ES	–	0.7-0.8 mm (0.028-0.032 in.)
KE125 1981 & later (A8 on)	B9ES	–	0.7-0.8 mm (0.028-0.032 in.)
KS125	B8HS	W24FS	0.6-0.7 mm (0.024-0.028 in.)
KX125 (1974-1976)	B9EV	W27ESG	0.6 mm (0.024 in.)

(continued)

SPARK PLUG APPLICATION AND GAP* (continued)

169-175 cc models	NGK	ND	Gap
F2 & F2TR	B7HS	W22FS	0.6-0.7 mm (0.024-0.028 in.)
F3	B8HS	W24FS	0.6-0.7 mm (0.024-0.028 in.)
F7	B9HS	W27FS	0.6-0.7 mm (0.024-0.028 in.)
KD175 (1976-1979)	B9HS	W27FS	0.6-0.7 mm (0.024-0.028 in.)
KE175 (1976-1982)	B9HS	W27FS	0.6-0.7 mm (0.024-0.028 in.)

238-350 cc models	NGK	ND	Gap
F4	B9HS	W27FS	0.6-0.7 mm (0.024-0.028 in.)
F21M	B8HN	W25FN	0.6-0.7 mm (0.024-0.028 in.)
F8	B8HS	W24FS	0.6-0.7 mm (0.024-0.028 in.)
F81M	B9HS	W27FS	0.6-0.7 mm (0.024-0.028 in.)
F5 & F9	B10H	W31FS	0.9-1.0 mm (0.035-0.039 in.)

*CAUTION: Make sure that the spark plug has the correct thread length (reach) for the application as well as the correct heat range. Occasionally a motorcycle may be equipped with a cylinder head which requires a spark plug with a different length of thread than the one listed in the following table, so it is important to check the actual thread length in the cylinder head as well as the following table. Spark plug threads and the threads in the cylinder head should be the same length.

APPROXIMATE FORK OIL CAPACITY

79-100 cc models	SAE grade	Ounces	cc
KD80 (1975, 1976 & 1980-1987)	5W/20	3.1	95
J Series	5W/20	4.6	135
MC1-A models	5W/20	3.1	95
G3 Models	30	4.4	130
D1	5W/20	4.6	135
G4TR	10W	5.7	174
G5	10W	5.7	174
G31M	20	5.8	170
KD100	5W/20	3.1	95
KE100 (1976-1978)	10W	5.7	174
	Maintain oil 395 mm from top		
KE100-A8 (1979)	10W	5.3-5.6	158-166
	Maintain oil 395 mm from top		
KE100 A9 - B13 (1980-1994)	10W/20	5.3-5.6	158-166
	Maintain oil 406.5-410.5 mm from top		
KH100	30	4.4	130
KM100	5W/20	3.1	95
KV100	10W	5.7	174

115-125 cc models	SAE grade	Ounces	cc
C2SS & C2TR (Early)	5W/20	4.0	120
C2SS & C2TR (Late)	5W/20	5.9	175
F6	10W	5.1	152
KD125	5W/20	5.1	150
KE125 (1976-1979)	5W/20	4.9-5.2	145-155
	Maintain oil 385-415 mm from top		
KE125-A7 & A8 (1980-1981)	5W/20	4.5	132
	Maintain oil 504-508 mm from top		
KE125-A9 through A12 (1982-1985)	5W/20	5.5	162
	Maintain oil 421-425 mm from top		
KS125	5W/20	5.1	150
	Maintain oil 385-415 mm from top		
KX125 (1974-1976)	5W/20	5.2	153
	Maintain oil 390 mm from top		

(continued)

APPROXIMATE FORK OIL CAPACITY (continued)

169-175 cc models	SAE grade	Ounces	cc
F2 & F2TR	5W/20	5.9	175
F3	5W/20	5.9	175
F7	10W	3.9	115
KD175 (1976-1979)	10W	5.1	150
KE175 (1976-1982)	10W	5.1	150

238-350 cc models	SAE grade	Ounces	cc
F4	10W	6.6	195
F21M	5W/20	6.8	200
F8	10W	5.9	175
F81M	10W	5.9	175
F5	10W	5.9	175
F9	10W	5.9	175

CLYMER

KAWASAKI

80-350cc ROTARY VALVE · 1966-1994

CHAPTER ONE

GENERAL INFORMATION

This book was written to provide service guidance to owners of Kawasaki motorcycles. Its contents cover all popular rotary valve single-cylinder models since 1966.

SERVICE HINTS

Most of the service procedures described in this book are straightforward and can be performed by anyone who is reasonably handy with tools. It is suggested, however, that you consider your own capabilities carefully before you attempt any operation which involves major disassembly of the engine.

Crankshaft disassembly, for example, requires the use of a press. It would be wiser to have that operation performed by a shop equipped for such work, rather than to try it with makeshift equipment. Other procedures require precision measurements. Unless you have the skills and equipment to make these measurements, call on a competent service outlet.

You will find that repairs will go much faster and easier if your machine is clean before you begin work. There are special cleaners for washing the engine and related parts. You just brush or spray on the cleaning solution, let it stand and rinse it away with a garden hose. Clean all oily or greasy parts with cleaning solvent as you remove them. *Never use gasoline as a cleaning agent.* Gasoline presents an extreme fire hazard. Be sure to work in a well ventilated area when you use cleaning solvent. Keep a fire extinguisher handy, just in case.

Special tools are required for some service procedures. These tools may be purchased at Kawasaki dealers. If you are on good terms with the dealer's service department people, you may be able to use theirs.

Much of the labor charge for repairs made by dealers is for removal and disassembly of other parts to reach the defective one. It is frequently possible for you to do all of this yourself, then take the affected subassembly, such as the crankshaft mentioned earlier, into the dealer for repair.

Once you decide to tackle the job yourself, read the entire section in this manual which pertains to the job. Study the illustrations and the text until you have a good idea of what is involved. If special tools are required, make arrangements to get them before you start the job. It is frustrating to get partly into a job and find that you are unable to complete it.

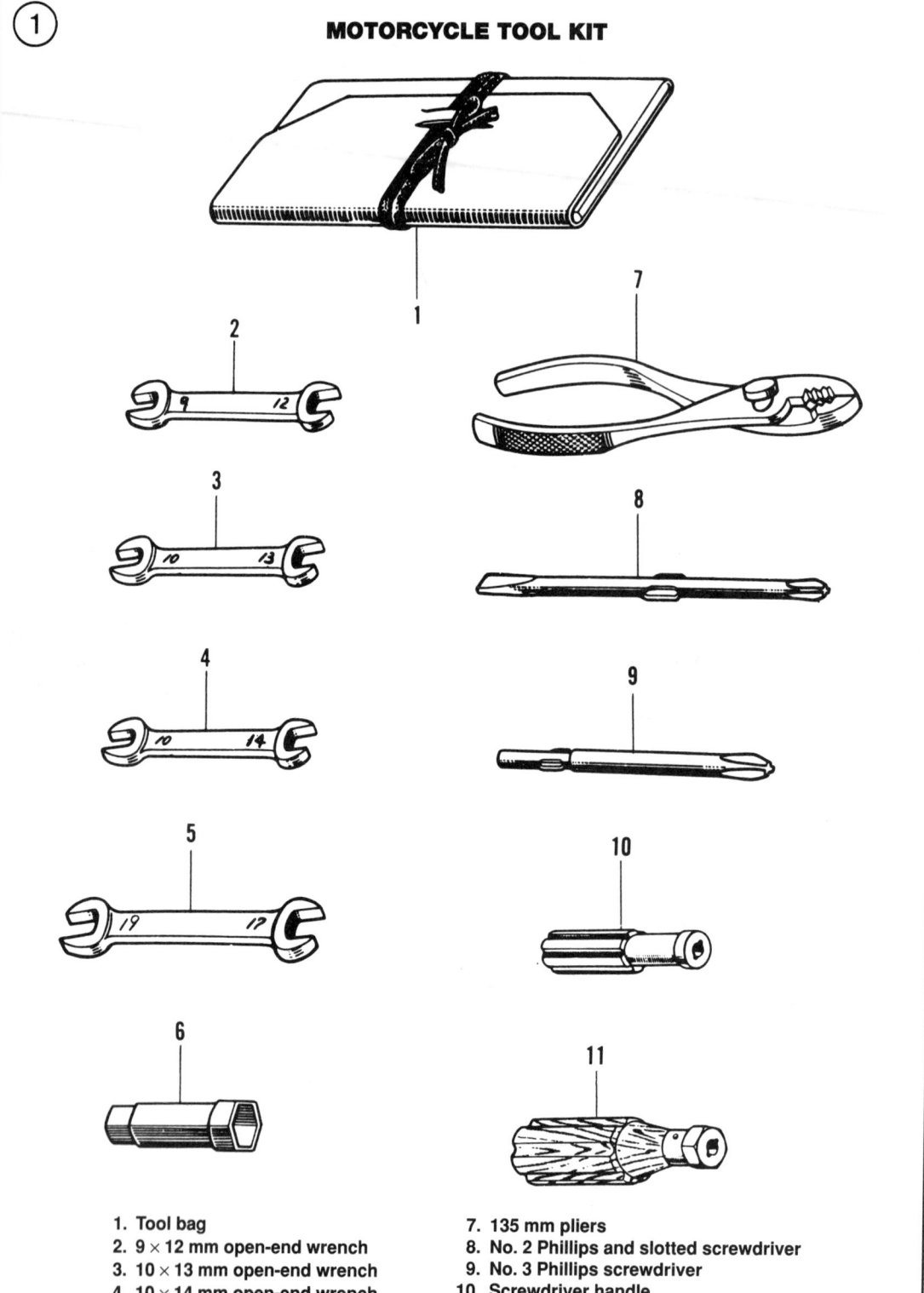

① **MOTORCYCLE TOOL KIT**

1. Tool bag
2. 9 × 12 mm open-end wrench
3. 10 × 13 mm open-end wrench
4. 10 × 14 mm open-end wrench
5. 17 × 19 mm open end wrench
6. Spark plug wrench

7. 135 mm pliers
8. No. 2 Phillips and slotted screwdriver
9. No. 3 Phillips screwdriver
10. Screwdriver handle
11. Screwdriver handle

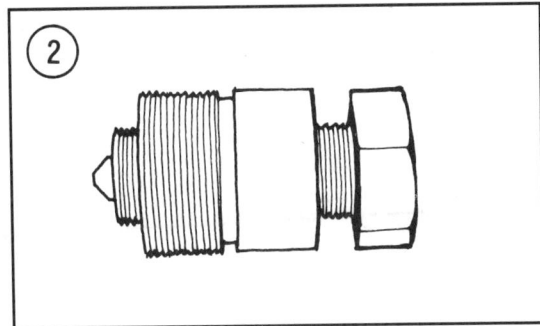

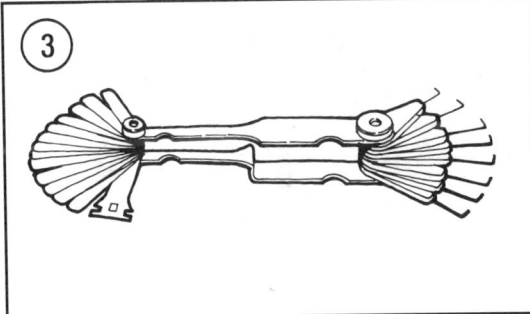

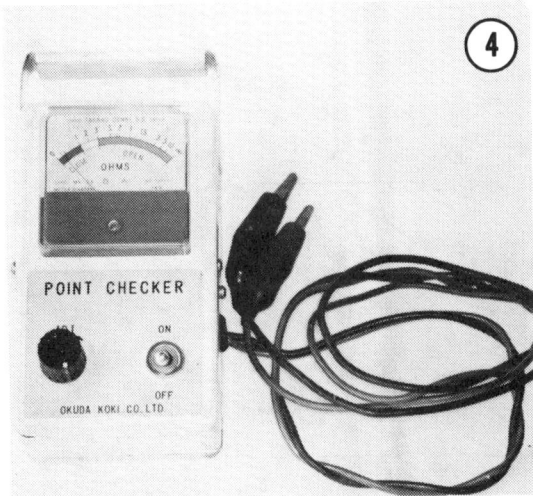

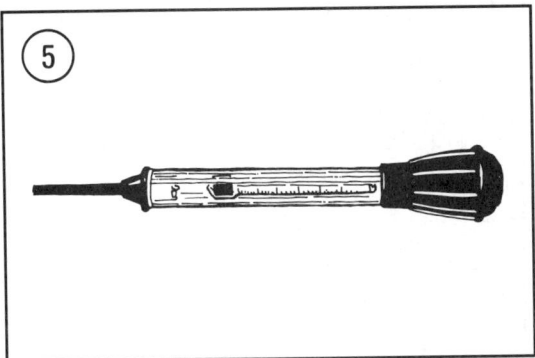

TOOLS

Every motorcyclist should carry a small tool kit to help make minor roadside adjustments and repairs. A suggested kit, available at most dealers, is shown in **Figure 1**.

For more extensive servicing, an assortment of ordinary hand tools is required. As a minimum, have the following available. Note that all threaded fasteners are metric sizes.

1. Combination wrenches
2. Socket wrenches
3. Assorted screwdrivers
4. Assorted pliers
5. Spark plug gauge
6. Spark plug wrench
7. Small hammer
8. Plastic mallet
9. Parts cleaning brush

A few special tools may also be required. The first four can be considered essential.

1. *Flywheel puller* (**Figure 2**). Bikes with magnetos require that the flywheel be removed to gain access to the breaker points. This tool is relatively inexpensive and is available at most motorcycle shops or by mail order from accessory dealers. Be sure to specify the model of your machine when ordering. There is no satisfactory substitute for this tool; but there have been many unhappy owners who bought expensive new crankshafts and flywheels after trying makeshift flywheel removal methods.

2. *Ignition gauge* (**Figure 3**). This tool combines round wire spark plug gap gauges with narrow breaker point feeler gauges. Most bikes with magnetos require that point gap be adjusted through a narrow slot in the flywheel. Standard feeler gauges will not fit through this slot, making point gap adjustment difficult or impossible. This tool is available at auto accessory stores.

3. *Timing tester* (**Figure 4**). This unit signals the instant when breaker points just open. On models with magnetos, this point is sometimes difficult to determine with a test light or ohmmeter, because the breaker points are shunted by a low-resistance coil.

4. *Hydrometer* (**Figure 5**). This tool measures charge of the battery and tells much about battery condition. A typical hydrometer is available at any auto parts store and through most mail order outlets.

5. *Multimeter, or VOM* (**Figure 6**). This instrument is invaluable for electrical system troubleshooting

and service. A few of its functions may be duplicated by locally fabricated substitutes, but for the serious hobbyist, it's a must. Its uses are described in the applicable sections of this book. It is available at electronics hobbyists stores and mail order outlets.

6. *Compression gauge* (**Figure 7**). An engine with low compression cannot be properly tuned and will not develop full power. The compression gauge shown has a flexible stem, which enables it to reach cylinders where there is little clearance between the cylinder head and frame. Inexpensive gauges are available at auto accessory stores or by mail order.

7. *Impact driver* (**Figure 8**). This tool might have been designed with the motorcyclist in mind. It makes removal of engine cover screws easy and eliminates damaged screw slots. Most hardware stores carry an impact driver.

EXPENDABLE SUPPLIES

Certain expendable supplies are also required. These include grease, oil, gasket cement, wiping rags, cleaning solvent and distilled water. Cleaning solvent is available at many service stations. Distilled water, required for battery service, is available at most supermarkets. It is sold for use in steam irons and is quite inexpensive.

MECHANIC'S TIPS

Removing Frozen Nuts and Screws

When a fastener rusts and cannot be removed, several methods may be used to loosen it. First apply penetrating oil liberally. Rap the fastener several times with a small hammer; don't hit it hard enough to cause damage.

For frozen screws, apply oil as described, then insert a screwdriver in the slot and rap the top of the screwdriver with a hammer. This loosens the rust so the screw can be removed in the normal way. If the screw head is too chewed up to use a screwdriver, grip the head with vise-type pliers and turn the screw out.

For a frozen bolt or nut, apply penetrating oil, then rap it with a hammer. Turn off with the proper size wrench. If the points are rounded off, grip with vise-type pliers as described for screws.

Stripped Threads

Occasionally, threads are stripped through carelessness or impact damage. Often the threads can be

cleaned up by running a tap (for internal threads) or die (for external threads) through the threads. See **Figure 9**.

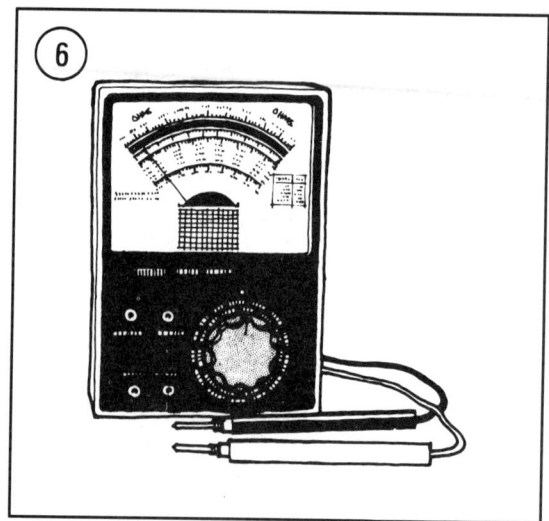

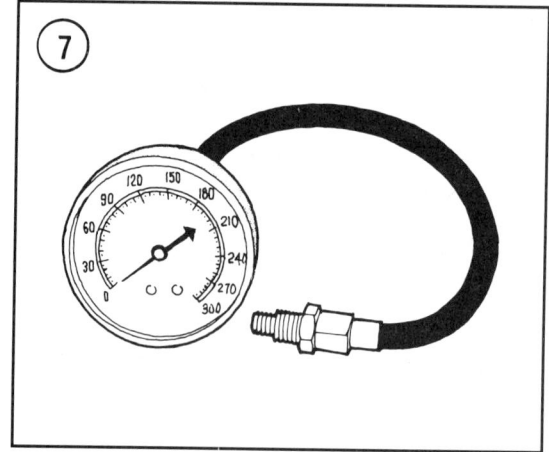

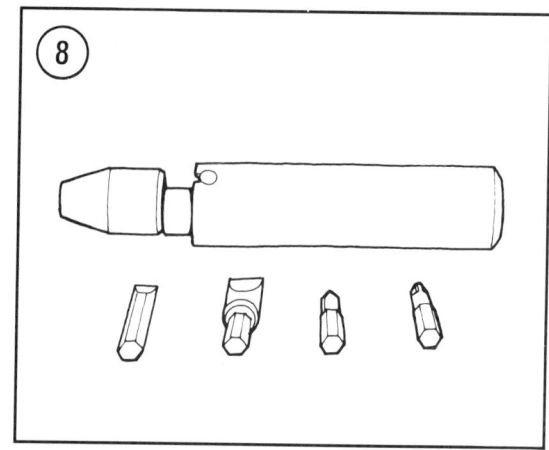

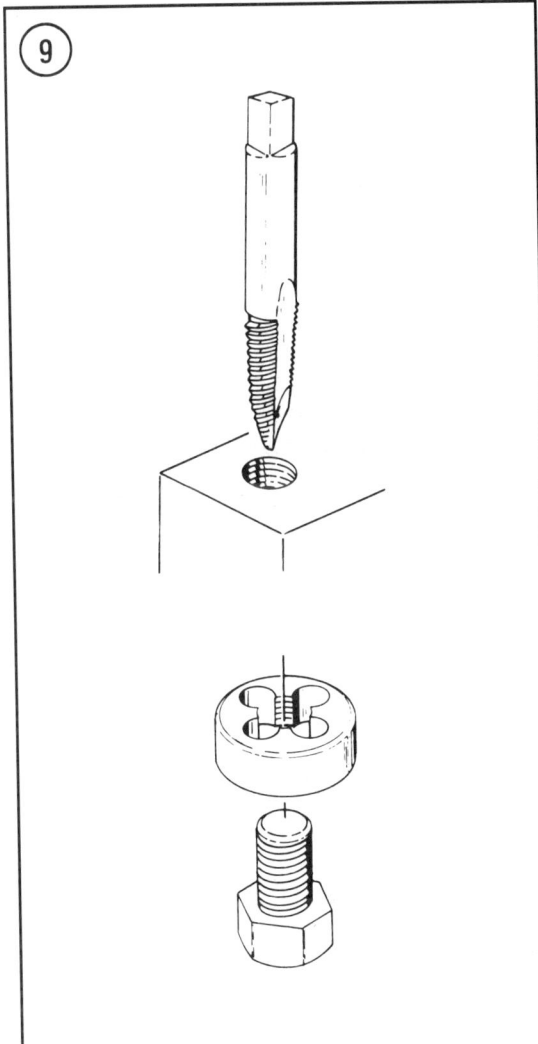

Broken Screw or Bolt

When the head breaks off a screw or bolt, several methods are available for removing the remaining portion.

If a large portion of the remainder projects out, try gripping it with vise-type pliers. If the projection portion is too small, try filing it to fit a wrench or cut a slot in it to fit a screwdriver. See **Figure 10**.

If the head breaks off flush, as it usually does, remove it with a screw extractor. Refer to **Figure 11**. Center-punch the broken part, then drill a hole into it. Drill sizes are marked on the tool. Tap the extractor into the broken part, then back it out with a wrench.

Removing Damaged Screws

WARNING
When removing screws by this method, always wear suitable eye protection.

CAUTION
Use clean rags to cover bearings or any other parts which might be harmed by metal chips produced during this procedure.

Figure 12 illustrates damaged screws typical of those on many bikes. Such screws may usually be removed easily by drilling. Select a bit with a diameter larger than that of the damaged screw, but smaller than its head, then drill into the screw head (**Figure 13**) until the head separates from the screw. The remainder of the screw may then be turned out easily. **Figure 14** illustrates one screw head removed in this manner. The other has been drilled to just the point where the head is separating from the screw body. Note that there is no damage to the plate which these screws retain.

SAFETY FIRST

Professional mechanics can work for years without sustaining serious injury. If you observe a few rules of common sense and safety, you can also enjoy many safe hours servicing your own machine. You can also hurt yourself or damage the bike if you ignore these rules:

1. Never use gasoline as a cleaning solvent.
2. Never smoke or use a torch near flammable liquids, such as cleaning solvent in open containers.

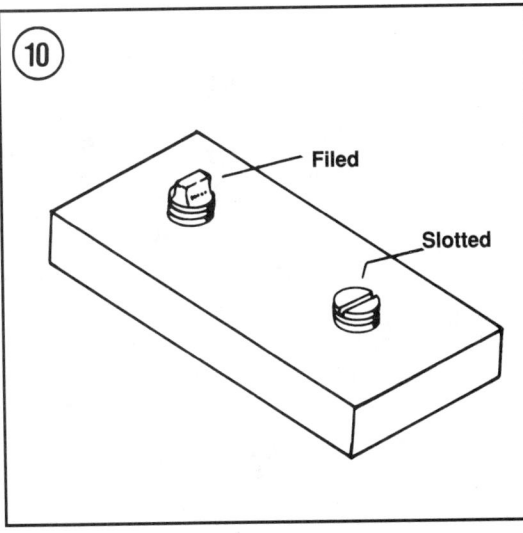

Filed

Slotted

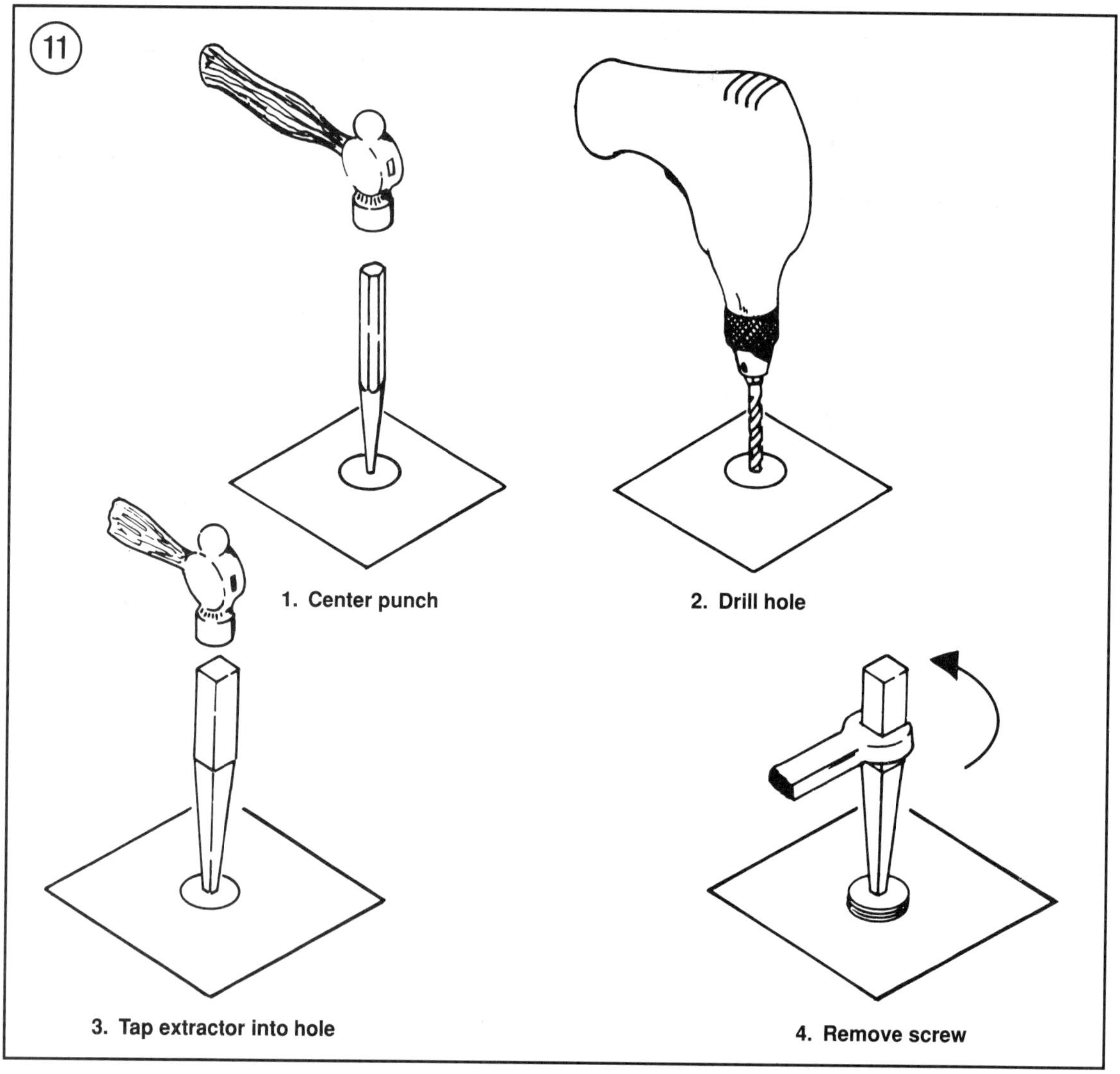

11
1. Center punch
2. Drill hole
3. Tap extractor into hole
4. Remove screw

12

13

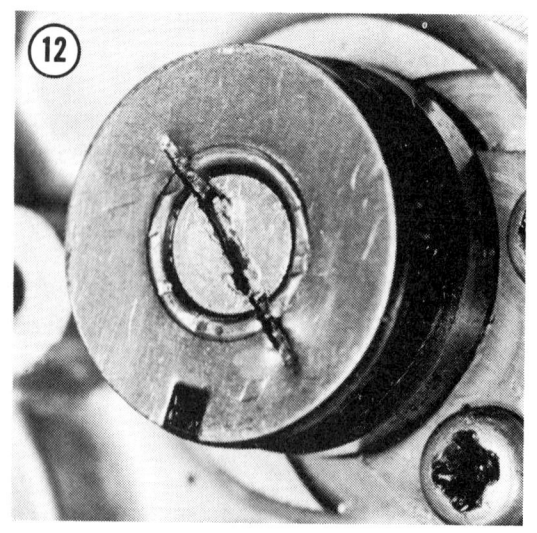

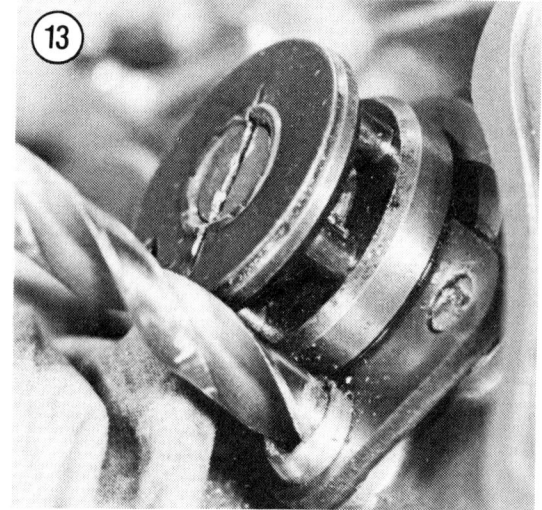

3. Never smoke or use a torch in an area where batteries are charging. Highly explosive hydrogen gas is formed during the charging process.

4. If welding or brazing is required on the machine, remove the fuel tank to a safe distance, at least 50 feet away.

5. Be sure to use proper size wrenches for nut turning.

6. If a nut is tight, think for a moment what would happen to your hand should the wrench slip. Be guided accordingly.

7. Keep your work area clean and uncluttered.

8. Wear safety goggles in all operations involving drilling, grinding, or use of a chisel.

9. Never use worn tools.

10. Keep a fire extinguisher handy. Be sure that it is rated for gasoline and electrical fires.

Table 1 MODEL IDENTIFICATION

80 cc	
1975	KD80
1976	KD80-A2
1980	KD80-M
1981	KD80-M2
1982	KD80-M3
1983	KD80-M4
1984	KD80-M5
1985	KD80-M6
1986	KD80-M7
1987	KD80-M8
85 cc	
1965	J1
1966-1967	J1L, J1TL & J1TRL
1973	MC1
1974	MC1-A & MC1M
1975	MC1-B & MC1M-A
90 cc	
1969-1970	G3SS & G3TR
1971	G3SS & G3TR-A
1972	G3SS-B & G3TR-B
1973	G3SS-C & G3TR-C
1974	G3SS-D & G3TR-D
100 cc	
1966	D1
1970	G4TR & G31M
1971	G4TR-A & G31M-A
1972	G4TR-B & G5
	(continued)

Table 1 MODEL IDENTIFICATION (continued)

100 cc (continued)	
1973	G4TR-C & G5-A
1974	G4TR-D & G5-B
1975	G3SS-E, G4TR-E & G5-C
1976	KD100-M1, KE100-A5, KH100-A1, KM100-A1 & KV100-A7
1977	KD100-M2, KE100-A6 & KM100-A2
1978	KD100-M3, KE100-A7 & KM100-A3
1979	KD100-M4, KE100-A8 & KM100-A4
1980	KD80-M & KE100-A9 & KM100-A6
1981	KE100-A10 & KM100-A7
1982	KE100-B1
1983	KE100-B2
1984	KE100-B3
1985	KE100-B3
1986	KE100-B5
1987	KE100-B6
1988	KE100-B7
1989	KE100-B8
1990	KE100-B9
1991	KE100-B10
1992	KE100-B11
1993	KE100-B12
1994	KE100-B13
120 cc	
1967-1969	C2SS & C2TR
125 cc	
1971	F6
1972	F6-A
1973	F6-B
1974	KS125, KX125
1975	KD125, KS125-A, KX125-A
1976	KD125-A2, KE125-A3, KX125-A3
1977	KD125-A3, KE125-A4
1978	KD125-A4, KE125-A5
1979	KD125-A5, KE125-A6
1980	KE125-A7
1981	KE125-A8
1982	KE125-A9
1983	KE125-A10
1984	KE125-A11
1985	KE125-A12
169–175 cc	
1967	F2 & F2TR
1968-1970	F3
1971	F7
1972	F7-A
1973	F7-B
1974	F7-C
1975	F7-D
1976	KD175-A1 & KE175-B1
1977	KD175-A2 & KE175-B2
1978	KD175-A3 & KE175-B3
1979	KD175-A4
1980	KE175-D2
1981	KE175-D3
1982	KE175-D4
(continued)	

Table 1 MODEL IDENTIFICATION (continued)

250 cc	
1968	F21M
1969	F4F21M
1970	F4
1971	F8 & F81M
1972	F8-A

350 cc	
1970	F5
1971	F5-A
1972	F9
1973	F9-A
1974	F9-B
1975	F9-C

Table 2 GENERAL SPECIFICATIONS

79-100 cc models	
KD80 (1975, 1976 & 1980-1987)	
General	
Bore and stroke (mm)	47 × 46
Displacement (cc)	79
Cylinder	
Standard bore diameter	47.008 mm (1.854 in.)
Transmission speeds	5 speeds
J series	
General	
Bore and stroke (mm)	47 × 47
Displacement (cc)	81.5
Cylinder	
Standard bore diameter	47.0 mm (1.850 in.)
Oil mix ratio	
Models without oil injection	1 part oil to 20 parts gasoline
Transmission speeds	4 speeds
MC1, MC1-A, MC1-B & MC1M	
General	
Bore and stroke (mm)	47 × 51.8
Displacement (cc)	89
Cylinder	
Standard bore diameter	47.0 mm (1.850 in.)
Transmission speeds	5 speeds
G3 models (except G3SS-E)	
General	
Bore and stroke (mm)	47 × 51.8
Displacement (cc)	89
Cylinder	
Standard bore diameter	47.0 mm (1.850 in.)
Transmission speeds	5 speeds
G3SS-E	
General	
Bore and stroke (mm)	49.5 × 51.8
Displacement (cc)	99
(continued)	

1

Table 2 GENERAL SPECIFICATIONS (continued)

79-100 cc models (continued)	
G3SS-E (continued)	
Cylinder	
Standard bore diameter	49.5 mm (1.949 in.)
Transmission speeds	5 speeds
D1	
General	
Bore and Stroke (mm)	52 × 47.8
Displacement (cc)	99
Cylinder	
Standard bore diameter	52.0 mm (2.047 in.)
Transmission speeds	4 speeds
G4TR	
General	
Bore and Stroke (mm)	49.5 × 51.8
Displacement (cc)	99
Cylinder	
Standard bore diameter	49.5 mm (1.949 in.)
Service limit	49.61 mm (1.9531 in.)
Transmission speeds	5 speeds 2 ranges
G5	
General	
Bore and Stroke (mm)	49.5 × 51.8
Displacement (cc)	99
Cylinder	
Standard bore diameter	49.5 mm (1.949 in.)
Transmission speeds	5 speeds
G31M	
General	
Bore and Stroke (mm)	49.5 × 51.8
Displacement (cc)	99
Cylinder	
Standard bore diameter	49.5 mm (1.949 in.)
Oil mix ratio	1 part oil to 20 parts gasoline
Transmission speeds	5 speeds
KD100	
General	
Bore and Stroke (mm)	49.5 × 51.8
Displacement (cc)	99
Cylinder	
Standard bore diameter	49.5 mm (1.949 in.)
Transmission speeds	5 speeds
KE100	
General	
Bore and Stroke (mm)	49.5 × 51.8
Displacement (cc)	99
Cylinder	
Standard bore diameter	49.508-49.523 mm (1.9491-1.9497 in.)
Service limit	49.61 mm (1.9531 in.)
Transmission speeds	5 speeds
(continued)	

Table 2 GENERAL SPECIFICATIONS (continued)

KH100

General	
Bore and Stroke (mm)	49.5 × 51.8
Displacement (cc)	99
Cylinder	
Standard bore diameter	49.508-49.523 mm (1.9491-1.9497 in.)
Service limit	49.61 mm (1.9531 in.)
Transmission speeds	5 speeds

KM100

General	
Bore and Stroke (mm)	49.5 × 51.8
Displacement (cc)	99
Cylinder	
Standard bore diameter	
KM100-A1, A2, A3 & A4	49.5 mm (1.949 in.)
KM100-A6 & A7	49.518 mm (1.950 in.)
Transmission speeds	5 speeds

KV100

General	
Bore and Stroke (mm)	49.5 × 51.8
Displacement (cc)	99
Cylinder	
Standard bore diameter	49.508-49.523 mm (1.9491-1.9497 in.)
Transmission speeds	5 speeds, 2 ranges

115-125 cc models

C2SS & C2TR

General	
Bore and Stroke (mm)	53 × 52.5
Displacement (cc)	115
Cylinder	
Standard bore diameter	53.0 mm (2.087in.)
Transmission speeds	
C2SS & C2TR (except 1969 C2TR)	4 speed
C2TR (1969)	4 speeds 2 ranges

F6

General	
Bore and Stroke (mm)	52 × 58.8
Displacement (cc)	124
Cylinder	
Standard bore diameter	52.0 mm (2.047 in.)
Transmission speeds	5 speeds

KD125

General	
Bore and Stroke (mm)	56.0 × 50.6
Displacement (cc)	124
Cylinder	
Standard bore diameter	56.0 mm (2.205 in.)
Transmission speeds	6 speeds

(continued)

Table 2 GENERAL SPECIFICATIONS (continued)

KE125	
General	
Bore and Stroke (mm)	56.0 × 50.6
Displacement (cc)	124
Cylinder	
Standard bore diameter	
KE125-A3, A4 & A5	56.0 mm (2.205 in.)
1979 & later (A6 on), standard	56.007 mm (2.205 in.)
Transmission speeds	6 speeds
KS125	
General	
Bore and Stroke (mm)	56.0 × 50.6
Displacement (cc)	124
Cylinder	
Standard bore diameter	56.0 mm (2.205 in.)
Transmission speeds	6 speeds
KX125 (1974-1976)	
General	
Bore and Stroke (mm)	56.0 × 50.6
Displacement (cc)	124
Cylinder	
Standard bore diameter	56.01 mm (2.205 in.)
Oil mix ratio	1 part oil to 20 parts gasoline
Transmission speeds	6 speeds
169-175 cc models	
F2 & F2TR	
General	
Bore and Stroke (mm)	62 × 56
Displacement (cc)	169
Cylinder	
Standard bore diameter	62.0 mm (2.441 in.)
Transmission speeds	4 speeds
F3	
General	
Bore and Stroke (mm)	62 × 56
Displacement (cc)	169
Cylinder	
Standard bore diameter	62.0 mm (2.441 in.)
Transmission speeds	4 speeds
F7	
General	
Bore and Stroke (mm)	61.5 × 58.8
Displacement (cc)	174
Cylinder	
Standard bore diameter	61.5 mm (2.421 in.)
Transmission speeds	5 speeds
KD175 (1976-1979) & KE175 (1976-1982)	
General	
Bore and Stroke (mm)	61.5 × 58.8
Displacement (cc)	174
(continued)	

Table 2 GENERAL SPECIFICATIONS (continued)

KD175 (1976-1979) & KE175 (1976-1982) (continued)	
Cylinder	
Standard bore diameter	61.5 mm (2.421 in.)
Transmission speeds	5 speeds

238-350 cc models	
F4	
General	
Bore and Stroke (mm)	70 × 62
Displacement (cc)	238
Cylinder	
Standard bore diameter	70.0 mm (2.756 in.)
Transmission speeds	4 speeds
F21M	
General	
Bore and Stroke (mm)	70 × 62
Displacement (cc)	238
Cylinder	
Standard bore diameter	70.0 mm (2.756 in.)
Oil mix ratio	1 part oil to 20 parts gasoline
Transmission speeds	4 speeds
F8	
General	
Bore and Stroke (mm)	68 × 68
Displacement (cc)	246.8
Cylinder	
Standard bore diameter	68.0 mm (2.667 in.)
Transmission speeds	5 speed
F81M	
General	
Bore and Stroke (mm)	68 × 68
Displacement (cc)	246.8
Cylinder	
Standard bore diameter	68.0 mm (2.667 in.)
Oil mix ratio	1 part oil to 20 parts gasoline
Transmission speeds	5 speed
F5	
General	
Bore and Stroke (mm)	80.5 × 68
Displacement (cc)	346
Cylinder	
Standard bore diameter	80.5 mm (3.169 in.)
Transmission speeds	5 speed
F9	
General	
Bore and Stroke (mm)	80.5 × 68
Displacement (cc)	346
Cylinder	
Standard bore diameter	80.5 mm (3.169 in.)
Transmission speeds	5 speed

CHAPTER TWO

TROUBLESHOOTING

Diagnosing motorcycle ills is relatively simple if you use orderly procedures and keep a few basic principles in mind.

Never assume anything. Don't overlook the obvious. If you are riding along and the bike suddenly quits, check the easiest, most accessible problem spots first. Is there gasoline in the tank? Is the gas petcock in the ON or RESERVE position? Has the spark plug wire fallen off? Check the ignition switch. Sometimes the weight of keys on a key ring may turn the ignition off suddenly.

If nothing obvious turns up in a cursory check, look a little further. Learning to recognize and describe symptoms will make repairs easier for you or a mechanic at the shop. Describe problems accurately and fully. Saying that "it won't run" isn't the same as saying "it quit on the highway at high speed and wouldn't start," or that "it sat in my garage for three months and then wouldn't start."

Gather as many symptoms together as possible to aid in diagnosis. Note whether the engine lost power gradually or all at once, what color smoke (if any) came from the exhaust and so on. Remember that the more complicated a machine is, the easier it is to troubleshoot because symptoms point to specific problems.

You don't need fancy equipment or complicated test gear to determine whether repairs can be attempted at home. A few simple checks could save a large repair bill and time lost while the bike sits in a dealer's service department. On the other hand, be realistic and don't attempt repairs beyond your abilities. Service departments tend to charge heavily for putting together a disassembled engine that may have been abused. Some won't even take on such a job—so use common sense; don't get in over your head.

OPERATING REQUIREMENTS

An engine needs three basics to run properly: correct fuel/air mixture, compression and a spark at the right time. If one or more are missing, the engine won't run. The electrical system is the weakest link of the three. More problems result from electrical breakdowns than from any other source. Keep that in mind before you begin tampering with carburetor adjustments and the like.

If a bike has been sitting for any length of time and refuses to start, check the battery (if the machine is so equipped) for a charged condition first and then look to the gasoline delivery system. This includes the tank, fuel petcocks, lines and the carburetor. Rust may have formed in the tank, obstructing fuel flow. Gasoline deposits may have gummed up carburetor jets and air passages. Gasoline tends to lose its potency after standing for long periods. Condensation may contaminate it with water. Drain old gas and try starting with a fresh tankful.

Compression, or the lack of it, usually enters the picture only in the case of older machines. Worn or broken pistons, rings and cylinder bores could prevent starting. Generally a gradual power loss and harder and harder starting will be readily apparent in this case.

STARTING DIFFICULTIES

Check gas flow first. Remove the gas cap and look into the tank. If gas is present, pull off a fuel line at the carburetor and see if gas flows freely. If none comes out, the fuel tap may be shut off, blocked by rust or foreign matter, or the fuel line may be stopped up or kinked. if the carburetor is getting usable fuel, turn to the electrical system next.

Check that the battery is charged by turning on the lights or by beeping the horn. Refer to your owner's manual for starting procedures with a dead battery. Have the battery recharged if necessary.

Pull off the spark plug cap, remove the spark plug and reconnect the cap. lay the plug against the cylinder head so its base makes a good connection and turn the engine over with the kickstarter. A fat, blue spark should jump across the electrodes. If there is no spark, or a weak one, there is electrical system trouble. Check for a defective plug by replacing it with a known good one. Don't assume a plug is good just because it's new.

Once the plug has been cleared of guilt, but there's still no spark, start backtracking through the system. If the contact at the end of the spark plug wire can be exposed, it can be held about 1/8 inch from the head while the engine is turned over to check for a spark. Remember to hold the wire only by its insulation to avoid a nasty shock. If the plug wires are dirty, greasy, or wet, wrap a rag around them so you don't get shocked. If you do feel a shock or see sparks along the wire, clean or replace the wire and/or its connections.

If there's no spark at the plug wire, look for loose connections at the coil and battery. If all seems in order here, check next for oily or dirty contact points. Clean points with electrical contact cleaner, or a strip of paper. On battery ignition models, with the ignition switch turned on, open and close the points manually with a screwdriver.

No spark at the points with this test indicates a failure in the ignition system. Refer to Chapter Six, *Electrical System* for check-out procedures for the entire system and individual components. Refer to

Chapter Three for checking and setting ignition timing.

Note that spark plugs of the incorrect heat range (too cold) may cause hard starting. Set gap to specifications. If you have just ridden through a puddle or washed the bike and it won't start, dry off the plug and plug wire. Water may have entered the carburetor and fouled the fuel under these conditions but a wet plug and wire are the more likely problem.

If a healthy spark occurs at the right time and there is adequate gas flow to the carburetor, check the carburetor itself at this time. Make sure all jets and air passages are clean, check float level and adjust if necessary. Shake the float to check for gasoline inside it and replace or repair as indicated. Check that the carburetor is mounted snugly and no air is leaking past the mounting flange. Check for a clogged air filter.

Compression may be checked in the field by turning the kickstarter by hand and noting that an adequate resistance is felt, or by removing the spark plug and placing a finger over the plug hole and feeling for pressure.

An accurate compression check gives a good idea of the condition of the basic working parts of the engine. Refer to *Compression Test* in Chapter Three for regular compression inspection.

Hard starting and low power can also be caused by a faulty primary compression in the crankcase. This can be caused by a leaking crankshaft seal, base gasket, or any crankcase leakage. If you suspect faulty crankcase compression, take the engine to your dealer for pressure testing.

1. Remove the plug from the cylinder to be tested and clean out any dirt or grease.
2. Insert the tip of the gauge into the hole, making sure it is seated correctly.
3. Open the throttle all the way.
4. Crank the engine several times and record the highest pressure reading on the gauge. Refer to Chapter Three, *Periodic Maintenance* to interpret results.

POOR IDLING

Poor idling may be caused by incorrect carburetor adjustment, incorrect timing, or ignition system defects. Check the gas cap vent for an obstruction. Also check for loose carburetor mounting bolts or a poor carburetor flange gasket.

MISFIRING

Misfiring can be caused by a weak spark or dirty plugs. Check for fuel contamination. Run the machine at night or in a darkened garage to check for spark leaks along the plug wires and under the spark plug cap. If misfiring occurs only at certain throttle settings, refer to the carburetor chapter for the specific carburetor circuits involved. Misfiring under heavy load, as when climbing hills or accelerating, is usually caused by bad spark plugs.

FLAT SPOTS

If the engine seems to die momentarily when the throttle is opened and then recovers, check for a dirty main jet in the carburetor, water in the fuel, or an excessively lean mixture.

POWER LOSS

Poor condition of rings, pistons, or cylinders will cause a lack of power and speed. Ignition timing should be checked.

OVERHEATING

If the engine seems to run too hot all the time, be sure you are not idling it for long periods. Air-cooled engines are not designed to operate at a standstill for any length of time. Heavy stop-and-go traffic is hard on a motorcycle engine. Spark plugs of the wrong heat range can burn pistons. An excessively lean gas mixture may cause overheating. Check ignition timing. Don't ride in too high a gear. Broken or worn rings may permit compression gases to leak past them, heating heads and cylinder excessively. Check oil level and use the proper grade lubricants.

BACKFIRING

Check that the timing is not advanced too far. Check fuel for contamination.

ENGINE NOISES

Experience is needed to diagnose accurately in this area. Noises are hard to differentiate and harder yet to describe. Deep knocking noises usually mean main bearing failure. A slapping noise generally comes from loose pistons. A light knocking noise during acceleration may be a bad connecting rod bearing. Pinging, which sounds like marbles being shaken in a tin can, is caused by ignition advanced too far or gasoline with too low an octane rating. Pinging should be corrected immediately or damage to pistons will result. Compression leaks at the head/cylinder joint will sound like a rapid on and off squeal.

PISTON SEIZURE

Piston seizure is caused by incorrect piston clearances when fitted, fitting rings with improper end gap, too thin an oil being used, incorrect spark plug heat range, or incorrect ignition timing. Overheating from any cause may result in seizure.

EXCESSIVE VIBRATION

Excessive vibration may be caused by loose motor mounts, worn engine or transmission bearings, loose wheels, worn swinging arm bushings, a generally poor running engine, broken or cracked frame, or one that has been damaged in a collision. See also *Poor Handling*.

CLUTCH SLIP OR DRAG

Clutch slip may be due to worn plates, improper adjustment, or glazed plates. A dragging clutch could result from damaged or bent plates, improper adjustment, or even clutch spring pressure.

POOR HANDLING

Poor handling may be caused by improper tire pressures, a damaged frame or swinging arm, worn shocks or front forks, weak fork springs, a bent or broken steering stem, misaligned wheels, loose or missing spokes, worn tires, bent handlebars, worn wheel bearings, or dragging brakes.

BRAKE PROBLEMS

Sticking brakes may be caused by broken or weak return springs, improper cable or rod adjustment, or dry pivot and cam bushings. Grabbing brakes may be caused by greasy linings which must be replaced. Brake grab may also be due to out-of-round drums or linings which have broken loose from the brake shoes. Glazed linings will cause loss of stopping power.

LIGHTING PROBLEMS

Bulbs which continuously burn out may be caused by excessive vibration, loose connections that permit sudden current surges, poor battery connections, or installation of the wrong type bulb.

A dead battery or one which discharges quickly may be caused by a faulty generator or rectifier. Check for loose or corroded terminals. Shorted bat-

tery cells or broken terminals will keep a battery from charging. Low water level will decrease a battery's capacity. A battery left uncharged after installation will sulfate, rendering it useless.

A majority of light and horn or other electrical accessory problems are caused by loose or corroded ground connections. Check those first and then substitute known good units for easier troubleshooting.

TROUBLESHOOTING GUIDE

The quick reference guide (**Table 1**) summarizes part of the troubleshooting process. Use this table to outline possible problem areas, then refer to the specific chapter or section involved.

2

Table 1 TROUBLESHOOTING GUIDE

Item	Problem or Cause	Things to Check
Loss of power	Poor compression	Piston rings and cylinder Head gaskets Crankcase leaks
	Overheated engine	Lubricating oil supply Clogged cooling fins Ignition timing Slipping clutch Carbon in combustion chamber
	Improper mixture	Dirty air cleaner Restricted fuel flow Gas cap vent hole
	Miscellaneous	Dragging brakes Tight wheel bearings Defective chain Clogged exhaust system
Steering	Hard steering	Tire pressures Steering damper adjustment Steering stem head Steering head bearings
	Pulls to one side	Unbalanced shock absorbers Drive chain adjustment Front/rear wheel alignment Unbalanced tires Defective swing arm Defective steering head
	Shimmy	Drive chain adjustment Loose or missing spokes Deformed rims Worn wheel bearings Wheel balance
	(continued)	

Table 1 TROUBLESHOOTING GUIDE (continued)

Item	Problem or Cause	Things to Check
Gearshifting difficulties	Clutch	Adjustment Springs Friction plates Steel plates Oil quantity
	Transmission	Oil quantity Oil grade Return spring or pin Change lever or spring Drum position plate Change drum Change forks
Brakes	Poor brakes	Worn linings Brake adjustment Oil or water on brake linings Loose linkage or cables
	Noisy brakes	Worn or scratched lining Scratched brake drums Dirt in brakes
	Unadjustable brakes	Worn linings Worn drums Worn brake cams

CHAPTER THREE

PERIODIC MAINTENANCE

REGULAR MAINTENANCE

This chapter covers all the regular maintenance you have to perform to keep your machine in top shape. In addition, while performing the routine jobs, you will probably notice any other developing problems at an early stage when they are simple and inexpensive to correct.

Tables are located at the end of the chapter.

Emission-Controlled Motorcycles

This manual covers both emission-controlled motorcycles manufactured after January 1, 1978 and non-controlled motorcycles built before that date. Only bikes that were designed as street-legal motorcycles are subject to emission controls.

If your motorcycle is emission-controlled, we urge you to follow all procedures specifically designated for your bike. If you don't follow the maintenance schedule in this manual, if you don't perform a tune-up according to these procedures, or if you alter engine parts or change their settings from the standard factory specifications (ignition timing, carburetor air screw, slide needle, exhaust system, etc.), your bike may not comply with federal emissions standards.

In addition, since most emission-controlled bikes are carburetted on the lean side, any changes to emission-related parts (such as exhaust system modifications) could cause the engine to run so lean that piston seizure could result.

Table 1 is a recommended minimum maintenance schedule. However, you will have to determine your own maintenance requirements based on the type of riding you do and the place you ride, whether it be on the road or in wet sand and mud.

Perform the maintenance at each TIME or MILE-AGE interval, whichever comes first.

RACING MAINTENANCE

If you have a motocross or enduro type racer, Table 2 is a pre-race checklist you should always run through before each event, even if it is as short as a moto. At the end of each race day, clean your machine thoroughly and inspect it carefully. Then give it a good general lubrication and make any adjustments necessary.

Table 3 is a maintenance schedule for racing machines. Full-time racing every weekend naturally requires more stringent maintenance than occasional sport and trail riding. You will have to determine your own maintenance requirements based on the type of riding you do and the terrain you ride on, whether it be dry desert dust or wet sand and mud.

ENGINE TUNE-UP

The number of definitions of the term "tune-up" is probably equal to the number of people defining it. For purposes of this book, we will define a tune-up as a general adjustment and/or maintenance of all service items to ensure continued peak operating efficiency of a motorcycle engine.

As part of a proper tune-up, some service procedures are essential. The following paragraphs discuss details of these procedures. Service operations should be performed in the order specified. Unless otherwise specified, the engine should be thoroughly cool before starting any tune-up service.

Spark Plug

As the first step in any tune-up, remove and examine the spark plug, because spark plug condition can tell much about engine condition and carburetor adjustment.

To remove the spark plug, first clean the area around its base to prevent dirt or other foreign material from entering the cylinder. Then unscrew the spark plug, using a suitable deep socket. If difficulty is encountered removing a spark plug, apply penetrating oil to its base and allow some 20 minutes for the oil to work in. It may also be helpful to rap the cylinder head lightly with a rubber or plastic mallet; this procedures sets up vibrations which help the penetrating oil to work in. Be careful not to break any cooling fins when tapping the cylinder head.

Figure 1 illustrates various conditions which might be encountered upon plug removal.

Normal condition–If plugs have a light tan or gray colored deposit and no abnormal gap wear or erosion, this indicates good engine, carburetion and ignition condition. The plug is of the proper heat range and may be serviced and returned to use.

Carbon fouled–Soft, dry, sooty deposits are evidence of incomplete combustion and can usually be attributed to rich carburetion. The condition is also sometimes caused by weak ignition, retarding timing, or low compression. Such a plug may usually be cleaned and returned to service, but the condition which causes fouling should be corrected.

Oil fouled–This plug exhibits a black insulator tip, damp oily film over the firing end and a carbon layer over the entire nose. Electrodes will not be worn. Common causes for this condition are listed below:

a. Improper fuel/oil mixture.

b. Wrong type of oil.

c. Idle speed too low.

d. Idle mixture too rich.

e. Clogged air filter.

f. Weak ignition.

g. Excessive idling.

h. Oil pump out of adjustment.

i. Wrong spark plugs (too cold).

Oil-fouled spark plugs may be cleaned in a pinch, but it is better to replace them. It is important to correct the cause of fouling before the engine is returned to service.

Gap bridging–Plugs with this condition exhibit gaps shorted out by combustion chamber deposits fused between electrodes. Any of the following may be the cause.

a. Improper fuel/oil mixture.

b. Clogged exhaust.

c. Oil pump misadjusted.

Be sure to locate and correct the cause of this spark plug condition. Such plugs must be replaced with new ones.

Overheated–Overheated spark plugs exhibit burned electrodes. The insulator tip will be light gray or even chalk white. The most common cause for this condition is using a spark plug of the wrong heat range (too hot). If it is known that the correct plug is used, other causes are lean fuel mixture, engine overloading or lugging, loose carburetor mounting, or timing advanced too far. Always correct the fault before putting the bike back into service. Such plugs cannot be salvaged; replace with new ones.

Worn out–Corrosive gases formed by combustion and high voltage sparks have eroded the electrodes. Spark plugs in this condition require more voltage to fire under hard acceleration; often more than the ignition system can supply. Replace them with new plugs of the same heat range.

Preignition–If electrodes are melted, preignition is almost certainly the cause. Check for loose carburetor mounting or overadvanced ignition timing. It is also possible that a plug of the wrong heat range (too hot) is being used. Find the cause of preignition before placing the engine back into service.

Refer to **Table 4** at the end of this chapter for spark plug specifications.

Spark plugs may usually be cleaned and regapped, which will restore them to near new condition. Since the effort involved is considerable, such service may

①

SPARK PLUG CONDITIONS

NORMAL USE

OIL FOULED

CARBON FOULED

OVERHEATED

GAP BRIDGED

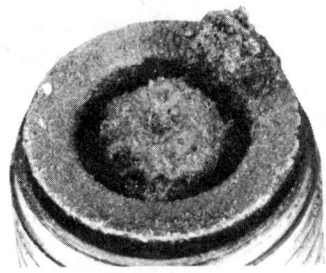

SUSTAINED PREIGNITION

WORN OUT

3

not be worth it; new spark plugs are relatively inexpensive.

For those who wish to service used plugs, the following procedure is recommended.

1. Clean all oily deposits from the spark plug with cleaning solvent, then blow dry with compressed air. If this precaution is not taken, oily deposits will cause gumming or caking of the sandblast cleaner.

2. Place the spark plug in a sandblast cleaner and blast 3-5 seconds, then turn on air only to remove particles from the plug.

3. Repeat Step 2 as required until the plug is cleaned. Prolonged sandblasting will erode the insulator and make the plug much more susceptible to fouling.

4. Bend the side electrode up slightly, then file the center electrode so that its edges are not rounded. The reason for this step is that less voltage is required to jump between sharp corners than between rounded edges.

5. Adjust spark plug gap to 0.035-0.039 in. (0.9-1.0 mm) for the F5 and F9, to 0.028-0.032 in. (0.7-0.8 mm) for the 1978 and later KE100 and to 0.024-0.028 in. (0.6-0.7 mm) for all other models except those with surface gap plugs. Surface gap spark plugs are not adjustable. Use a round wire gauge for measurement (**Figure 2**). Always adjust spark plug gap by bending the side electrode, not the center electrode.

It will be easier to turn the engine over for other service operations if the spark plug is not installed until it is time to start the engine.

Compression Test

An engine requires adequate compression to develop full power. If for any reason compression is low, the engine will not develop full power. A compression test, or even better, a series of them over the life of the bike, will tell much about engine condition.

To make a compression test, proceed as follows:

1. Start the engine, then ride the bike long enough to warm it thoroughly.

2. Remove the spark plug.

3. Screw the compression gauge into the spark plug hole, or if a press-in type gauge is used, hold it firmly in position.

4. With the ignition switch OFF, crank the engine briskly with the kickstarter several times; the compression gauge indication will increase with each kick. Continue to crank the engine until the gauge shows no more increase, then record the gauge indication.

Example:

    1st kick: 90 psi
    2nd kick: 140 psi
    3rd kick: 160 psi
    4th kick: 170 psi
    5th kick: 170 psi

Because of differences in engine design, carbon deposits and other factors, no definite compression readings can be specified for any one engine.

A series of measurements made over a period of time may reveal an indication of trouble ahead, long before the engine exhibits serious symptoms.

It is for the reasons outlined in the foregoing paragraphs that a serious motorcycle hobbyist will want to own and use a compression gauge and also keep a permanent record of its findings. It should be pointed out, however, that measurements taken with different gauges are not necessarily conclusive, be-

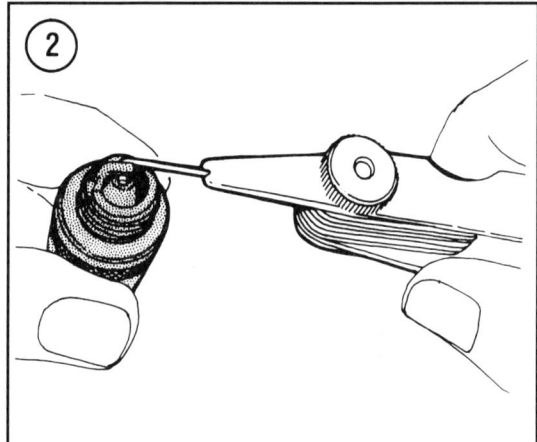

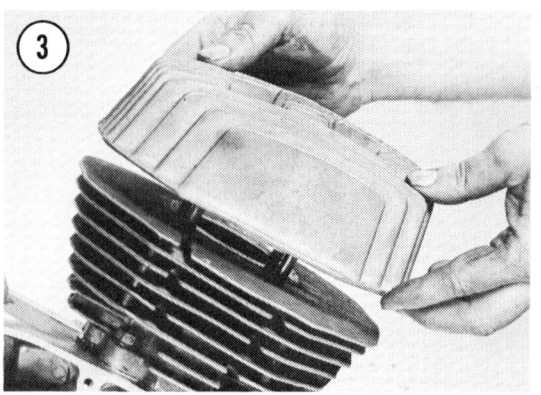

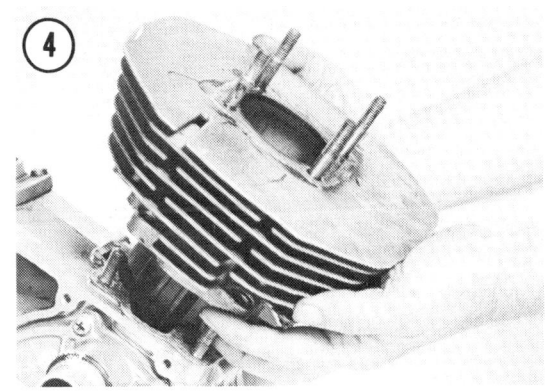

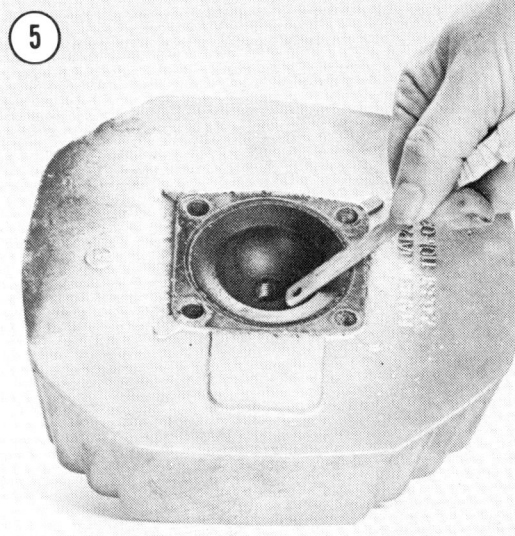

cause of production tolerances, calibration errors and other factors.

Carbon Removal

Two-stroke engines are particularly susceptible to carbon formation. Deposits form on the inside of the cylinder head, on top of the piston and within the exhaust port. Combustion chamber deposits can abnormally increase compression ration, causing overheating, preignition and possible severe engine damage. Carbon deposits within the exhaust port, exhaust pipe and muffler restrict engine breathing, causing loss of power.

To remove carbon from the engine, first remove the cylinder head (**Figure 3**) and cylinder (**Figure 4**). It is usually unnecessary to remove the piston. Be sure to stuff a clean rag into the crankcase opening to prevent entry of foreign material.

Always allow the engine to cool to avoid possible cylinder head warpage. To remove the cylinder head proceed as follows.

1. Remove the spark plug.

2. Following a crisscross sequence, loosen each cylinder head retaining nut 1/2 turn at a time until each one turns freely. This procedures minimizes chances for cylinder head warpage.

3. Lift the cylinder head from the cylinder. If it sticks, tap it lightly with a rubber mallet. Do not pry it off; doing so may cause damage to sealing surfaces.

4. Reverse the procedure to install the head. Always use a new cylinder head gasket. Torque cylinder head nuts as follows:

   8 mm nuts: 15 ft.-lbs.

   10 mm nuts: 25 ft.-lbs.

An easy method for removing cylinder head deposits is to use the rounded end of a hacksaw blade as a scraper, as shown in **Figure 5**. Be very careful not to cause any damage to the sealing surface.

The same tool may be used for removing carbon deposits from piston heads (**Figure 6**). After removing all deposits from the piston head, clean all carbon and gum from the piston ring grooves using a ring groove cleaning tool or broken piston ring (**Figure 7**). Any deposits left in the grooves will cause the piston rings to stick, thereby causing gas blow-by and loss of power.

To remove piston rings, it is only necessary to spread the top ring with a thumb on each end (**Figure 8**), then remove it upward. Repeat the procedure for each remaining ring. When replacing rings, be sure that the ends of the rings engage the locating pins in the grooves (**Figure 9**).

Finally, scrape all carbon deposits from the cylinder exhaust port, as shown in **Figure 10**. A blunted screwdriver is a suitable tool for this job.

Reverse the removal procedure to install the cylinder. Be sure to lubricate the piston and cylinder liberally before installation. Note that when replacing the cylinder, it is necessary to compress each piston ring as it enters the cylinder. A ring compressor tool makes the job easier, but the rings may be compressed by hand with little difficulty.

Breaker Points

Normal use of a motorcycle causes the breaker points to burn and pit gradually. If they are not too pitted, they can be dressed with a few strokes of a clean point file. Do not use emery cloth or sandpaper,

because particles can remain on the points and cause arcing and burning. If a few strokes of a file do not smooth the points completely, replace them.

Oil or dirt may get on the points, resulting in poor performance or even premature failure. Common causes for this condition are defective oil seals, improper or excessive breaker cam lubrication, or lack of care when the breaker point cover is removed.

Points should be cleaned and regapped every 2,500 miles (4,000 km). To clean the points, first dress them lightly with a clean point file, then remove all residue with lacquer thinner. Close the points on a piece of clean white paper such as a business card. Continue to pull the card through the closed points until no discoloration or residue re-

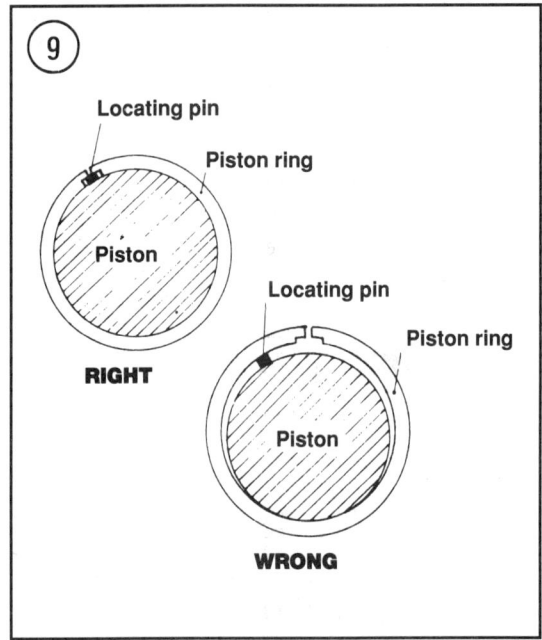

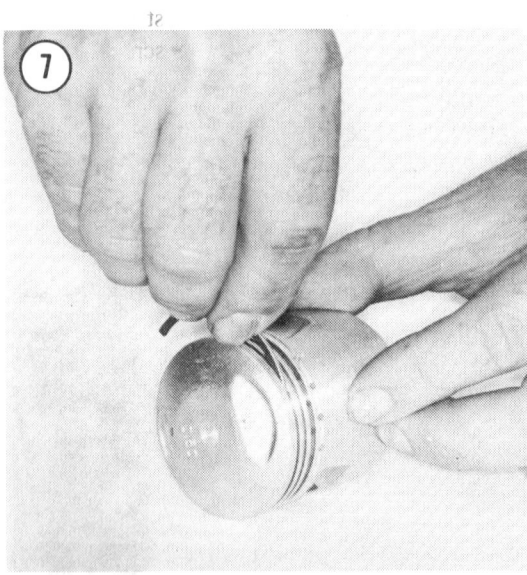

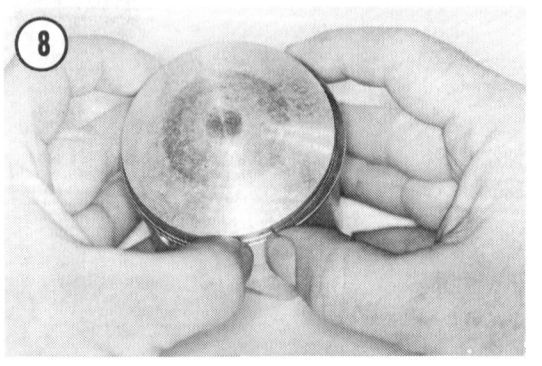

mains on the card. Finally, rotate the engine and observe the points as they open and close. If they do not meet squarely, replace them.

If poor engine performance has been traced to oil-fouled points, correct the cause before returning the motorcycle to service.

To service or replace breaker points on models with magneto ignition, proceed as follows.

1. Remove gearshift lever. Note that its clamping bolt must be removed completely before the lever can be pulled from the shaft.

2. Remove left crankcase cover. An impact driver makes it easy to loosen the cover screws without damaging them.

3. Remove flywheel retaining nut and its lockwasher.

4. Screw a flywheel puller (left-hand thread) into the flywheel to its full depth. Be sure that the puller screw is backed out fully when installing the puller. Turn the puller screw clockwise to remove the flywheel.

5. Refer to **Figure 11**. Remove both wires, then remove point retaining screw (A).

6. After the new points are installed, tighten screw (A) just enough so that the stationary contact does not slip, but not so much that the contact cannot be moved by a screwdriver twisted in pry slots (B). Move the stationary contact until both points just barely make contact.

7. Install flywheel, lockwasher and flywheel retaining nut.

8. Adjust ignition timing.

Breaker point service on models with battery ignition is similar to that on models with magnetos, however, point gap must be adjusted separately.

1. Remove ignition cover from left side of engine.

2. Turn engine counterclockwise until breaker points are open to their widest distance apart. Measure point gap (**Figure 12**), using a clean feeler gauge. If point gap is 0.012-0.016 in. (0.30-0.40 mm), no adjustment is required.

3. If adjustment is required, refer to **Figure 13**. Loosen screws (A) just enough so that stationary contact (B) may be moved to adjust point gap to 0.012-0.016 in. (0.30-0.40 mm). A screwdriver inserted into pry slots (C) makes adjustment easy.

4. Tighten screws (A), then recheck adjustment.

5. Adjust ignition timing.

Ignition Timing
(Models With Magnetos)

It is necessary to adjust ignition timing whenever breaker points are serviced. Proceed as follows:

1. Refer to **Figure 14**. Turn engine counterclockwise until mark (A) on flywheel aligns with index (B) on crankcase.

2. Connect a timing tester to the breaker point terminal and a good engine ground. Follow the manufacturer's instructions.

3. Refer to **Figure 15**. Loosen screw (C) slightly, then move stationary contact with a screwdriver inserted into pry slots (D) and (E) until the timing tester indicates that the breaker points just open. Be sure to tighten screw (C) after adjustment.

4. Check the adjustment by rotating the flywheel counterclockwise. The points must just begin to open as mark (A, **Figure 14**) on the flywheel aligns with mark (B) on the crankcase.

5. When timing is adjusted correctly, maximum point gap will be 0.012-0.016 in. (0.3-0.4 mm). It is not necessary to adjust point gap separately on the models.

Note that magnetos on F8 models have slotted mounting holes for adjustment. It is necessary that the marks on the magneto base and crankcase be aligned before adjustment.

Ignition Timing
(Models With Starter-Generator)

Refer to **Figure 16**, then proceed as follows:

1. Turn engine counterclockwise until mark on timing pointer (A) aligns with index pointer (B).

2. Connect a test light, ohmmeter, timing tester to the terminal on the breaker points. Also connect to a good ground.

3. Loosen timing plate screws (C) slightly, then move timing plate (D) up or down as required, until the breaker points just open. Tighten screws (C).

4. Recheck the adjustment by turning the engine clockwise slightly, then counterclockwise slowly. The points must open just as timing pointer (A) aligns with index pointer (B).

Ignition Timing (CDI)

Because a signal pulse is generated only when the engine is running, it is not possible to time the ignition statically, as in the case with ignition sys-

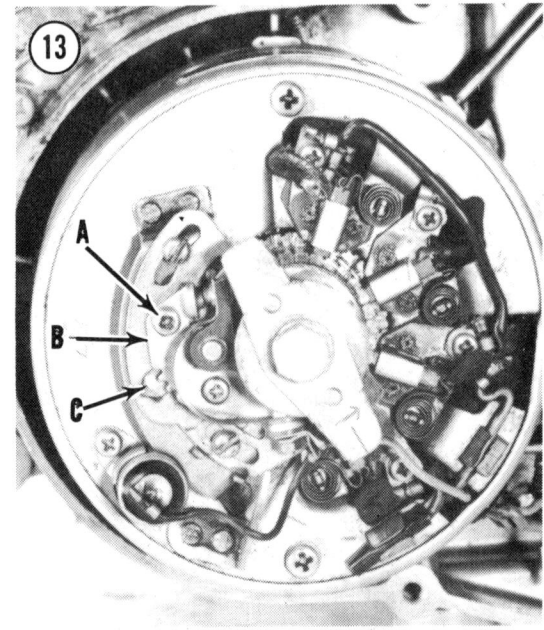

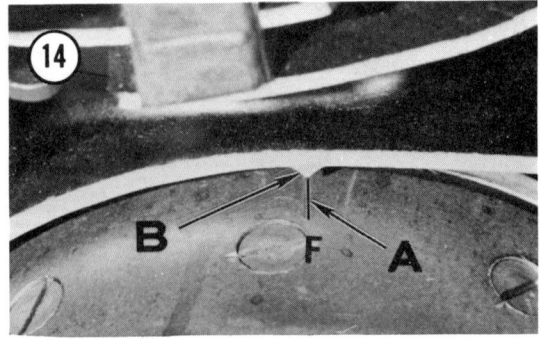

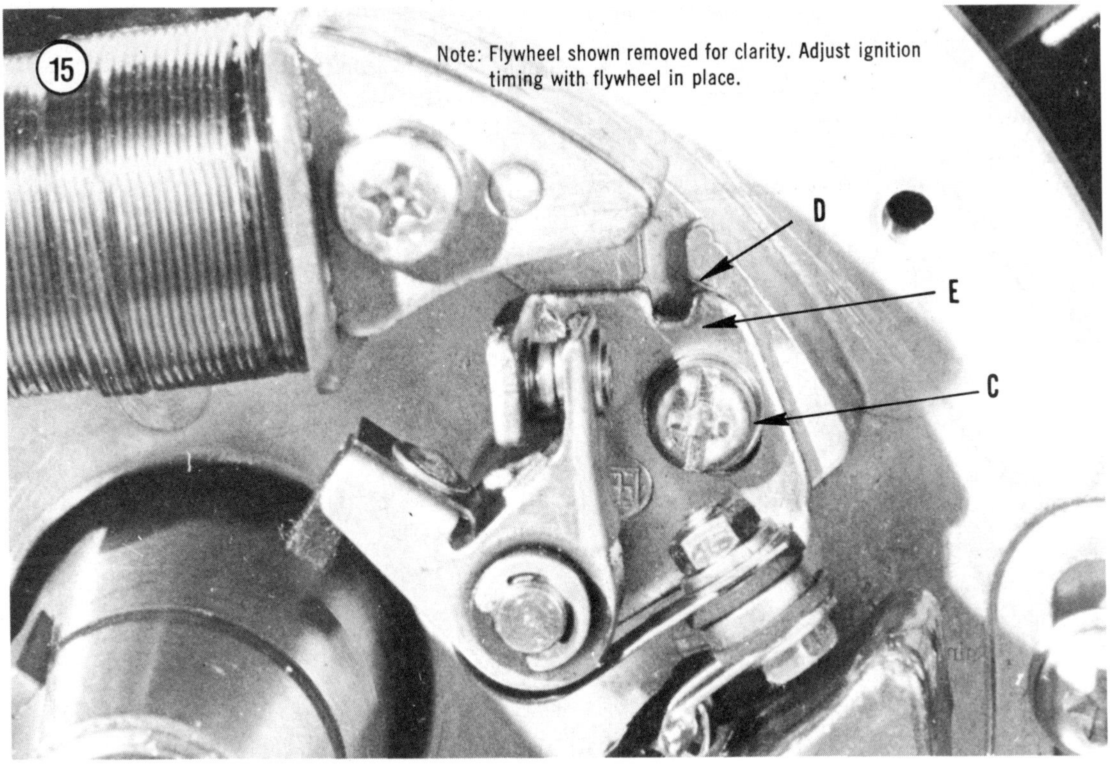
15
Note: Flywheel shown removed for clarity. Adjust ignition timing with flywheel in place.
D
E
C

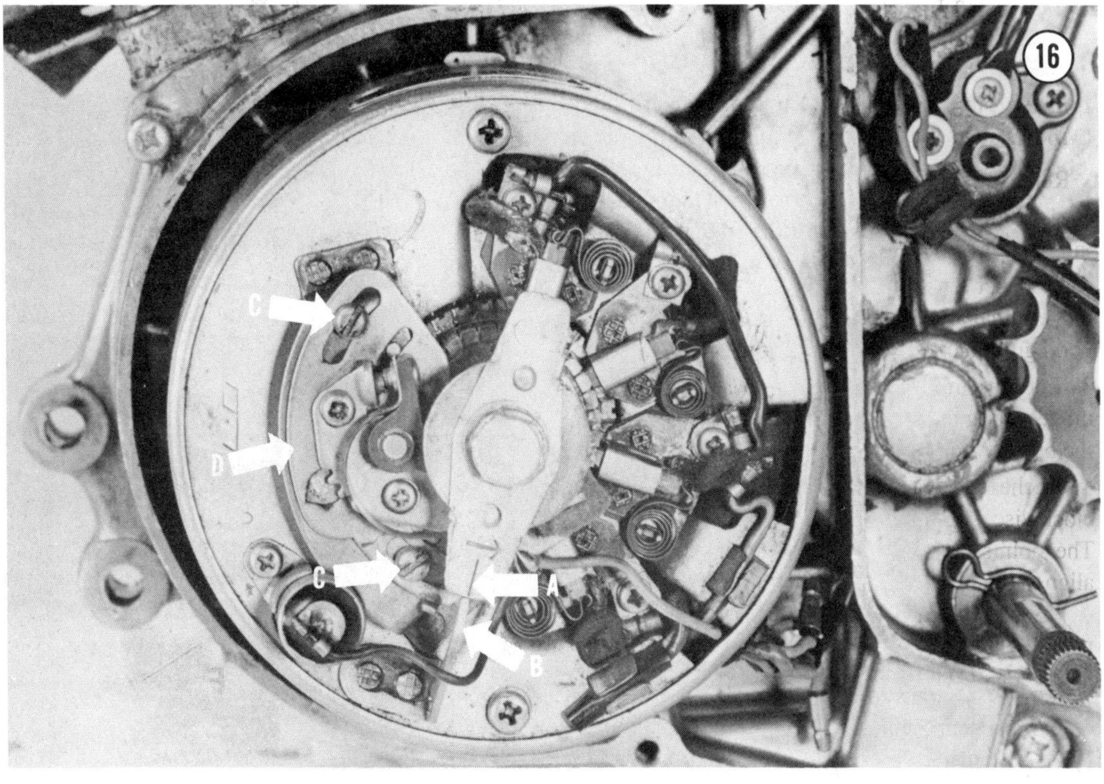
16
C
D
C
A
B

tems which use breaker points. To check timing, proceed as follows.

1. Remove chaincase and magneto cover.
2. Connect a timing light (**Figure 17**).
3. Start the engine and run it at 6,000 rpm.
4. Direct the timing light on the timing marks on the flywheel and crankcase, as shown in **Figure 18**. Timing is correct if both marks are aligned.

NOTE
Figure 19 shows flywheel removed for clarity. Adjust timing with flywheel in place.

If the marks are not aligned, ignition timing must be adjusted. Refer to **Figure 19**, then proceed as follows.

1. Insert a screwdriver through the hole in the flywheel, then loosen stator screws at locations (A), (B) and (C).
2. Rotate the magneto base with a screwdriver inserted into notch (D): counterclockwise rotation retards timing; clockwise rotation advances timing.
3. Tighten screws at locations (A), (B) and (C).
4. Reconnect the timing light and recheck timing with the light. Repeat the procedure as necessary.

Air Cleaner Service

As part of any tune-up, air cleaner elements should be cleaned or replaced, as required. A clogged air cleaner results in an overrich mixture, causing power loss and poor gas mileage. Be sure that the air cleaner element is not torn and that it fits so that no dirt can leak past its edges.

Replace paper air cleaner elements if they become torn, punctured, or so clogged that dirt cannot be removed and/or after cleaning them five times.

Some models are equipped with polyurethane foam air cleaner elements. Wash such elements in solvent, dry thoroughly, then wet lightly but thoroughly with engine oil before installation. Replace the element if it is torn or punctured.

Fuel Strainer

Remove and clean the fuel strainer. Blow dry with compressed air. On models with automatic fuel cocks, be sure that there are no leaks in the signal tube from the carburetor to the fuel cock. Air leaks will result in poor fuel flow.

Carburetor Adjustment

Carburetor adjustment is left as the last step to be done on the engine, because it cannot be done accurately until all other adjustments are correct. The carburetor must also be adjusted with the engine thoroughly warmed, while most other adjustments either must be or are more easily done with the engine cold.

Idle speed and idle mixture are normally the only carburetor adjustments performed at the time of engine tune-up. If other adjustments seem to be required, refer to Chapter Five for details of major carburetor service. Refer to **Figure 20**.

The idle fuel/air mixture affects low speed emissions, as well as idling stability and smooth transition to partial throttle openings. The idle mixture

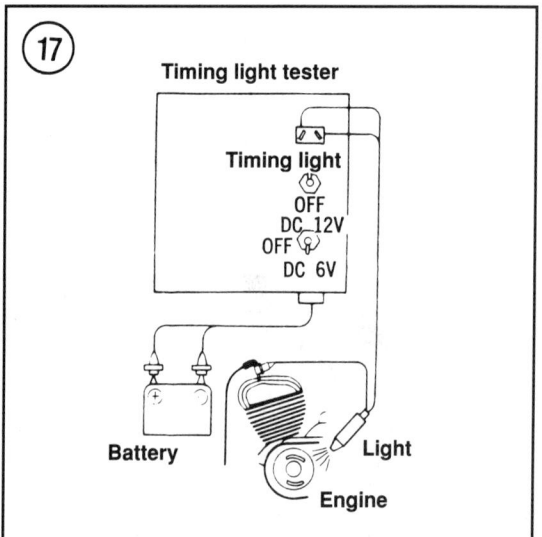

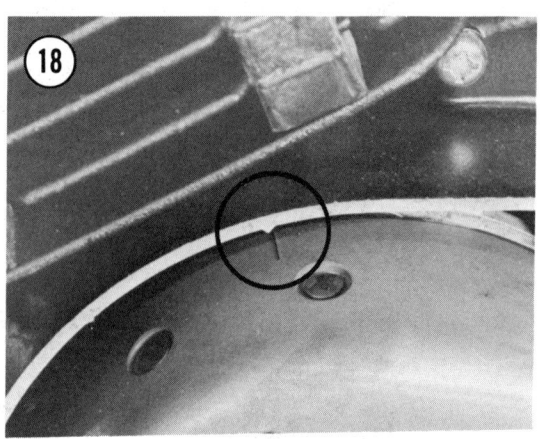

should *not* be adjusted on emission-controlled bikes unless the factory setting has been altered. There should be a dab of yellow paint securing the mixture screw on emission-controlled models.

1. Turn in the idle mixture screw (A) until it seats lightly, then back it out 1 to 1 3/4 turns. See **Table 6** at the end of this chapter for your motorcycle's standard idle mixture screw setting.

2. Start the engine, then ride the bike long enough to warm it thoroughly.

3. Turn the idle speed adjuster (B) until the engine runs slower and begins to falter.

4. *Non-emission controlled bikes only:* Turn the idle mixture screw as required to make the engine run smoothly. Repeat steps 3 and 4 to achieve the lowest stable idle speed.

5. *Emission-controlled bikes:* Turn the idle speed adjuster to achieve the lowest stable idle speed.

Oil Pump and Throttle Cable Adjustment

Since oil pump and throttle valve operation are related, it is essential to adjust the oil pump and throttle cables so that they operate simultaneously.

1. With the engine at normal operating temperature, adjust idle speed.

2. Refer to **Figure 21**. Loosen throttle cable locknut (a), then turn cable adjuster (A) to provide 0.08-0.12 in. Play at the grip. Repeat the procedure for the starter cable. Tighten the locknuts.

3. Refer to **Figure 22**. Remove throttle cable play by turning adjuster (A) at the top of the carburetor. The idle speed should just start to increase.

4. Refer to **Figure 23**. Loosen locknut on pump cable then turn cable adjuster until mark on lever aligns with mark on lever stop (A). Be sure to tighten cable adjuster locknut.

5. Refer to **Figure 22**. Readjust throttle cable play to 0.08-0.12 in.

BATTERY SERVICE

Tune-up time is also battery service time. Complete battery service information is contained in Chapter Six. Briefly, the following items should be attended to regularly.

1. Test state of charge. Recharge if at half charge (1.220 specific gravity) or less.

2. Add distilled water if required.

3. Clean battery top.

4. Clean and tighten terminals.

TRANSMISSION

Oil Change

To change oil, first ride the bike until it is thoroughly warm. Place a flat pan under the engine, then remove the oil drain plug from the bottom of the engine and allow oil to drain. It may be helpful to rock the motorcycle from side to side and also forward and backward to get out as much as possible.

Replace the drain plug, then refill with fresh engine oil which meets API specifications MS or SE. Maintain oil level between both marks on the dipstick. On models with a level inspection screw, add oil until it runs out of the screw hole.

CLUTCH ADJUSTMENT

Adjust the clutch at 2,500 mile (4,000 km) intervals, or more often if required. Complete clutch adjustment procedures are discussed in Chapter Four.

ELECTRICAL EQUIPMENT

Check all electrical equipment for proper operation–lights, horn, starter, etc. Refer to Chapter Six for electrical system service.

DRIVE CHAIN

Clean and adjust the drive chain every 500 miles (800 km). Adjust drive chain tension to provide 3/4-1 in. (20-25 mm) up-and-down play in the center of the lower chain run. Both wheels should be on the ground and a rider in the saddle when this measurement is made. Be sure to adjust the rear brake after chain tension adjustment.

BRAKES

Adjust front and rear brakes every 2,500 miles (4,000 km), or more often as needed. Remove wheels and check brake lining at 2,500 mile (4,000 km) intervals. Check and service wheel bearings at the same time.

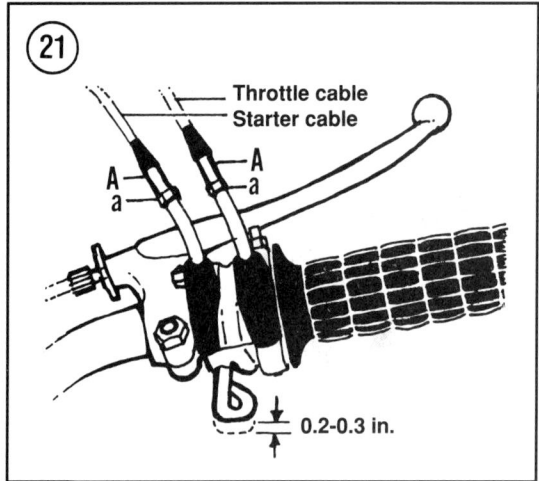

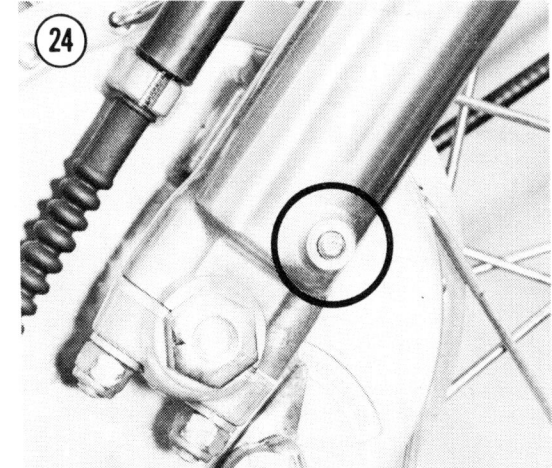

WHEELS AND TIRES

Check wheels for bent rims and loose or missing spokes. Complete wheel inspection and service procedures are detailed in Chapter Seven.

Check tires for worn treads, cuts and proper inflation. Inflate tires to the value specified in **Table 7**.

FORK OIL

Replace fork oil at 5,000 mile (8,000 km) intervals. To do so, place a pan under each fork leg, then remove the drain plug at the lower end of each fork leg (**Figure 24**). Replace with fresh fork oil through the upper fork bolts. Refill quantities are listed in **Table 8**.

Complete fork service is described in Chapter Seven.

STEERING HEAD BEARINGS

Check steering bearings for looseness or binding. *If any exists, find and correct the cause immediately.* Complete service instructions are in Chapter Seven.

SWINGING ARM

Disassemble the swinging arm and grease its pivot shaft and bushings every 5,000 miles (8,000 km). Complete service procedures are in Chapter Seven.

Table 1 MAINTENANCE SCHEDULE

Initial 800 km (500 miles)	Check idle speed
	Check throttle grip play
	Check oil pump and carburetor synchronization
	Clean and gap spark plug
	Check ignition timing
	Check cylinder head nuts
	Check battery (at least once each month)
	Check brake play
	Check brake light switch
	Adjust clutch
	Check steering for play
	Check spokes for tightness
	Check wheel for runout
	Check all fasteners (nuts and bolts) for tightness
	Change transmission oil (at least once each year)
	(continued)

Table 1 MAINTENANCE SCHEDULE (continued)

Every 300 km (180 miles)	Lubricate drive chain
Every 800 km (500 miles)	Check and adjust drive chain slack
Every 4,000 km (2,500 miles)	Check idle speed Check throttle grip play Check oil pump and carburetor synchronization Clean and gap spark plug Check ignition timing Clean air filter Check battery (at least once each month) Check brake play Check brake light switch Check brake lining for wear Adjust clutch Check steering for play Check spokes for tightness Check wheel for runout Check drive chain for wear Check tires for wear Perform general lubrication
Every 8,000 km (5,000 miles)	Service all items listed in 4,000 km (2,500 miles) service interval. Install new air filter (after every 5 cleanings) Clean fuel system and filter Check cylinder head nuts Check all fasteners (nuts and bolts) for tightness Change transmission oil (at least once each year) Change fork oil Lubricate swing arm
Every 12,000 km (7,200 miles)	Service all items listed in 4,000 km (2,500 miles) service interval.
Every 16,000 km (9,600 miles)	Service all items listed in 8,000 km (5,000 miles) service interval. Lubricate brake camshafts (at least every two years)

Every 20,000 km (12,000 miles)	Service all items listed in 4,000 km (2,500 miles)
	   service interval.
	Lubricate wheel bearings (at least every two years)
	Lubricate speedometer gear (at least every two years)
	Lubricate steering stem bearings (at least every two
	   years)

Every 24,000 km (14,400 miles)	Service all items listed in 8,000 km (5,000 miles) service interval.
Every 4 years	Replace all fuel hoses.

Table 2 PRE-RACE CHECKLIST

ENGINE	
Transmission oil	Level correct
Gearshift	Not bent, smooth operation
Engine compression	Normal – piston ring OK
(continued)	

Table 2 PRE-RACE CHECKLIST (continued)

ENGINE (continued)	
Spark plug	Clean, gapped, torqued
Cylinder and head	Bolts/nuts torqued
Engine mounts	Bolts/nuts torqued
Air cleaner	Clean, no leaks
Throttle	Cable play OK, smooth operation
Carburetor	Idle adjusted
Kill switch	Functions
Clutch	Cable play OK, smooth operation
Exhaust system	Secure, no dents, cracks
CHASSIS	
Drive chain	Adjusted, lubricated
Brakes	Adjusted, smooth operation
Tires	Pressure OK, no damage
Spokes	Evenly tightened
Wheel rims	No deep dents, runout OK
Steering	Smooth, but not loose, no binding cables
Front suspension	No leaks, smooth operation, air pressure checked
Rear suspension	No leaks, smooth operation
Nuts, bolts, fasteners	All tight, cotter pins and safety clips secure
Frame	Check for cracks
General lubrication	Performed
Fuel system	Clean, no water or dirt
Fuel tank	Enough fuel, mounts secure
Fuel valve	ON

Table 3 RACING MAINTENANCE SCHEDULE

EVERY 3 RACES	
Piston	Clean, inspect
Piston rings	Replace
Small end bearing	Inspect
Transmission oil	Change
EVERY 6 RACES	
Small end bearing	Replace
Drive chain	Replace
Brake camshaft	Lubricate
Fork oil	Change
EVERY 12 RACES	
Big end bearing	Inspect
Sprockets	Inspect
Brake wear	Inspect
Wheel bearings	Lubricate
Steering bearings	Lubricate

Table 4 SPARK PLUG APPLICATION AND GAP

79-100 cc models	NGK	ND	Gap
KD80 (1975, 1976 & 1980-1987)	B7HS	W22FS	0.6-0.7 mm (0.024-0.028 in.)
J Series	B6H	W17F	0.6-0.7 mm (0.024-0.028 in.)
MC1-A, MC1-B & MC1M	B7HS	W25FN	0.6-0.7 mm (0.024-0.028 in.)
G3SS	B8HS	W24FS	0.6-0.7 mm (0.024-0.028 in.)
G3TR	B7HS	W25FS	0.6-0.7 mm (0.024-0.028 in.)
(continued)			

Table 4 SPARK PLUG APPLICATION AND GAP (continued)

79-100 cc models	NGK	ND	Gap (continued)
D1	B7H	W22F	0.6-0.7 mm (0.024-0.028 in.)
G4TR	B7HS	W25FN	0.6-0.7 mm (0.024-0.028 in.)
G5	B8HS	W24FS	0.6-0.7 mm (0.024-0.028 in.)
G31M	B8HN	W25FN	0.6-0.7 mm (0.024-0.028 in.)
KD100	B7HS	W22FS	0.6-0.7 mm (0.024-0.028 in.)
KE100 1978 & earlier	B8HS	W24FS	0.6-0.7 mm (0.024-0.028 in.)
KE100 1979 & later (A8 on)	B8ES	W24ES	0.7-0.8 mm (0.028-0.032 in.)
KH100	B8HS	W24FS	0.6-0.7 mm (0.024-0.028 in.)
KM100	B7HS	W22FS	0.6-0.7 mm (0.024-0.028 in.)
KV100	B7HS	W22FS	0.6-0.7 mm (0.024-0.028 in.)
115-125 cc models	**NGK**	**ND**	**Gap**
C2SS & C2TR	B7HS	W22FS	0.6-0.7 mm (0.024-0.028 in.)
F6	B8HS	W24FS	0.6-0.7 mm (0.024-0.028 in.)
KD125	B8HS	W24FS	0.6-0.7 mm (0.024-0.028 in.)
KE125 1979 & earlier	B8HS	W24FS	0.6-0.7 mm (0.024-0.028 in.)
KE125-A7 1980	B9ES	–	0.7-0.8 mm (0.028-0.032 in.)
KE125 1981 & later (A8 on)	B9ES	–	0.7-0.8 mm (0.028-0.032 in.)
KS125	B8HS	W24FS	0.6-0.7 mm (0.024-0.028 in.)
KX125 (1974-1976)	B9EV	W27ESG	0.6 mm (0.024 in.)
169-175 cc models	**NGK**	**ND**	**Gap**
F2 & F2TR	B7HS	W22FS	0.6-0.7 mm (0.024-0.028 in.)
F3	B8HS	W24FS	0.6-0.7 mm (0.024-0.028 in.)
F7	B9HS	W27FS	0.6-0.7 mm (0.024-0.028 in.)
KD175 (1976-1979)	B9HS	W27FS	0.6-0.7 mm (0.024-0.028 in.)
KE175 (1976-1982)	B9HS	W27FS	0.6-0.7 mm (0.024-0.028 in.)
238-350 cc models	**NGK**	**ND**	**Gap**
F4	B9HS	W27FS	0.6-0.7 mm (0.024-0.028 in.)
F21M	B8HN	W25FN	0.6-0.7 mm (0.024-0.028 in.)
F8	B8HS	W24FS	0.6-0.7 mm (0.024-0.028 in.)
F81M	B9HS	W27FS	0.6-0.7 mm (0.024-0.028 in.)
F5 & F9	B10H	W31FS	0.9-1.0 mm (0.035-0.039 in.)

CAUTION: Make sure that the spark plug has the correct thread length (reach) for the application as well as the correct heat range. Occasionally a motorcycle may be equipped with a cylinder head which requires a spark plug with a different length of thread than the one listed in the following table, so it is important to check the actual thread length in the cylinder head as well as the following table. Spark plug threads and the threads in the cylinder head should be the same length.

Table 5 IGNITION TIMING

79-100 cc models	Piston position	° BTDC	*Breaker point gap
KD80 (1975, 1976 & 1980-1987)	1.86 mm (0.073 in.)	20	**
J Series	1.58 mm (0.062 in.)	19	0.30-0.40 mm (0.012-0.016 in.)
MC1-A, MC1-B & MC1M	1.96 mm (0.077 in.)	20	**
G3SS & G3TR	1.96 mm (0.077 in.)	20	0.30-0.40 mm (0.012-0.016 in.)
D1	1.58 mm (0.062 in.)	19	0.30-0.40 mm (0.012-0.016 in.)
G4TR	1.96 mm (0.077 in.)	20	0.30-0.40 mm (0.012-0.016 in.)
G5	1.96 mm (0.077 in.)	20	0.30-0.40 mm (0.012-0.016 in.)
G31M	2.58 mm (0.099 in.)	23	0.30-0.40 mm (0.012-0.016 in.)
KD100	1.96 mm (0.077 in.)	20	**
KE100 1978 & earlier	1.96 mm (0.077 in.)	20	**
KE100 1979 & later (A8 on)	2.58 mm (0.099 in.)	23 @ 1,300 rpm	**
KH100 & KM100	1.96 mm (0.077 in.)	20	**
KV100	1.96 mm (0.077 in.)	20	**

(continued)

Table 5 IGNITION TIMING (continued)

115-125 cc models	Piston position	° BTDC	*Breaker point gap
C2SS & C2TR	1.78 mm (0.070 in.)	19	0.30-0.40 mm (0.012-0.016 in.)
F6	2.94 mm (0.116 in.)	23	0.30-0.40 mm (0.012-0.016 in.)
KD125	1.96 mm (0.077 in.)	20	**
KE125 1979 & earlier	2.52 mm (0.099 in.)	23 @1,300 rpm	**
KE125-A7 1980	2.52 mm (0.099 in.)	23 @1,300 rpm	**
KE125 1981 & later (A8 on)	2.52 mm (0.099 in.)	21 @1,300 rpm	**
KS125	2.52 mm (0.099 in.)	21 @1,300 rpm	**
KX125 (1974-1976)	1.91 mm (0.075 in.)	20 @6,000 rpm	Breakerless CDI
169-175 cc models	**Piston position**	**° BTDC**	***Breaker point gap**
F2 & F2TR	2.09 mm (0.082 in.)	20	0.30-0.40 mm (0.012-0.016 in.)
F3	2.75 mm (0.108 in.)	23	0.30-0.40 mm (0.012-0.016 in.)
F7	2.94 mm (0.116 in.)	23 @6,000 rpm	Breakerless CDI
KD175 (1976-1979)	2.69 mm (0.102 in.)	22 @4,000 rpm	Breakerless CDI
KE175 (1976-1982)	2.69 mm (0.102 in.)	22 @4,000 rpm	Breakerless CDI
238-350 cc models	**Piston position**	**° BTDC**	***Breaker point gap**
F4 & F21M	3.09 mm (0.121 in.)	23	0.30-0.40 mm (0.012-0.016 in.)
F8	2.59 mm (0.101 in.)	20	0.30-0.40 mm (0.012-0.016 in.)
F81M	2.34 mm (0.092 in.)	19	0.30-0.40 mm (0.012-0.016 in.)
F5 & F9	3.41 mm (0.134 in.)	23 @6,000 rpm	Breakerless CDI

* On all models so equipped, ignition timing is changed when breaker point gap is changed, so timing and breaker point gap should both be checked.
** On models indicated, timing is set by changing breaker point gap.

Table 6 CARBURETOR IDLE MIXTURE SCREW AND SPEED SETTINGS

79-100 cc models	*Idle mixture screw	Idle speed
KD80 (1975, 1976 & 1980-1987)	1 1/2 turns open	**
J Series	1 1/2 turns open	**
MC1-A, MC1-B & MC1M	1 1/2 turns open	**
G3SS & G3TR	1 1/4-1 1/2 turns open	**
D1	1 3/4 turns open	**
G4TR	1 1/4-1 1/2 turns open	**
G5	1 1/2 turns open	**
G31M	1 1/2 turns open	**
KD100	1 1/4 turns open	**
KE100	1 1/2 turns open	**
KH100	1 1/4 turns open	**
KM100	1 1/4 turns open	**
KV100	1 1/4 turns open	**
115-125 cc models	***Idle mixture screw**	**Idle speed**
C2SS & C2TR	1 1/2 turns open	**
F6	1 3/4 turns open	**
KD125	1 1/2 turns open	**
KE125-A3, A4 & A5 (1976-1978)	1 1/2 turns open	**
KE125-A6 -A12 (1979-1985)	1 1/4 turns open	**
KS125	1 1/2 turns open	**
KX125 (1974-1976)	1 1/2 turns open	**
169-175 cc models	***Idle mixture screw**	**Idle speed**
F2 & F2TR	1 3/4 turns open	**
F3	1 3/4 turns open	**
F7	1 1/2-1 3/4 turns open	**

(continued)

Table 6 CARBURETOR IDLE MIXTURE SCREW AND SPEED SETTINGS (continued)

169-175 cc models	*Idle mixture screw	Idle speed (continued)
KD175 (1976-1979)	1 1/4 turns open	**
KE175 (1976-1982)	1 1/4 turns open	**
238-350 cc models	***Idle mixture screw**	**Idle speed**
F4	1 1/4 turns open	**
F21M	1 1/4 turns open	**
F8	1 3/4 turns open	**
F81M	1 1/4 turns open	**
F5	1 3/4 turns open	**
F9	1 1/2 turns open	**

* Idle mixture (pilot screw) settings are approximate and should be set for optimum running.
** Engine idle speed should be adjusted as slow as possible while maintaining smooth running without stalling.

Table 7 TIRE SIZE AND INFLATION PRESSURE

79-100 cc models	Front	psi	Rear	psi
KD80 (1975, 1976 & 1980-1987)	2.50-16	18	2.75-14	18
J Series	2.50-17	22	2.50-17	28
MC1-A & MC1M	2.50-16	23	2.75-14	26
MC1-B	2.50-16	25	3.00-14	28
G3 models	2.50-18	23	2.75-18	28
D1	2.50-17	22	2.50-17	28
G4TR	3.00-18	25	3.00-18	25 (under 215 lb.) 32 (over 215 lb.)
G5	*2.75-19	25	3.00-18	25 (under 215 lb.) 32 (over 215 lb.)
G31M	3.25-18	–	3.25-18	–
KD100	2.25-18	18	2.75-14	18
KE100 (1976-1981)	2.75-19	25	3.00-18	25 (under 215 lb.) 32 (over 215 lb.)
KE100 B2 - B13 (1982-1994)	2.75-19	21	3.00-17	28 (under 215 lb.) 32 (over 215 lb.)
KH100	2.75-18	21	3.00-18	28 (under 215 lb.) 32 (over 215 lb.)
KM100	2.50-16	25	3.00-14	28
KV100	3.00-18	25	3.00-18	25 (under 215 lb.) 32 (over 215 lb.)
115-125 cc models	**Front**	**psi**	**Rear**	**psi**
C2SS	2.75-18	22	3.00-18	28
C2TR	3.00-18	22	3.00-18	28
F6	3.00-18	23	3.25-18	28
KD125	2.75-21	25	3.50-18	25
KE125	2.75-21	25	3.50-18	25
KS125	2.75-21	25	3.50-18	25
KX125 (1974-1976)	3.00-21	–	4.10-18	–
169-175 cc models	**Front**	**psi**	**Rear**	**psi**
F2	2.50-18	22	2.75-18	28
F2TR	2.75-18	22	3.00-18	28
F3	3.00-19	22	3.50-18	28
F7	3.00-19	23	3.50-18	23 (under 215 lb.) 28 (over 215 lb.)
KD175 (1976-1979)	2.75-21	18	3.50-18	18 (under 215 lb.) 21 (over 215 lb.)

(continued)

Table 7 TIRE SIZE AND INFLATION PRESSURE (continued)

169-175 cc models	Front	psi	Rear	psi
KE175 (1976-1982)	2.75-21	25	3.50-18	25 (under 215 lb.) 28 (over 215 lb.)

238-350 cc models	Front	psi	Rear	psi
F4	3.25-19	24	4.00-18	31
F21M	3.50-19	–	4.00-18	–
F8	3.25-19	24	4.00-18	31
F81M	3.00-21	–	4.00-18	–
F5	3.00-21	24	4.00-18	28 (under 215 lb.) 32 (over 215 lb.)
F9	3.00-21	24	4.00-18	28 (under 215 lb.) 32 (over 215 lb.)

* Some early G5 models are equipped with 2.75-18 front tire.

Table 8 APPROXIMATE FORK OIL CAPACITY

79-100 cc models	SAE Grade	oz.	cc
KD80 (1975, 1976 & 1980-1987)	5W/20	3.1	95
J Series	5W/20	4.6	135
MC1-A models	5W/20	3.1	95
G3 models	30	4.4	130
D1	5W/20	4.6	135
G4TR	10W	5.7	174
G5	10W	5.7	174
G31M	20	5.8	170
KD100	5W/20	3.1	95
KE100 (1976-1978)	10W	5.7	174
	Maintain oil 395 mm from top		
KE100-A8 (1979)	10W	5.3-5.6	158-166
	Maintain oil 395 mm from top		
KE100 A9 - B13 (1980-1994)	10W/20	5.3-5.6	158-166
	Maintain oil 406.5-410.5 mm from top		
KH100	30	4.4	130
KM100	5W/20	3.1	95
KV100	10W	5.7	174

115-125 cc models	SAE Grade	oz.	cc
C2SS & C2TR (Early)	5W/20	4.0	120
C2SS & C2TR (Late)	5W/20	5.9	175
F6	10W	5.1	152
KD125	5W/20	5.1	150
KE125 (1976-1979)	5W/20	4.9-5.2	145-155
	Maintain oil 385-415 mm from top		
KE125-A7 & A8 (1980-1981)	5W/20	4.5	132
	Maintain oil 504-508 mm from top		
KE125-A9 - A12 (1982-1985)	5W/20	5.5	162.6
	Maintain oil 421-425 mm from top		
KS125	5W/20	5.1	150
	Maintain oil 385-415 mm from top		
KX125 (1974-1976)	5W/20	5.2	153
	Maintain oil 390 mm from top		

169-175 cc models	SAE Grade	oz.	cc
F2 & F2TR	5W/20	5.9	175
F3	5W/20	5.9	175

(continued)

Table 8 APPROXIMATE FORK OIL CAPACITY (continued)

169-175 cc models	SAE Grade	oz.	cc (continued)
F7	10W	3.9	115
KD175 (1976-1979)	10W	5.1	150
KE175 (1976-1982)	10W	5.1	150
238-350 cc models	**SAE Grade**	**oz.**	**cc**
F4	10W	6.6	195
F21M	5W/20	6.8	200
F8	10W	5.9	175
F81M	10W	5.9	175
F5	10W	5.9	175
F9	10W	5.9	175

CHAPTER FOUR

ENGINE, TRANSMISSION AND CLUTCH

This chapter describes removal, disassembly, service and reassembly of the engine, transmission and clutch. It is suggested that the engine be serviced without removing it from the chassis except for overhaul of the crankshaft assembly, transmission or bearings. Operating principles of rotary valve 2-stroke engines are also discussed in this chapter.

Tables 1-12 are at the end of the chapter.

ROTARY VALVE ENGINES

Figures 1-4 illustrate the 4 phases of the operating cycle. During this discussion, assume that the crankshaft is rotating counterclockwise. In **Figure 1**, as the piston travels downward, a transfer, or scavenging port (A) is opened. Exhaust gases leave the cylinder through exhaust port (B), which is opened by downward movement of piston (C). A fresh fuel/air charge, which has previously been compressed slightly, travels from crankcase (D) through transfer port (A) as the port opens.

Figure 2 illustrates the second phase. As the crankshaft rotates, the piston moves upward, closing the exhaust and transfer ports. Fresh fuel/air mixture is trapped in the cylinder and compressed by upward movement of the piston. Notice also that a low pressure area is created in the crankcase as the piston moves upward. Rotary valve (E), which is attached to the crankshaft and rotates with it, opens intake port (F). The upward movement of the piston then

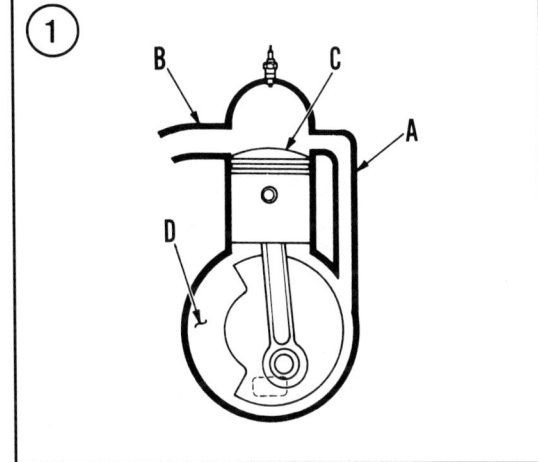

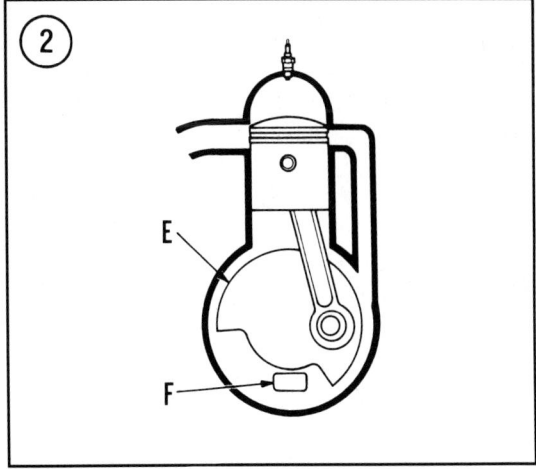

draws a fresh fuel/air charge into the crankcase through the intake port.

The third phase is shown in **Figure 3**. As the piston approaches top dead center, spark plug (G) fires, igniting the air/fuel mixture. The piston is then driven downward by the expanding gases. The rotary valve also closes as the piston reaches top dead center. As the piston continues downward, the mixture trapped in the crankcase is compressed.

When the piston uncovers the exhaust port, the fourth phase begins, as shown in **Figure 4**. The exhaust gases leave the cylinder through the exhaust port. Further movement of the piston opens the transfer port and the cycle is then repeated.

Figure 5 and **Figure 6** are typical examples of a late-model rotary valve disc and the cover which provides the carburetor mount.

ENGINE LUBRICATION

It can be seen from the foregoing discussion that the engine cannot receive its lubrication from an oil supply in the crankcase. Oil splash in the crankcase would be carried into the cylinder with the fuel/air charge, resulting in high oil consumption and spark plug fouling. Kawasaki 2-stroke engines use one of three methods for engine lubrication.

Fuel and Oil Mixture

Some competition models are lubricated by oil premixed with the fuel. Sufficient oil is added to the fuel to provide adequate lubrication for the engine under the high speed and load conditions found in

competition. Under low speed and load conditions, however, the engine receives more oil than is necessary, resulting in possible plug fouling. In addition, oil starvation can occur in prolonged periods during which the engine turns at high speeds with the throttle closed, as when descending a long hill. These

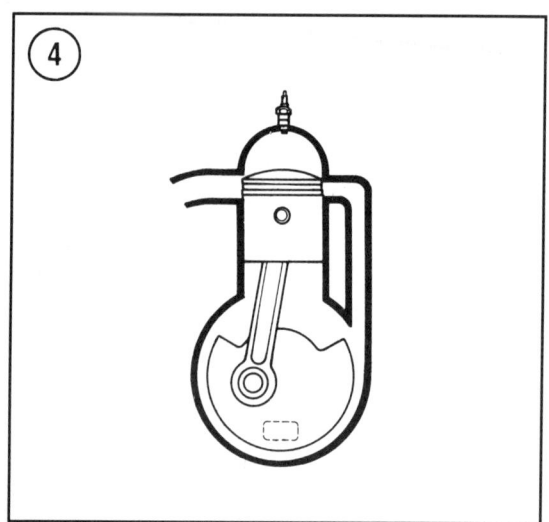

Rotary Disc

Valve Cover

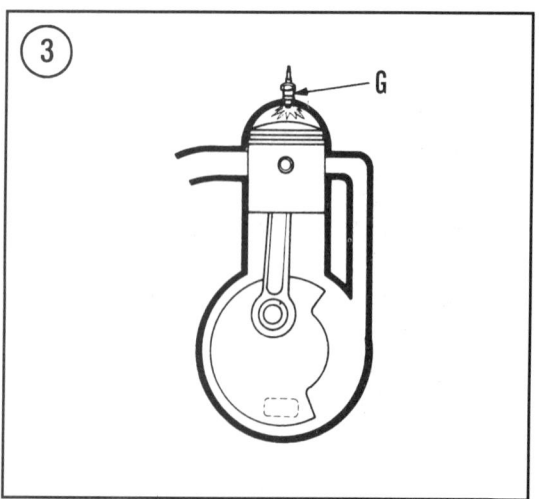
G

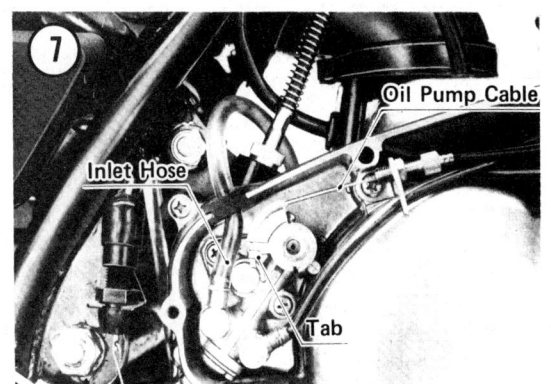

Oil Pump Cable

Inlet Hose

Tab

situations don't occur during competition, but could cause problems for machines intended for street use.

Superlube System

To overcome objections to the oil/fuel mixture lubrication method, Kawasaki developed its Super-lube system. This system is used on most models. A separate engine-driven oil pump (**Figure 7** and **Figure 8**) supplies oil to the engine induction tract (**Figure 9**). The output from the pump is controlled not only by engine speed, but also by throttle posi-

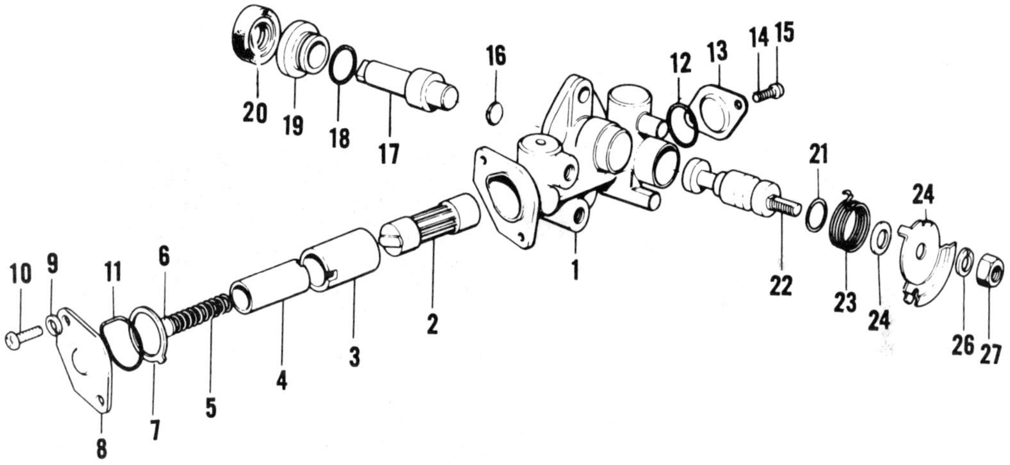

4

OIL PUMP

1. Pump body	15. Lockwasher
2. Plunger	16. Spacer
3. Valve sleeve	17. Pump shaft
4. Plunger follower	18. O-ring
5. Plunger spring	19. Bushing
6. Spring seat	20. Oil seal
7. Valve sleeve stopper	21. V-ring
8. Cap	22. Control cam
9. Lockwasher	23. Pump lever spring
10. Screw	24. Pump lever
11. O-ring	25. Washer
12. O-ring	26. Lockwasher
13. Cap	27. Nut
14. Screw	

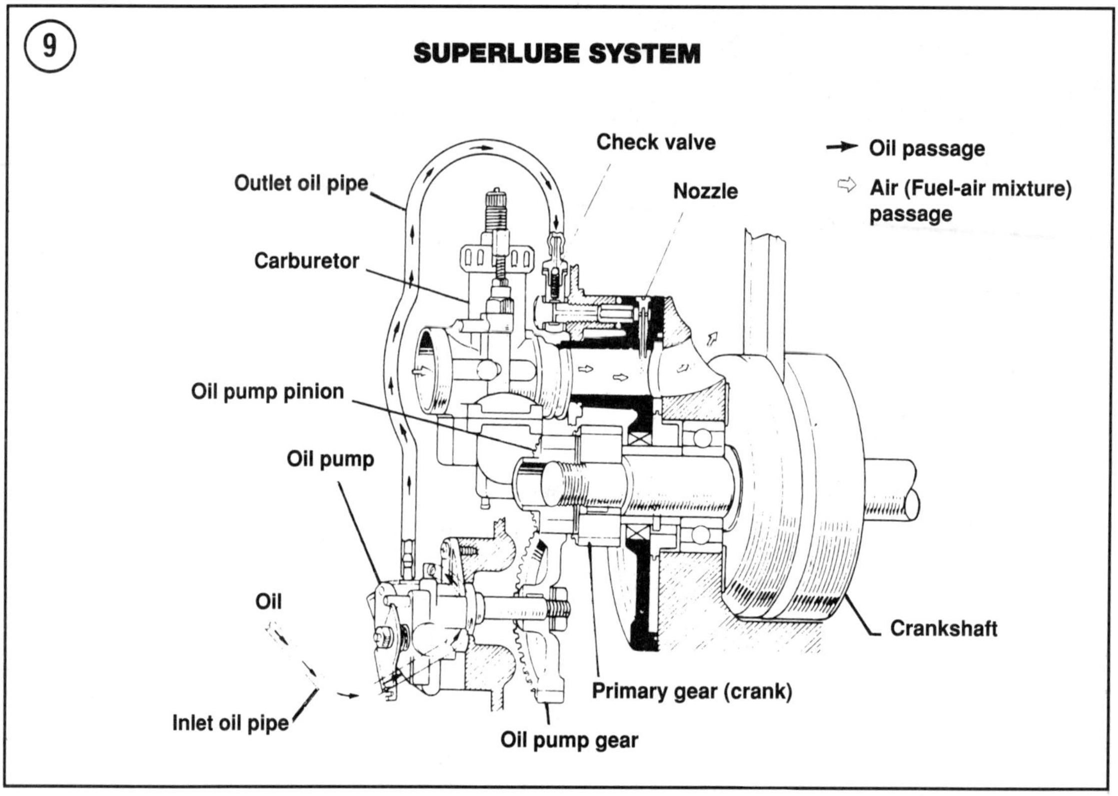

SUPERLUBE SYSTEM

9

Check valve

Nozzle

Outlet oil pipe

→ Oil passage

⇨ Air (Fuel-air mixture) passage

Carburetor

Oil pump pinion

Oil pump

Oil

Inlet oil pipe

Oil pump gear

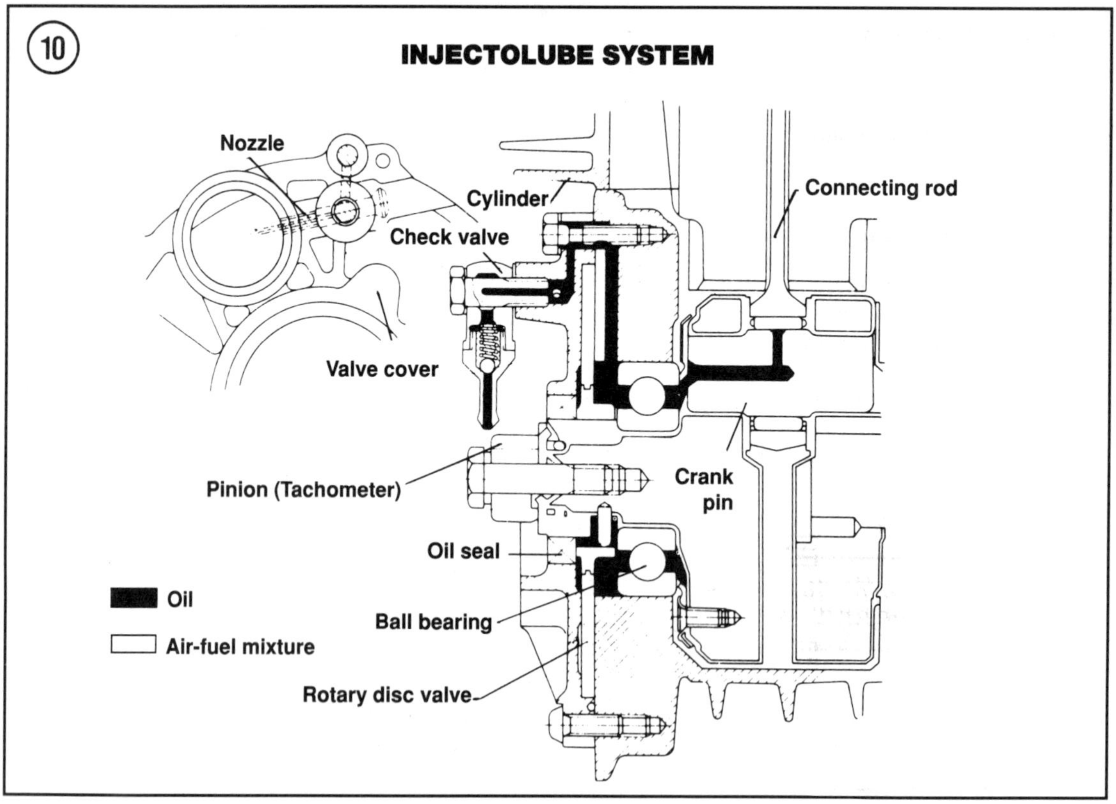

Primary gear (crank)

Crankshaft

INJECTOLUBE SYSTEM

10

Nozzle

Cylinder

Connecting rod

Check valve

Valve cover

Pinion (Tachometer)

Crank pin

Oil seal

Oil

Air-fuel mixture

Ball bearing

Rotary disc valve

tion, which is closely related to engine load. The engine is thereby supplied with the proper amount of oil under all operating conditions.

Injectolube System

Injectolube, used on larger models, is similar to the Superlube system in that it supplies oil to the engine in varying quantities. The oil pump has an additional output, however, which supplies oil under pressure to the main bearings (**Figure 10**) in the engine.

Checking the Oil Pump

> *CAUTION*
> *Operate the engine on a 20:1 fuel/oil mixture during the following procedure. Failure to do so may result in severe engine damage.*

1. Remove the oil pump outlet tube at the check valve.
2. Start the engine and run it at 2,000 rpm.
3. Hold the end of the oil outlet tube over a suitable collecting vessel.
4. Pull the oil pump lever to the fully upward position.
5. Measure the quantity of oil pumped in 3 minutes. The proper oil volume should be as specified in **Table 1**.

Bleeding the Oil Pump

Air will enter the oil pump whenever the pump is disconnected or the oil tank has run dry. After such an occurrence, the oil pump must be bled.

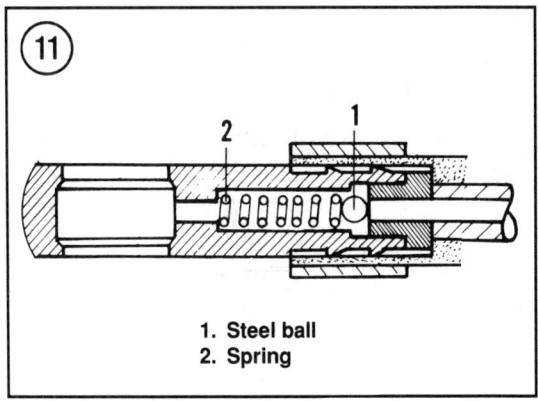

1. Steel ball
2. Spring

> *CAUTION*
> *Operate the engine on a 20:1 fuel/oil mixture during the following procedure. Failure to do so may result in severe engine damage.*

To bleed the oil pump, start the engine and run it at approximately 2,000 rpm. Pull up the control lever and operate the engine until no more air bubbles appear. If after a short time, bubbles continue to appear, check connections at the suction side of the pump, pump discharge port and banjo connection.

Finally, remove the banjo bolt at the oil pump suction inlet and fill the tube with oil until no more bubbles appear.

Oil Pump Check Valve

The check valve (**Figure 11**) prevents oil from flowing away from the engine when it is not running, thereby preventing dry starts. Avoid disassembly of the check valve. If it is assembled carelessly, it will not operate properly. In the event of malfunction, the check valve should be replaced.

PREPARATION FOR ENGINE DISASSEMBLY

1. Thoroughly clean the engine exterior of dirt, oil and foreign material using one of the cleaners formulated for the purpose.
2. Be sure that you have the proper tools for the job. See *General Information*, Chapter One.
3. As you remove parts from the engine, place them in trays in the order of their disassembly. Doing so will make assembly faster and easier and will ensure correct installation of all engine parts.
4. Note that the disassembly procedures vary slightly between the different models. Be sure to read all steps carefully and follow those which apply to your engine.

ENGINE REMOVAL

Engine removal is generally similar for all models. The following steps are set forth as a guide.

1. If the engine runs, start it and let it run for a few minutes to warm the oil. Then remove the drain plug and drain the transmission oil.

2. Remove the exhaust pipe at the cylinder and the muffler attaching bolts. The muffler and exhaust pipe may then be removed together.

3. Remove the air cleaner assembly.

4. Turn the fuel petcock to OFF, then remove the fuel line at the carburetor.

5. Remove the carburetor (**Figure 12**). A hole is provided in the cover for access to its attaching screw.

6. Remove the inner wire from the oil pump control lever. Remove the banjo bolt and the inlet oil line from the oil pump. Be sure to plug the tube to prevent oil from flowing out. Remove the fitting screw and withdraw the tachometer cable.

7. Slacken the outer clutch cable, remove the inner cable from the clutch release lever (**Figure 13**), then remove the clutch cable.

8. Remove the gear change pedal, then the left crankcase cover.

9. Remove the master link, then the drive chain. It may be necessary to rotate the rear wheel to position the master link for convenient removal. When installing the chain, be sure to position the master link clip as shown in **Figure 14**.

10. Disconnect all wiring at the flywheel magneto or generator.

11. Remove the spark plug cap.

12. Remove all engine mount bolts.

13. Straddle the machine and remove the engine from the frame.

14. Reverse the removal procedure to install the engine. Be sure to check the following items before starting the engine:

    a. Oil supply

    b. Transmission oil level

    c. Clutch adjustment

    d. Oil pump and throttle cables

    e. Drive chain adjustment

    f. Engine mounting bolts

    g. Ignition timing

CYLINDER AND CYLINDER HEAD

Kawasaki 2-stroke engines are equipped with several types of cylinders: cast iron, aluminum alloy with iron liner, alloy with chrome plated bore (G31M) and on emission-controlled models, alloy with tungsten coated bore (ELECTRO-FUSE).

Service procedures are the same for all types except where noted.

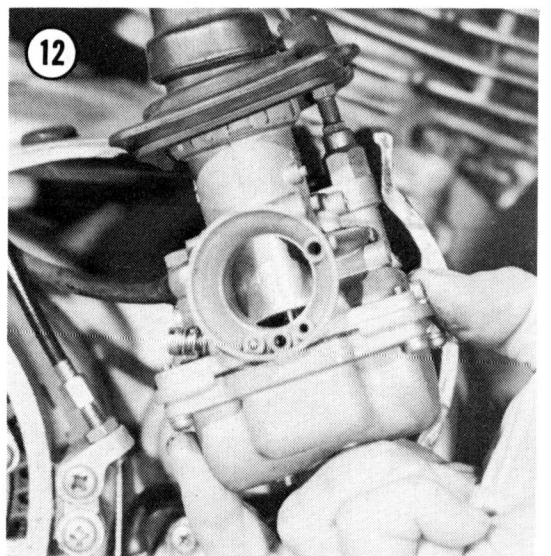

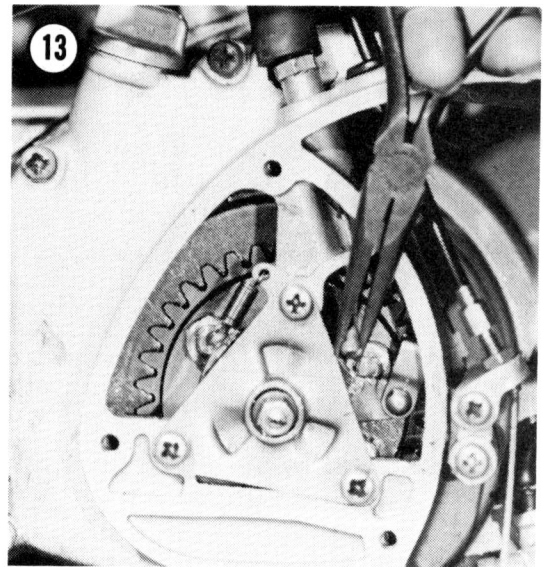

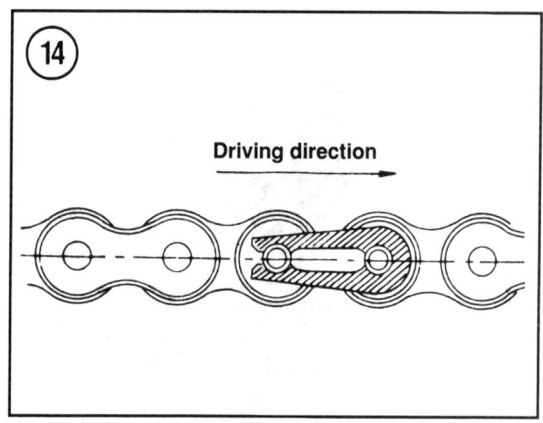

Driving direction

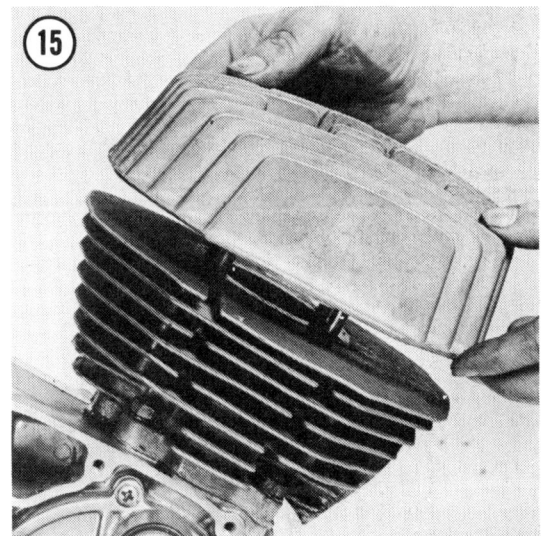

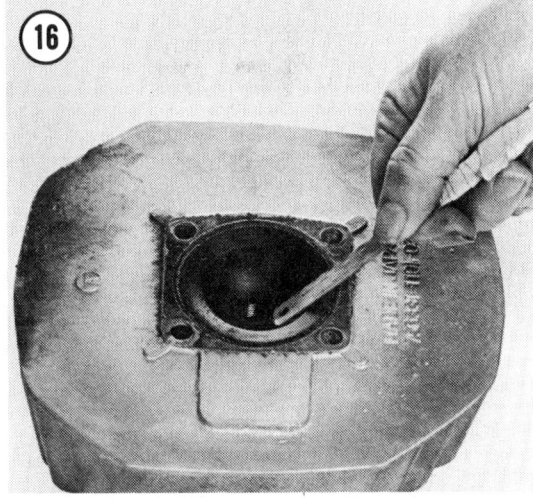

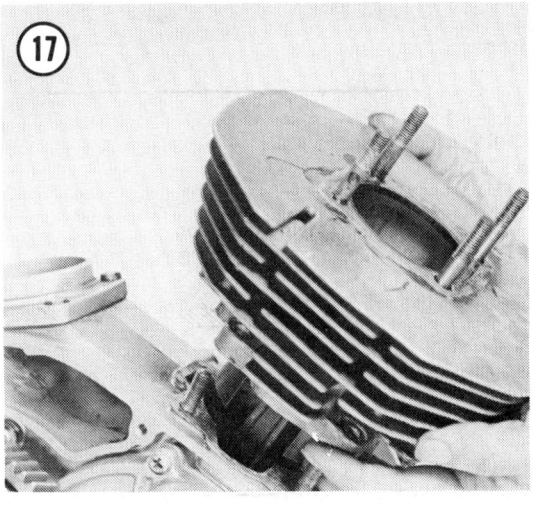

Cylinder Head Removal/Installation

With the engine cold, loosen each cylinder head nut a little bit at a time, in crisscross order, until all are loose. Then remove all nuts. Lift the cylinder head from the cylinder (**Figure 15**). It may be necessary to tap the had lightly with a rubber mallet to free it; if so, take care not to break any cooling fins.

Upon installation, always use a new cylinder head gasket. Torque cylinder head nuts in crisscross order to 18 ft.-lb. (2.5 mkg) for 8 mm nuts and 25 ft.-lb. (4.0 mkg) for 10 mm nuts.

Removing Carbon Deposits

Carbon deposits in the combustion chamber cause increased compression ratio and may lead to preignition, overheating and excessive fuel consumption. To remove these deposits, scrape them off with the rounded end of a hacksaw blade, as shown in **Figure 16**. Be careful not to damage the gasket surface.

Cylinder Removal

With the cylinder head and any cylinder base nuts removed, tap the cylinder around the exhaust port with a plastic mallet, then pull it away from the crankcase (**Figure 17**). Stuff a clean rag into the crankcase opening to prevent entry of any foreign material.

Checking the Cylinder: Electro-Fuse
(1978-1/2 and later KE100, KM100, KE125)

Measure the cylinder inside diameter in one place: front-to-back, 1 in. (25 mm) below the top of the cylinder. If the cylinder has worn past the service limit shown in **Table 2**, the cylinder should be replaced. When installing a new cylinder, give the bike the same break-in procedure you would use on a new machine.

CAUTION
Electro-Fuse cylinders can not be bored oversize. The coating will be destroyed.

Checking the Cylinder: Iron Liner

Measure cylinder wall wear at locations (a), (b), (c) and (d) with a cylinder gauge or inside micrometer, as shown in **Figure 18**. Position the instrument parallel and then at right angles to the crankshaft at each depth. If any measurement exceeds 0.006 in.

(0.15 mm) over the standard value, or if the difference between any measurement exceeds 0.002 in (0.05 mm), rebore and hone the cylinder to the next oversize, or replace the cylinder. Pistons are available in oversizes of 0.02 in. (0.50 mm) and 0.04 in. (1.00 mm). After boring and honing, the difference between maximum and minimum diameter must not be more than 0.0004 in. (0.01 mm). Standard measurements are listed in **Table 2**.

Removing Carbon Deposits

Scrape carbon deposits from around the cylinder exhaust port, as shown in **Figure 19**. The rounded end of a hacksaw blade is a suitable tool for carbon removal.

Cylinder Installation

Be sure that each piston ring end gap is aligned with its locating pin in the ring groove. Lubricate the piston and cylinder, then insert the piston into the lower end of the cylinder. It will be necessary to compress each piston ring as it goes into the cylinder. Always use a new cylinder base gasket upon reassembly.

PISTON, PISTON PIN
AND PISTON RINGS

Remove the clip at each end of the piston pin with needlenose pliers (**Figure 20**). Press out the piston pin (**Figure 21**). A tool is available for this job, but it can be done by hand if the piston is first heated by wrapping in rags soaked in hot water. Also remove the upper end bearing (**Figure 22**).

Piston Rings

Remove the piston rings by spreading the top ring with a thumb on each end, as shown in **Figure 23**. Then remove the ring from the top of the piston. Repeat this procedure for the remaining ring or rings. Expander rings used on some models may be removed easily by prying the ends with a narrow screwdriver.

Measure each ring for wear by inserting it 0.2 in. (5 mm) into the BOTTOM of the cylinder where the cylinder is least worn (**Figure 24**). Seat the ring squarely in the cylinder by pushing it in slightly with a piston. Measure the installed end gap with a feeler gauge. A new ring should have an installed gap no

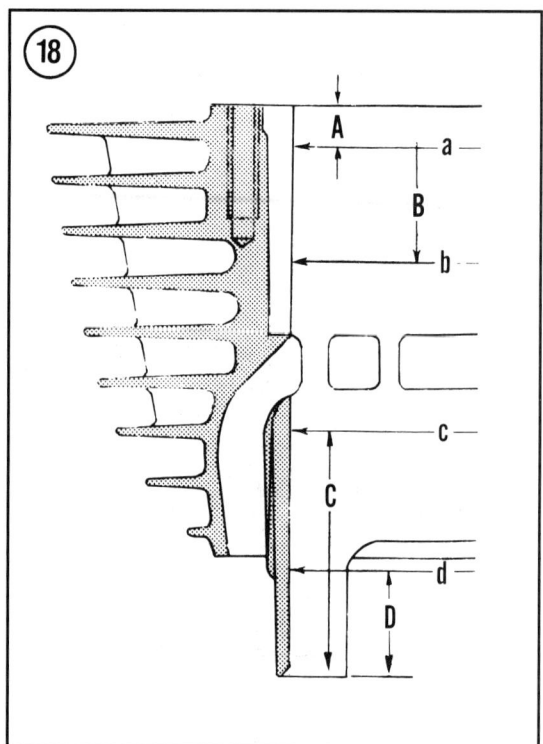

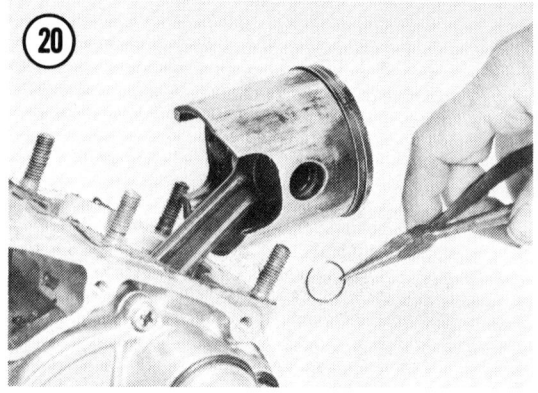

smaller than the minimum shown in **Table 3**. If it is less, file the ends of the ring until the minimum gap is reached. As old rings wear, the gap will increase. Discard any rings whose installed gap exceeds the maximum shown in **Table 3**.

Scrape carbon deposits from the head of the piston (**Figure 25**). Then clean all carbon and gum from the piston ring grooves (**Figure 26**) using a broken piston ring, or a ring groove cleaning tool. Any deposits left in the grooves will cause the rings to stick, leading to gas blow-by and loss of power.

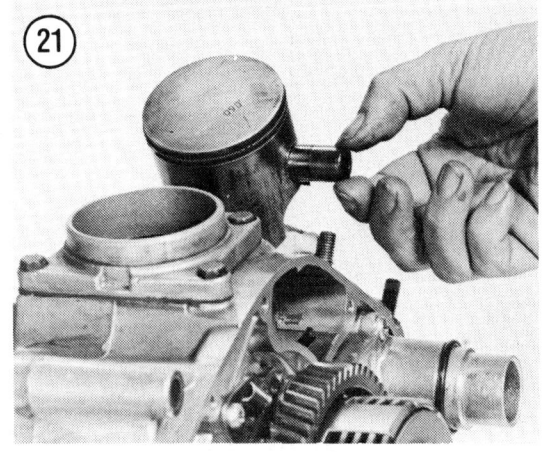

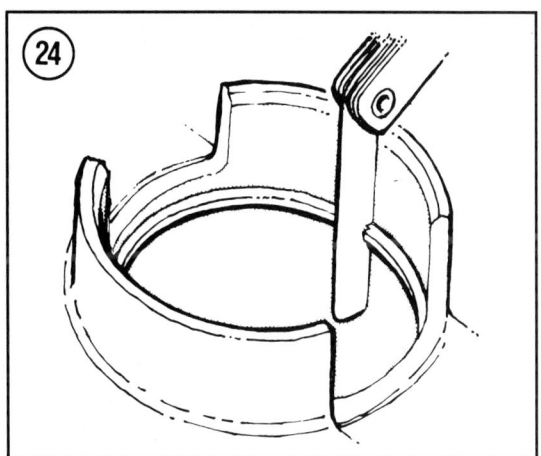

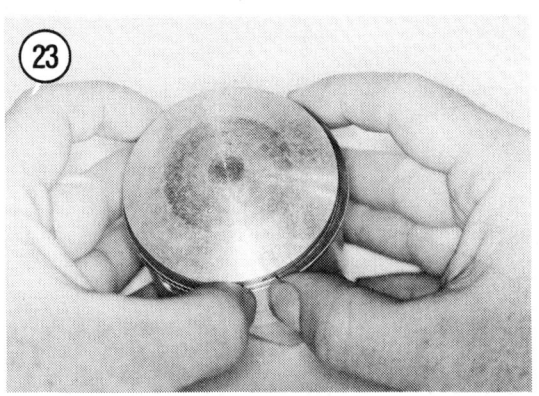

To check fit of the piston ring in its groove, slip the outer surface of the ring into the groove next to the locating pin, then roll the ring completely around the piston (**Figure 27**). If any binding occurs, determine and correct the cause before proceeding.

When replacing rings, install the lower one first. Be sure that any printing on the ring is toward the top of the piston. Spread the rings carefully with your thumbs, just enough to slip them over the piston. Align end gaps with the locating pin in each ring groove.

Checking and Correcting Piston Clearance

Piston clearance is the difference between maximum piston diameter and minimum cylinder diameter. Measure outside diameter of the piston skirt (**Figure 28**) at right angles to the piston pin. The measurement should be made 0.2 in. (5 mm) from the bottom of the piston. Proper piston clearances are listed in **Table 4**.

A piston showing signs of seizure will result in noise, loss of power and damage to the cylinder wall. If a piston is reused without correction, another seizure will develop. To correct this condition, lightly smooth the affected area with No. 400 emery paper or a fine oilstone (**Figure 29**).

Install the piston with arrow mark (**Figure 30** pointing toward the front of the machine. This is vital because the hole for the piston pin is offset slightly to prevent piston slap.

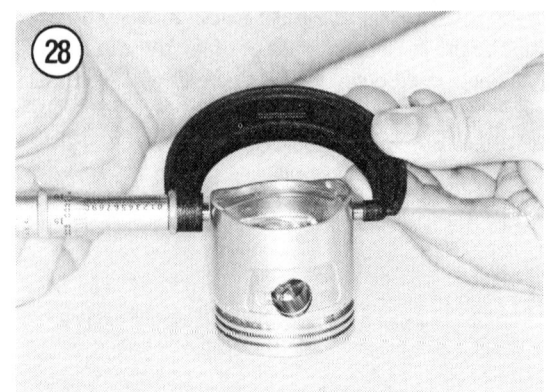

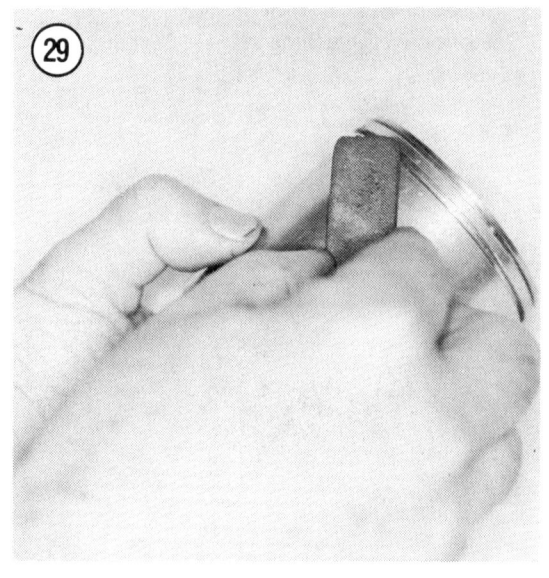

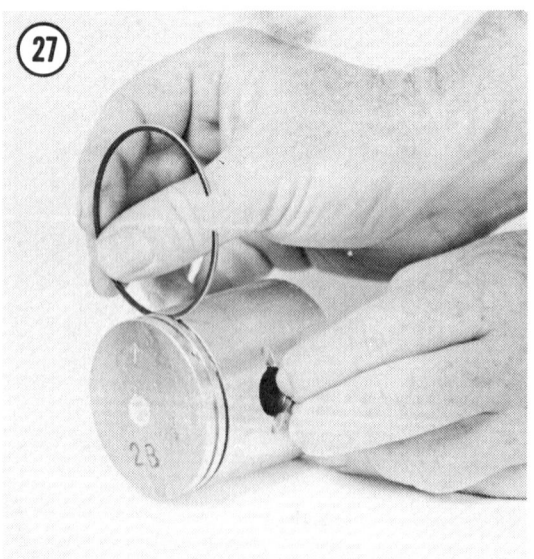

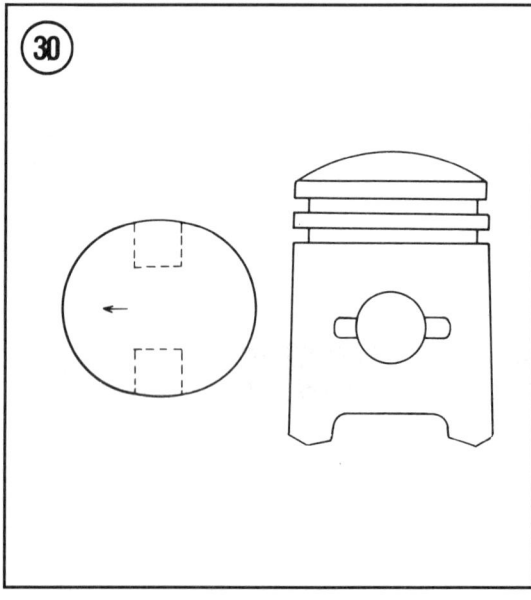

LEFT CRANKCASE COVER

The left crankcase cover protects the generator or magneto, engine sprocket and bearings from dust and dirt. Covers on smaller models are of one-piece construction. Larger models use a 2-piece cover, consisting of an engine cover and a front chaincase cover.

Removal (Smaller Models)

To remove the cover on these models, proceed as follows:
1. Completely remove gearshift pedal clamp bolt.
2. Pull gearshift pedal from its shaft.
3. Remove cover attaching screws, then pull cover from engine.

Removal (F Series)

1. Remove breaker contact cover on models so equipped.
2. Remove chaincase cover.
3. Remove left engine cover.

Installation (All Models)

Reverse the removal procedure to install the crankcase cover. Be sure that the gearshift shaft oil seal is in good condition. be sure that the clutch release lever on F series models operates through an angle of about 90-100°.

FLYWHEEL MAGNETO AND STARTER-GENERATOR

Only removal and installation of these components is discussed in this chapter. Refer to Chapter Two for troubleshooting or to Chapter Three for routine service.

Removal (Smaller Models)

1. Remove the flywheel mounting nut, then use a puller (**Figure 31**) to remove the flywheel.

NOTE
Feed a rolled-up rag between the primary reduction gears on the other side

of the engine to prevent the flywheel from turning.

2. Remove the wiring from the neutral indicator switch.

3. Remove the screws from the magneto base, then remove the magneto base.

4. Remove the Woodruff key from the shaft.

Removal (Larger Models)

1. Remove the flywheel nut. Insert a screwdriver through one of the holes in the flywheel into the hole in the magneto base to prevent the flywheel from turning.

2. Pull the flywheel from the shaft, using a flywheel puller.

Magneto Installation (All Models)

1. Reverse the removal procedure to install the magneto.

2. Be sure to align mark (A) on the magneto base (**Figure 32**) with mark (B) on the crankcase. Failure to do so will make proper ignition timing impossible.

3. Tighten flywheel nut to 36 ft.-lb. (5 mkg) for all models except F5, F7, F8 and F9. Tighten flywheel nuts to 72 ft.-lb. (10 mkg) on those models.

Starter-Generator
Removal/Installation

1. Remove both yoke mounting screws.

2. Pull yoke from engine (**Figure 33**).

3. Using a suitable puller, remove armature (**Figure 34**).

4. Remove Woodruff key from crankshaft.

5. Reverse the removal procedure to install the starter-generator. It is much easier to install the yoke

if all brushes are held up by their springs (**Figure 35**) until the mounting screws are in place. Don't forget to snap brush springs back into position.

ENGINE SPROCKET

Removal

1. Use a blunted chisel to straighten the tab on the lockwasher.

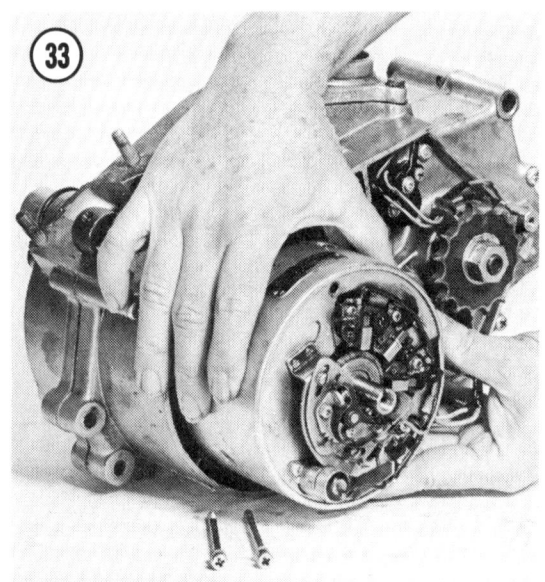

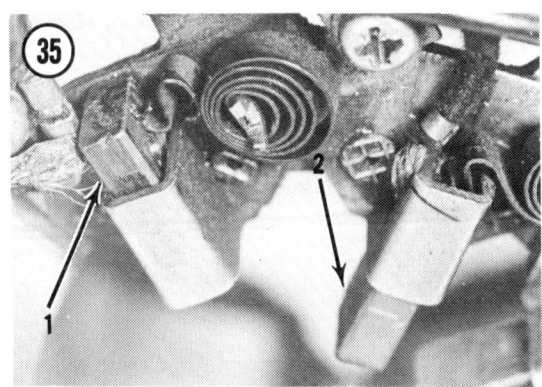

2. Loosen the mounting nut and remove sprocket (**Figure 36**).

Inspection

Inspect sprocket teeth for wear. Excessive wear results in shortened drive chain life. Replace the sprocket if it is worn. **Figure 37** compares worn and serviceable sprockets.

Installation

Reverse the removal procedure to install the sprocket. Be sure to insert the tang on the lockwasher into the hole in the sprocket and also be sure that one edge of the lockwasher is bent up against the sprocket nut.

RIGHT CRANKCASE COVER

Removal (Smaller Models)

1. Remove the kickstarter pinch bolt, then slide the kickstarter pedal from the shaft.
2. Remove the carburetor cover.
3. Remove the carburetor and the clutch cable from the clutch release mechanism (**Figure 38**).
4. Remove the oil pump cover, then remove the oil pump cable and oil inlet tube. Plug the tube to prevent loss of oil.
5. Remove the screws which attach the crankcase cover and pull the cover away from the engine. It is

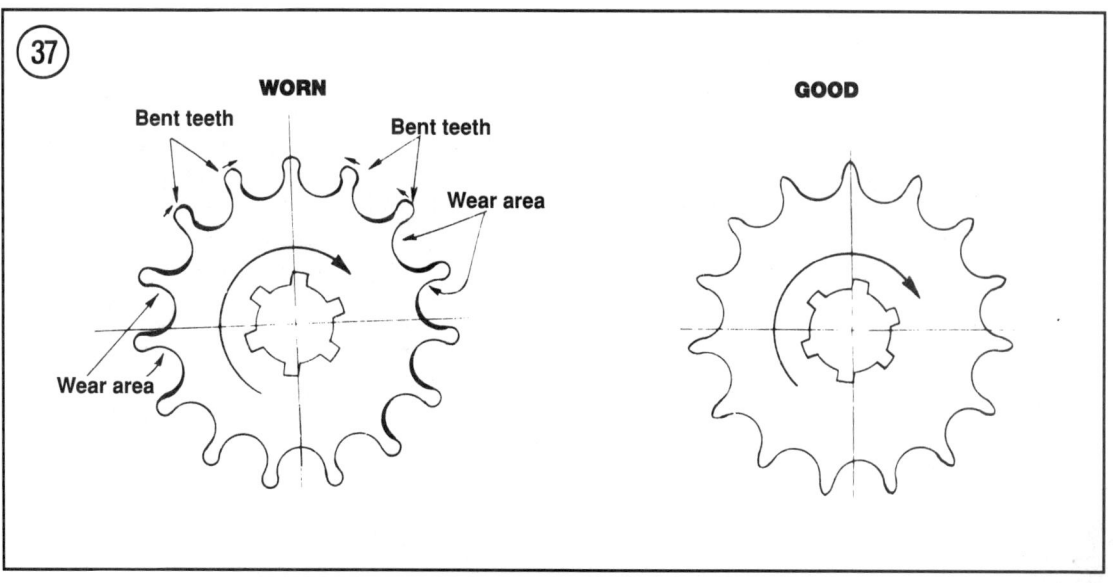

not necessary to remove the oil pump, the clutch release mechanism or the oil outlet tube.

Removal (Larger Models)

Right crankcase cover removal is similar, except that the clutch release mechanism is located on the other side of the engine, on the front chaincase cover.

Inspection

1. Make certain that the oil drain tube under the carburetor is not clogged.
2. Check the oil seal around the kickstarter shaft. Replace it if it is damaged or shows evidence of leakage.
3. Inspect the gasket. Replace it if damaged.

Installation

Reverse the removal procedure to install the cover. Take particular care that the O-rings on the valve cover and check valves are installed correctly (**Figure 39**). Also be sure that the clutch holder assembly and oil pump gear are correctly positioned. Rotate the flywheel, if necessary, to mesh the oil pump gears.

PRIMARY DRIVE GEAR

Removal (Smaller Models)

1. Use a blunted chisel to straighten the tab on the lockwasher.

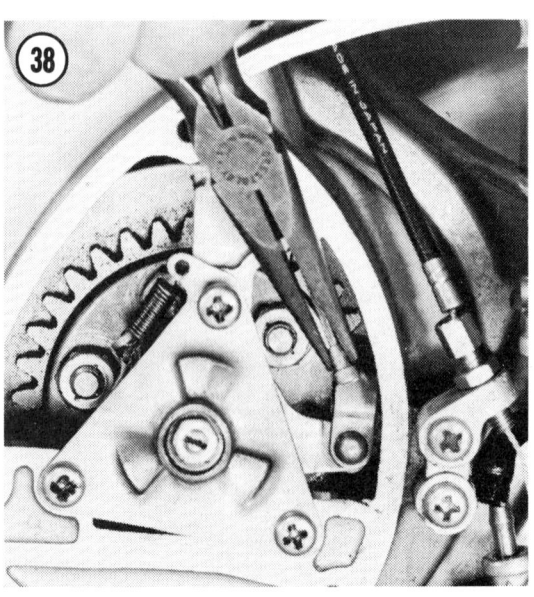

2. Prevent crankshaft from turning by feeding a rolled-up rag between both primary reduction gears.
3. Remove the primary drive gear nut, then pull off the gear (**Figure 40**). Remove Woodruff key.

Removal (Larger Models)

1. Use a blunted chisel to straighten the lockwasher on the oil pump pinion.
2. Prevent the crankshaft from turning, then remove the oil pump pinion nut.
3. Remove the lockwasher and primary drive gear from the crankshaft.
4. Remove the Woodruff key.

Inspection

Check the gear teeth for wear or damage. Slight roughness may be smoothed with an oilstone. Replace the gear if damage cannot be dressed.

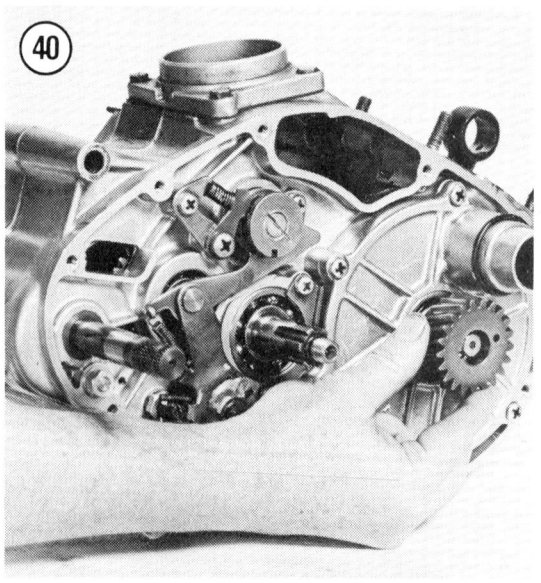

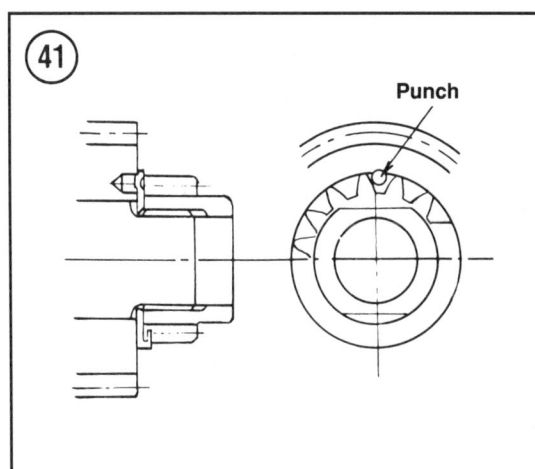

Installation

Reverse the removal procedure to install the gear. Torque the primary gear or oil pump gear nut to 36 ft.-lb. (5 mkg). Be sure to bend the tab on the lockwasher tightly against one flat on the nut. On models F5, F8 and F9, punch the lockwasher into the small hole on the pinion, as shown in **Figure 41**.

CLUTCH

Operation (Type 1 Clutch)

Figure 42 and **Figure 43** are exploded and sectional views of the clutch and clutch release mecha-

TYPE 1 CLUTCH
(F5, F6, F7, F8, F81M & F9)

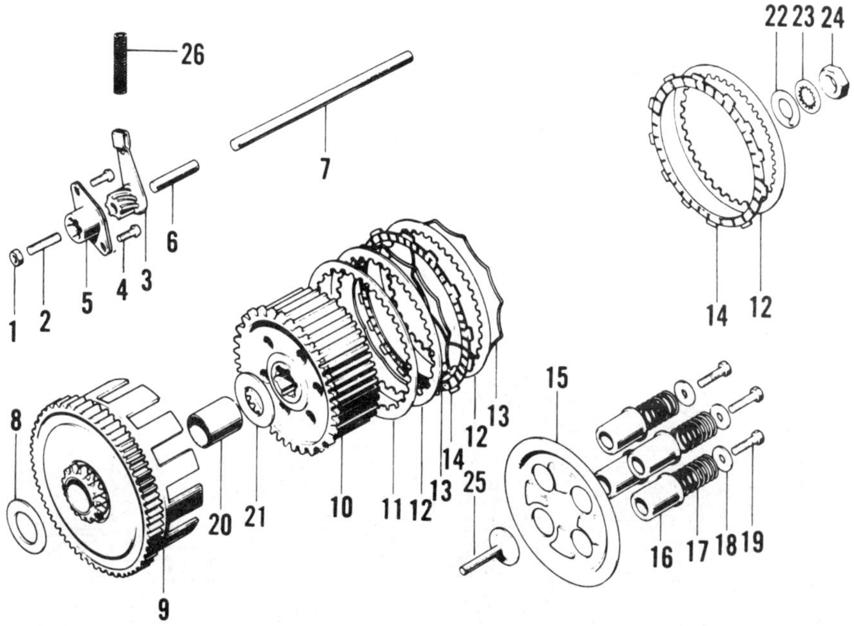

1. Nut	10. Hub	19. Bolt
2. Screw	11. Clutch wheel	20. Bushing
3. Inner release	12. Clutch plate	21. Washer
4. Screw	13. Ring	22. Washer
5. Outer release housing	14. Friction plate	23. Lockwasher
6. Push rod	15. Spring plate	24. Nut
7. Push rod	16. Guide	25. Push crown
8. Washer	17. Spring	26. Spring
9. Clutch housing	18. Spring holder	

nism used principally on F series. As the rider operates the clutch lever, the clutch cable pulls release lever (3), causing it to rotate in release housing (5). As the release lever rotates, helical splines force the lever to move away from the release housing. As the release lever moves, short (6) and long (7) pushrods move with it and disengage the clutch. Screw (2) and locknut (1) are used to adjust the clutch.

Release Mechanism (Type 1 Clutch)

To remove the clutch release mechanism on these models, proceed as follows.

1. Remove the front chain cover. On F6 and F7 models, it is necessary to remove the breaker plate cover.

2. Remove the clutch cable from the clutch release lever.

3. Remove the retaining screws from the clutch release housing. Remove the clutch release housing from the chain cover.

4. Pull short pushrod out through oil seal.

5. Check the assembled parts for wear or play by moving the release lever. Replace both parts if any large scratches or cracks are evident, as these impair clutch action.

6. Assemble the release lever and release housing, then install the clutch release housing into the front chaincase cover. Consider the operating angle of the clutch release lever, as it is pulled by the clutch cable. This angle should be about 90-100°. Tighten the mounting screws evenly to prevent warpage of the release housing.

Types 2 and 3 Clutches (1981 and Earlier)

Figure 44 and **Figure 45** are exploded and sectional views of Type 2 clutches. Type 3 clutches, shown in **Figure 46**, are similar.

Type 2 (1982 and Later)

The clutch shown in **Figure 47** is used on 1982 and later KE100 models. It is similar to other Type 2 clutches, but the pusher (16, **Figure 47**) is piloted

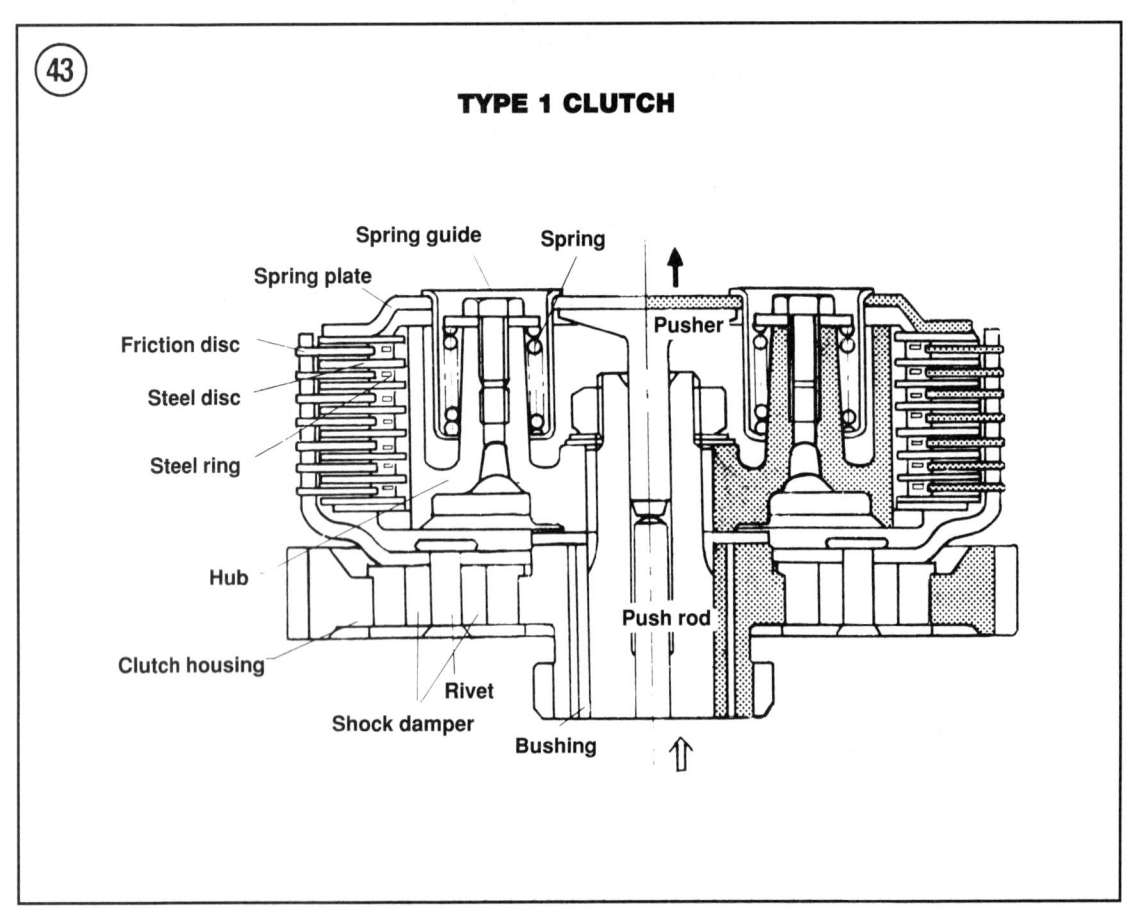

43

TYPE 1 CLUTCH

- Spring guide
- Spring
- Spring plate
- Pusher
- Friction disc
- Steel disc
- Steel ring
- Hub
- Push rod
- Clutch housing
- Rivet
- Shock damper
- Bushing

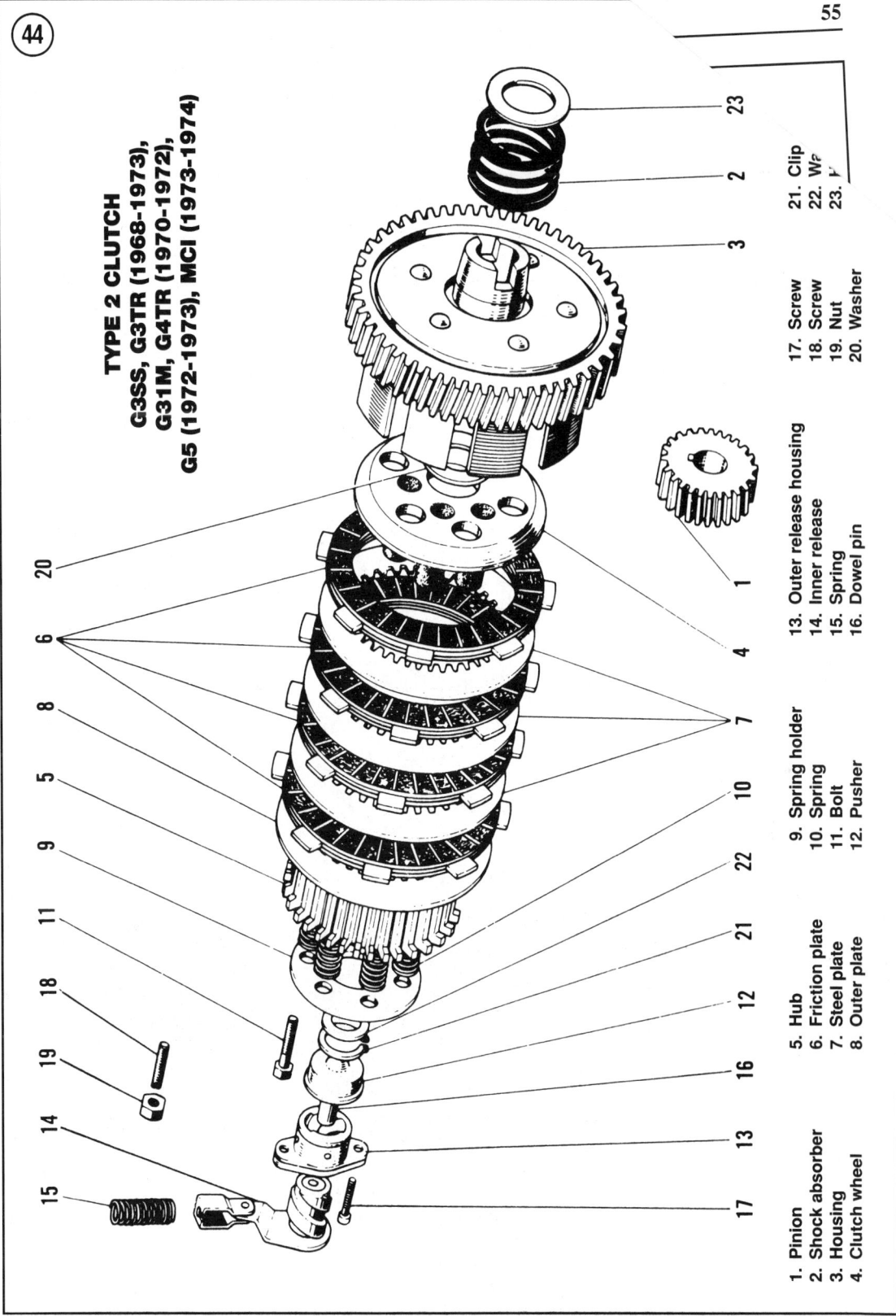

TYPE 2 CLUTCH
G3SS, G3TR (1968-1973),
G31M, G4TR (1970-1972),
G5 (1972-1973), MCI (1973-1974)

1. Pinion
2. Shock absorber
3. Housing
4. Clutch wheel
5. Hub
6. Friction plate
7. Steel plate
8. Outer plate
9. Spring holder
10. Spring
11. Bolt
12. Pusher
13. Outer release housing
14. Inner release
15. Spring
16. Dowel pin
17. Screw
18. Screw
19. Nut
20. Washer
21. Clip
22. W?
23. ?

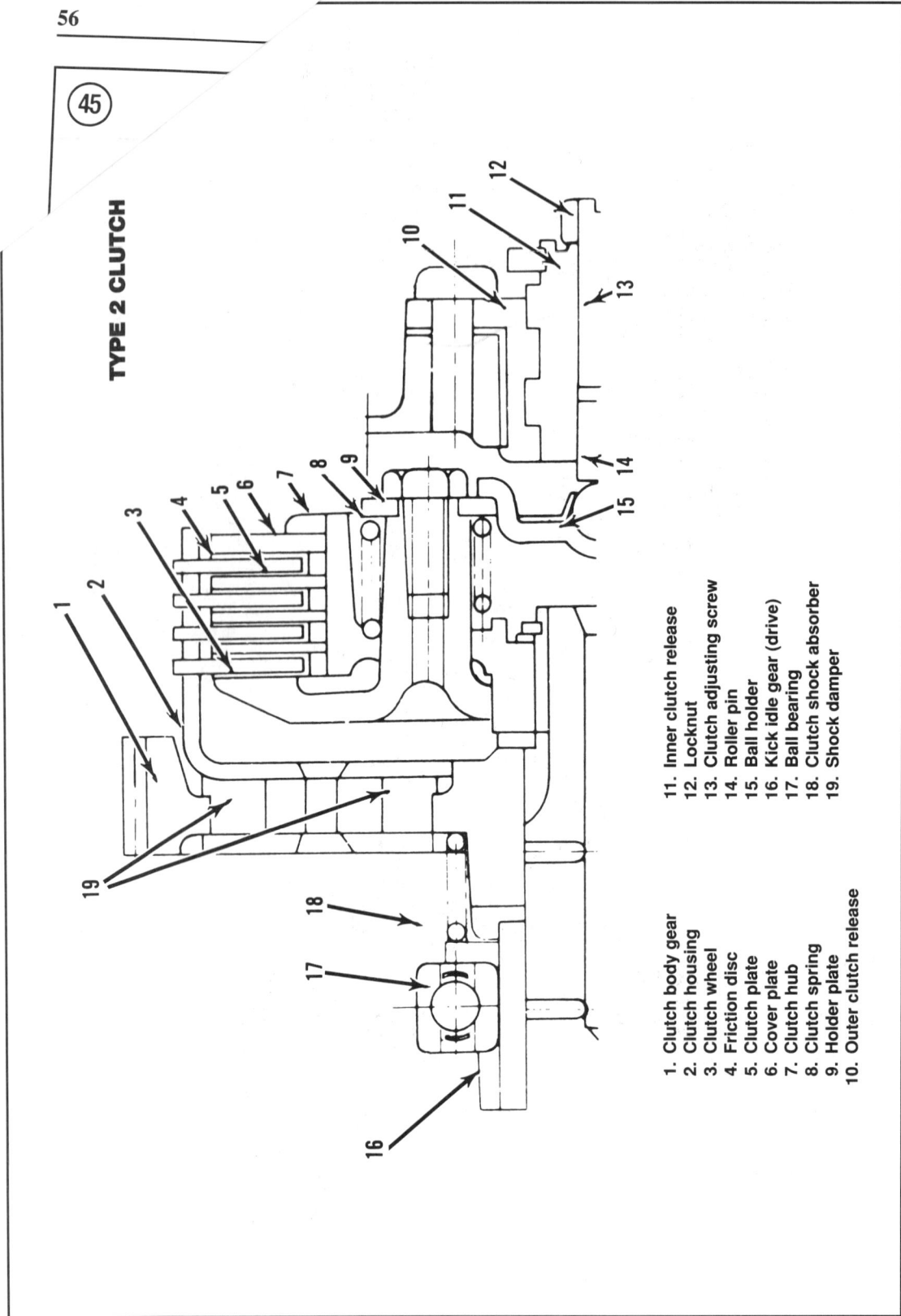

(45)

TYPE 2 CLUTCH

1. Clutch body gear
2. Clutch housing
3. Clutch wheel
4. Friction disc
5. Clutch plate
6. Cover plate
7. Clutch hub
8. Clutch spring
9. Holder plate
10. Outer clutch release
11. Inner clutch release
12. Locknut
13. Clutch adjusting screw
14. Roller pin
15. Ball holder
16. Kick idle gear (drive)
17. Ball bearing
18. Clutch shock absorber
19. Shock damper

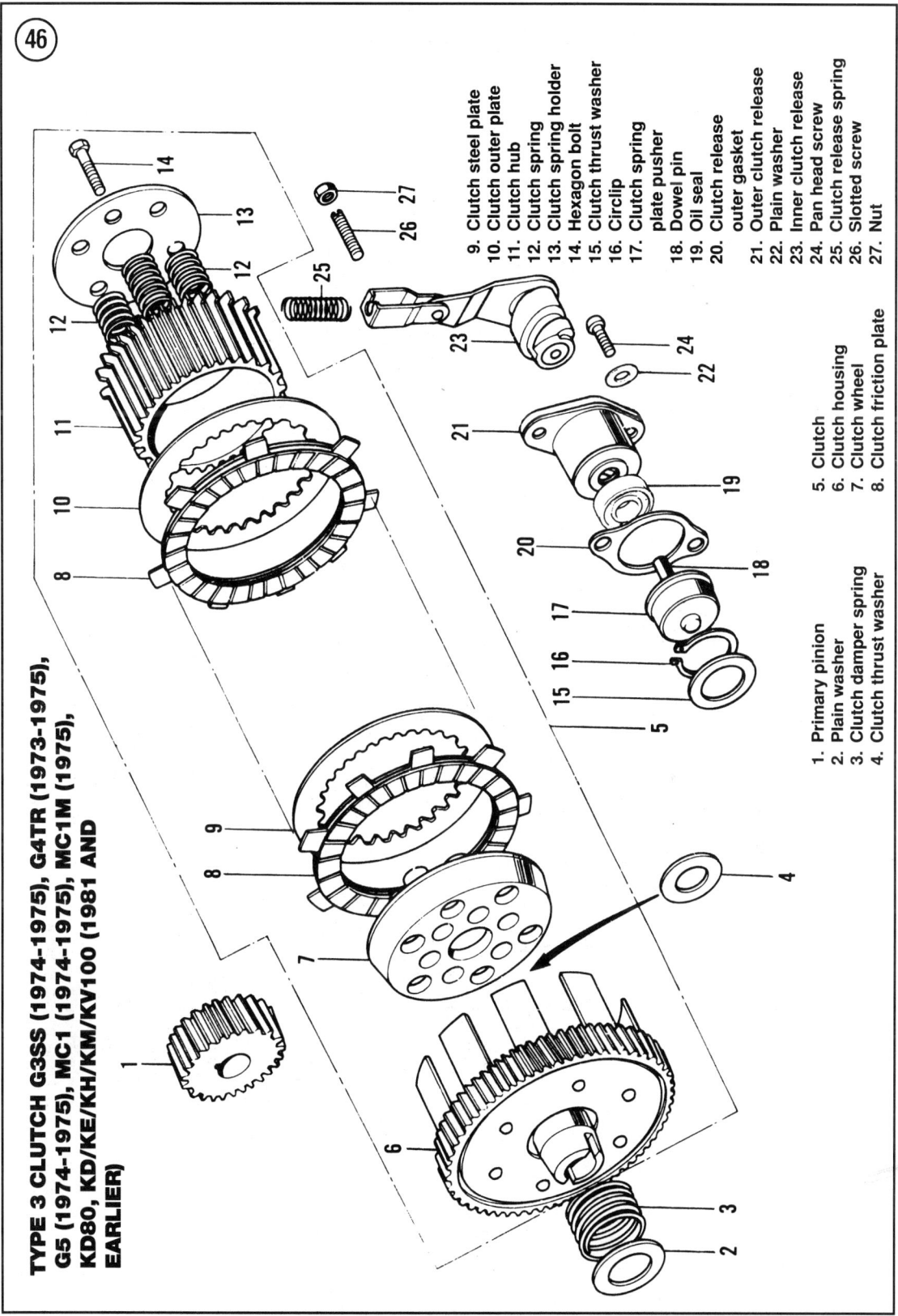

TYPE 3 CLUTCH G3SS (1974-1975), G4TR (1973-1975), G5 (1974-1975), MC1 (1974-1975), MC1M (1975), KD80, KD/KE/KH/KM/KV100 (1981 AND EARLIER)

1. Primary pinion
2. Plain washer
3. Clutch damper spring
4. Clutch thrust washer
5. Clutch
6. Clutch housing
7. Clutch wheel
8. Clutch friction plate
9. Clutch steel plate
10. Clutch outer plate
11. Clutch hub
12. Clutch spring
13. Clutch spring holder
14. Hexagon bolt
15. Clutch thrust washer
16. Circlip
17. Clutch spring plate pusher
18. Dowel pin
19. Oil seal
20. Clutch release outer gasket
21. Outer clutch release
22. Plain washer
23. Inner clutch release
24. Pan head screw
25. Clutch release spring
26. Slotted screw
27. Nut

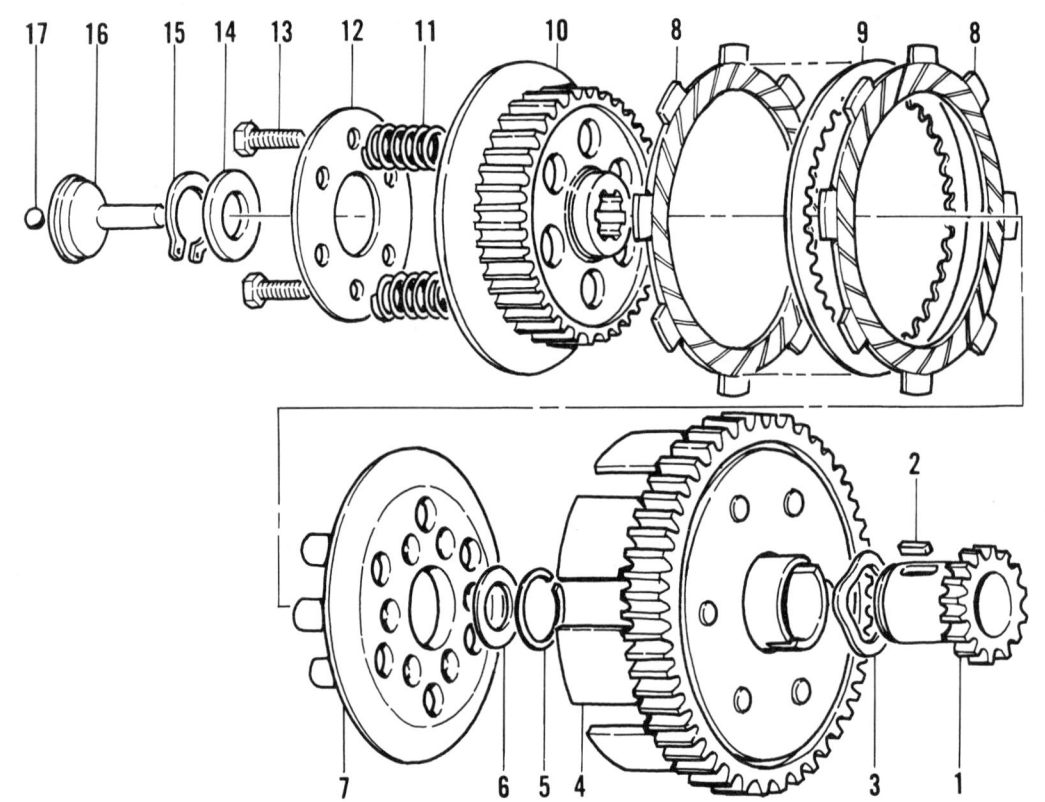

**TYPE 2 CLUTCH
(1982-ON KE100)**

1. Kick gear
2. Key
3. Washer
4. Clutch housing
5. Circlip
6. Thrust washer
7. Clutch wheel
8. Clutch friction plate
9. Clutch steel plate
10. Clutch hub
11. Clutch springs
12. Clutch spring holder
13. Bolts
14. Thrust washer
15. Circlip
16. Clutch spring
    plate pusher
17. Thrust ball

into the transmission input shaft. The clutch housing (4, **Figure 47**) drives idler gear (1, **Figure 47**) with key (2, **Figure 47**).

The grooves of some clutch friction discs are angled tangentially and should be installed as shown in **Figure 48** when viewed from the right side.

Operation (Types 2 and 3 Clutches)

The clutch release mechanism on Types 2 and 3 clutches is similar to that of Type 1, except that it is mounted on the right side of the engine. Because this release mechanism is on the same side of the engine as the clutch, the 2 pushrods are not required. A short steel pin in the center of the splined portion of the release lever operates the clutch.

Removal, inspection and installation procedures are similar to those for type 1 clutches.

Operation (Type 4 Clutch)

Figure 49 is an exploded view of this clutch. **Figure 50** is a sectional view of its release mechanism. The steel balls in release ball assembly (20) normally rest in depressions in clutch release plate (19). As the rider operates the clutch lever on the handlebar, the clutch cable pulls the arm on the clutch release plate, causing it to rotate. As the clutch release plate rotates, the balls are forced out of the depression. The balls then force the release plate and cam plate (5) apart. Roller (18) then moves pusher (14) to release the clutch.

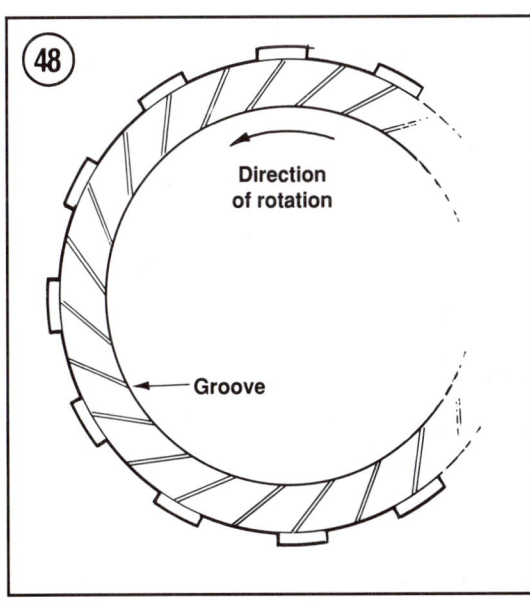

Release Mechanism

To remove the release mechanism, refer to **Figure 51**. Remove the retaining screws, then take off the assembly. Inspect all parts carefully and replace any that are worn or damaged.

Reverse the removal procedure to install the clutch release mechanism.

Type 5 Clutch

Figure 52 is an exploded view of this clutch. Operation and service is similar to that of Type 4 clutches.

Clutch Disassembly

Clutch removal and disassembly is generally similar for all models. Note that it is usually not necessary to disassemble the clutch if service on it is not required, as in the case of removal in preparation for crankcase disassembly. In such cases, it is only necessary to remove the clutch retaining hardware, then pull the entire assembly free.

1. Remove nuts, clutch spring plate and springs (**Figure 53**).
2. Feed a rolled-up rag between both primary reduction gears to prevent the clutch from turning, then remove the clutch hub nut.
3. Remove clutch hub, pressure plate, steel plates and friction plates (**Figure 54**).
4. Remove clutch housing (**Figure 55**).
5. Slide clutch bushing and thrust washer from shaft. Take care to note how thrust washer is installed.

Clutch Inspection

Measure free length of each clutch spring as shown in **Figure 56**. If free length is shorter than the standard length by the amount of the wear limit specified in **Table 5**, replace all springs.

Measure thickness of each friction disc at several places as shown in **Figure 57**. Replace any disc that is worn unevenly or more than the wear tolerance listed in **Table 6**.

Measure gap (a) between the splines on the clutch friction discs and the clutch housing (**Figure 58**) using a feeler gauge. Gap must be 0.002-0.018 in. (0.05-0.45 mm) to prevent noisy operation. Replace the friction plates if the gap is too large.

Check the gear teeth on the clutch housing for burrs, nicks or damage. Smooth any such defects

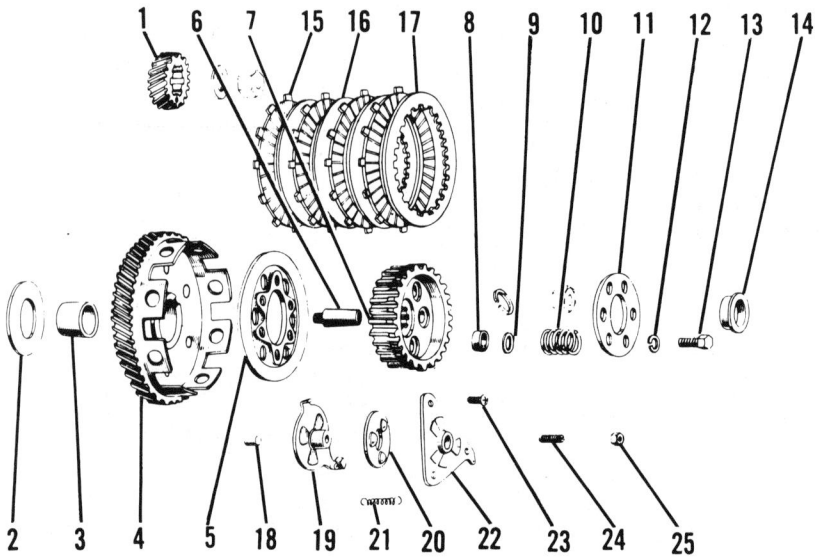

**TYPE 4 CLUTCH
(C2SS, C2TR, F3, F4)**

1. Pinion
2. Washer
3. Bushing
4. Housing
5. Cam plate
6. Stud
7. Hub
8. Damper
9. Washer
10. Spring
11. Spring plate
12. Lockwasher
13. Bolt
14. Pusher
15. Friction plate
16. Steel plate
17. Outer plate
18. Roller
19. Release plate
20. Release ball assembly
21. Spring
22. Cam plate
23. Screw
24. Screw
25. Nut

with an oilstone. If the oilstone doesn't smooth out the damage, replace clutch housing.

Insert the bushing into the needle bearing in the clutch housing (**Figure 59**). Replace the bushing if there is noticeable play. Excessive play results in gear noise.

Clutch Installation

Reverse the applicable disassembly procedure to reassemble the clutch. Be sure that all thrust washers are in position. An easy way to compress the clutch assembly during reassembly is to make a simple tool from a socket wrench of appropriate diameter, large washers and a length of threaded rod or bolt of suitable length (**Figure 60**).

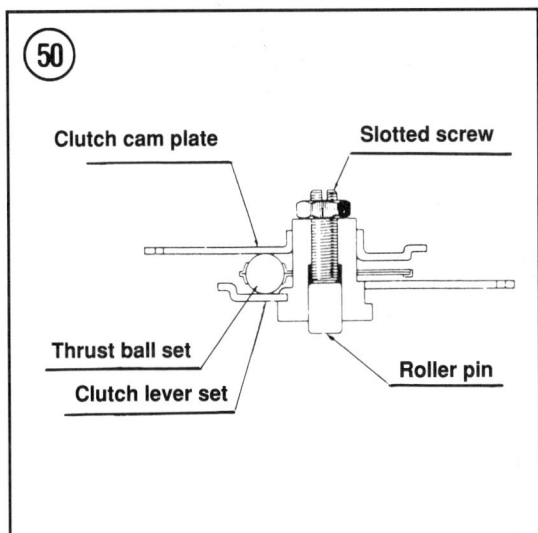

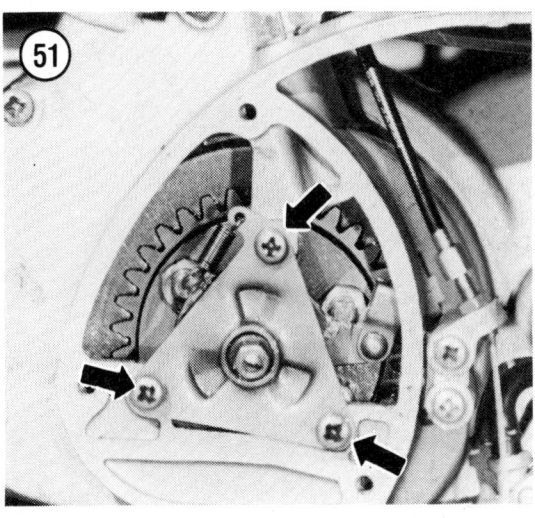

Clutch Adjustment (Types 1 and 2)

Figure 61 is a sectional view of a typical clutch adjustment mechanism on these machines. Refer to this illustration, then proceed as follows.

1. Refer to **Figure 62**. Loosen locknut (a), then back off adjustment screw (A) several turns.

2. Refer to **Figure 63**. Loosen locknut (b), then turn clutch cable adjuster (B) to set the angle of the clutch release lever to 90°, as shown in **Figure 64**.

3. Refer back to **Figure 62**. Turn adjustment screw (A) clockwise until it seats lightly, then hold it in that position and tighten locknut (a). Be sure that screw (A) does not turn any further as you tighten the locknut or clutch slippage may result.

4. Refer to **Figure 65**. Adjust play at the clutch lever to 0.5-0.7 in. (13-18 mm). To do so, loosen locknut (c), then rotate cable adjuster (C) as required. Dont forget to tighten the locknut.

The illustrations for the foregoing procedure apply to F5, F8, F9 and F81M models. Remove the breaker contact cover to gain access to the adjustment screw on F6 and F7 models. On G series models, remove the carburetor cover. The adjustment procedure is similar for all models.

Clutch Adjustment (Type 4)

To adjust the clutch on these models, proceed as follows.

1. Refer to **Figure 66**. Loosen locknut (D) and cable adjustment screw (C).

2. Refer to **Figure 67**. Loosen locknut (B), then turn adjusting screw (A) until the clutch release cable is completely slack.

3. Refer to **Figure 68**. Loosen locknut (F). Turn adjustment screw (E) in until it seats, then back it out 1/4-1/2 turn. Tighten locknut (F) securely.

4. Adjust play in the clutch lever to 0.5-0.7 in. (13-18 mm). Loosen locknut (c), then rotate cable adjuster (C) as required (**Figure 65**). Tighten locknut.

Clutch Adjustment (Type 3)

To adjust the clutch on these models, proceed as follows.

1. Remove the carburetor cover.

2. Refer to **Figure 69**. Loosen the locknut, turn the adjuster in fully to give play to the cable, then tighten the locknut.

4

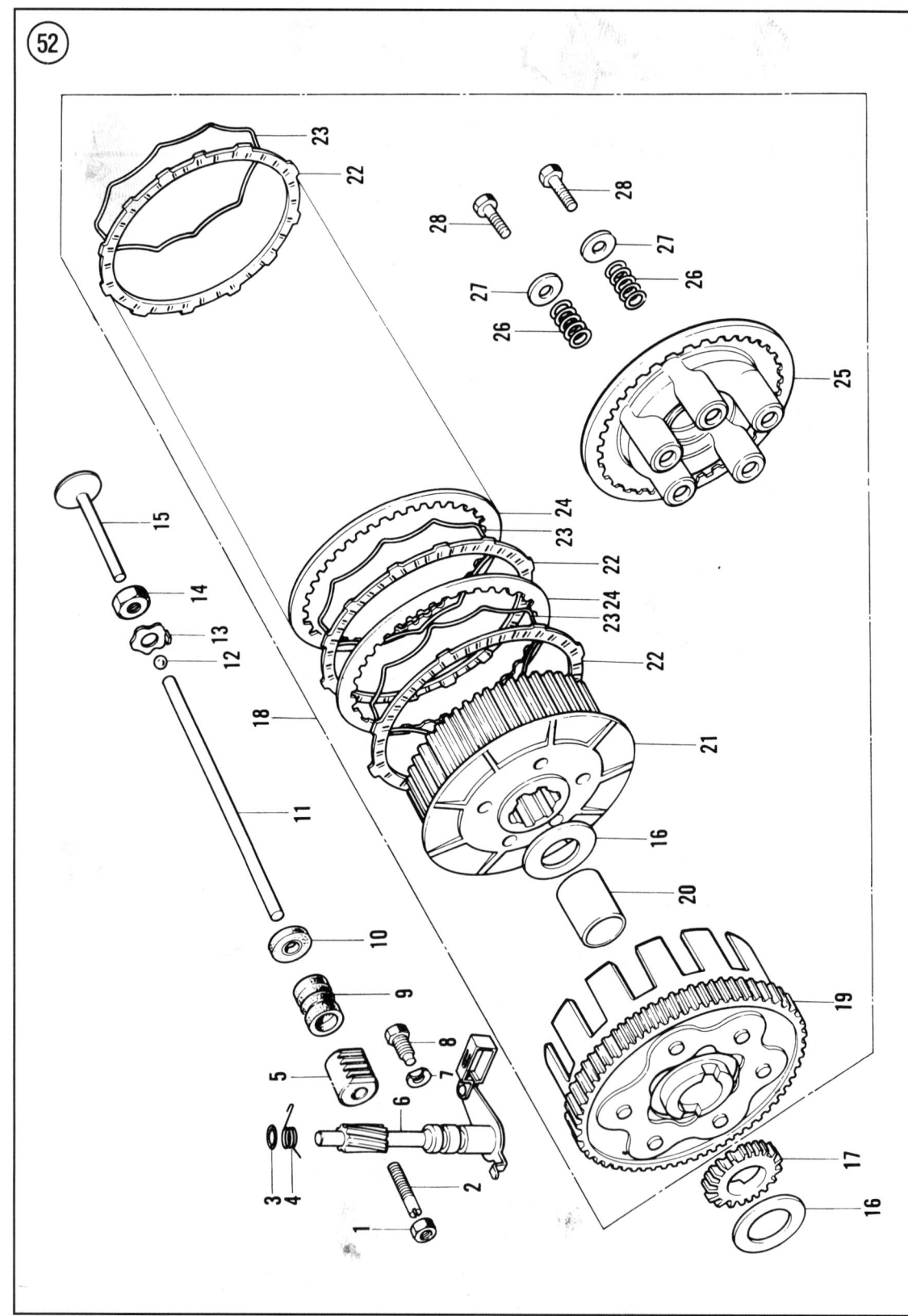

TYPE 5 CLUTCH (KD/KE/KS/KX125; KD/KE175 [WITH TYPE 3 CLUTCH RELEASE])

1. Nut
2. Slotted screw
3. O-ring
4. Clutch release return spring
5. Clutch release pushrod
6. Clutch release shaft
7. Lockwasher
8. Bolt
9. Collar
10. Oil seal
11. Clutch pushrod
12. Steel ball
13. Lockwasher
14. Nut
15. Clutch spring plate pusher
16. Clutch thrust washer
17. Kickstarter pinion
18. Clutch
19. Clutch housing
20. Clutch bushing
21. Clutch hub
22. Clutch friction plate
23. Clutch steel ring
24. Clutch steel plate
25. Clutch spring plate
26. Clutch spring
27. Plain washer
28. Hexagon head bolt

3. Refer to **Figure 70**. Loosen the locknut, then back out the adjusting screw several turns.

4. Refer to **Figure 71**. Loosen the locknut, then turn the adjusting nut as required until the angle between the clutch release lever and clutch cable is 80°. Tighten the locknut.

5. Refer back to **Figure 70**. Turn in the adjusting screw until there is approximately 1/16-1/8 in. (2-3 mm) play at the clutch lever (**Figure 72**). Be sure to tighten the locknut.

6. Minor adjustments may be made at the clutch hand lever.

Clutch Adjustment (Type 5)

1. Slide clutch lever dust cover out of the way.

2. Refer to **Figure 73**. Loosen the locknut slightly, then turn the adjuster to provide 0.20-0.24 in. (5-6 mm) gap between the adjuster and locknut.

4

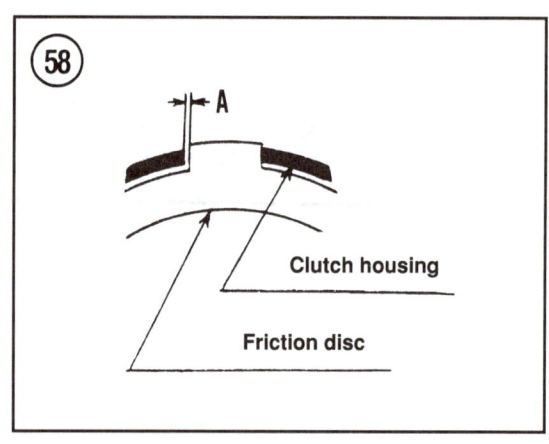

Clutch housing

Friction disc

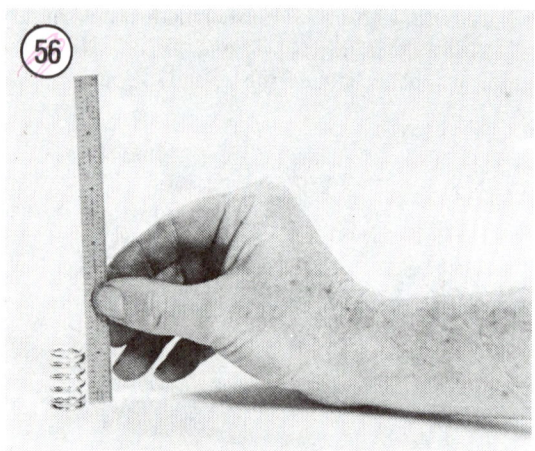

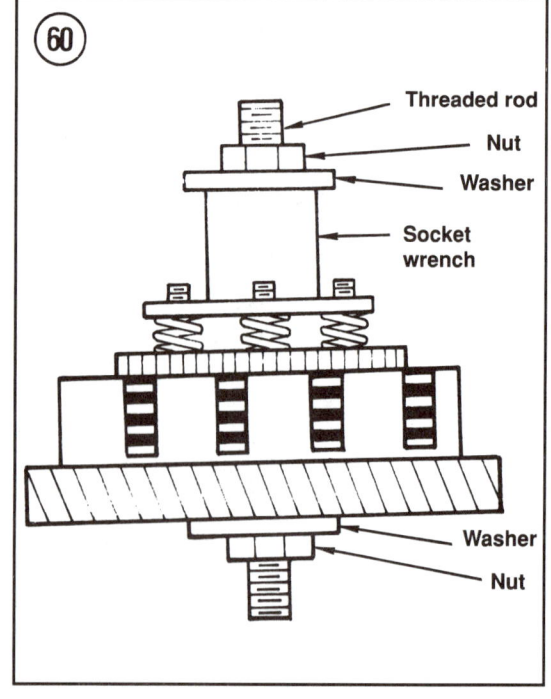

Threaded rod

Nut

Washer

Socket wrench

Washer

Nut

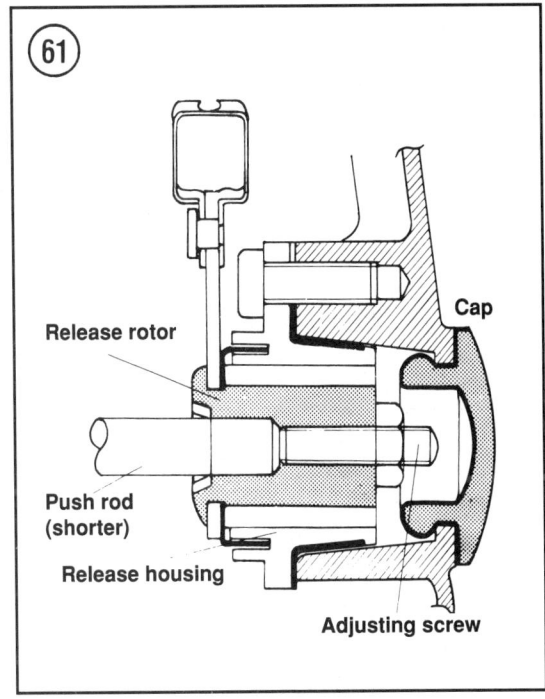

Cap

Release rotor

Push rod
(shorter)

Release housing

Adjusting screw

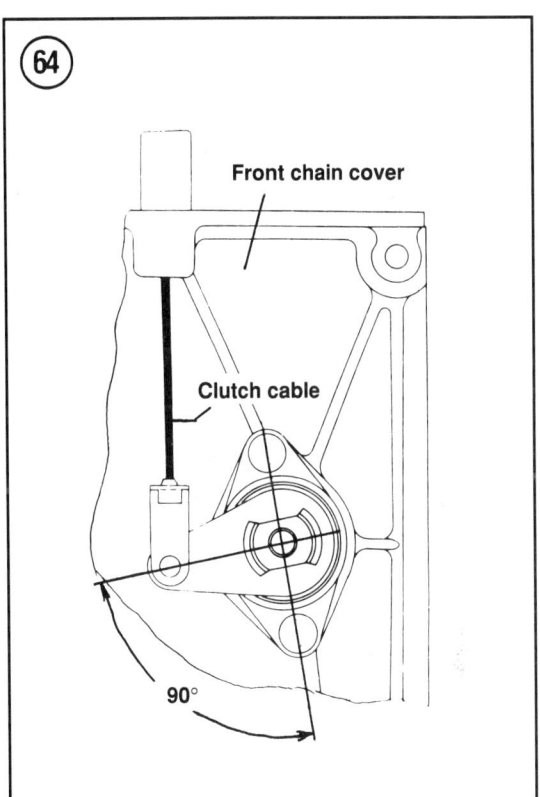

Front chain cover

Clutch cable

90°

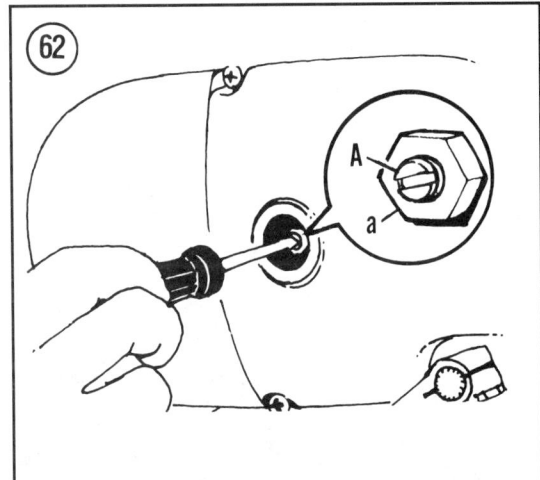

A

a

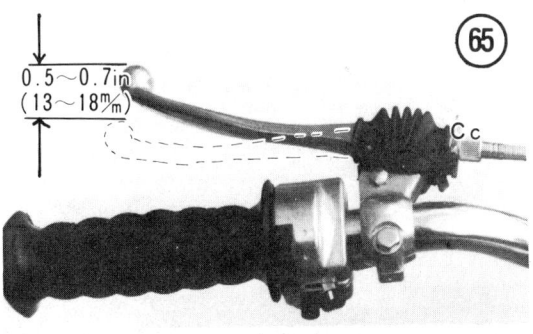

0.5~0.7in
(13~18ᵐm)

Cc

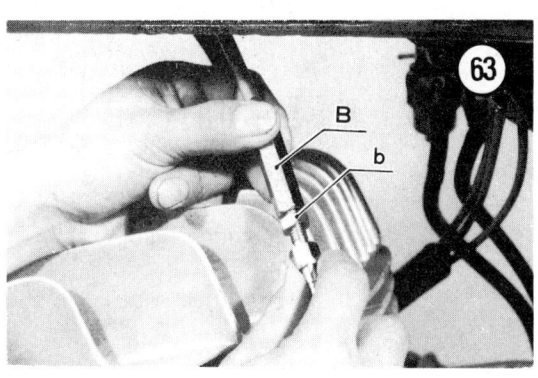

B

b

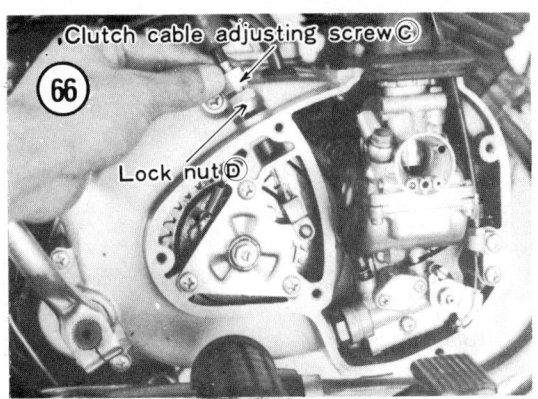

Clutch cable adjusting screw C

Lock nut D

4

3. Refer to **Figure 74**. Loosen the locknut, then turn the adjusting nut to provide plenty of free play in the cable.

4. Remove the clutch adjustment hole cover.

5. Refer to **Figure 75**. Loosen the locknut. Back out the adjustment screw until it turns freely if it does not already do so.

6. Refer back to **Figure 74**. Turn the adjusting nut in the cable until the projection on the clutch release lever (**Figure 76**) is parallel with the seam between the left engine cover and left crankcase half.

7. Turn the adjustment screw (**Figure 77**) in until it seats lightly, then tighten the locknut. Do not allow the screw to turn when tightening the locknut.

8. Refer back to **Figure 74**. Remove any play at the clutch hand lever by returning the cable adjustment nut. Then tighten the locknut.

9. Refer back to **Figure 73**. Adjust hand lever play to 1/16-1/8 in. (2-3 mm) using the adjuster, then tighten the locknut.

10. Replace both covers.

ROTARY VALVE

The rotary valve system consists of the crankshaft, disc valve, crankcase and disc cover. **Figure 78** is a sectional view of the valve mechanism.

On early rotary valve models, the disc is made from phenolic resin. The boss in the center of the disc is of steel and is attached to the crankshaft with a dowel pin. Valve discs on later models are of steel.

The valve floats back and forth a distance of 0.12 in. (0.3 mm). This floating action permits the valve to seat against the O-ring on the valve cover and

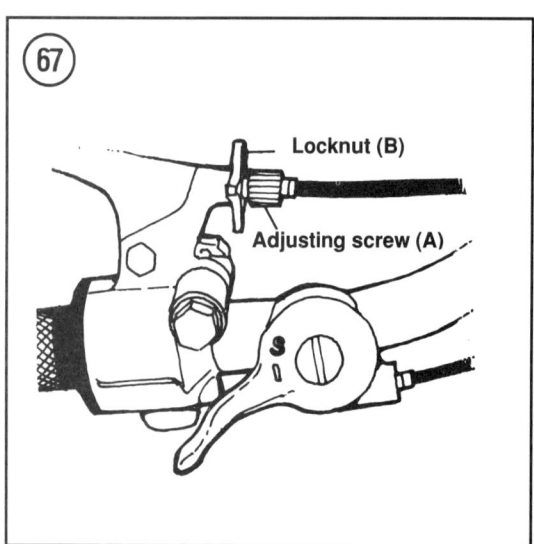

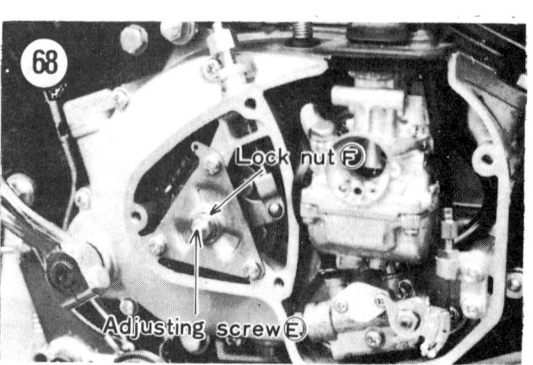

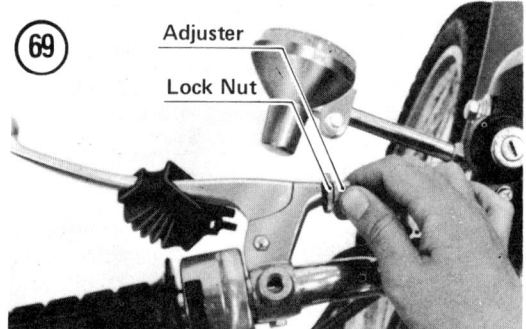

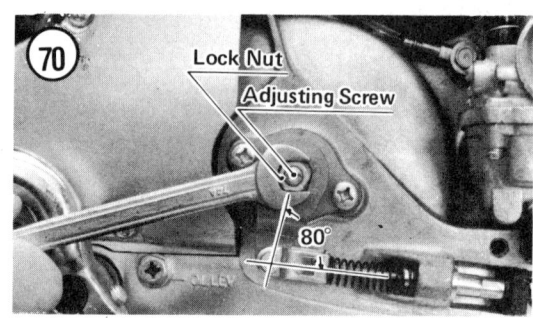

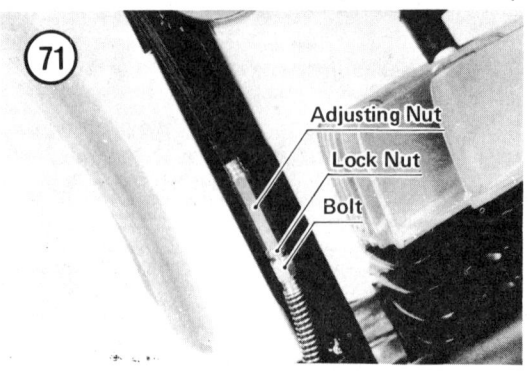

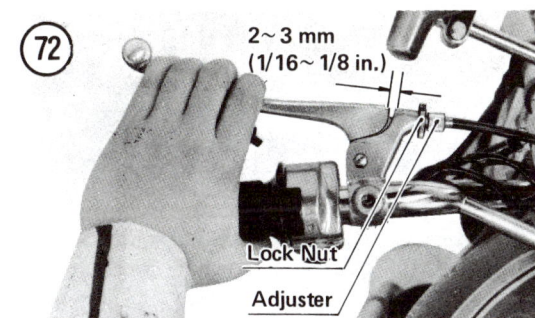

2~3 mm
(1/16~ 1/8 in.)

Lock Nut

Adjuster

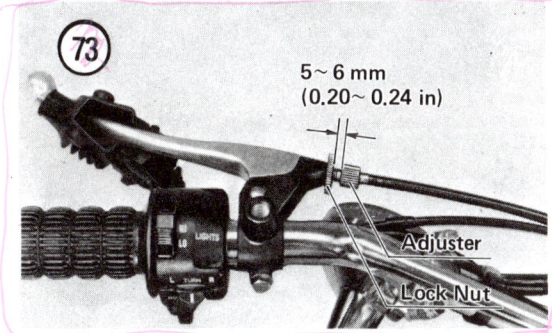

5~ 6 mm
(0.20~ 0.24 in)

Adjuster

Lock Nut

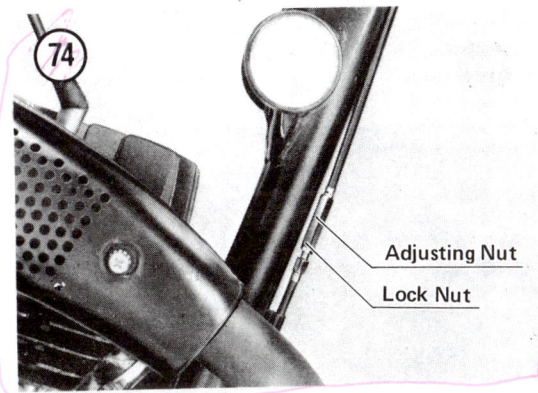

Adjusting Nut

Lock Nut

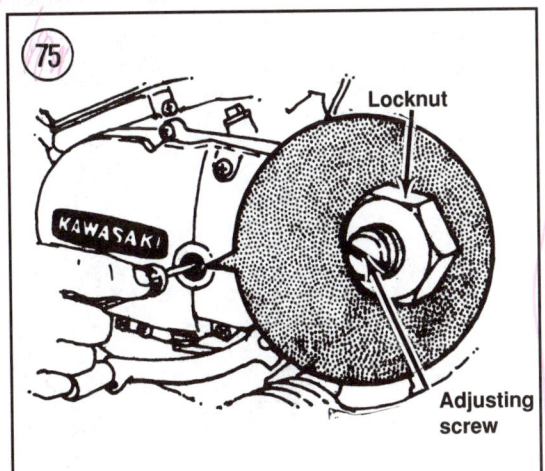

Locknut

KAWASAKI

Adjusting
screw

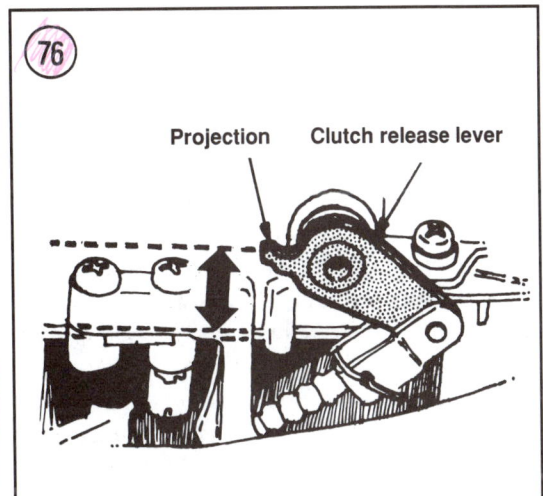

Projection   Clutch release lever

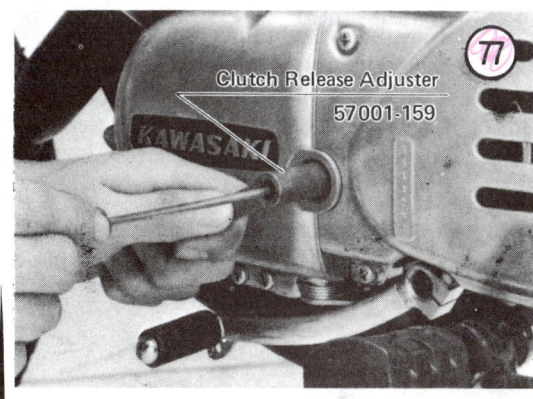

Clutch Release Adjuster
57001-159

KAWASAKI

4

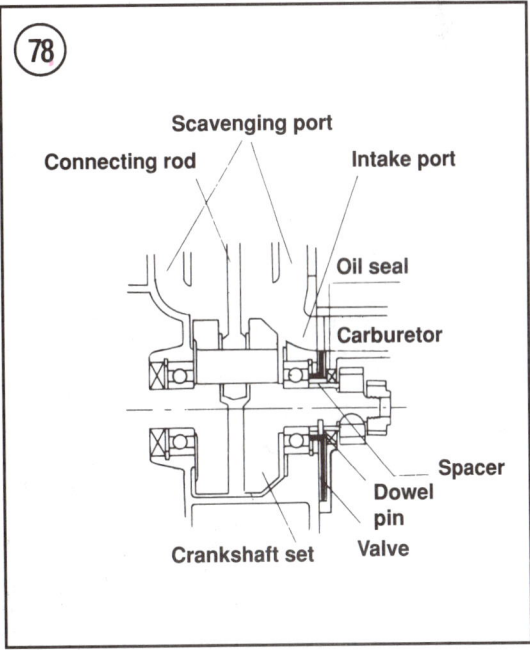

Scavenging port

Connecting rod   Intake port

Oil seal

Carburetor

Spacer

Dowel
pin

Crankshaft set   Valve

thereby seal the crankcase during the downstroke of the piston.

Removal

To remove the rotary valve, proceed as follows.

1. Remove the valve cover retaining screws, then pull off the valve cover (**Figure 79**).

2. Slide the valve disc (**Figure 80**) from its shaft.

3. Refer to **Figure 81**. Remove the spacer, O-ring and dowel (A) from the crankshaft.

Inspection

Figure 82 illustrates the valve cover. Examine the oil seal (B) for scratches, lip deformation or other damage. Check for any damage to the O-ring (A). Replace the valve cover in the event of deep scratches or if it is worn more than the wear limit specified in **Table 7**. **Figure 83** illustrates the measurement.

Measure thickness of the valve disc as shown in **Figure 84**. Replace the disc if it is worn beyond the wear limit or if there are any scratches or damage on its surface. Thickness should be as specified in **Table 8**.

Installation

Reverse the removal procedure to install the rotary valve. Observe the following notes.

1. Apply engine oil to both sides of the valve disc before installation.

2. Insert the smaller O-ring into the spacer on the crankshaft. Install the larger O-ring in the groove on the valve cover.

3. Tighten the valve cover screws in the order shown in **Figure 85**.

4. On models F6 and F7, be sure to align the mark on the valve with the pin on the crankshaft.

GEARSHIFT MECHANISM

Figure 86 illustrates the external parts of a typical gearshift mechanism. As the rider presses the gearshift pedal, the shaft turns and moves the change lever. The change lever meshes with pins on the shift drum (part of the transmission assembly). Therefore, as the pedal is moved, the shift drum rotates. Grooves on the shift drum cause shift forks in the transmission to slide from side to side, thereby selecting the various gear ratios (**Figure 87**).

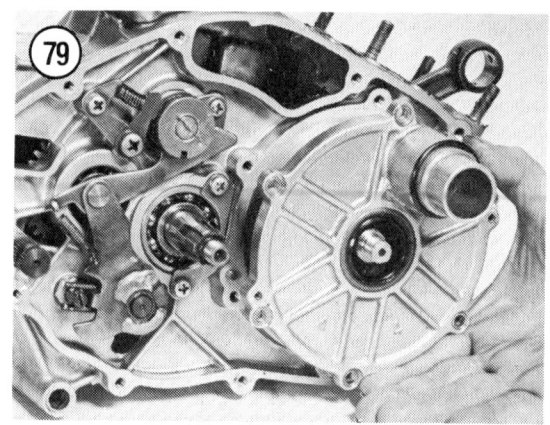

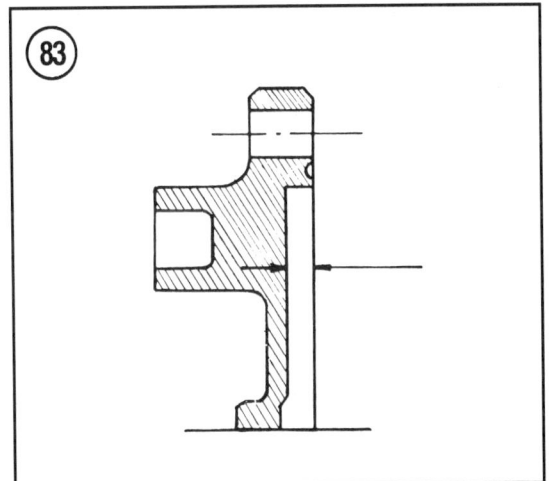

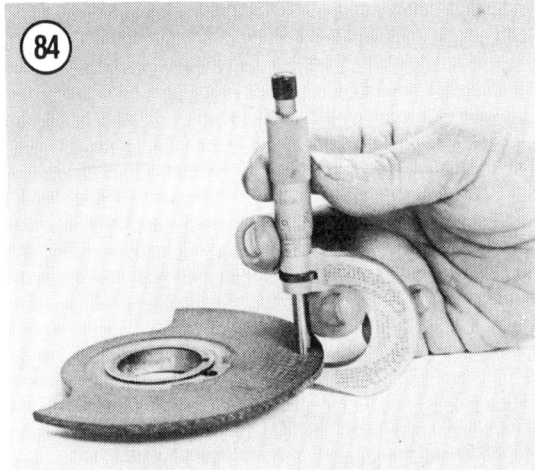

The set levers are also meshed with the pins on the change drums. They keep the drum in position after each step of rotation on the drum.

The five speed shift mechanism used on 1980 and later KE100 models operates in the same way as earlier models, but the shift forks are located on shift rails as shown in **Figure 88**. Differences in the disassembly, inspection and reassembly procedures are evident.

Removal

To remove the gearshift mechanism, proceed as follows.

1. Carefully note how both set levers are installed (**Figure 89**).

2. Remove the shifter shaft retaining clip (A, **Figure 90**) and thrust washer.

3. Disengage set levers from gear change drum.

4. Pull out shifter shaft and levers as an assembly (**Figure 91**).

5. Note how return spring is installed, then remove it (**Figure 92**).

Inspection

Check return spring tension. Replace the spring if it is weak or cracked. Inspect the set lever spring for cracks or weakness. Be sure that the return spring set pin is not loose. If it is, missed shifts will result. Be sure that the locknut is tight.

Installation

Reverse the removal procedure to install the shift mechanism. Observe the following notes.

1. Be sure to install each spring correctly.

2. On F series models, adjust shift lever position by turning the return spring setting pin as required.

CRANKCASE

The crankcase is made in 2 halves of diecast aluminum alloy. They are assembled without a gasket; only gasket cement, such as Kawasaki bond is used. Two dowel pins hold the crankcase halves in alignment when they are bolted together. **Figure 93** is an exploded view of a typical crankcase assembly.

TYPICAL GEARSHIFT MECHANISM

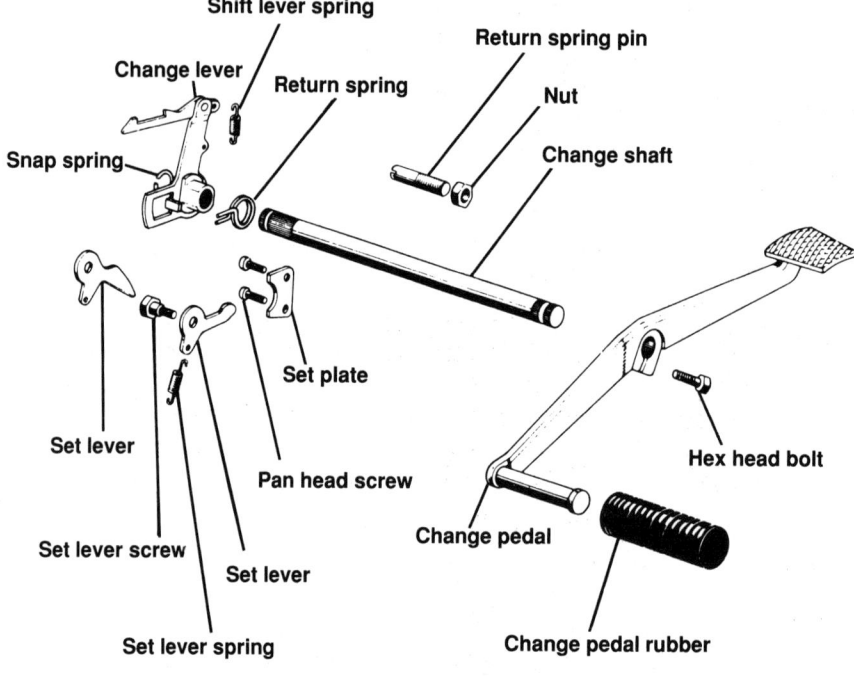

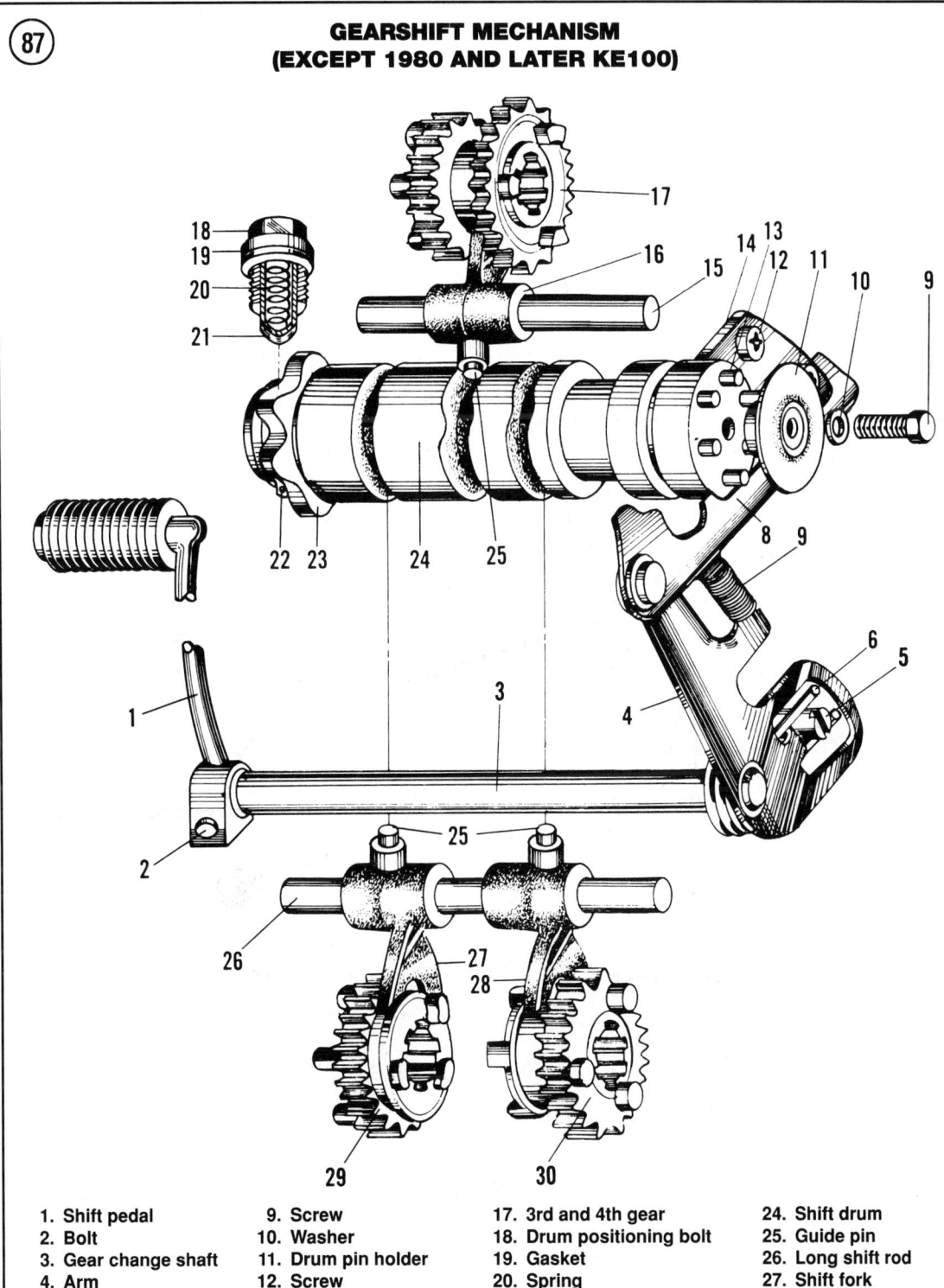

GEARSHIFT MECHANISM
(EXCEPT 1980 AND LATER KE100)

1. Shift pedal	9. Screw	17. 3rd and 4th gear
2. Bolt	10. Washer	18. Drum positioning bolt
3. Gear change shaft	11. Drum pin holder	19. Gasket
4. Arm	12. Screw	20. Spring
5. Return spring pin	13. Drum pin	21. Drum positioning pin
6. Return spring	14. Shift drum stopper	22. Circlip
7. Spring	15. Short shift rod	23. Drum operating disc
8. Shift pawl	16. Shift fork	

24. Shift drum
25. Guide pin
26. Long shift rod
27. Shift fork
28. Shift fork
29. 6th gear
30. 5th gear

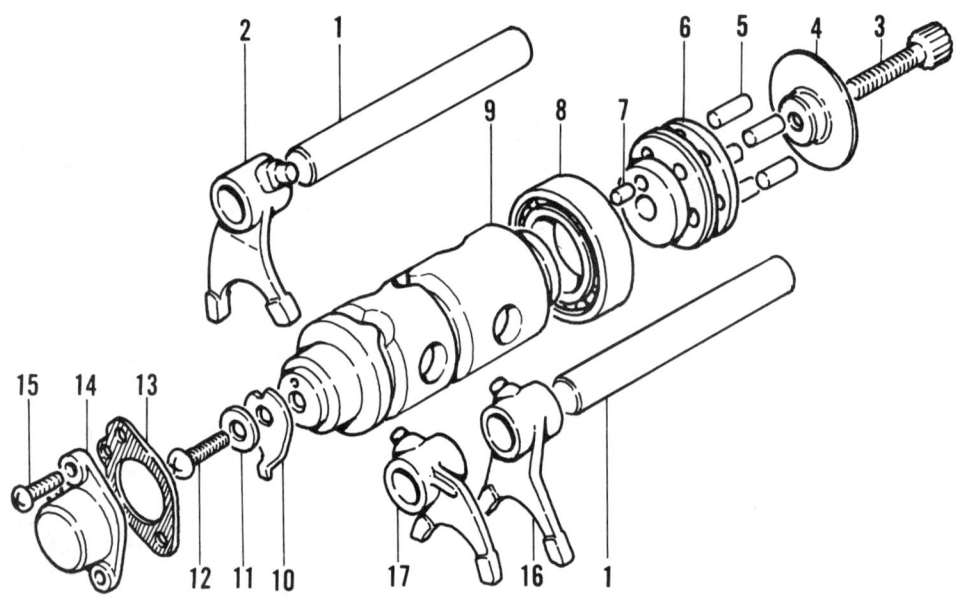

88

5-SPEED SHIFT MECHANISM
(1980-ON KE100)

1. Shift rod
2. Shift fork (4th & 5th)
3. Bolt
4. Pin holder
5. Pins
6. Bearing holder
7. Pin
8. Ball Bearing
9. Shift drum
10. Rotor
11. Washer
12. Screw
13. Gasket
14. Neutral switch
15. Screws
16. Shift fork (1st & 2nd)
17. Shift fork (3rd)

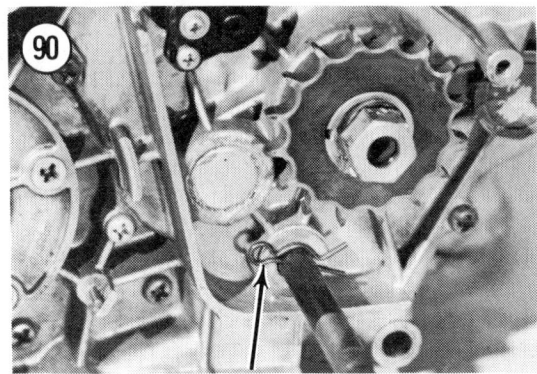

Crankcase Disassembly

Crankcase disassembly is generally similar for all models. Note that later models require a crankcase splitting tool.

1. Remove neutral indicator switch. Also remove snap rings from gearshift rods on models so equipped.

2. Remove air cleaner adapter (**Figure 94**).

3. Remove the shift drum retaining plate (**Figure 95**).

4. Remove all crankcase screws. An impact tool will make this job much easier.

5. Using a rawhide mallet, alternately tap the left end of the crankshaft and transmission output shaft to split both crankcase halves or use a crankcase splitting tool for those models mentioned.

6. Lift left crankcase away (**Figure 96**). Leave all internal components in the right crankcase half (**Figure 97**).

7. Remove the bearing retainers, then pry out the oil seals. Finally, press the bearings from the crankcase halves.

Inspection

Check each oil supply hole. If any are clogged, blow them out with compressed air. Also check the transmission breather hole. If dust or dirt clogs this hole, internal pressure will build up and cause oil leakage.

Check the crankshaft main bearings and transmission bearings for rust, wear, pitting or excess radial clearance. If radial clearance of any bearing is more than 0.002 in. (0.5 mm), replace the bearings. Before examining them, clean the bearings with solvent and dry them with compressed air. Do not spin bearings with an air blast. Transmission bearings are particularly susceptible to damage from metal particles or other foreign material in the transmission oil. Crankshaft bearings may become damaged if the air filter is damaged or missing. **Figure 98** illustrates a crankshaft bearing which failed after only a few miles of operation without an air filter. One end of each transmission shaft is supported in a bushing. These bushings are lubricated by oil carried through a groove on the shaft. Examine these bushings carefully for wear and replace them if necessary.

The crankcase oil seals maintain crankcase pressure. If these seals leak, primary compression leakage will occur and lead to poor engine performance and possible crankshaft failure. It is good practice to

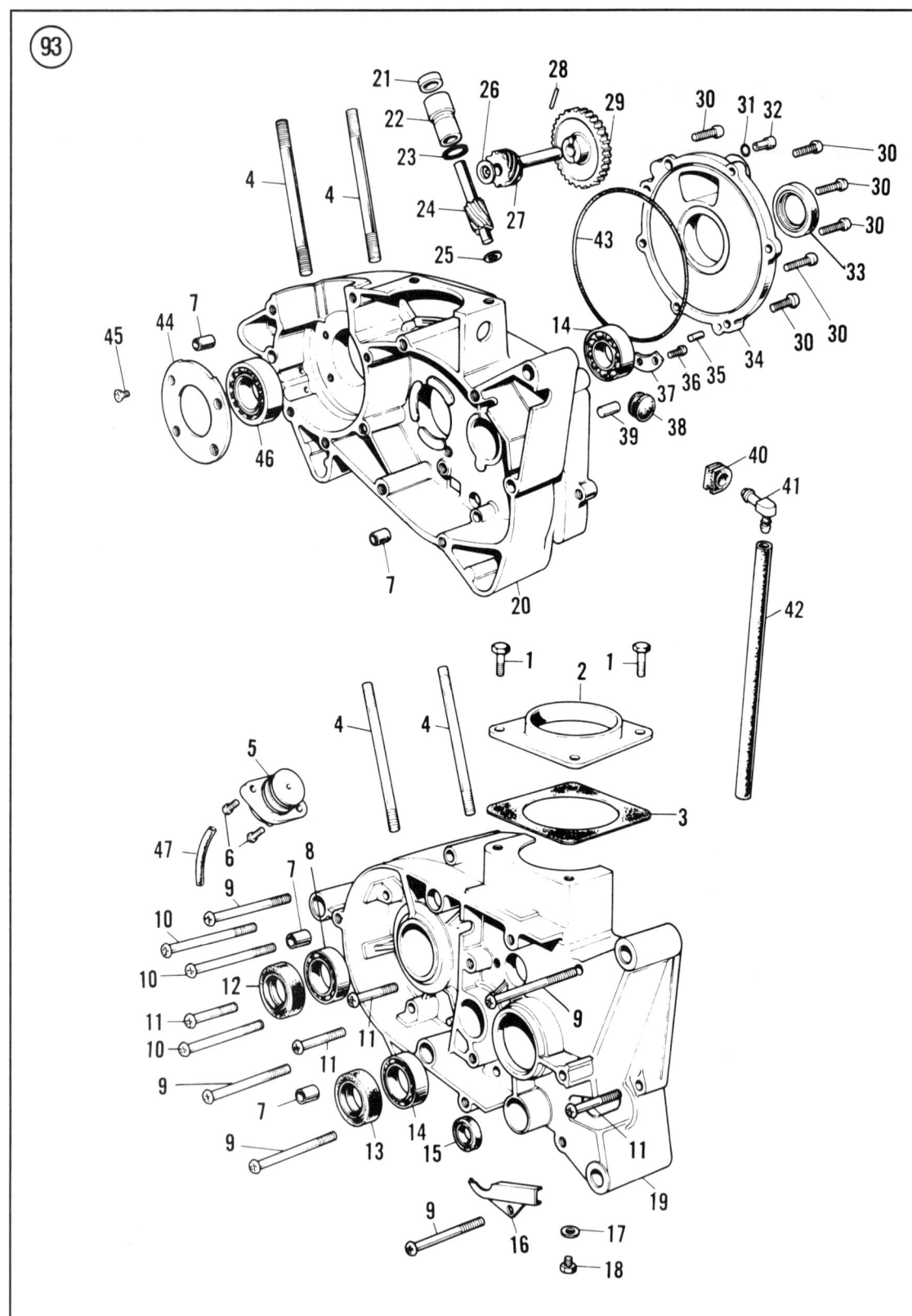

CRANKCASE ASSEMBLY

1. Bolt
2. Tube
3. Gasket
4. Stud
5. Pump
6. Screw
7. Dowel pin
8. Bearing
9. Screw
10. Screw
11. Screw
12. Oil seal
13. Oil seal
14. Bearing
15. Oil seal
16. Cover
17. Gasket
18. Plug
19. Left crankcase
20. Right crankcase
21. Oil seal
22. Bushing
23. O-ring
24. Gear
25. Washer
26. Washer
27. Gear
28. Dowel pin
29. Gear
30. Screw
31. O-ring
32. Check valve
33. Oil seal
34. Cover
35. Dowel pin
36. Screw
37. Bearing retainer
38. Grommet
39. Dowel pin
40. Grommet
41. Breather
42. Tube
43. O-ring
44. Bearing retainer
45. Screw
46. Bearing
47. Tube

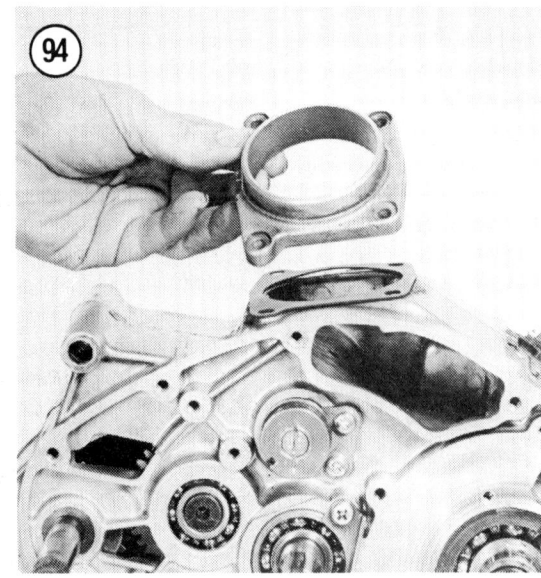

4

replace these seals each time the engine is over-hauled. Also, check the oil seals on the transmission and shifter shafts.

Crankcase Reassembly

1. Begin reassembly by pressing in each bearing until its side is flush with the inner side of the crankcase, as shown in **Figure 99**. Lubricate the bearings with engine oil during installation. This work will be easier if the crankcase is heated to approximately 200° F in an oven. Do not use a torch for heating, as warping or cracking may result.

2. Press the oil seals in from the magneto side until they are flush with the outside of the crankcase, as shown in **Figure 100**. Markings on the oil seals should be toward the magneto, or visible after they are installed. Always install new oil seals when replacing bearings. Lubricate seal lips with engine oil upon installation.

3. On machines so equipped, lubricate the needle bearing, then press it in until it stops.

4. Lubricate the transmission drive shaft bushing then press it in from the gearshift pedal side.

5. Install the crankshaft into the right crankcase half, except on M series. If the crankshaft must be pressed in, use a wedge between crank wheels to maintain crankshaft alignment.

6. Insert the kick shaft.

7. Install the transmission and shifter drum as a unit. On models with a ball on the end of the transmission drive shaft, a little grease will hold the ball in position during assembly.

8. Apply gasket cement to the mating surfaces of the crankcase halves.

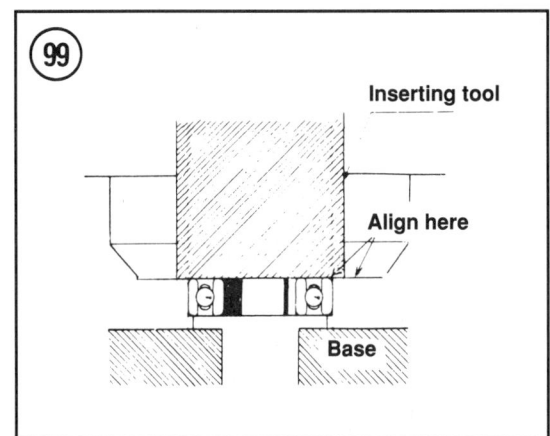

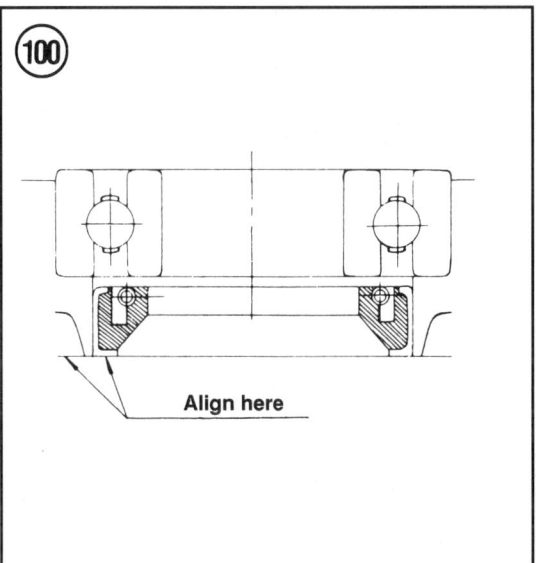

9. On G series models, install the ball and shim at the end of the transmission drive shaft.

10. Assemble both crankcase halves. Tap the left half with a plastic mallet to seat it against the right half. Take care not to damage oil seals.

11. Install and tighten the crankcase screws.

After assembly, be sure that the crankshaft and transmission gears rotate smoothly. Check the gearshift mechanism for smoothness and positive operation. Be sure that the kick gear and kick ratchet operate properly.

KICKSTARTER

Several different types of kickstarter mechanisms are used on Kawasaki machines. Refer to the applicable section for the procedure to follow for your machine.

To remove the kickstarter, first take careful note of how it is installed, then lift it from the crankcase (**Figure 101**).

Type 1 Kickstarter

Figure 102 is an exploded view of this kickstarter mechanism. As the rider presses the kickstarter

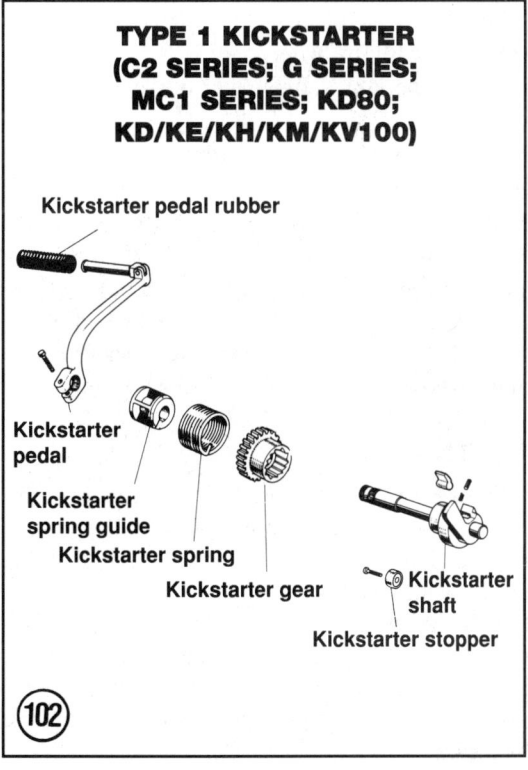

TYPE 1 KICKSTARTER
(C2 SERIES; G SERIES;
MC1 SERIES; KD80;
KD/KE/KH/KM/KV100)

Kickstarter pedal rubber

Kickstarter pedal

Kickstarter spring guide

Kickstarter spring

Kickstarter gear

Kickstarter shaft

Kickstarter stopper

pedal, the kick shaft rotates clockwise (**Figure 103**). As the kick shaft rotates, the kick pawl spring and kick pawl pin push the kick pawl away from the kick pawl stopper and into engagement with the internal teeth of the kick gear. After the engine starts and the kick pedal is released, the kick shaft returns to its original position. At this time, the kick pawl stopper (**Figure 104**) contacts the kick pawl and holds it away from the kick gear, thereby releasing the mechanism during normal running.

To disassemble this mechanism, proceed as follows.

1. Slide the kick gear from the kickstarter shaft.

2. Disassemble the pawl, pawl pin and pawl spring.

3. Remove the kick stopper from the left crankcase half.

After disassembly, inspect the following items.

1. Check the inner teeth of the kick gear for wear. If these teeth are worn or rounded, the pawl will slip. Replace the gear if the teeth are worn or damaged.

2. Check for wear on the tip of the kick pawl. Wear results in slippage. Replace the pawl if the tip is worn.

3. Be sure there is no foreign material in the pawl pin hole. Check for freedom of movement of the pawl pin and pawl spring.

Installation is generally the reverse of removal. Observe the following notes.

1. Install the kick stopper into the left crankcase half.

2. Insert the pawl spring, then the pawl pin, into the hole in the kick shaft.

3. Install the kick pawl. Hold the kick pawl down, then install the kick gear.

4. Insert one end of the kick spring into the hole in the right crankcase half. Twist the outer end of the spring clockwise approximately 120° and insert it into the hole on the kick shaft (**Figure 105**).

Type 2 Kickstarter

Figure 106 and **Figure 107** are exploded and sectional views of this kickstarter. When the pedal is pressed, the kick gear slides along the kick shaft and meshes with the low gear on the output shaft, thereby turning the engine. When the engine starts, the kick gear is driven by the gear on the output idle gear and is forced to disengage. When the kick pedal is released, the kick shaft turns clockwise and is stopped by the kick stopper.

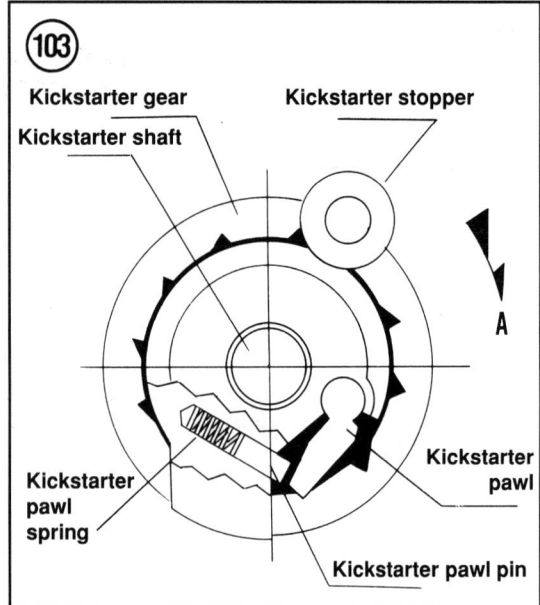

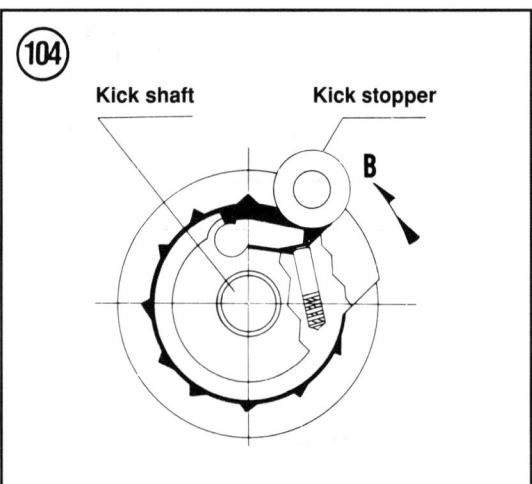

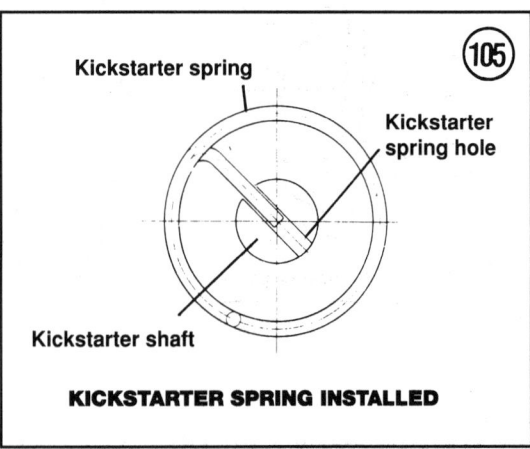

TYPE 2 KICKSTARTER
(F5 [1970]; F6; F7)

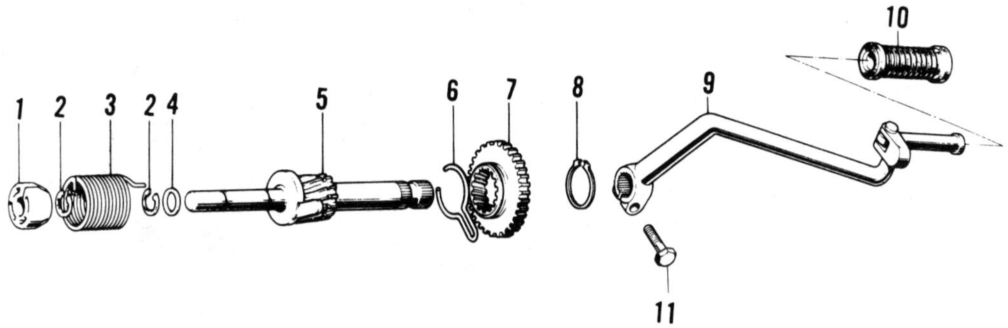

1. Spring guide
2. Snap ring
3. Spring
4. Shim
5. Shaft
6. Gear holder
7. Kickstarter gear
8. Snap ring
9. Pedal
10. Pedal cover
11. Bolt

4

TYPE 2 KICKSTARTER

Kickstarter gear

Spring

Kickstarter gear

Kickstarter shaft

Spring guide

Gear holder

Oil seal

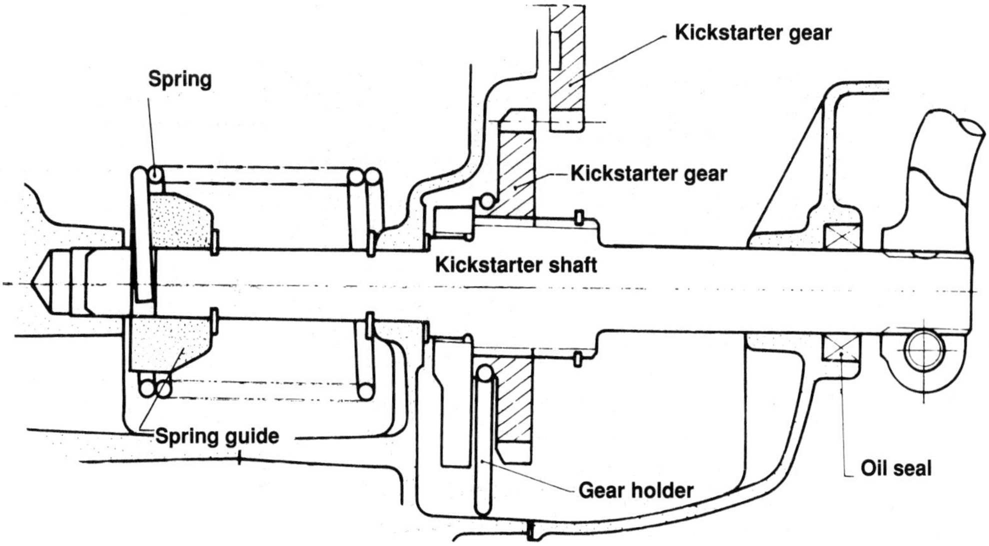

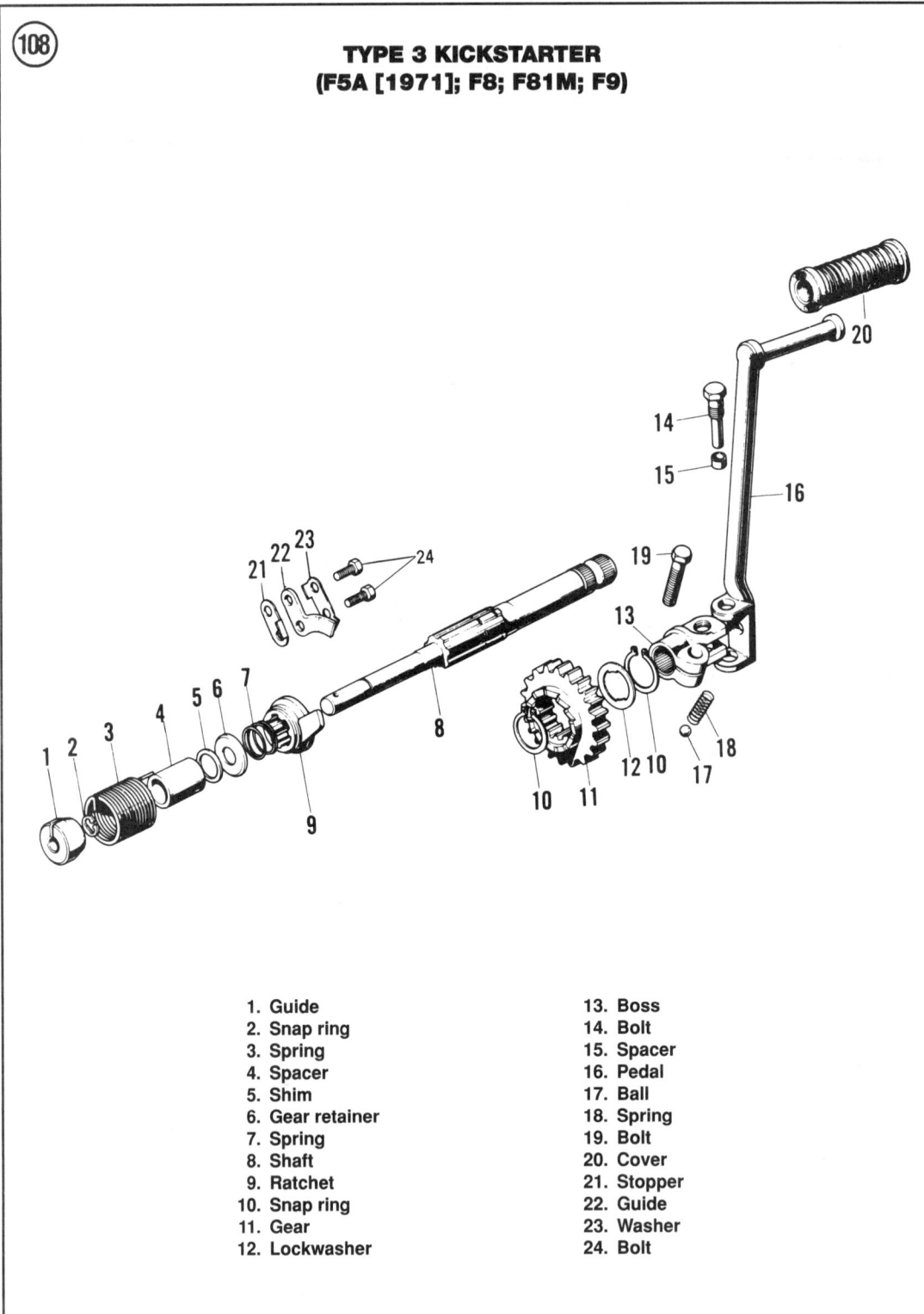

TYPE 3 KICKSTARTER
(F5A [1971]; F8; F81M; F9)

1. Guide
2. Snap ring
3. Spring
4. Spacer
5. Shim
6. Gear retainer
7. Spring
8. Shaft
9. Ratchet
10. Snap ring
11. Gear
12. Lockwasher
13. Boss
14. Bolt
15. Spacer
16. Pedal
17. Ball
18. Spring
19. Bolt
20. Cover
21. Stopper
22. Guide
23. Washer
24. Bolt

To disassemble this kickstarter, proceed as follows.

1. Remove the spring guide, the spring and both snap rings.

2. Remove the snap rings and the kick gear from the kick shaft.

After disassembly check the following items.

1. Check the kick gear guide and kick gear splines for wear and free movement.

2. Check the kick shaft for bends or cracks.

3. Check the teeth of the kick gear for wear or damage.

Installation is generally the reverse of removal. Observe the following notes.

1. Insert the kick shaft into the right crankcase half. Be sure shim is in place, then install the snap rings.

2. Insert one end of the spring into the hole in the right crankcase half. Twist the spring clockwise approximately 120°, then insert the other end into the hole in the kick shaft.

3. Slide the spring guide onto the kick shaft.

4. Install the kick gear and gear holder from outside the right crankcase half, then install the snap ring into its groove on the kick shaft.

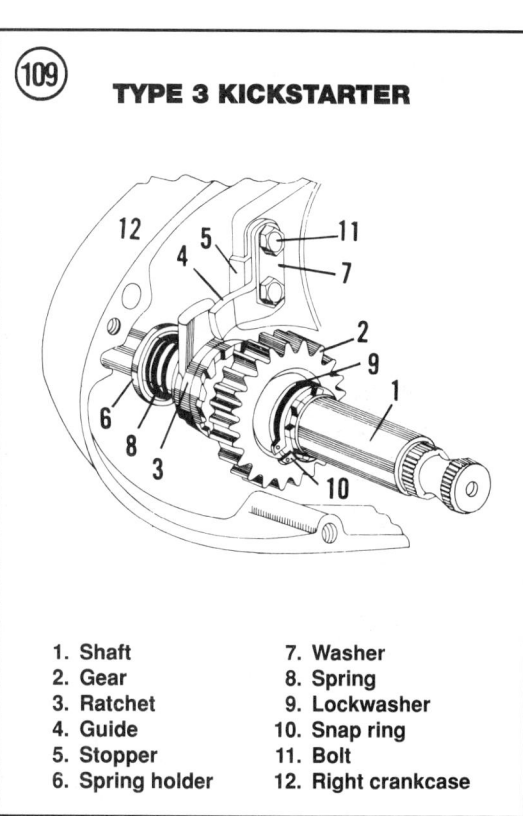

(109) TYPE 3 KICKSTARTER

1. Shaft	7. Washer
2. Gear	8. Spring
3. Ratchet	9. Lockwasher
4. Guide	10. Snap ring
5. Stopper	11. Bolt
6. Spring holder	12. Right crankcase

Type 3 Kickstarter

Figure 108 is an exploded view of this kickstarter. **Figure 109** illustrates its operation. The ratchet slides along the splined portion of the kick shaft. When the rider presses the kick pedal, the ratchet slides past the kick guide until it separates from the guide plate. The spring then forces the ratchet against the teeth on the side of the kick gear, causing the kick gear to turn. The kick gear is always meshed with the kickstarter idler gear in the transmission.

When the engine starts, the kick gear is driven by the kick idler gear in the transmission. The teeth on the side of the kick gear slide over the teeth on the ratchet until the kick starter pedal is released. When the kickstarter pedal is released, the ratchet is forced to move away from the kick gear by the guide plate.

NOTE
F8 and early F5 models before engine No. 07269 do not use the kick guide plate. Helical splines on the kick shaft force the ratchet against the side of the kick gear.

To disassemble this mechanism, proceed as follows.

1. Remove the kick gear snap ring, then pull the kick gear from the kick shaft.

2. Remove the ratchet, spring holder plate and spring.

After disassembly, check the following items.

1. Check that the ratchet slides against the kick guide properly.

2. Be sure that the kick shaft is not bent or scratched.

3. Check for worn or damaged teeth on the kick gear.

Installation is generally the reverse of removal. Observe the following notes.

1. Install the kick guide and the kick stopper into the crankcase. Be sure both screws are tight.

2. Insert the kick shaft into its hole.

3. Install the spring holder, shim, spacer and snap ring.

4. Insert one end of the return spring into the hole in the crankcase. Twist the spring approximately 120° and insert the other end into the hole in the kick shaft.

5. Slide the spring guide onto the kick shaft.

4

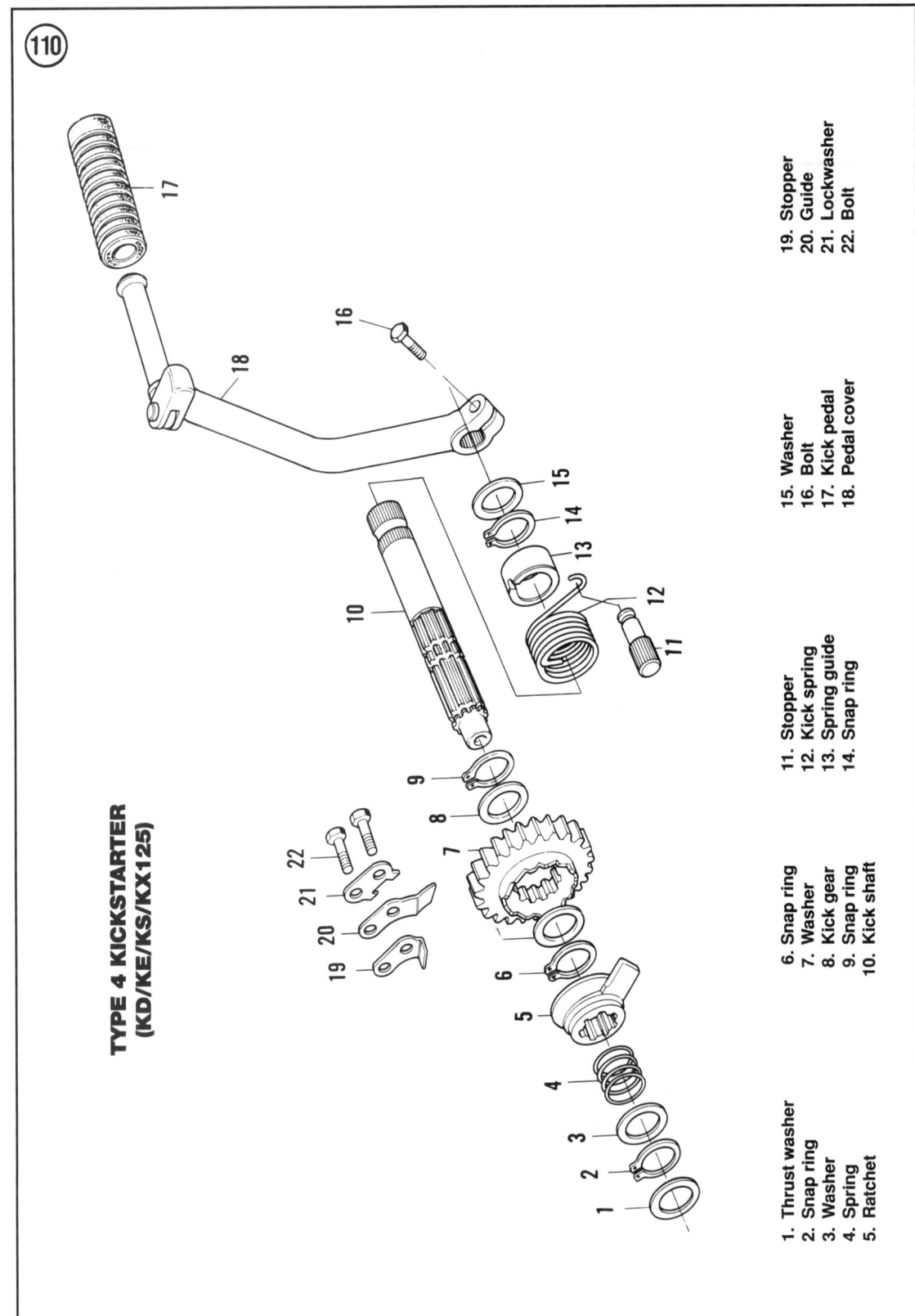

⑩

TYPE 4 KICKSTARTER
(KD/KE/KS/KX125)

1. Thrust washer
2. Snap ring
3. Washer
4. Spring
5. Ratchet

6. Snap ring
7. Washer
8. Kick gear
9. Snap ring
10. Kick shaft

11. Stopper
12. Kick spring
13. Spring guide
14. Snap ring

15. Washer
16. Bolt
17. Kick pedal
18. Pedal cover

19. Stopper
20. Guide
21. Lockwasher
22. Bolt

6. Slide the ratchet onto the kick shaft. Be sure that the marks on the kick shaft and the ratchet are aligned.

7. Install the kick gear and kick gear snap ring.

Type 4 Kickstarter

Figure 110 is an exploded view of this kickstarter. Operation, disassembly, service and installation are similar to Type 3 kickstarter.

Type 5 Kickstarter

Figure 111 is an exploded view of this kickstarter. Its operation, disassembly, service and installation are similar to that of Type 3.

CRANKSHAFT

The crankshaft operates under conditions of high stress. Dimensional tolerances are critical. It is necessary to locate and correct defects in the crankshaft to prevent more serious trouble later. **Figure 112** illustrates part of a typical crankshaft assembly.

To remove the crankshaft, first be sure that the dowel (A, **Figure 113**) has been removed. Start it by tapping its end with a rawhide mallet, then lift it out (**Figure 114**).

Inspection

There are several measurement locations on the crankshaft assembly. Measurements to be made are big end radial clearance, big end side clearance and small end radial clearance.

Measure big end radial clearance with dial indicator. If clearance exceeds the wear limit, replace the crankpin and needle bearing. It may also be necessary to replace the connecting rod. **Table 9** specifies wear limits.

Measure side clearance as shown in **Figure 115** using a feeler gauge. If side clearance exceeds the wear limit, replace the side washers. **Table 10** specifies wear limits. If measuring equipment is not available, refer to **Figure 116**. Move the upper end of the connecting rod from side to side. Measure movement of the upper end. If this movement is no greater than 0.10 in. (2.5 mm), the lower end bearing is not worn. Be careful not to mistake side play for upper end movement.

Measure piston pin radial clearance at measurement location (A) in **Figure 117**. If clearance exceeds 0.002 in. (0.05 mm), replace the needle bearing and piston pin. Standard clearance for all models is 0.00012-0.00086 in. (0.0030-0.022 mm).

If this measurement is difficult, clean and dry the piston pin, upper end bearing and connecting rod. Assemble them without lubrication. Then check for any perceptible play in the upper end (**Figure 118**).

4

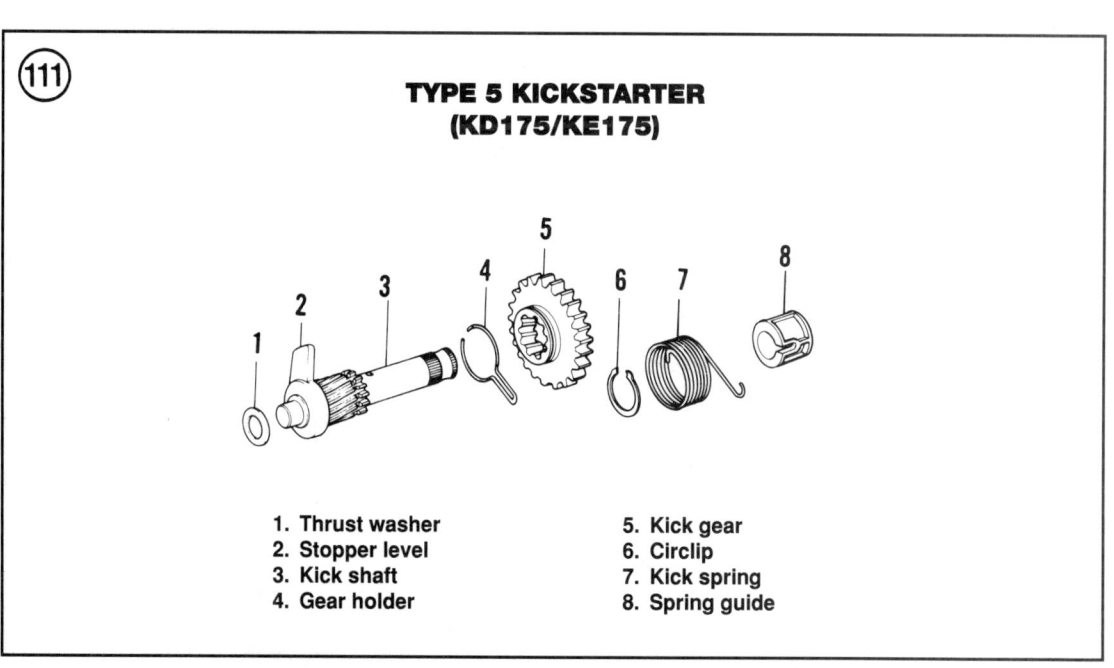

(111)

TYPE 5 KICKSTARTER
(KD175/KE175)

1. Thrust washer
2. Stopper level
3. Kick shaft
4. Gear holder
5. Kick gear
6. Circlip
7. Kick spring
8. Spring guide

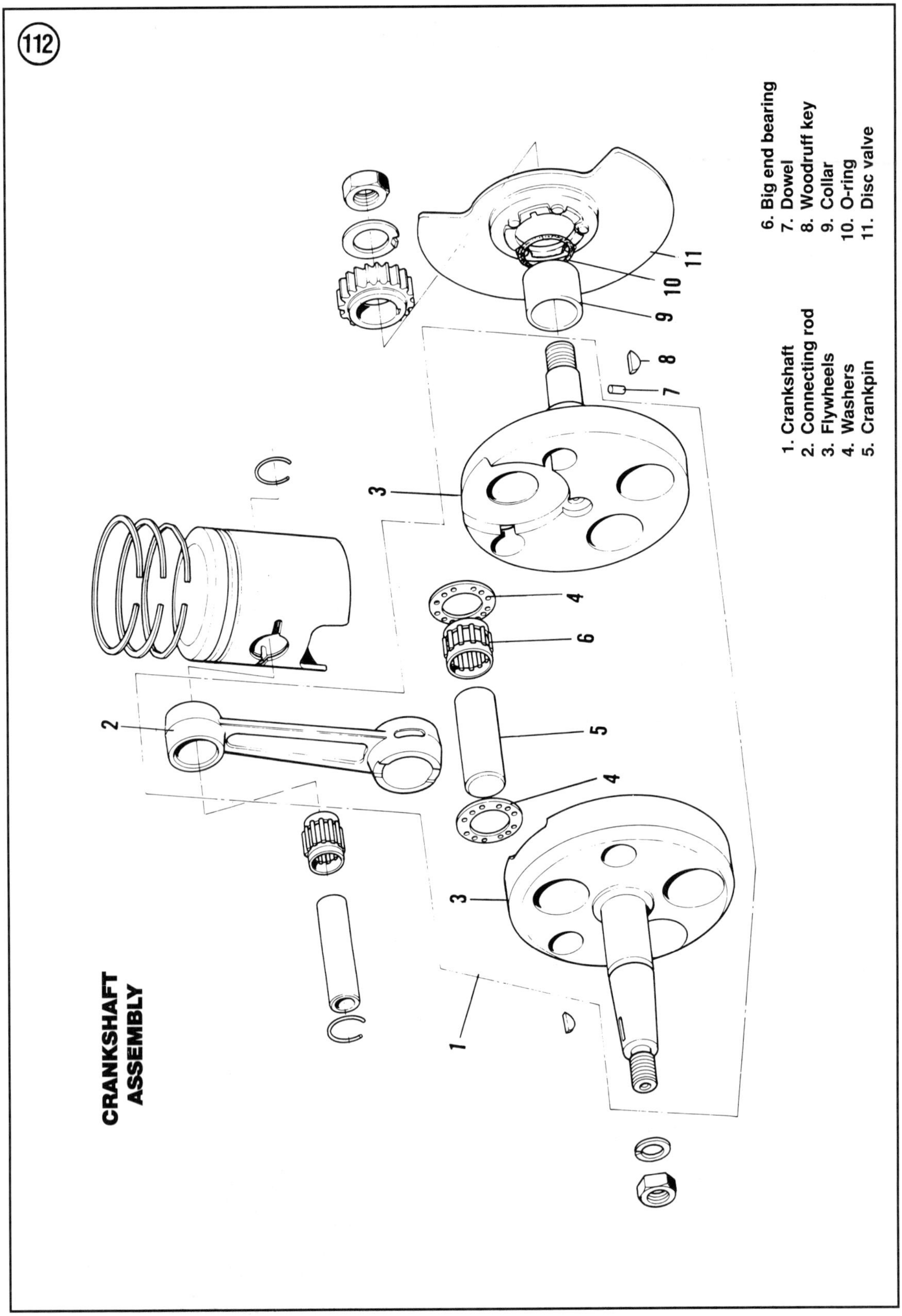
112
CRANKSHAFT ASSEMBLY
1. Crankshaft
2. Connecting rod
3. Flywheels
4. Washers
5. Crankpin
6. Big end bearing
7. Dowel
8. Woodruff key
9. Collar
10. O-ring
11. Disc valve
1
2
3
3
4
4
5
6
7
8
9
10
11

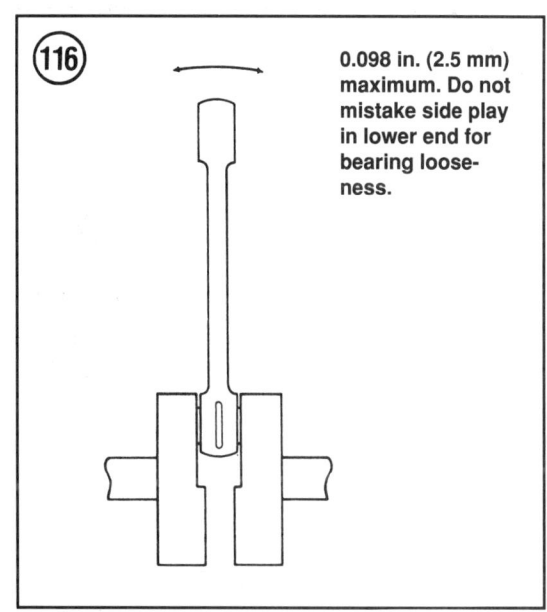

0.098 in. (2.5 mm) maximum. Do not mistake side play in lower end for bearing looseness.

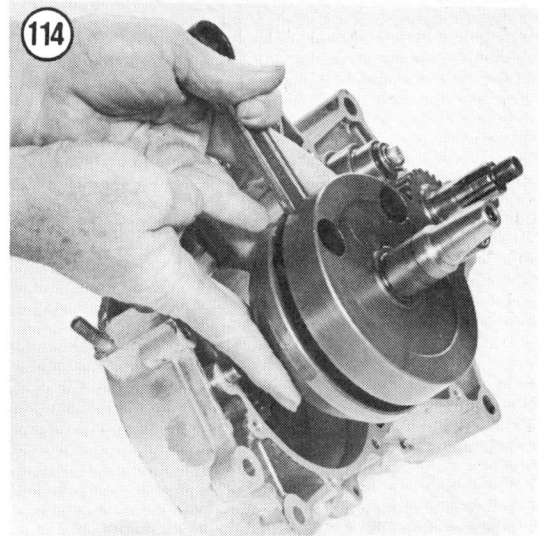

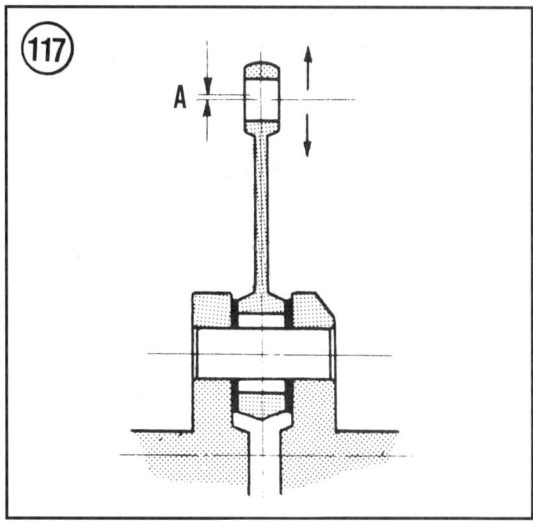

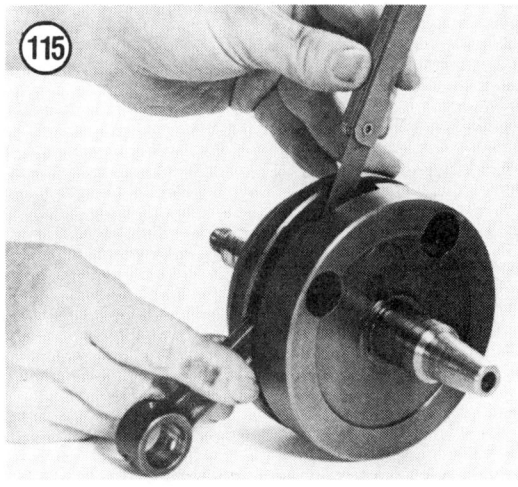

If any exists, replace the piston pin and bearing. In extreme cases it may be necessary to replace the connecting rod also.

Crankshaft Runout

Mount the crankshaft in a lathe, V-blocks or other suitable centering device. Rotate the crankshaft through a complete revolution and measure runout at the main bearing journals, as shown in **Figure 119**. If the dial indicator reading is greater than the repair limit, disassemble the crankshaft and replace the crankpin. If runout exceeds the standard limit, but does not exceed the repair limit, it may be corrected. Standard runout limit for all models is 0.0012 in. (0.03 mm). The repair limit is 0.004 in. (0.10 mm) for all models.

Crankshaft Overhaul

Crankshaft overhaul requires a press of 10-12 tons (9,000-11,000 kg) capacity, holding jigs and a crankshaft alignment jig. Do not attempt to overhaul the crankshaft unless this equipment is available.

1. Place the crankshaft assembly in a suitable jig, then press out the crankpin from the drive side first (**Figure 120**).

2. Remove the spacers, connecting rod and lower end bearing (**Figure 121**).

3. Press the crankpin out from the magneto side (**Figure 122**).

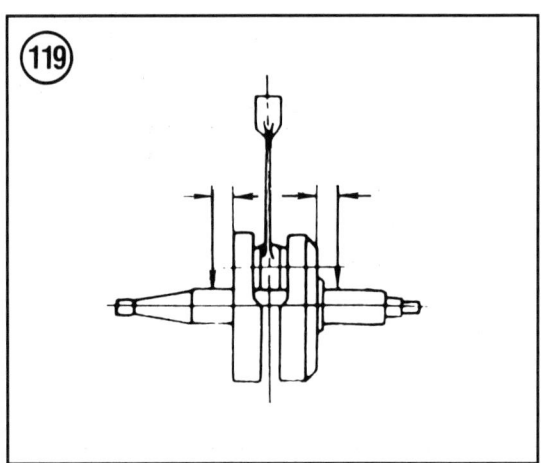

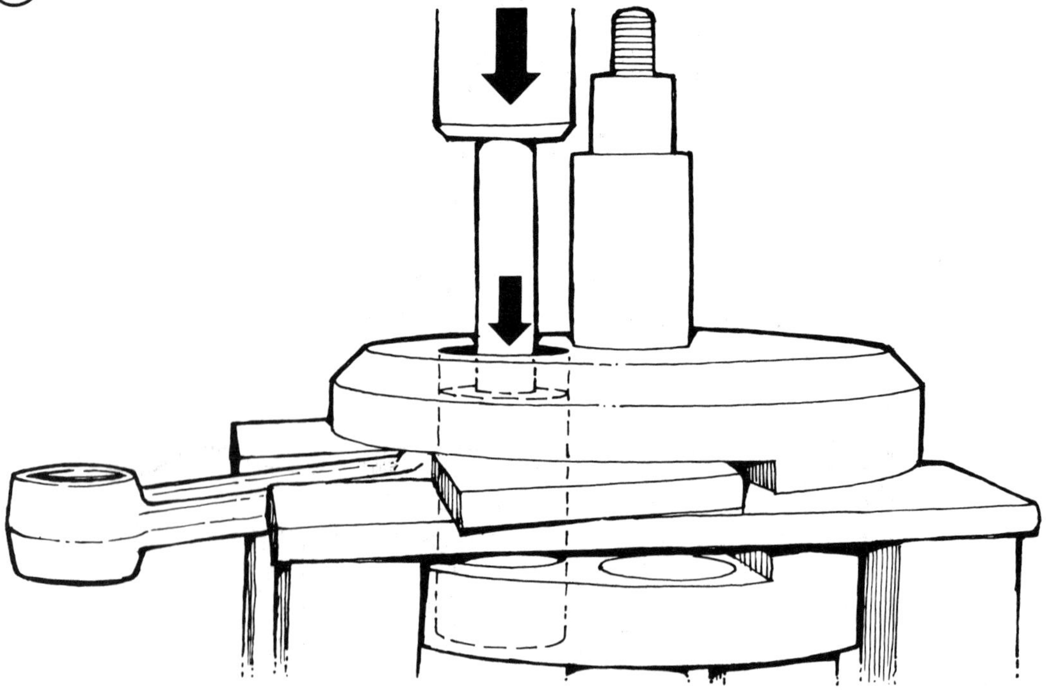

4

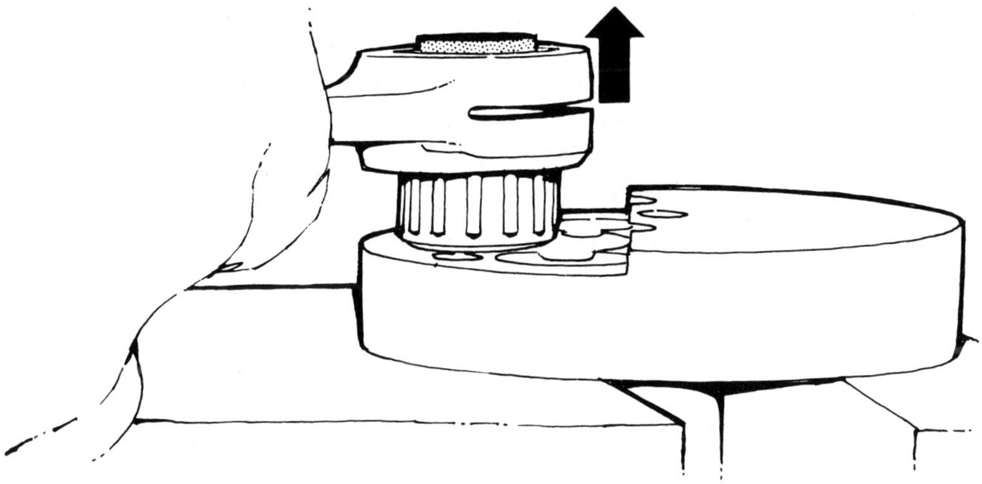

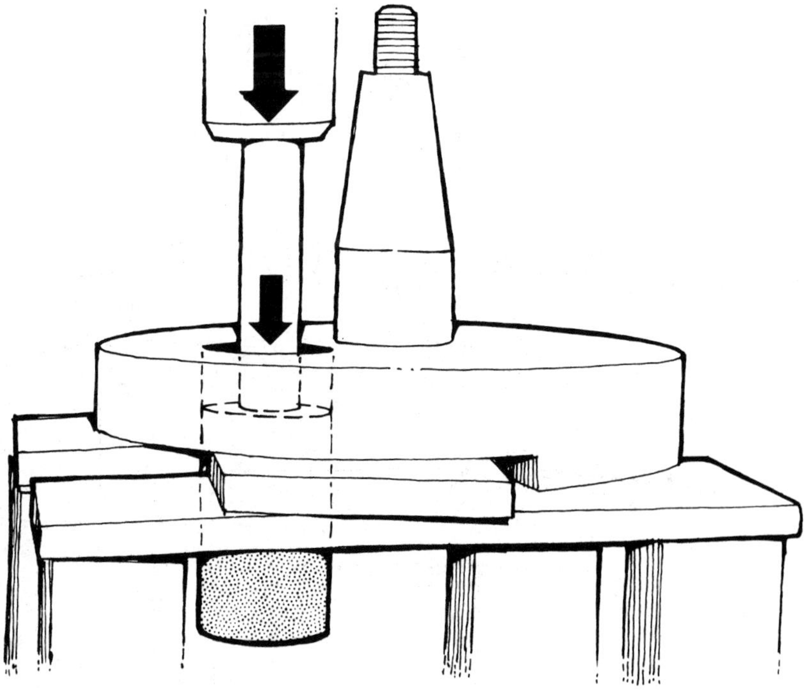

123

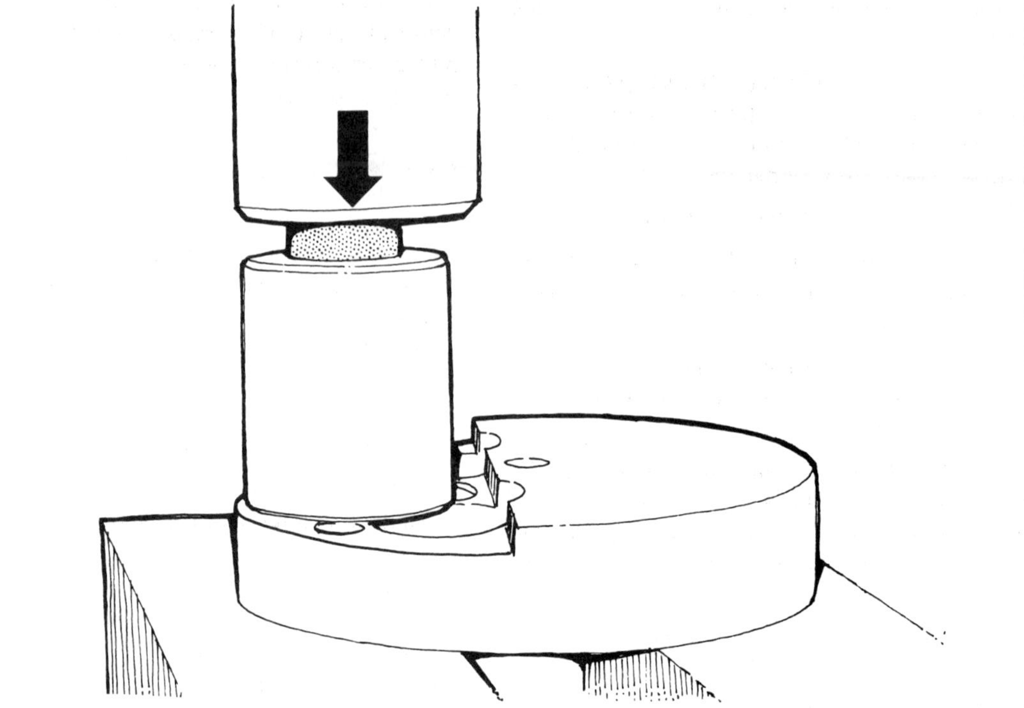

124

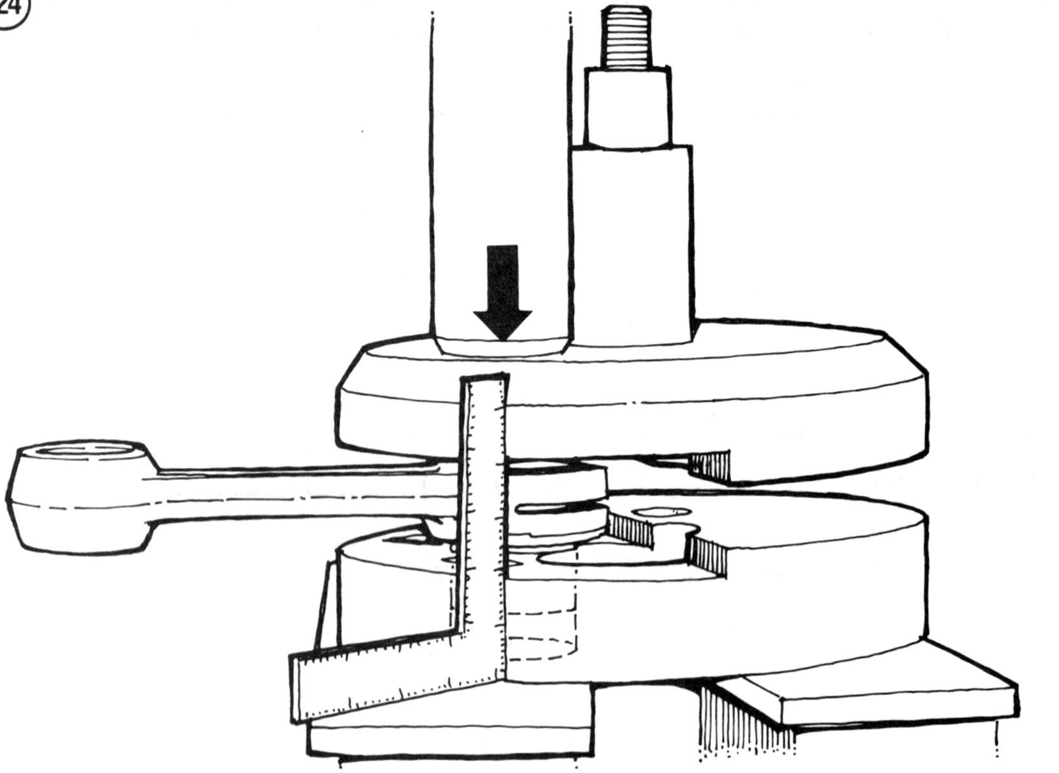

4. Carefully remove all residue from the crank wheels.

5. Using a suitable alignment fixture, press the replacement crankpin into the magneto side crank wheel (**Figure 123**) until the end of the crankpin is flush with the outside of the crank wheel.

6. Install a side washer, then the bearing.

7. Install the connecting rod, then the remaining side washer. There is no front or back to the connecting rod; it fits either way.

8. Using a small square for initial alignment (**Figure 124**), start pressing the drive side crank wheel onto the crankpin.

9. Select feeler gauge of appropriate thickness (**Table 10**), then insert it between the upper spacer and drive side crank wheel. Continue pressing the drive side crank wheel onto the crankpin until the feeler gauge fits tightly.

10. Release all pressure from the press. The feeler gauge will then slip out easily.

11. Align the crankshaft assembly.

If after a crankshaft seizure, either crankshaft half is damaged, replace the entire crankshaft assembly. Otherwise, disassemble the crankshaft and replace the connecting rod, needle bearing, side washers and crankpin.

Defective crankshaft seals are the most common cause of catastrophic crankshaft failures. Always replace crankcase oil seals when crankshaft is removed for service.

Crankshaft Alignment

After any crankshaft service, it is necessary to align the assembly so that both crank wheels and the shafts extending from them all rotate on a common center. Mount the assembled crankshaft in a suitable alignment fixture, as described under *Crankshaft Runout*, then slowly rotate the crankshaft through one or more complete turns and observe both dial indicators. One of several indications will be observed.

1. Neither dial indicator needle begins its swing at the same time and the needles will move in opposite directions during part of the crankshaft rotation cycle. Each needle will probably indicate a different amount of total travel. This condition is caused by eccentricity (both crank wheels not being on the same center), as shown in **Figure 125**. To correct this situation, slowly rotate the crankshaft assembly until the drive side dial gauge indicates its maximum. Mark the rim of the drive side crank wheel at the point in line with the plungers on both dial gauges. Remove the crankshaft assembly from the jig, then

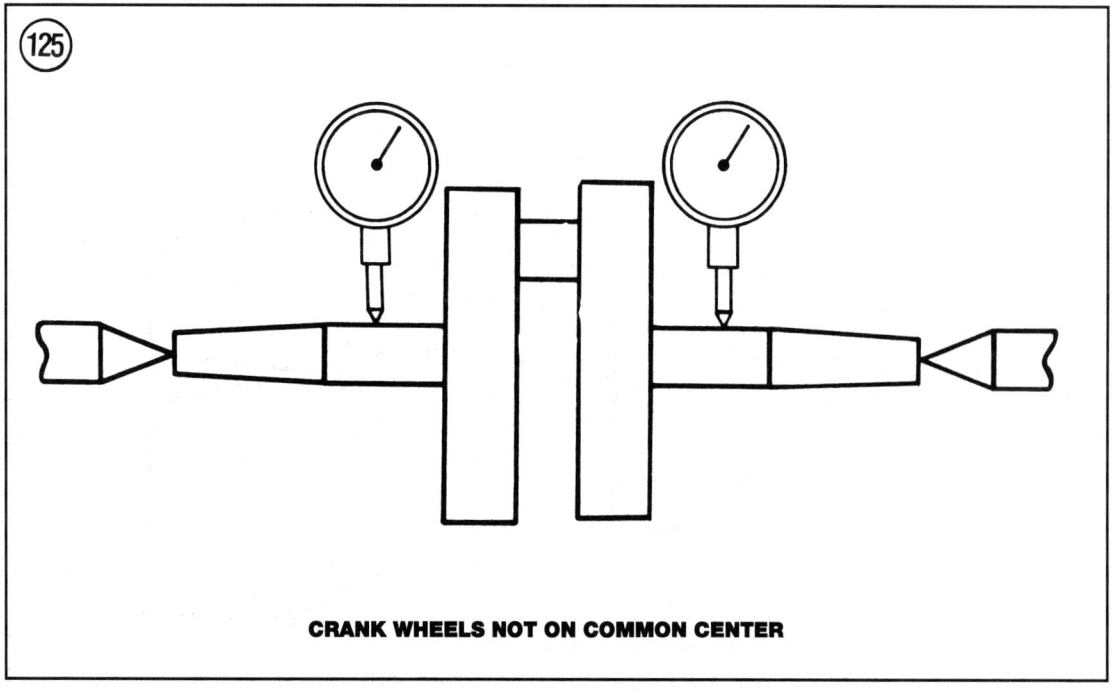

CRANK WHEELS NOT ON COMMON CENTER

while holding the magneto side crank wheel in one hand, strike the chalk mark a sharp blow with a brass or lead mallet (**Figure 126**). Recheck alignment after each blow and continue this procedure until both dial gauges begin and end their swings at the same time.

2. After the foregoing adjustment is completed, the crank wheels may still be pinched (**Figure 127**) or spread (**Figure 128**). Both dial indicators will indicate maximum travel when the crankpin is toward the dial gauges if the crank wheels are pinched. Correct this condition by removing the crankshaft assembly, then drive a wedge or chisel between the crank wheels at a point opposite maximum dial gauge indication. Recheck alignment after each adjustment. Continue this procedure until the dial gauges indicate no more than 0.0012 in. (0.03 mm) runout on each side. If the dial gauges indicate their maximum when the crankpin is on the side of the alignment test jig away from the dial gauges, the crank wheels are spread. Correct this condition by tapping the outside of one of the wheels toward the other with a brass or lead mallet. Recheck alignment after each blow. Continue adjustment until runout is within the tolerance specified in the foregoing paragraph.

NOTE
It may be necessary to repeat the correction for eccentricity during the correction procedure for pinch or spread.

TRANSMISSION

Kawasaki bikes are variously equipped with 4-, 5- and 6-speed transmissions. Although service procedures for the various transmissions are similar, individual gear ratios differ, depending on transmission usage. Service procedures are similar for all models; differences will be pointed out where they exist.

Type 1 Transmission
(Except 1982 and Later KE100)

Figure 129 and **Figure 130** are exploded and sectional views of this transmission, which is used on G series models, except for the G4.

As the gearshift mechanism rotates the shift drum, the shift forks move in slots in the drum to position the shift forks and thereby select the different gear positions within the transmission. The change drum is provided with 6 pins. Each time the gearshift pedal

is operated, the drum rotates 1/6 of a revolution. Each step selects one gear ratio.

The steel ball at the end of the drive shaft eliminates the influence of thrust produced by clutch action and makes gear changes easier. The idler gears transmit the kick gear rotation to the primary gear, through the gear in the clutch housing. The transmission switch mounts on the crankcase. It causes the neutral indicator lamp to light when the transmission is in neutral position.

Type 1 Transmission
(1982 and Later KE100)

The transmission of 1982 and later KE100 models is similar to other Type 1 transmissions, except that the left end of the transmission input shaft is supported by a roller bearing and two thrust washers are located between the left half of the crankcase and the 5th speed gear (**Figure 131**).

When disassembling, be careful not to lose the steel ball (2, **Figure 131**). Threads of adjusting plug (5, **Figure 131**) are coated with "Loctite" or equivalent and it may be difficult to remove. The adjusting plug does not need to be removed unless the end needs to be adjusted following assembly.

When assembling, roller bearing (7, **Figure 131**) should be pressed into left half of crankcase until it is 1 mm below flush as shown at A, **Figure 131**. Install the steel washer (9, **Figure 131**) next to the

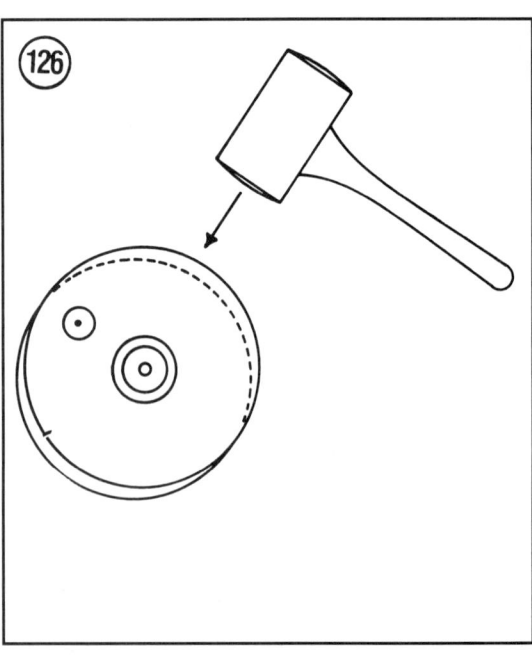
⑫⑥

127

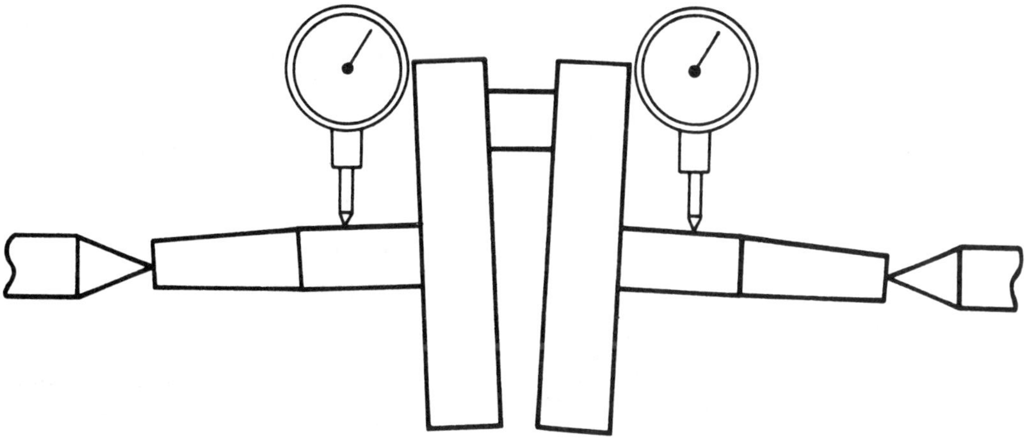

CRANK WHEELS PINCHED TOGETHER

128

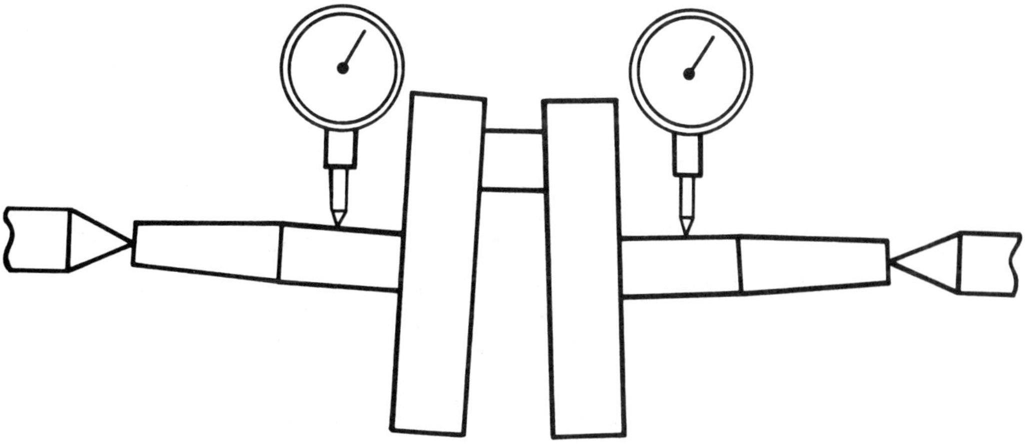

CRANK WHEELS SPREAD APART

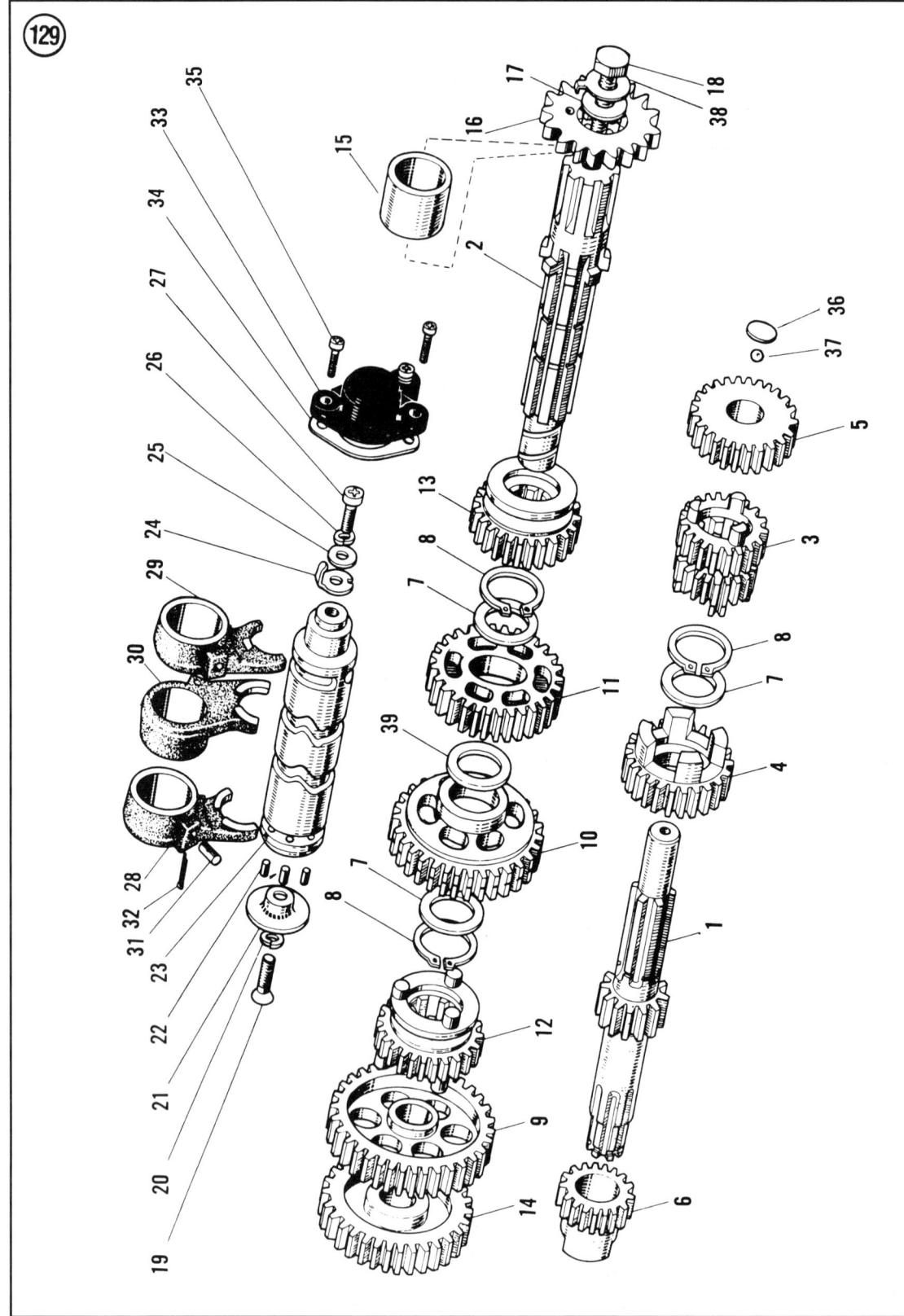

TYPE 1 TRANSMISSION
(G SERIES [EXCEPT G4TR]; MC1 SERIES; KD80; KD/KE/KH/KM100)

1. Drive shaft
2. Output shaft
3. 2nd and 3rd drive gear
4. 4th drive gear
5. 5th drive gear
6. Starter pinion
7. Washer
8. Snap ring
9. 1st output gear
10. 2nd output gear
11. 3rd output gear
12. 4th output gear
13. 5th output gear
14. Kickstarter idler gear
15. Spacer
16. Sprocket
17. Washer
18. Bolt
19. Screw
20. Lockwasher
21. Change drum pin plate
22. Drum pin
23. Drum
24. Switch rotor
25. Washer
26. Lockwasher
27. Screw
28. Fork
29. Fork
30. Fork
31. Guide pin
32. Cotter pin
33. Switch
34. Gasket
35. Screw
36. Washer
37. Ball
38. Lockwasher
39. Washer

4

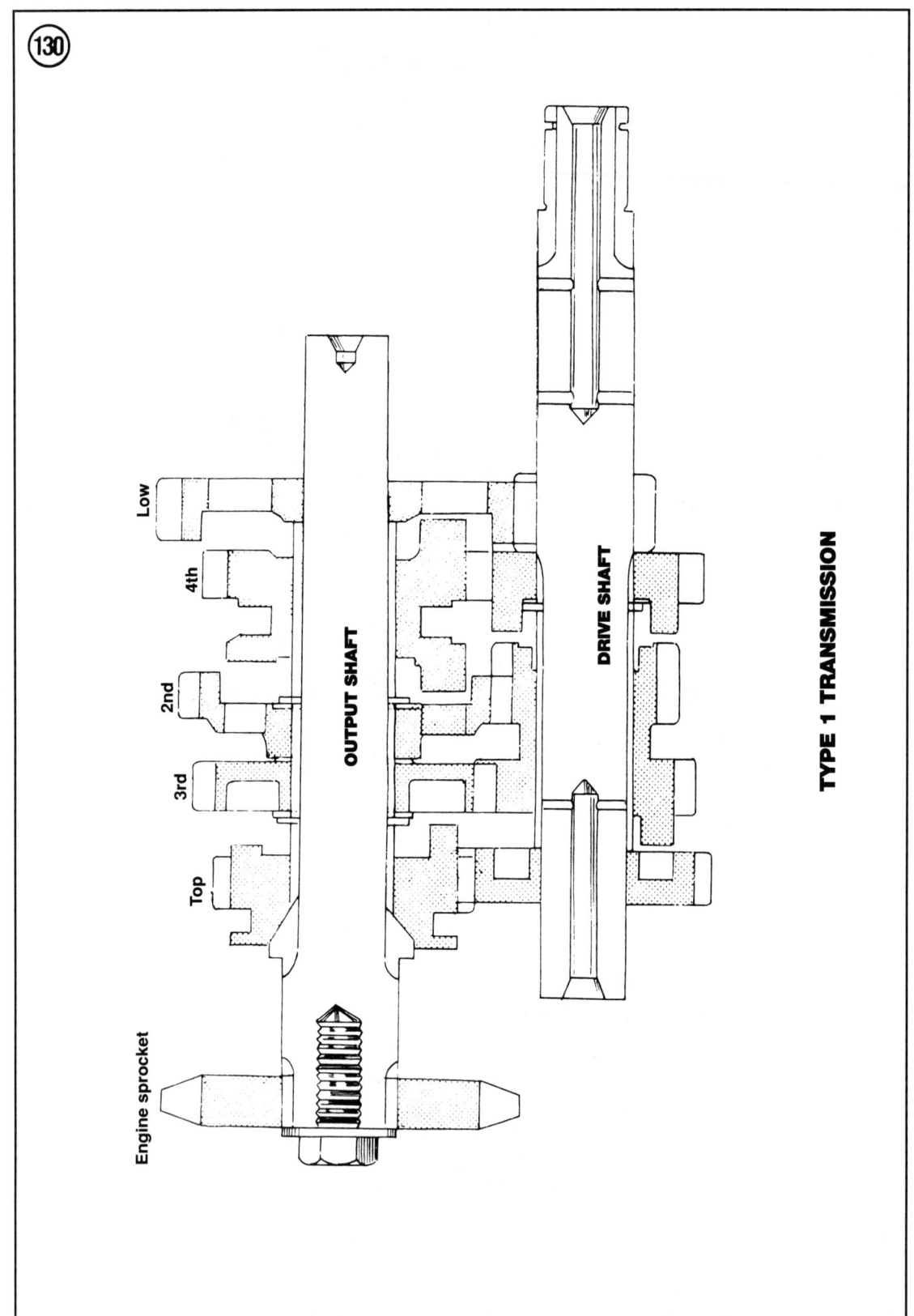

(130)

Engine sprocket

Low   4th   2nd   3rd   Top

OUTPUT SHAFT

DRIVE SHAFT

TYPE 1 TRANSMISSION

TYPE 1 TRANSMISSION

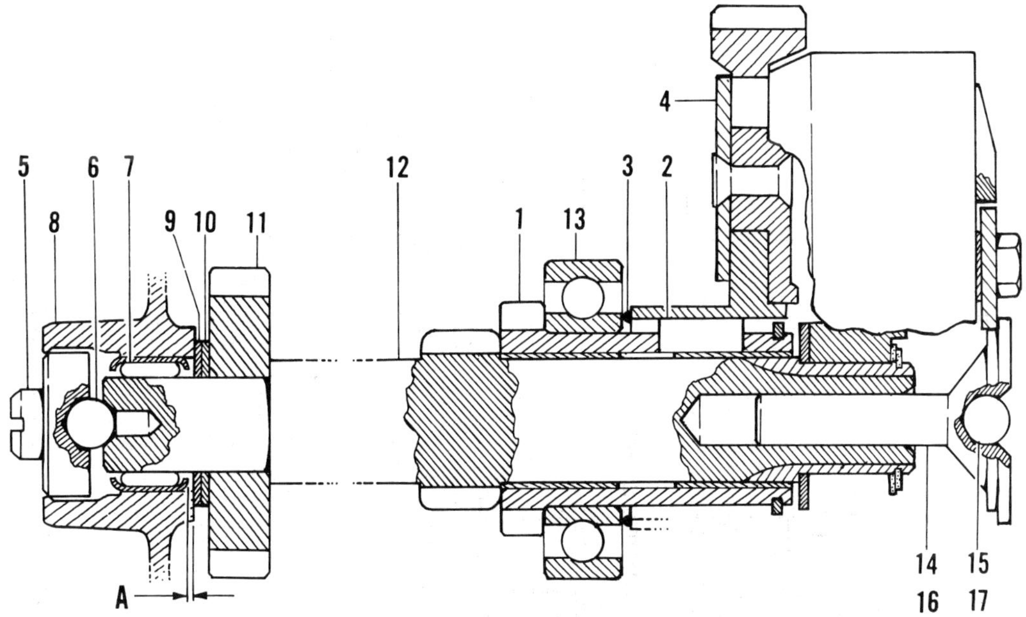

1. Idler gear
2. Drive key
3. Wave washer
4. Clutch
5. Adjusting plug
6. Steel ball
7. Roller bearing
8. Crankcase left half
9. Steel washer
10. Copper washer
11. Gear (5th speed)
12. Output shaft
13. Ball bearing
14. Clutch pusher
15. Steel ball

aluminum crankcase and the copper washer (10, **Figure 131**) next to the steel 5th speed gear (11, **Figure 131**).

Be sure that steel ball (6, **Figure 131**) is in place when assembling. Output shaft (12, **Figure 131**) should have no end play or binding. If end play is incorrect, it will be necessary to remove adjusting plug (5, **Figure 131**). Coat threads of plug with "Loctite" or equivalent thread lock, then turn plug into crankcase, against steel ball (6, **Figure 131**), until shaft end play is just removed without causing shaft to bind.

Type 2 Transmission

Figure 132 is an exploded view of this transmission. it features dual-range operation, which provides greater reduction for off-road operations.

Type 3 Transmission

Figure 133 and **Figure 134** are exploded and sectional views of this transmission used on the F series models. The selector forks slide along guide bars, instead of sliding on the shift cam. The pins on the shift forks are inserted into grooves on the shift drum. Rotation of the shift drum moves the shift forks to select the desired gear ration.

Three balls are spaced every 120° around the output shaft. They are used to set the neutral position, which is between first and second gear position.

Type 4 Transmission

Figure 135 is an exploded view of this transmission. The shift drum is provided with 5 pins. Each movement of the gearshift pedal rotates the drum 1/5 revolution. Each step selects one gear position or neutral. The shift forks move in grooves in the shift drum to select the gear ratios.

Type 5 Transmission

This transmission has 6 speeds. **Figure 136** and **Figure 137** are sectional and exploded views of the transmission. Service procedures are similar to those of other transmission.

Type 6 Transmission

Figure 138 is an exploded view of this transmission. Note that all shift forks slide on rails rather than on the shift cam itself.

Transmission Disassembly

1. Lift transmission from crankcase as a unit (**Figure 139**).
2. Remove shift forks from shift drum by removing cotter pins and shift fork pins.
3. On some models the shift forks slide on guide rods. They are removed when the shift fork pins are removed from the shift drum.
4. Remove each gear (**Figure 140**) by removing its associated snap ring and thrust washer.

Inspection

1. Measure clearance between each shift fork and the groove on its associated gear as shown in **Figure 141**. Standard clearance is 0.004-0.01 in. (0.1-0.25 mm). Replace the gear and/or the fork if the clearance exceeds 0.024 in. (0.6 mm). Replace the shift fork if there are any burrs or other damage.
2. Any burrs, pits or roughness on the gear teeth will cause wear on the mating gear. Replace any gear with such defects. Examine its mating gear carefully and replace it if there is any doubt about its condition.
3. Check dog clutch teeth (A, **Figure 142**) for wear or damage.
4. Be sure that all sliding gears operate smoothly on their splines.

Transmission Assembly

To assemble the transmission, reverse the disassembly procedure. Observe the following notes.
1. Position the shift forks in the grooves in the gears, then insert the transmission and shift drum into right crankcase half as an assembly.
2. On G series models, be sure that the kick gear and both idler gears are completely engaged.
3. Clean the steel balls (F series) with cleaning solvent, then grease them to hold them in position during installation. Be sure that the balls move properly.
4. Secure the gearshift drum to the right crankcase half with the setting plate.

DRAIN PUMP

Some models are equipped with a drain pump which removes any gasoline and oil which may accumulate inside the carburetor chamber. **Figure**

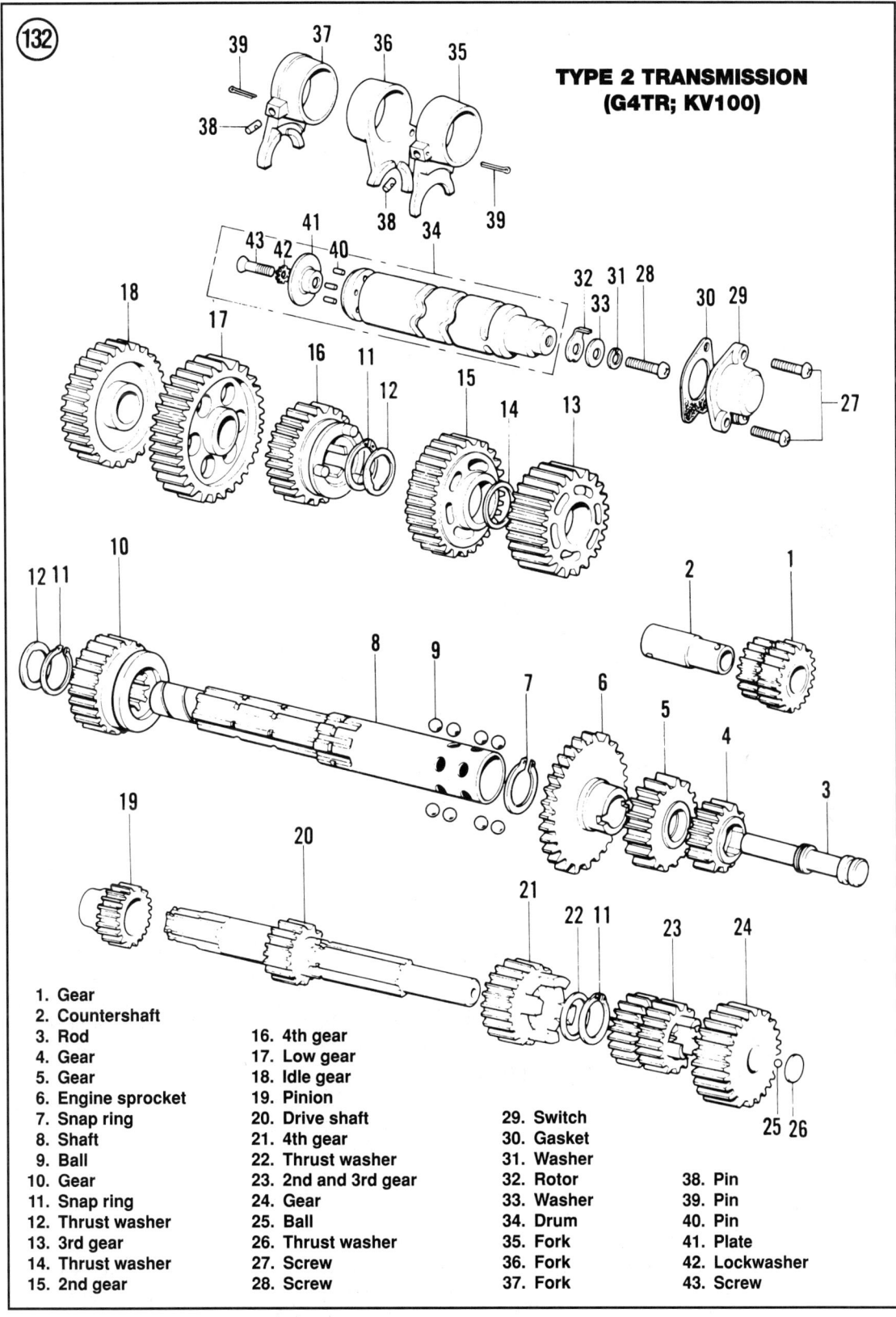

TYPE 2 TRANSMISSION
(G4TR; KV100)

4

1. Gear
2. Countershaft
3. Rod
4. Gear
5. Gear
6. Engine sprocket
7. Snap ring
8. Shaft
9. Ball
10. Gear
11. Snap ring
12. Thrust washer
13. 3rd gear
14. Thrust washer
15. 2nd gear
16. 4th gear
17. Low gear
18. Idle gear
19. Pinion
20. Drive shaft
21. 4th gear
22. Thrust washer
23. 2nd and 3rd gear
24. Gear
25. Ball
26. Thrust washer
27. Screw
28. Screw
29. Switch
30. Gasket
31. Washer
32. Rotor
33. Washer
34. Drum
35. Fork
36. Fork
37. Fork
38. Pin
39. Pin
40. Pin
41. Plate
42. Lockwasher
43. Screw

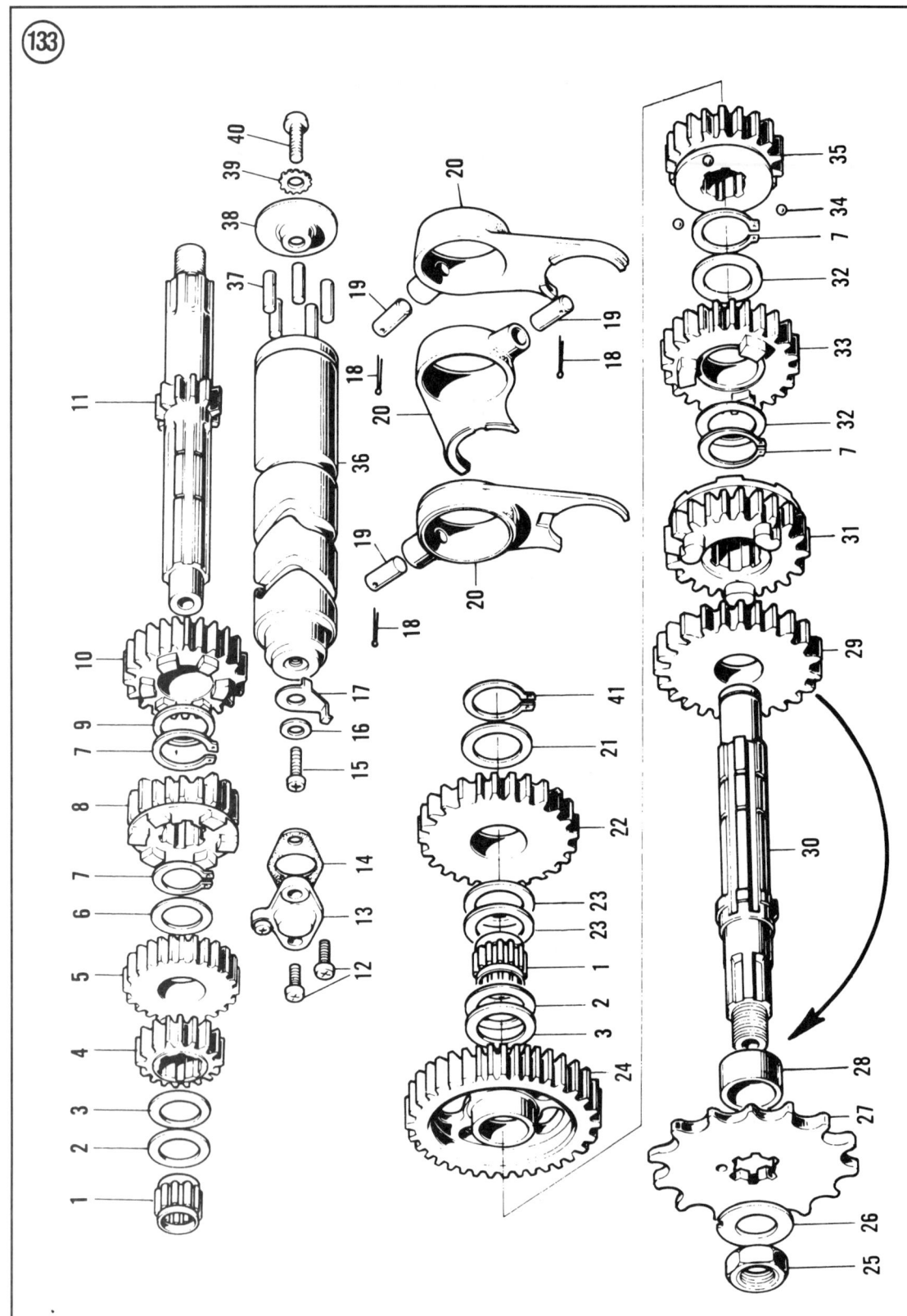

TYPE 3 TRANSMISSION
(F6; F7; KD/KE175)

1. Bearing
2. Washer
3. Washer
4. 2nd drive gear
5. 4th drive gear
6. Washer
7. Snap ring
8. 3rd drive gear
9. Washer
10. 5th drive gear
11. Drive shaft
12. Switch
13. Switch
14. Gasket
15. Screw
16. Washer
17. Switch rotor
18. Cotter pin
19. Pin
20. Fork
21. Fork
22. Kickstarter idler gear
23. Washer
24. 1st output gear
25. Nut
26. Washer
27. Sprocket
28. Spacer
29. 2nd output gear
30. Output shaft
31. 4th output gear
32. Lockwasher
33. 3rd output gear
34. Ball
35. 5th output gear
36. Drum
37. Rollers
38. Plate
39. Washer
40. Screw
41. Snap ring

4

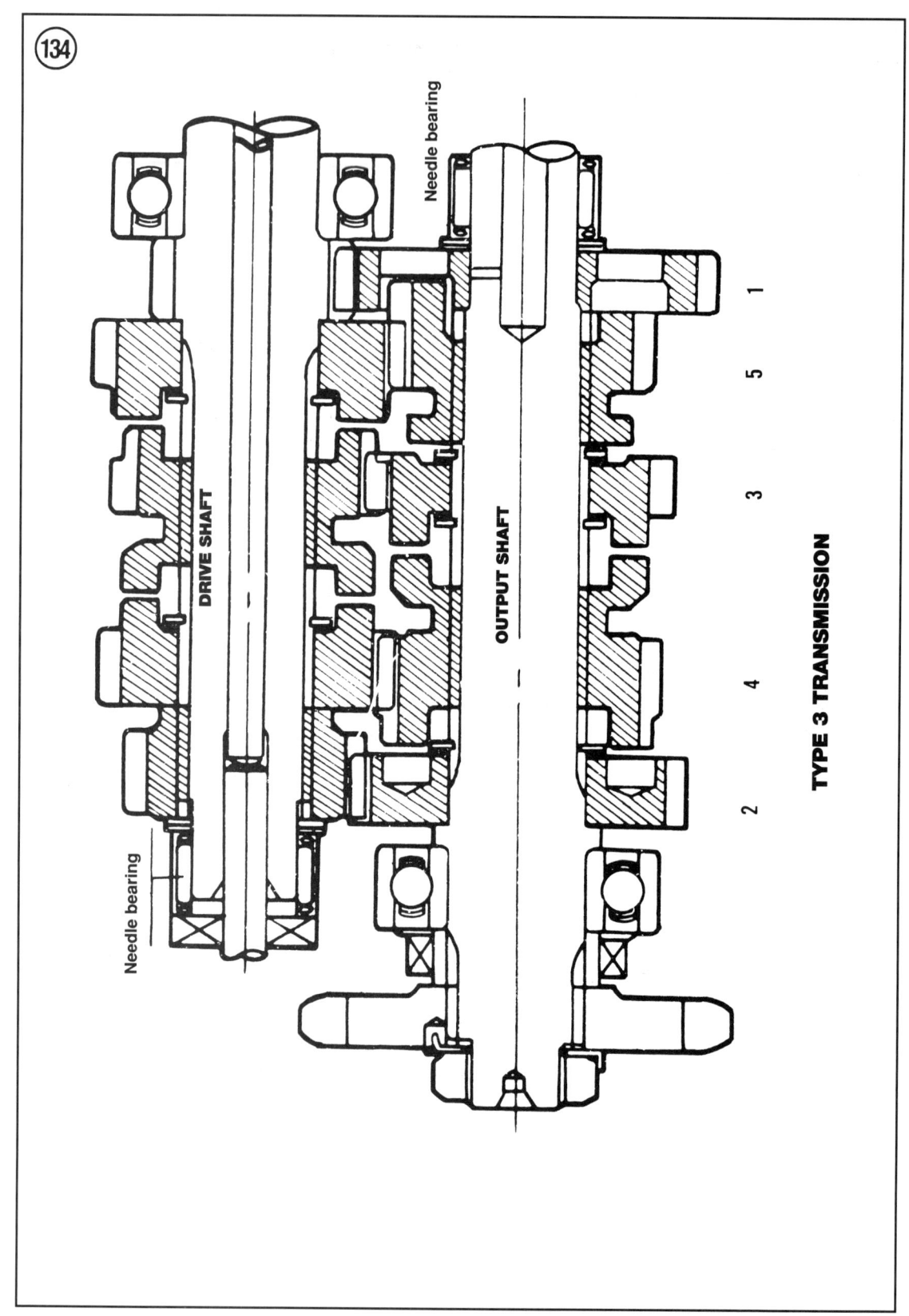

(134)

Needle bearing

DRIVE SHAFT

OUTPUT SHAFT

Needle bearing

1

5

3

4

2

TYPE 3 TRANSMISSION

TYPE 4 TRANSMISSION
(C2SS; F3; F4)

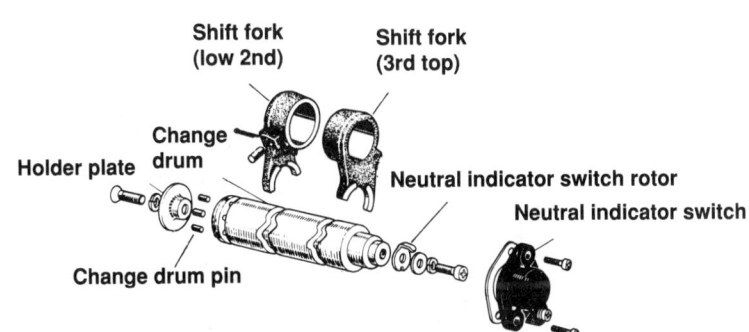

Shift fork (low 2nd)

Shift fork (3rd top)

Change drum

Holder plate

Neutral indicator switch rotor

Neutral indicator switch

Change drum pin

4

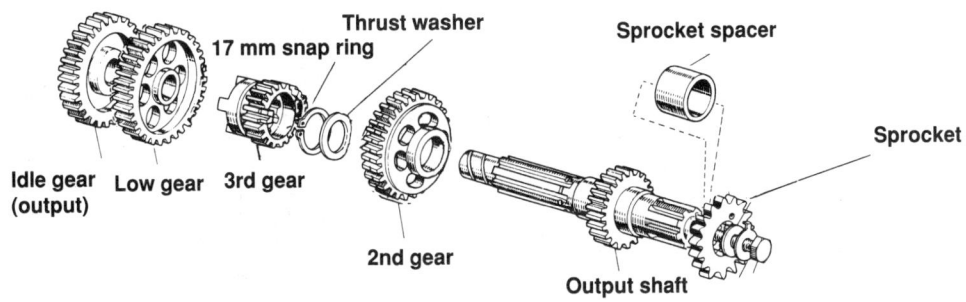

Thrust washer

17 mm snap ring

Sprocket spacer

Sprocket

Idle gear (output)

Low gear

3rd gear

2nd gear

Output shaft

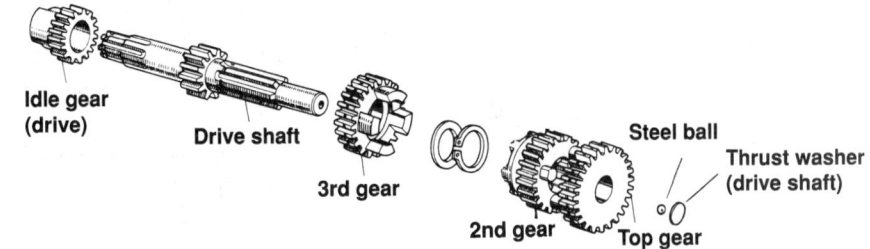

Idle gear (drive)

Drive shaft

3rd gear

2nd gear

Steel ball

Thrust washer (drive shaft)

Top gear

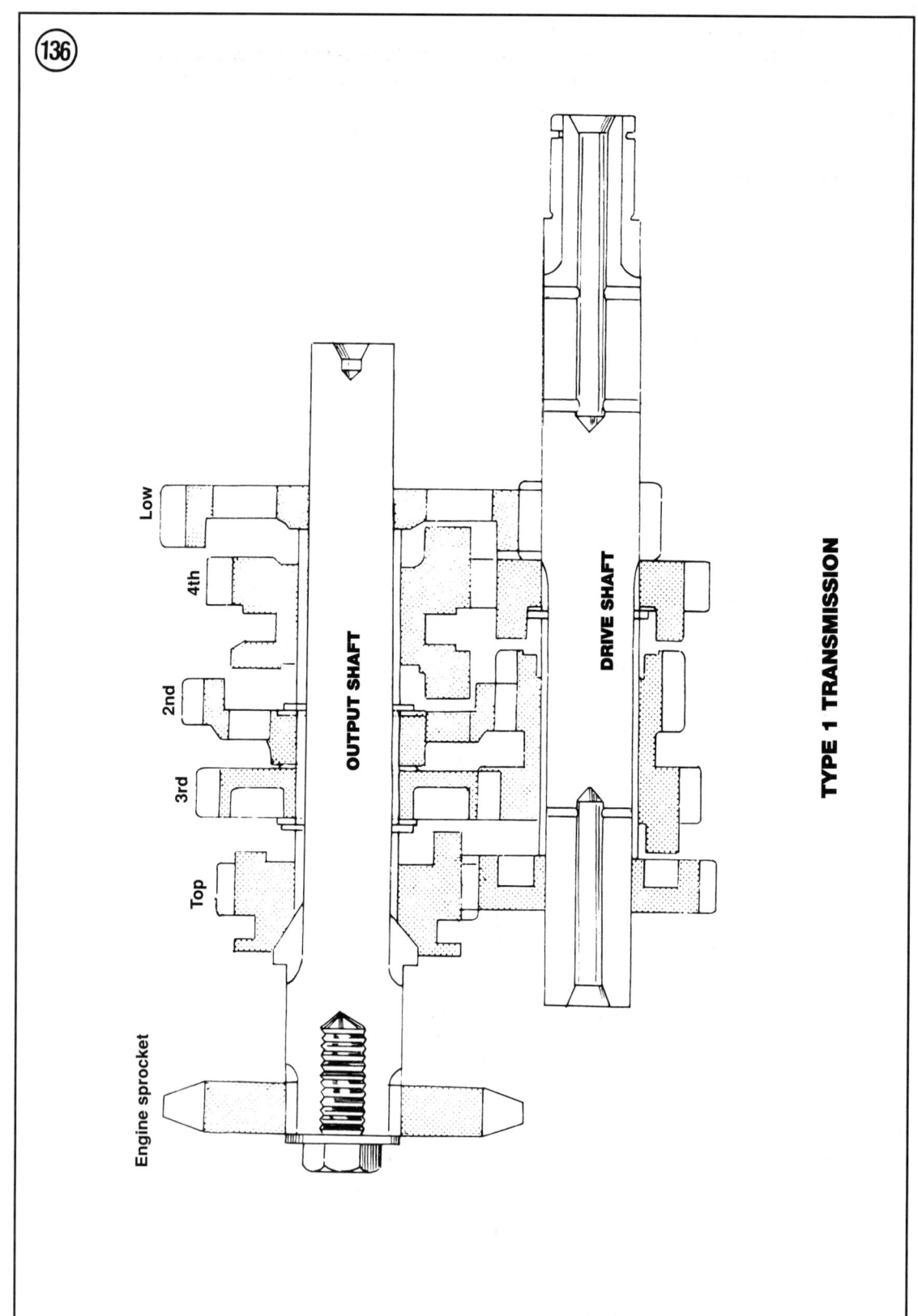

(136)

TYPE 1 TRANSMISSION

143 is a sectional view of the pump. Upward movement of the piston causes a lowered pressure in the crankcase, consequently, the diaphragm is pulled inward toward the crankcase. As the diaphragm moves inward, inlet valve (A) opens and exhaust valve (B) closes. As the inlet valve opens, contents of the carburetor chamber are drawn into the pump.

As the piston moves down in the cylinder, the crankcase is pressurized. Crankcase pressure forces the diaphragm away from the crankcase. Pressure built up in the pump by the outward movement o the diaphragm closes the inlet valve and opens the discharge valve. When the discharge valve opens, contents of the pump are expelled.

Figures 137-143 and Tables 1-12 are on the following pages.

4

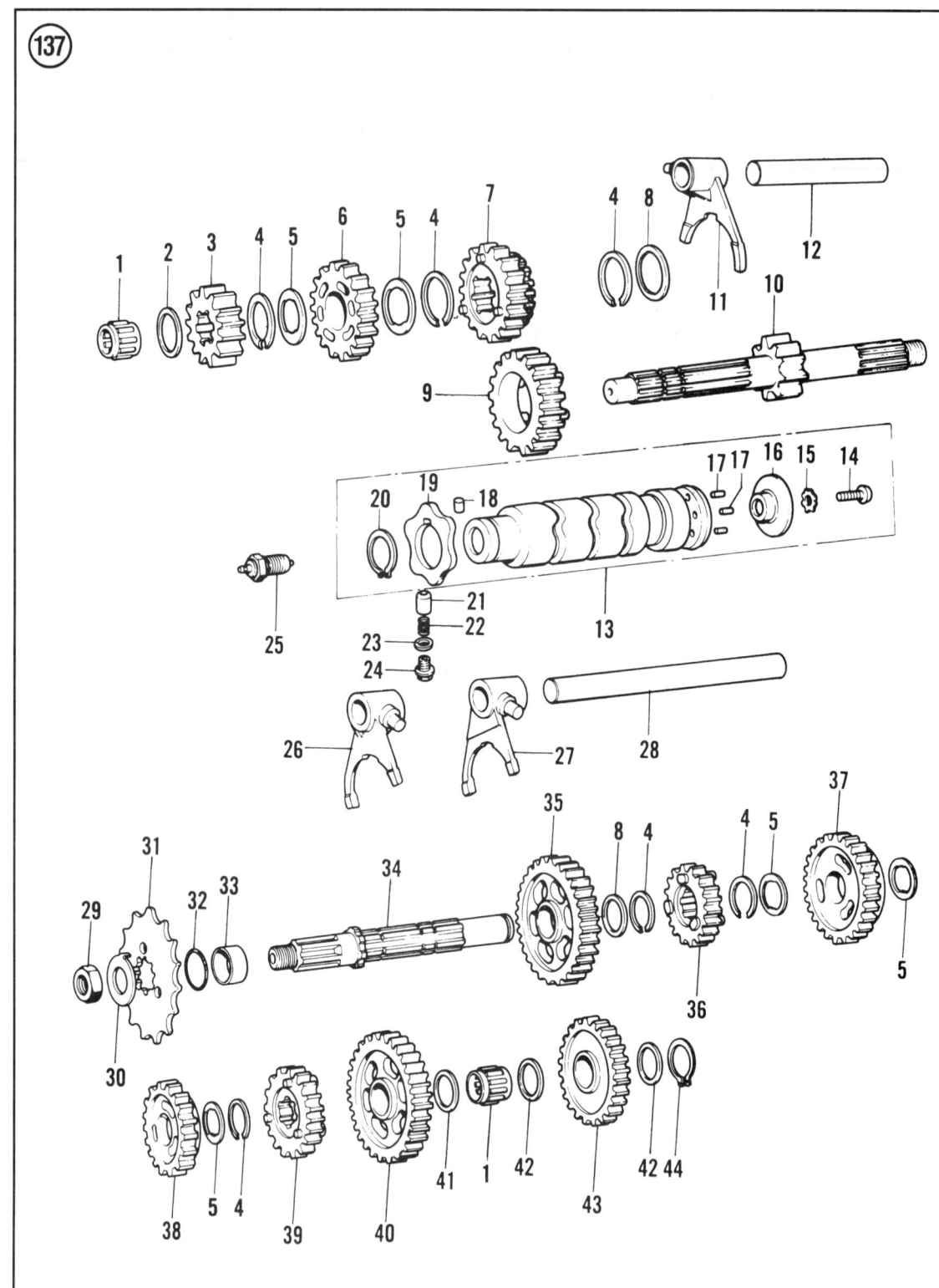

TYPE 5 TRANSMISSION
(KD/KE/KS/KX125)

1. Needle bearing
2. Thrust washer
3. Drive shaft 2nd gear
4. Snap ring
5. Lockwasher
6. Drive shaft top gear
7. Drive shaft 3rd and 4th gear
8. Thrust washer
9. Drive shaft 5th gear
10. Drive shaft
11. 5th and top selector fork
12. Shift rod
13. Gear change drum
14. Pan head screw
15. Lockwasher
16. Gear change drum pin plate
17. Gear change drum pin
18. Dowel
19. Gear change drum operating disc
20. Snap ring
21. Neutral positioning pin
22. Neutral positioning pin spring
23. Gasket
24. Bolt
25. Neutral switch
26. 2nd and 3rd selector fork
27. Low and 4th selector fork
28. Shift rod
29. Nut
30. Lockwasher
31. Engine sprocket
32. O-ring
33. Engine sprocket collar
34. Output shaft
35. 2nd gear, output shaft
36. Top gear, output shaft
37. 3rd gear, output shaft
38. 4th gear, output shaft
39. 5th gear, output shaft
40. Low gear, output shaft
41. Thrust washer
42. Plain washer
43. Kickstarter idle gear
44. Snap ring

4

TYPE 6 TRANSMISSION

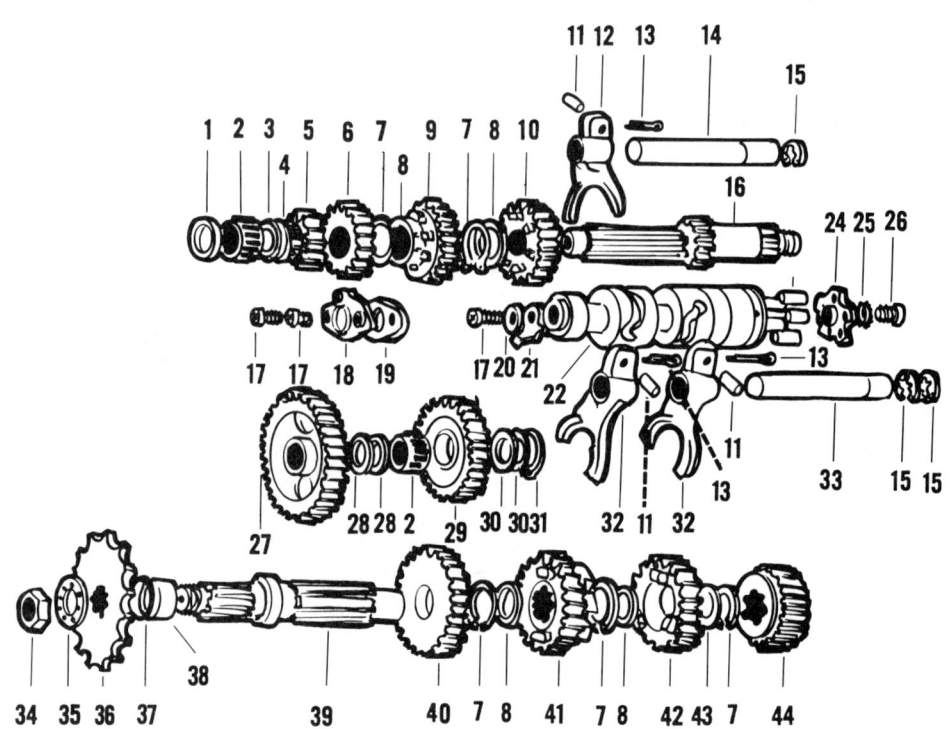

1. Oil seal
2. Needle bearing
3. Washer
4. Thrust washer (bronze)
5. Input 2nd gear
6. Input 4th gear
7. Washer (25 mm)
8. Circlip (24 mm)
9. Input 3rd gear
10. Input 3rd gear
11. Shift fork pin
12. Shift fork
13. Cotter pin
14. Shift rod (113 mm)
15. Circlip (10 mm)
16. Input shaft
17. Screw (6 × 20 mm)
18. Neutral indicator switch
19. Gasket
20. Washer (6 mm)
21. Neutral switch rotor
22. Shift drum
23. Pins
24. End plate
25. Lockwasher (6 mm)
26. Screw (6 × 20 mm)
27. Output 1st gear
28. Thrust washer
29. Kickstarter idle gear
30. Thrust washer
31. Circlip (19 mm)
32. Shift forks
33. Shift rod (119 mm)
34. Nut (18 mm)
35. Lockwasher
36. Sprocket (14 T standard)
37. O-ring
38. Collar
39. Output shaft
40. Output 2nd gear
41. Output 4th gear
42. Output 3rd gear
43. Washer
44. Output 5th gear

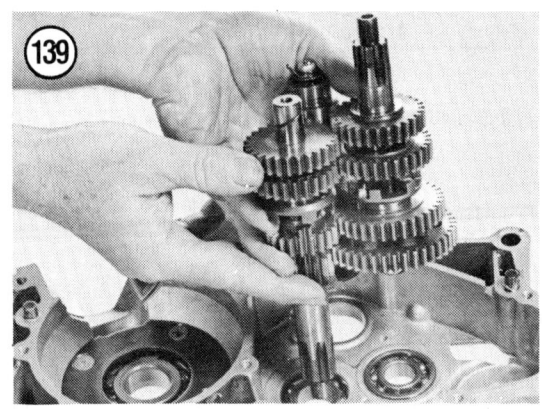

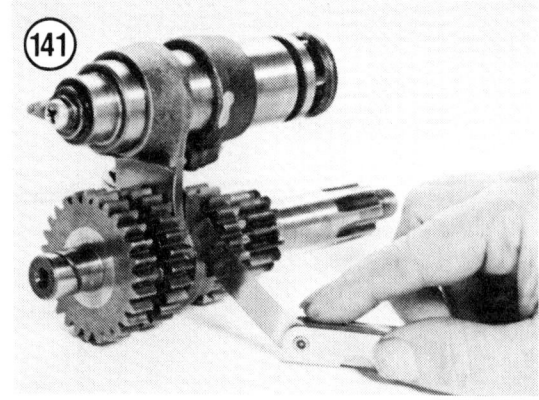

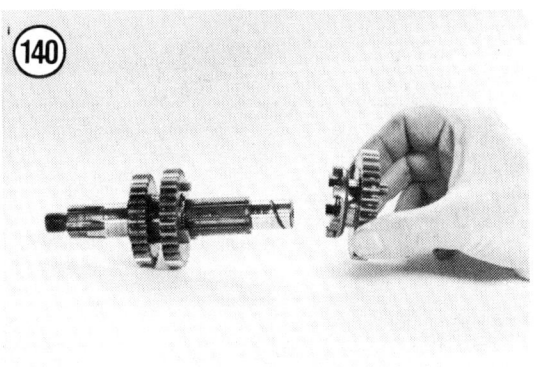

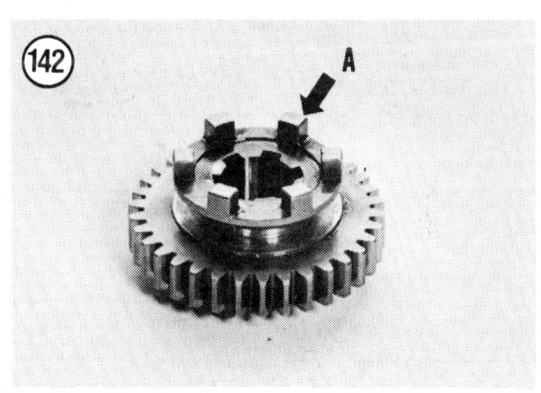

139

141

140

142
A

143
DRAIN PUMP
Cover
A
B
Housing
Gasket
Diaphragm
C
Crankcase

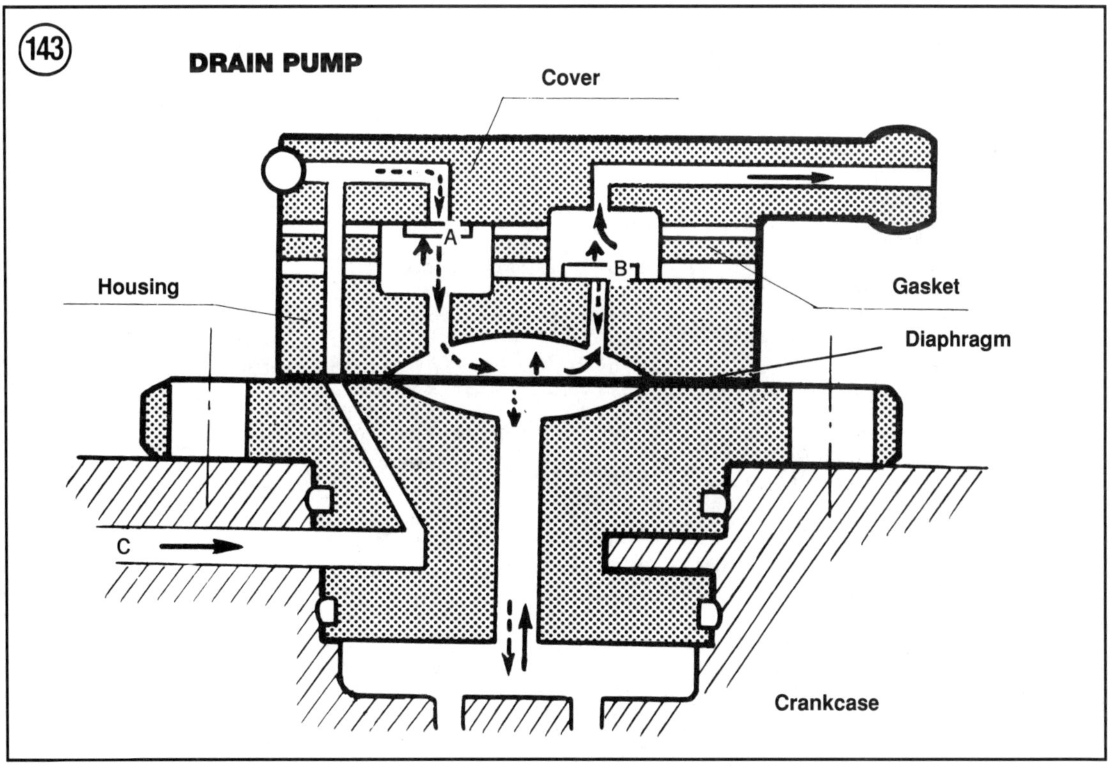

Table 1 OIL PUMP OUTPUT/3 MINUTES @ 2000 RPM

79-100 cc models	Output cc	oz.
KD80 (1975, 1976 & 1980-1987)	2.8	0.095
J Series		
Models with oil pump	2.8	0.095
Oil mix ratio without oil injection	1 part oil to 20 parts gasoline	
MC1, MC1-A, MC1-B & MC1M	2.8	0.095
G3 models (except G3SS-E)	2.8	0.095
G3SS-E	2.8	0.095
D1 oil mix ratio	1 part oil to 20 parts gasoline	
G4TR	2.8	0.095
G5	2.8	0.095
G31M oil mix ratio	1 part oil to 20 parts gasoline	
KD100	2.8	0.095
KE100		
1978 & earlier models	2.8	0.095
1979 & later (A8 on)	3.6-4.1	0.122-0.139
KH100, KM100 & KV100	2.8	0.095

115-125 cc models	Output cc	oz.
C2SS & C2TR	3.1	0.11
F6	4.1	0.14
KD125	3.4	0.115
KE125	3.4	0.115
KS125	3.4	0.115
KX125 (1974-1976) oil mix ratio	1 part oil to 20 parts gasoline	

169-175 cc models	Output cc	oz.
F2 & F2TR	5.5	0.19
F3	5.5	0.19
F7	5.5	0.19
KD175 (1976-1979)		
& KE175 (1976-1982)	4.1	0.14

238-350 cc models	Output cc	oz.
F4	6.0	0.20
F21M oil mix ratio	1 part oil to 20 parts gasoline	
F8	6.0	0.20
F81M oil mix ratio	1 part oil to 20 parts gasoline	
F5	10.0	0.34
F9	10.0	0.34

Table 2 CYLINDER DIAMETER

79-100 cc models	Standard diameter mm (in.)	*Service limit mm (in.)
KD80 (1975, 1976 & 1980-1987)	47.008 (1.854)	
J Series	47.0 (1.850)	
MC1, MC1-A, MC1-B & MC1M	47.0 (1.850)	
G3 models (except G3SS-E)	47.0 (1.850)	
G3SS-E	49.5 (1.949)	
D1	52.0 (2.047)	
G4TR & G5	49.5 (1.949)	
G31M	49.5 (1.949)	
KD100	49.5 (1.949)	(continued)

Table 2 CYLINDER DIAMETER (continued)

79-100 cc models	Standard diameter mm (in.)	*Service limit mm (in.)
KE100	49.508-49.523 (1.9491-1.9497)	49.61 (1.9531)
KH100	49.508-49.523 (1.9491-1.9497)	49.61 (1.9531)
KM100-A1, A2, A3 & A4	49.5 (1.949)	
KM100-A6 & A7	49.518 (1.950)	49.58 (1.952)
KV100	49.508-49.523 (1.9491-1.9497)	49.61 (1.9531)

115-125 cc models	Standard diameter mm (in.)	*Service limit mm (in.)
C2SS & C2TR	53.0 (2.087)	
F6	52.0 (2.047)	
KD125	56.0 (2.205)	
KE125-A3, A4 & A5	56.0 (2.205)	
KE125-A6 on (1979 & later)	56.007 (2.205)	56.08 (2.208)
KS125	56.0 (2.205)	
KX125 (1974-1976)	56.01 (2.205)	

169-175 cc models	Standard diameter mm (in.)	*Service limit mm (in.)
F2 & F2TR	62.0 (2.441)	
F3	62.0 (2.441)	
F7	61.5 (2.421)	
KD175 (1976-1979) & KE175 (1976-1982)	61.5 (2.421)	

238-350 cc models	Standard diameter mm (in.)	*Service limit mm (in.)
F4 & F21M	70.0 (2.756)	
F8 & F81M	68.0 (2.667)	
F5 & F9	80.5 (3.169)	

* Refer to text for service limits for cast iron cylinders.

Table 3 PISTON RING INSTALLED GAP

79-100 cc models	
KD80 (1975, 1976 & 1980-1987)	0.15-0.65 mm (0.006-0.026 in.)
J Series	0.15-0.65 mm (0.006-0.026 in.)
MC1, MC1-A, MC1-B & MC1M	0.15-0.65 mm (0.006-0.026 in.)
G3SS & G3TR	0.15-0.65 mm (0.006-0.026 in.)
D1	0.15-0.65 mm (0.006-0.026 in.)
G4TR, G5 & G31M	0.15-0.65 mm (0.006-0.026 in.)
KD100, KE100, KH100, KM100 & KV100	0.15-0.65 mm (0.006-0.026 in.)
115-125 cc models	
C2SS & C2TR	0.15-0.30 mm (0.006-0.012 in.)
F6	0.15-0.65 mm (0.006-0.026 in.)
KD125, KE125 & KS125	0.15-0.65 mm (0.006-0.026 in.)
KX125 (1974-1976)	0.15-0.65 mm (0.006-0.026 in.)
169-175 cc models	
F2 & F2TR	0.20-0.65 mm (0.008-0.026 in.)
F3 & F7	0.20-0.65 mm (0.008-0.026 in.)
KD175 (1976-1979) & KE175 (1976-1982)	0.20-0.65 mm (0.008-0.026 in.)

(continued)

Table 3 PISTON RING INSTALLED GAP (continued)

238-350 cc models	
F4 & F21M	0.20-0.65 mm (0.008-0.026 in.)
F8 & F81M	0.20-0.65 mm (0.008-0.026 in.)
F5 & F9	0.25-0.65 mm (0.010-0.026 in.)

Table 4 PISTON TO CYLINDER CLEARANCE

79-100 cc models	
KD80 (1975, 1976 & 1980-1987)	0.028 mm (0.001 in.)
J Series	0.026 mm (0.001 in.)
MC1, MC1-A, MC1-B & MC1M	0.028 mm (0.001 in.)
G3 models (except G3SS-E)	0.028 mm (0.001 in.)
G3SS-E	0.028 mm (0.001 in.)
D1	0.040 mm (0.0016 in.)
G4TR & G5	0.028 mm (0.001 in.)
G31M	0.091 mm (0.0036 in.)
KD100	0.046 mm (0.002 in.)
KE100, KH100 & KV100	0.032-0.042 mm (0.0013-0.0017 in.)
115-125 cc models	
C2SS & C2TR	0.004-0.040 mm (0.00016-0.0016 in.)
F6	0.072 mm (0.0028 in.)
KD125	0.069 mm (0.0027 in.)
KE125-A3, A4 & A5	0.069 mm (0.0027 in.)
KE125-A6 on (1979 & later)	0.066 mm (0.0026 in.)
KS125	0.069 mm (0.0027 in.)
KX125 (1974-1976)	0.046 mm (0.0018 in.)
169-175 cc models	
F2 & F2TR	0.072 mm (0.0028 in.)
F3	0.072 mm (0.0028 in.)
F7	0.064 mm (0.0025 in.)
KD175 (1976-1979) & KE175 (1976-1982)	0.040 mm (0.0016 in.)
238-350 cc models	
F4	0.082 mm (0.003 in.)
F21M	0.127 mm (0.005 in.)
F8	0.157 mm (0.006 in.)
F81M	0.082 mm (0.003 in.)
F5	0.200 mm (0.0078 in.)
F9	0.100 mm (0.004 in.)

Table 5 CLUTCH SPRING SPECIFICATIONS

79-100 cc models	Type	Standard length	Service limit
KD80 (1975, 1976 & 1980-1987)	3	21.6 mm (0.85 in.)	20 mm (0.79 in.)
J Series	2	24.8 mm (0.98 in.)	24 mm (0.94 in.)
MC1, MC1-A & MC1M (1973-1974)	2	21.6 mm (0.85 in.)	20 mm (0.79 in.)
MC1-B, & MC1M-A (1974-1975)	3	21.6 mm (0.85 in.)	20 mm (0.79 in.)
G3SS & G3TR	2	21.6 mm (0.85 in.)	20 mm (0.79 in.)
D1	2	24.8 mm (0.98 in.)	23 mm (0.91 in.)
G4TR (1970-1972)	2	21.6 mm (0.85 in.)	20 mm (0.79 in.)
G4TR (1973-1975)	3	21.6 mm (0.85 in.)	20 mm (0.79 in.)
G5 (1972-1973)	2	21.6 mm (0.85 in.)	20 mm (0.79 in.)
G5 (1974-1975)	3	21.6 mm (0.85 in.)	20 mm (0.79 in.)
G31M	2	21.6 mm (0.85 in.)	20 mm (0.79 in.)

(continued)

Table 5 CLUTCH SPRING SPECIFICATIONS (continued)

79-100 cc models	Type	Standard length	Service limit
KD100, KE100, KH100, KM100 & KV100	3	21.6 mm (0.85 in.)	20 mm (0.79 in.)
115-125 cc models	**Type**	**Standard length**	**Service limit**
C2SS & C2TR	4	21.6 mm (0.85 in.)	19.6 mm (0.77 in.)
F6	1	34.5 mm (1.36 in.)	31 mm (1.22 in.)
KD125, KE125, KS125 & KX125 (1974-1976)	5	33.1 mm (1.30 in.)	31.6 mm (1.24 in.)
169-175 cc models	**Type**	**Standard length**	**Service limit**
F2, F2TR & F3	4	24.5 mm (0.96 in.)	22.3 mm (0.88 in.)
F7	1	34.5 mm (1.36 in.)	31 mm (1.22 in.)
KD175	5	34.5 mm (1.36 in.)	33 mm (1.30 in.)
238-350 cc models	**Type**	**Standard length**	**Service limit**
F4 & F21	4	24.5 mm (0.96 in.)	22.3 mm (0.88 in.)
F8	1	33.6 mm (1.32 in.)	30.1 mm (1.19 in.)
F81M	1	2.8 mm (0.11 in.)	2.5 mm (0.10 in.)
F5 & F9	1	33.6 mm (1.32 in.)	30.1 mm (1.19 in.)

Table 6 CLUTCH PLATE SPECIFICATIONS

79-100 cc models	Standard thickness	Service limit
KD80 (1975, 1976 & 1980-1987)	3.2 mm (0.13 in.)	2.8 mm (0.11 in.)
J Series	3.7 mm (0.146 in.)	3.35 mm (0.132 in.)
MC1, MC1-A, MC1-B, MC1M & MC1M-A	3.2 mm (0.13 in.)	2.8 mm (0.11 in.)
G3SS & G3TR	3.2 mm (0.13 in.)	2.8 mm (0.11 in.)
D1	3.7 mm (0.146 in.)	3.35 mm (0.132 in.)
G4TR	3.2 mm (0.13 in.)	2.8 mm (0.11 in.)
G5	3.2 mm (0.13 in.)	2.8 mm (0.11 in.)
G31M	3.2 mm (0.13 in.)	2.8 mm (0.11 in.)
KD100, KE100, KH100, KM100 & KV100	3.2 mm (0.13 in.)	2.8 mm (0.11 in.)
115-125 cc models	**Standard thickness**	**Service limit**
C2SS & C2TR	4.3 mm (0.17 in.)	3.9 mm (0.15 in.)
F6	4.0 mm (0.16 in.)	3.6 mm (0.14 in.)
KD125, KE125 & KS125	3.0 mm (0.12 in.)	2.5 mm (0.10 in.)
KX125 (1974-1976)	3.0 mm (0.12 in.)	2.5 mm (0.10 in.)
169-175 cc models	**Standard thickness**	**Service limit**
F2, F2TR & F3	4.0 mm (0.16 in.)	3.6 mm (0.14 in.)
F7	3.1 mm (0.12 in.)	2.8 mm (0.11 in.)
KD175 (1976-1979) & KE175 (1976-1982)	3.0 mm (0.12 in.)	2.5 mm (0.10 in.)
238-350 cc models	**Standard thickness**	**Service limit**
F4 & F21	4.0 mm (0.16 in.)	3.6 mm (0.14 in.)
F8	2.8 mm (0.11 in.)	2.5 mm (0.10 in.)
F81M	2.8 mm (0.11 in.)	2.5 mm (0.10 in.)
F5 & F9	2.8 mm (0.11 in.)	2.5 mm (0.10 in.)

Table 7 ROTARY VALVE COVER SPECIFICATIONS

79-100 cc models	Standard depth	Service limit
KD80 (1975, 1976 & 1980-1987)	3.4 mm(0.13 in.)	4.0 mm (0.16 in.)
J Series	3.4 mm(0.13 in.)	4.0 mm (0.16 in.)
MC1, MC1-A, MC1-B & MC1M	3.4 mm(0.13 in.)	4.0 mm (0.16 in.)
G3 models	3.4 mm(0.13 in.)	4.0 mm (0.16 in.)
G4TR	3.4 mm(0.13 in.)	4.0 mm (0.16 in.)
	(continued)	

Table 7 ROTARY VALVE COVER SPECIFICATIONS (continued)

79-100 cc models	Standard depth	Service limit
G5	3.4 mm (0.13 in.)	4.0 mm (0.16 in.)
KD100	3.4 mm (0.13 in.)	4.0 mm (0.16 in.)
KE100		
1978 & earlier models	3.4 mm (0.13 in.)	4.0 mm (0.16 in.)
1979 & later (-8 on)	0.85 mm (0.033 in.)	1.5 mm (0.06 in.)
KH100	3.4 mm (0.13 in.)	4.0 mm (0.16 in.)
KM100		
KM100-A1, A2, A3 & A4	3.4 mm (0.13 in.)	4.0 mm (0.16 in.)
KM100-A6 & A7	1.15 mm (0.045 in.)	1.5 mm (0.06 in.)
KV100	3.4 mm (0.13 in.)	4.0 mm (0.16 in.)
115-125 cc models	**Standard depth**	**Service limit**
C2SS & C2TR	3.5 mm (0.14 in.)	4.0 mm (0.16 in.)
F6	3.5 mm (0.14 in.)	4.0 mm (0.16 in.)
KD125	0.85 mm (0.003 in.)	1.2 mm (0.047 in.)
KE125		
KE125-A3, A4 & A5	0.85 mm (0.033 in.)	1.2 mm (0.047 in.)
1979 & later (A6 on)	0.85 mm (0.033 in.)	1.5 mm (0.06 in.)
KS125	0.85 mm (0.033 in.)	1.2 mm (0.047 in.)
KX125 (1974-1976)	0.85 mm (0.033 in.)	1.2 mm (0.047 in.)
169-175 cc models	**Standard depth**	**Service limit**
F2 & F2TR	3.5 mm (0.14 in.)	4.0 mm (0.16 in.)
F3	3.5 mm (0.14 in.)	4.0 mm (0.16 in.)
F7	3.5 mm (0.14 in.)	4.0 mm (0.16 in.)
KD175 (1976-1979) & KE175 (1976-1982)	1.15 mm (0.045 in.)	1.5 mm (0.060 in.)
238-350 cc models	**Standard depth**	**Service limit**
F4	3.5 mm (0.14 in.)	4.0 mm (0.16 in.)
F21M	3.5 mm (0.14 in.)	4.0 mm (0.16 in.)
F8	0.8 mm (0.03 in.)	–
F81M	0.8 mm (0.03 in.)	–
F5	0.8 mm (0.03 in.)	–
F9	0.8 mm (0.03 in.)	–

Table 8 ROTARY VALVE DISC THICKNESS

79-100 cc models	Standard	Wear limit
KD80 (1975, 1976 & 1980-1987)	3.1 mm (0.12 in.)	2.8 mm (0.11 in.)
J Series	3.1 mm (0.12 in.)	2.8 mm (0.11 in.)
MC1, MC1-A, MC1-B & MC1M	3.1 mm (0.12 in.)	2.8 mm (0.11 in.)
G3SS & G3TR	3.1 mm (0.12 in.)	2.8 mm (0.11 in.)
G4TR	3.1 mm (0.12 in.)	2.8 mm (0.11 in.)
G5	3.1 mm (0.12 in.)	2.8 mm (0.11 in.)
KD100	3.1 mm (0.12 in.)	2.8 mm (0.11 in.)
KE100		
1978 & earlier models	3.1 mm (0.12 in.)	2.8 mm (0.11 in.)
1979 & later (-8 on)	0.7 mm (0.028 in.)	0.5 mm (0.02 in.)
KH100	3.1 mm (0.12 in.)	2.8 mm (0.11 in.)
KM100		
KM100-A1, A2, A3 & A4, standard	3.1 mm (0.12 in.)	
Service limit	2.8 mm (0.11 in.)	
KM100-A6 & A7	0.7 mm (0.028 in.)	0.5 mm (0.02 in.)
KV100	3.1 mm (0.12 in.)	2.8 mm (0.11 in.)
115-125 cc models	**Standard**	**Wear limit**
C2SS & C2TR	3.1 mm (0.12 in.)	2.8 mm (0.11 in.)
F6	3.1 mm (0.12 in.)	2.8 mm (0.11 in.)

(continued)

Table 8 ROTARY VALVE DISC THICKNESS (continued)

115-125 cc models	Standard	Wear limit
KD125	0.4 mm (0.016 in.)	0.25 mm (0.01 in.)
KE125		
KE125-A3, A4 & A5, standard	0.4 mm (0.016 in.)	
Service limit	0.25 mm (0.01 in.)	
1979 & later (A6 on), standard	0.7 mm (0.028 in.)	
Service limit	0.5 mm (0.02 in.)	
KS125	0.4 mm (0.016 in.)	0.25 mm (0.01 in.)
KX125 (1974-1976)	0.4 mm (0.016 in.)	0.25 mm (0.01 in.)
169-175 cc models	**Standard**	**Wear limit**
F2 & F2TR	3.1 mm (0.12 in.)	2.8 mm (0.11 in.)
F3	3.1 mm (0.12 in.)	2.8 mm (0.11 in.)
F7	3.1 mm (0.12 in.)	2.8 mm (0.11 in.)
KD175 (1976-1979) & KE175 (1976-1982)	0.7 mm (0.028 in.)	0.5 mm (0.02 in.)
238-350 cc models	**Standard**	**Wear limit**
F4	3.1 mm (0.12 in.)	2.8 mm (0.11 in.)
F21M	3.1 mm (0.12 in.)	2.8 mm (0.11 in.)
F8	0.5 mm (0.02 in.)	0.4 mm (0.01 in.)
F81M	0.5 mm (0.02 in.)	0.4 mm (0.01 in.)
F5	0.5 mm (0.02 in.)	0.4 mm (0.01 in.)
F9	0.5 mm (0.02 in.)	0.4 mm (0.01 in.)

4

Table 9 CONNECTING ROD BIG END RADIAL PLAY

79-100 cc models	Standard play	Service limit
KD80 (1975, 1976 & 1980-1987)	0.40 mm (0.016 in.)	0.60 mm (0.024 in.)
J Series	0.021 mm (0.0009 in.)	0.20 mm (0.008 in.)
MC1, MC1-A, MC1-B & MC1M	0.034 mm (0.0013 in.)	0.08 mm (0.003 in.)
G3SS & G3TR	0.034 mm (0.0013 in.)	0.08 mm (0.003 in.)
D1	0.2 mm (0.008 in.)	—
G4TR	0.034 mm (0.0013 in.)	0.08 mm (0.003 in.)
G5	0.034 mm (0.0013 in.)	0.08 mm (0.003 in.)
G31M	0.034 mm (0.0013 in.)	0.08 mm (0.003 in.)
KD100, KE100, KH100, KM100 & KV100	0.034 mm (0.0013 in.)	0.08 mm (0.003 in.)
115-125 cc models	**Standard play**	**Service limit**
C2SS & C2TR	0.021 mm (0.0009 in.)	0.20 mm (0.008 in.)
F6	0.014 mm (0.0006 in.)	0.06 mm (0.0023 in.)
KD125, KE125, KS125 & KX125 (1974-1976)	0.024 mm (0.0009 in.)	0.08 mm (0.003 in.)
169-175 cc models	**Standard play**	**Service limit**
F2 & F2TR	0.014 mm (0.0006 in.)	0.06 mm (0.0023 in.)
F3	0.014 mm (0.0006 in.)	0.06 mm (0.0023 in.)
F7	0.014 mm (0.0006 in.)	0.06 mm (0.0023 in.)
KD175 (1976-1979) & KE175 (1976-1982)	0.019 mm (0.0007 in.)	0.07 mm (0.0028 in.)
238-350 cc models	**Standard play**	**Service limit**
F4	0.014 mm (0.0006 in.)	0.06 mm (0.0023 in.)
F21M	0.014 mm (0.0006 in.)	0.06 mm (0.0023 in.)
F8	0.05 mm (0.0019 in.)	0.06 mm (0.0023 in.)
F81M	0.05 mm (0.0019 in.)	0.06 mm (0.0023 in.)
F5	0.05 mm (0.0019 in.)	0.06 mm (0.0023 in.)
F9	0.05 mm (0.0019 in.)	0.06 mm (0.0023 in.)
(continued)		

Table 10 CONNECTING ROD BIG END SIDE PLAY

79-100 cc models	Standard play	Service limit
KD80 (1975, 1976 & 1980-1987)	0.034 mm (0.0013 in.)	0.08 mm (0.003 in.)
J Series	0.40 mm (0.016 in.)	0.60 mm (0.024 in.)
MC1, MC1-A, MC1-B & MC1M	0.40 mm (0.016 in.)	0.60 mm (0.024 in.)
G3SS & G3TR	0.40 mm (0.016 in.)	0.60 mm (0.024 in.)
D1	0.30 mm (0.012 in.)	—
G4TR	0.40 mm (0.016 in.)	0.60 mm (0.024 in.)
G5	0.40 mm (0.016 in.)	0.60 mm (0.024 in.)
G31M	0.40 mm (0.016 in.)	0.60 mm (0.024 in.)
KD100, KE100, KH100, KM100 & KV100	0.40 mm (0.016 in.)	0.60 mm (0.024 in.)
115-125 cc models	**Standard play**	**Service limit**
C2SS & C2TR	0.28 mm (0.011 in.)	0.45 mm (0.018 in.)
F6	0.38 mm (0.015 in.)	0.60 mm (0.024 in.)
KD125, KE125, KS125 & KX125 (1974-1976)	0.375 mm (0.015 in.)	0.60 mm (0.024 in.)
169-175 cc models	**Standard play**	**Service limit**
F2 & F2TR	0.38 mm (0.015 in.)	0.60 mm (0.024 in.)
F3	0.38 mm (0.015 in.)	0.60 mm (0.024 in.)
F7	0.38 mm (0.015 in.)	0.60 mm (0.024 in.)
KD175 (1976-1979) & KE175 (1976-1982)	0.375 mm (0.015 in.)	0.60 mm (0.024 in.)
238-350 cc models	**Standard play**	**Service limit**
F4	0.43 mm (0.017 in.)	0.60 mm (0.024 in.)
F21M	0.43 mm (0.017 in.)	0.60 mm (0.024 in.)
F8	0.43 mm (0.017 in.)	0.60 mm (0.024 in.)
F81M	0.43 mm (0.017 in.)	0.60 mm (0.024 in.)
F5	0.43 mm (0.017 in.)	0.60 mm (0.024 in.)
F9	0.43 mm (0.017 in.)	0.60 mm (0.024 in.)

Table 11 PORT TIMING SPECIFICATIONS

79-100 cc models	(degrees, minutes)
KD80 (1975, 1976 & 1980-1987)	
Rotary valve intake, open-close	120 BTDC-55 ATDC
Transfer ports	55 from BDC
Exhaust port	75 from BDC
J Series	
Rotary valve intake, open-close	110 BTDC-45 ATDC
Transfer ports	56, 30 from BDC
Exhaust port	74, 50 from BDC
MC1, MC1-A, MC1-B & MC1M	
Rotary valve intake, open-close	120 BTDC-55 ATDC
Transfer ports	54, 52 from BDC
Exhaust port	75, 02 from BDC
G3 models (except G3SS-E)	
Rotary valve intake, open-close	120 BTDC-55 ATDC
Transfer ports	57, 30 from BDC
Exhaust port	84, 30 from BDC*
G3SS-E	
Rotary valve intake, open-close	120 BTDC-55 ATDC
Transfer ports	58, 35 from BDC
Exhaust port	84, 16 from BDC
D1	
Rotary valve intake, open-close	110 BTDC-45 ATDC
Transfer ports	56, 20 from BDC
Exhaust port	74, 20 from BDC
G4TR	
Rotary valve intake, open-close	120 BTDC-55 ATDC

(continued)

Table 11 PORT TIMING SPECIFICATIONS (continued)

79-100 cc models	(degrees, minutes)
Transfer ports	
1973 & earlier models	57, 30 from BDC
1974 & later (-D on)	58, 35 from BDC
Exhaust port	
1973 & earlier models	84, 30 from BDC
1974 & later (-D on)	84, 16 from BDC
G5	
Rotary valve intake, open-close	120 BTDC-55 ATDC
Transfer ports	
1972 & 1973 models	57, 30 from BDC
1974 & later (-B on)	58, 35 from BDC
Exhaust port	
1972 & 1973 models	84, 30 from BDC
1974 & later (-B on)	84, 16 from BDC
G31M	
Rotary valve intake, open-close	140 BTDC-70 ATDC
Transfer ports	62 from BDC
Exhaust port	93 from BDC
KD100	
Rotary valve intake, open-close	120 BTDC-55 ATDC
Transfer ports	55 from BDC
Exhaust port	77 from BDC
KE100	
Rotary valve intake, open-close	120 BTDC-55 ATDC
Transfer ports	
1978 & earlier models	58, 35 from BDC
1979 & later (-A8 on)	59 from BDC
Exhaust port	
1978 & earlier models	84, 16 from BDC
1979 & later (-A8 on)	84, 30 from BDC
KH100	
Rotary valve intake, open-close	120 BTDC-55 ATDC
Transfer ports	58, 35 from BDC
Exhaust port	84, 16 from BDC
KM100	
Rotary valve intake, open-close	120 BTDC-55 ATDC
Transfer ports	58, 35 from BDC
Exhaust port	84, 16 from BDC
KV100	
Rotary valve intake, open-close	120 BTDC-55 ATDC
Transfer ports	58, 35 from BDC
Exhaust port	84, 16 from BDC

115-125 cc models	(degrees, minutes)
C2SS & C2TR	
Rotary valve intake, open-close	
Early models	110 BTDC-45 ATDC
Later models	110 BTDC-55 ATDC
Transfer ports	
Early models	57, 30 from BDC
Later models	60 from BDC
Exhaust port	
Early models	78, 30 from BDC
Later models	82 from BDC
F6	
Rotary valve intake, open-close	115 BTDC-55 ATDC
Transfer ports	57, 30 from BDC
Exhaust port	87 from BDC

(continued)

Table 11 PORT TIMING SPECIFICATIONS (continued)

KD125	
Rotary valve intake, open-close	115 BTDC-55 ATDC
Transfer ports	56 from BDC
Exhaust port	83 from BDC
KE125	
Rotary valve intake, open-close	115 BTDC-55 ATDC
Transfer ports	56 from BDC
Exhaust port	
KE125-A3, A4 & A5	83 from BDC
1979 & later (A6 on)	80 from BDC
KS125	
Rotary valve intake, open-close	115 BTDC-55 ATDC
Transfer ports	56 from BDC
Exhaust port	83 from BDC
KX125 (1974-1976)	
Rotary valve intake, open-close	135 BTDC-65 ATDC
Transfer ports	64 from BDC
Exhaust port	92 from BDC

169-175 cc models	**(degrees, minutes)**
F2 & F2TR	
Rotary valve intake, open-close	110 BTDC-45 ATDC
Transfer ports	60 from BDC
Exhaust port	86 from BDC
F3	
Rotary valve intake, open-close	110 BTDC-60 ATDC
Transfer ports	57, 46 from BDC
Exhaust port	86, 50 from BDC
F7	
Rotary valve intake, open-close	115 BTDC-55 ATDC
Transfer ports	55, 30 from BDC
Exhaust port	82 from BDC
KD175 (1976-1979) & KE175 (1976-1982)	
Rotary valve intake, open-close	115 BTDC-55 ATDC
Transfer ports	55 from BDC
Exhaust port	83 from BDC

238-350 cc models	**(degrees, minutes)**
F4	
Rotary valve intake, open-close	110 BTDC-45 ATDC
Transfer ports	57, 30 from BDC
Exhaust port	78, 30 from BDC
F21M	
Rotary valve intake, open-close	120 BTDC-60 ATDC
Transfer ports	62 from BDC
Exhaust port	85 from BDC
F8	
Rotary valve intake, open-close	110 BTDC-50 ATDC
Transfer ports	59 from BDC
Exhaust port	83 from BDC
F81M	
Rotary valve intake, open-close	130 BTDC-65 ATDC
Transfer ports	59 from BDC
Exhaust port	87, 40 from BDC
F5	
Rotary valve intake, open-close	110 BTDC-50 ATDC
Transfer ports	57 from BDC
Exhaust port	82 from BDC

(continued)

Table 11 PORT TIMING SPECIFICATIONS (continued)

F9	
Rotary valve intake, open-close	120 BTDC-60 ATDC
Transfer ports	57 from BDC
Exhaust port	82 from BDC

* Exhaust port timing for G3SS-C, G3SS-D, G3TR-C & G3TR-D models is 83° from BDC.

Table 12 TIGHTENING TORQUES*

KD80, MC1-A, MC1-B, MC1M, G3SS, G3TR, G4TR, G31M & G5	
Cylinder head nuts	11.8-14.7 N•m (104-130 in.-lb.)
J Series and D1	
Cylinder head nuts	7.9-9.7 N•m (70-86 in.-lb.)
KD100, KE100, KH100, KM100 & KV100	
Clutch spring bolts (M5)	3.95-5.08 N•m (35-45 in.-lb.)
Cylinder head nuts (M8)	21.7 N•m (16 ft.-lb.)
Engine mounting bolts (M10)	25.8-33.9 N•m (19-25 ft.-lb.)
Front axle nut (M10)	33.9-44.7 N•m (25-33 ft.-lb.)
Front fork clamp bolts, upper (M8)	15.6-21.7 N•m (11.5-16.0 ft.-lb.)
Front fork clamp bolts, lower (M10)	25.8-33.9 N•m (19-25 ft.-lb.)
Front fork top bolts	14.9-19.7 N•m (11.0-14.5 ft.-lb.)
Handlebar clamp bolts (M8)	15.6-21.7 N•m (11.5-16.0 ft.-lb.)
Magneto flywheel nut (M10)	48.8 N•m (36 ft.-lb.)
Oil hose banjo bolts	3.95-5.08 N•m (35-45 in.-lb.)
Primary gear nut (M12)	69.2-73.2 N•m (51-54 ft.-lb.)
Rear axle nut (M10)	33.9-44.7 N•m (25-33 ft.-lb.)
Rear shock absorber	
Bolts (M10)	25.8-33.9 N•m (19-25 ft.-lb.)
Nuts (M12)	25.8-33.9 N•m (19-25 ft.-lb.)
Rear sprocket nuts (M8)	19.7-21.7 N•m (14.5-16.0 ft.-lb.)
Spark plug	24.4-29.8 N•m (18-22 ft.-lb.)
Sprocket bolt (M8)	21.7-24.4 N•m (16-18 ft.-lb.)
Steering stem head bolt	29.8-48.8 N•m (22-36 ft.-lb.)
Steering stem head clamp bolt (M8)	15.6-21.7 N•m (11.5-16.0 ft.-lb.)
Steering stem lock nut	17.6-21.7 N•m (13-16 ft.-lb.)
Swing arm pivot shaft nut (M10)	17.6-21.7 N•m (13-16 ft.-lb.)
Torque link nut (M10)	25.8-33.9 N•m (19-25 ft.-lb.)
C2SS & C2TR	
Cylinder head nuts	7.9-9.7 N•m (70-86 in.-lb.)
F6	
Cylinder head nuts	19.0 N•m (14 ft.-lb.)
Magneto flywheel nut	94.9 N•m (70 ft.-lb.)
KD125 & KE125 (1979 & earlier) & KS125	
Carburetor rim bolts	3.95-5.08 N•m (35-45 in.-lb.)
Clutch hub nut	39.3-48.8 N•m (29-36 ft.-lb.)
Clutch spring bolts	2.5 N•m (22 in.-lb.)
Cylinder head nuts	23.7-27.1 N•m (17.5-20.0 ft.-lb.)
Engine mounting	
M8 bolts	15.6-21.7 N•m (11.5-16.0 ft.-lb.)
M10 bolts	25.8-33.9 N•m (19-25 ft.-lb.)
Front axle clamp nuts	(11.5-16.0 ft.-lb.)
Front axle nut	33.9-44.7 N•m (25-33 ft.-lb.)
Front fork clamp bolts (M8)	15.6-21.7 N•m (11.5-16.0 ft.-lb.)
Front fork top bolts	14.9-19.7 N•m (11.0-14.5 ft.-lb.)
Handlebar clamp bolts	15.6-21.7 N•m (11.5-16.0 ft.-lb.)
Magneto flywheel nut	58.3-69.2 N•m (43-51 ft.-lb.)
Oil hose banjo bolts	4.4 N•m (39 in.-lb.)
Primary gear nut	44.7-48.8 N•m (33-46 ft.-lb.)

(continued)

Table 12 TIGHTENING TORQUES (continued)

Rear axle nut	69.2-88.1 N•m (51-65 ft.-lb.)
Rear shock absorber	
Bolts	25.8-33.9 N•m (19-25 ft.-lb.)
Nuts	25.8-33.9 N•m (19-25 ft.-lb.)
Rear sprocket nuts	19.7-21.7 N•m (14.5-16.0 ft.-lb.)
Shift drum positioning bolt	14.9 N•m (11 ft.-lb.)
Spark plug	24.4-29.8 N•m (18-22 ft.-lb.)
Sprocket nut	54.23-63.7 N•m (40-47 ft.-lb.)
Steering base clamp bolt (M10)	19.7-29.8 N•m (14.5-22.0 ft.-lb.)
Steering stem head bolt	29.8 N•m (22 ft.-lb.)
Steering stem head clamp bolt	15.6-21.7 N•m (11.5-16.0 ft.-lb.)
Steering stem lock nut	17.6-21.7 N•m (13-16 ft.-lb.)
Swing arm pivot shaft nut	39.3-58.3 N•m (29-43 ft.-lb.)
Torque link nut	19.7-21.7 N•m (14.5-16.0 ft.-lb.)
KE125-A7 on (1980 & later)	
Refer to earlier KE125 models except the following.	
Front axle nut	69.2-88.1 N•m (51-65 ft.-lb.)
Front fork bottom Allen bolts	12.9-22.4 N•m (9.5-16.5 ft.-lb.)
Front fork clamp bolts	
Upper	16.3-23.7 N•m (12.0-17.5 ft.-lb.)
Lower	25.8-33.9 N•m (19-25 ft.-lb.)
Front fork drain bolt	7.8 N•m (69 in.-lb.)
Steering stem head bolt	48.8-58.3 N•m (36-43 ft.-lb.)
Swing arm pivot shaft nut	48.8-69.2 N•m (36-51 ft.-lb.)
Torque link nut	24.4-39.3 N•m (18-29 ft.-lb.)
KX125 (1974-1976)	
Cylinder head nuts	21.7 N•m (16 ft.-lb.)
Engine mounting nuts	
M8	15.6-21.7 N•m (11.5-16.0 ft.-lb.)
M10	25.8-33.9 N•m (19-25 ft.-lb.)
Front axle clamp nuts	15.6-21.7 N•m (11.5-16.0 ft.-lb.)
Front axle nut	33.9-44.7 N•m (25-33 ft.-lb.)
Front brake cam lever	6.9-7.8 N•m (61-69 in.-lb.)
Front fork clamp bolts	
Upper	15.6-21.7 N•m (11.5-16.0 ft.-lb.)
Lower	15.6-21.7 N•m (11.5-16.0 ft.-lb.)
Handlebar clamp bolts	15.6-21.7 N•m (11.5-16.0 ft.-lb.)
Rear axle nut	69.2-108.5 N•m (51-80 ft.-lb.)
Rear brake cam lever	6.9-7.8 N•m (61-69 in.-lb.)
Rear shock absorber	
Bolts	25.8-33.9 N•m (19-25 ft.-lb.)
Nuts	25.8-33.9 N•m (19-25 ft.-lb.)
Rear sprocket nuts	19.7-21.7 N•m (14.5-16 ft.-lb.)
Steering base bolt	19.7-29.8 N•m (14.5-22.0 ft.-lb.)
Steering stem head bolt	29.8 N•m (22 ft.-lb.)
Steering stem head clamp bolt	14.9-22.4 N•m (11.0-16.5 ft.-lb.)
Swing arm pivot shaft nut	39.3-58.3 N•m (29-43 ft.-lb.)
Torque link nut	17.63-23.1 N•m (13-17 ft.-lb.)
F2, F2TR & F3	
Cylinder head nuts	21.7 N•m (16 ft.-lb.)
F7	
Cylinder head nuts	19.0 N•m (14 ft.-lb.)
Magneto flywheel nut	94.9 N•m (70 ft.-lb.)
F4 & F21M	
Cylinder head nuts	21.7 N•m (16 ft.-lb.)
F8 & F81M	
Cylinder head (tighten large nuts first)	
Small bolts	19.0 N•m (14 ft.-lb.)
Large nuts	33.9 N•m (25 ft.-lb.)
Magneto flywheel nut	94.9 N•m (70 ft.-lb.)

(continued)

Table 12 TIGHTENING TORQUES (continued)

F5			
Cylinder head (tighten large nuts first)			
Small bolts	19.0 N·m (14 ft.-lb.)		
Large nuts	33.9 N·m (25 ft.-lb.)		
Magneto flywheel nut	94.9 N·m (70 ft.-lb.)		
F9			
Magneto flywheel nut	94.9 N·m (70 ft.-lb.)		
Standard tightening torques			
Thread diameter	mkg	N·m	ft.-lb.
5 mm	0.35-0.50	3.4-4.9	2.5-3.6 (30-43 in.-lb.)
6 mm	0.60-0.80	5.9-7.8	4.3-5.8 (52-69 in.-lb.)
8 mm	1.4-1.9	14-19	10.0-13.5
10 mm	2.6-3.5	25-34	19-25
12 mm	4.5-6.2	44-61	33-45
14 mm	7.4-10.0	73-98	54-72
16 mm	11.5-16.0	115-155	83-115
18 mm	17.0-23.0	165-225	125-165
20 mm	23-33	225-325	165-240

*The following is a partial list of recommended torque values for specific fasteners of specific models. Refer to the list of torque values for standard thread sizes if the application for a specific model is not listed.

Table 13 ENGINE SPECIFICATIONS

79-100 cc models	
KD80 (1975, 1976 & 1980-1987)	
General	
Bore and stroke (mm)	47 × 46
Displacement (cc)	79
Cylinder	
Standard bore diameter	47.008 mm (1.854 in.)
Piston to cylinder clearance	0.028 mm (0.001 in.)
Piston rings	
End gap	0.15-0.65 mm (0.006-0.026 in.)
Crankshaft and connecting rod	
Crankpin to rod clearance, standard	0.034 mm (0.0013 in.)
Service limit	0.08 mm (0.003 in.)
Big end side play, standard	0.40 mm (0.016 in.)
Service limit	0.60 mm (0.024 in.)
Oil pump output/3 minutes @ 2000 rpm	2.8 cc (0.095 oz.)
Port timing (degrees, minutes)	
Rotary valve intake, open-close	120 BTDC-55 ATDC
Transfer ports	55 from BDC
Exhaust port	75 from BDC
Rotary valve thickness, standard	3.1 mm (0.12 in.)
Service limit	2.8 mm (0.11 in.)
Rotary valve cover depth, standard	3.4 mm (0.13 in.)
Service limit	4.0 mm (0.16 in.)
Clutch type	3
Transmission speeds	5 speeds (Type 1)
J Series	
General	
Bore and stroke (mm)	47 × 47
Displacement (cc)	81.5
Cylinder	
Standard bore diameter	47.0 mm (1.850 in.)
Piston to cylinder clearance	0.026 mm (0.001 in.)

(continued)

Table 13 ENGINE SPECIFICATIONS (continued)

Piston rings	
End gap	0.15-0.65 mm (0.006-0.026 in.)
Crankshaft and connecting rod	
Crankpin to rod clearance, standard	0.021 mm (0.0009 in.)
Service limit	0.20 mm (0.008 in.)
Big end side play, standard	0.40 mm (0.016 in.)
Service limit	0.60 mm (0.024 in.)
Oil pump output/3 minutes @ 2000 rpm	
J1L, J1TL & J1TRL models	2.8 cc (0.095 oz.)
Oil mix ratio	
Models without oil injection	1 part oil to 20 parts gasoline
Port timing (degrees, minutes)	
Rotary valve intake, open-close	110 BTDC-45 ATDC
Transfer ports	56, 30 from BDC
Exhaust port	74, 50 from BDC
Rotary valve thickness, standard	3.1 mm (0.12 in.)
Service limit	2.8 mm (0.11 in.)
Rotary valve cover depth, standard	3.4 mm (0.13 in.)
Service limit	4.0 mm (0.16 in.)
Clutch type	2
Transmission speeds	4 speeds (* Type 1)
MC1, MC1-A, MC1-B & MC1M	
General	
Bore and stroke (mm)	47 × 51.8
Displacement (cc)	89
Cylinder	
Standard bore diameter	47.0 mm (1.850 in.)
Piston to cylinder clearance	0.028 mm (0.001 in.)
Piston rings	
End gap	0.15-0.65 mm (0.006-0.026 in.)
Crankshaft and connecting rod	
Crankpin to rod clearance, standard	0.034 mm (0.0013 in.)
Service limit	0.08 mm (0.003 in.)
Big end side play, standard	0.40 mm (0.016 in.)
Service limit	0.60 mm (0.024 in.)
Oil pump output/3 minutes @ 2000 rpm	2.8 cc (0.095 oz.)
Port timing (degrees, minutes)	
Rotary valve intake, open-close	120 BTDC-55 ATDC
Transfer ports	54, 52 from BDC
Exhaust port	75, 02 from BDC
Rotary valve thickness, standard	3.1 mm (0.12 in.)
Service limit	2.8 mm (0.11 in.)
Rotary valve cover depth, standard	3.4 mm (0.13 in.)
Service limit	4.0 mm (0.16 in.)
Clutch type	
MC1, MC1-A & MC1M (1973-1974)	2
MC1-B, & MC1M-A (1974-1975)	3
Transmission speeds	5 speeds (Type 1)
G3 models (except G3SS-E)	
General	
Bore and stroke (mm)	47 × 51.8
Displacement (cc)	89
Cylinder	
Standard bore diameter	47.0 mm (1.850 in.)
Piston to cylinder clearance	0.028 mm (0.001 in.)
Piston rings	
End gap	0.15-0.65 mm (0.006-0.026 in.)
Crankshaft and connecting rod	
Crankpin to rod clearance, standard	0.034 mm (0.0013 in.)
Service limit	0.08 mm (0.003 in.)

(continued)

Table 13 ENGINE SPECIFICATIONS (continued)

Crankshaft and connecting rod (continued)	
Big end side play	0.40 mm (0.016 in.)
Service limit	0.60 mm (0.024 in.)
Oil pump output/3 minutes @ 2000 rpm	2.8 cc (0.095 oz.)
Port timing (degrees, minutes)	
Rotary valve intake, open-close	120 BTDC-55 ATDC
Transfer ports	57, 30 from BDC
Exhaust port	84, 30 from BDC**
Rotary valve thickness, standard	3.1 mm (0.12 in.)
Service limit	2.8 mm (0.11 in.)
Rotary valve cover depth, standard	3.4 mm (0.13 in.)
Service limit	4.0 mm (0.16 in.)
Clutch type	2
Transmission speeds	5 speeds (Type 1)
G3SS-E	
General	
Bore and stroke (mm)	49.5 × 51.8
Displacement (cc)	99
Cylinder	
Standard bore diameter	49.5 mm (1.949 in.)
Piston to cylinder clearance	0.028 mm (0.001 in.)
Piston rings	
End gap	0.15-0.65 mm (0.006-0.026 in.)
Crankshaft and connecting rod	
Crankpin to rod clearance, standard	0.034 mm (0.0013 in.)
Service limit	0.08 mm (0.003 in.)
Big end side play, standard	0.40 mm (0.016 in.)
Service limit	0.60 mm (0.024 in.)
Oil pump output/3 minutes @ 2000 rpm	2.8 cc (0.095 oz.)
Port timing (degrees, minutes)	
Rotary valve intake, open-close	120 BTDC-55 ATDC
Transfer ports	58, 35 from BDC
Exhaust port	84, 16 from BDC
Rotary valve thickness, standard	3.1 mm (0.12 in.)
Service limit	2.8 mm (0.11 in.)
Rotary valve cover depth, standard	3.4 mm (0.13 in.)
Service limit	4.0 mm (0.16 in.)
Clutch type	2
Transmission speeds	5 speeds (Type 1)
D1	
General	
Bore and stroke (mm)	52 × 47.8
Displacement (cc)	99
Cylinder	
Standard bore diameter	52.0 mm (2.047 in.)
Piston rings	
End gap	0.15-0.65 mm (0.006-0.026 in.)
Crankshaft and connecting rod	
Crankpin to rod clearance, standard	0.2 mm (0.008 in.)
Big end side play, standard	0.30 mm (0.012 in.)
Port timing (degrees, minutes)	
Rotary valve intake, open-close	110 BTDC-45 ATDC
Transfer ports	56, 20 from BDC
Exhaust port	74, 20 from BDC
Clutch type	2
Transmission speeds	4 speeds (Type 4)
G4TR	
General	
Bore and stroke (mm)	49.5 × 51.8
Displacement (cc)	99

(continued)

4

Table 13 ENGINE SPECIFICATIONS (continued)

Cylinder	
Standard bore diameter	49.5 mm (1.949 in.)
Piston to cylinder clearance	0.028 mm (0.001 in.)
Piston rings	
End gap	0.15-0.65 mm (0.006-0.026 in.)
Crankshaft and connecting rod	
Crankpin to rod clearance, standard	0.034 mm (0.0013 in.)
Service limit	0.08 mm (0.003 in.)
Big end side play, standard	0.40 mm (0.016 in.)
Service limit	0.60 mm (0.024 in.)
Oil pump output/3 minutes @ 2000 rpm	2.8 cc (0.095 oz.)
Port timing (degrees, minutes)	
Rotary valve intake, open-close	120 BTDC-55 ATDC
Transfer ports	
1973 & earlier models	57, 30 from BDC
1974 & later (-D on)	58, 35 from BDC
Exhaust port	
1973 & earlier models	84, 30 from BDC
1974 & later (-D on)	84, 16 from BDC
Rotary valve thickness, standard	3.1 mm (0.12 in.)
Service limit	2.8 mm (0.11 in.)
Rotary valve cover depth, standard	3.4 mm (0.13 in.)
Service limit	4.0 mm (0.16 in.)
Clutch type	
G4TR, G4TR-A & G4TR-B (1970-1972)	2
G4TR-C, G4TR-D & G4TR-E (1973-1975)	3
Transmission speeds	5 speeds 2 Ranges (Type 2)
G5	
General	
Bore and stroke (mm)	49.5 × 51.8
Displacement (cc)	99
Cylinder	
Standard bore diameter	49.5 mm (1.949 in.)
Piston to cylinder clearance	0.028 mm (0.001 in.)
Piston rings	
End gap	0.15-0.65 mm (0.006-0.026 in.)
Crankshaft and connecting rod	
Crankpin to rod clearance, standard	0.034 mm (0.0013 in.)
Service limit	0.08 mm (0.003 in.)
Big end side play, standard	0.40 mm (0.016 in.)
Service limit	0.60 mm (0.024 in.)
Oil pump output/3 minutes @ 2000 rpm	2.8 cc (0.095 oz.)
Port timing (degrees, minutes)	
Rotary valve intake, open-close	120 BTDC-55 ATDC
Transfer ports	
1972 & 1973 models	57, 30 from BDC
1974 & later (-B on)	58, 35 from BDC
Exhaust port	
1972 & 1973 models	84, 30 from BDC
1974 & later (-B on)	84, 16 from BDC
Rotary valve thickness, standard	3.1 mm (0.12 in.)
Service limit	2.8 mm (0.11 in.)
Rotary valve cover depth, standard	3.4 mm (0.13 in.)
Service limit	4.0 mm (0.16 in.)
Clutch type	
G5 & G5-A (1972-1973)	2
G5-B & G5-C (1974-1975)	3
Transmission speeds	5 speeds (Type 1)

(continued)

Table 13 ENGINE SPECIFICATIONS (continued)

G31M

General	
Bore and stroke (mm)	49.5 × 51.8
Displacement (cc)	99
Cylinder	
Standard bore diameter	49.5 mm (1.949 in.)
Piston to cylinder clearance	0.091 mm (0.0036 in.)
Piston rings	
End gap	0.15-0.65 mm (0.006-0.026 in.)
Crankshaft and connecting rod	
Crankpin to rod clearance, standard	0.034 mm (0.0013 in.)
Service limit	0.08 mm (0.003 in.)
Big end side play, standard	0.40 mm (0.016 in.)
Service limit	0.60 mm (0.024 in.)
Oil mix ratio	1 part oil to 20 parts gasoline
Port timing (degrees, minutes)	
Rotary valve intake, open-close	140 BTDC-70 ATDC
Transfer ports	62 from BDC
Exhaust port	93 from BDC
Clutch type	2
Transmission speeds	5 speeds (Type 1)

KD100

General	
Bore and stroke (mm)	49.5 × 51.8
Displacement (cc)	99
Cylinder	
Standard bore diameter	49.5 mm (1.949 in.)
Piston to cylinder clearance	0.046 mm (0.002 in.)
Piston rings	
End gap	0.15-0.65 mm (0.006-0.026 in.)
Crankshaft and connecting rod	
Crankpin to rod clearance, standard	0.034 mm (0.0013 in.)
Service limit	0.08 mm (0.003 in.)
Big end side play, standard	0.40 mm (0.016 in.)
Service limit	0.60 mm (0.024 in.)
Oil pump output/3 minutes @ 2000 rpm	2.8 cc (0.095 oz.)
Port timing (degrees, minutes)	
Rotary valve intake, open-close	120 BTDC/55 ATDC
Transfer ports	55 from BDC
Exhaust port	77 from BDC
Rotary valve thickness, standard	3.1 mm (0.12 in.)
Service limit	2.8 mm (0.11 in.)
Rotary valve cover depth, standard	3.4 mm (0.13 in.)
Service limit	4.0 mm (0.16 in.)
Clutch type	3
Transmission speeds	5 speeds (Type 1)

KE100

General	
Bore and stroke (mm)	49.5 × 51.8
Displacement (cc)	99
Cylinder	
Standard bore diameter	49.508-49.523 mm (1.9491-1.9497 in.)
Service limit	49.61 mm (1.9531 in.)
Piston to cylinder clearance	0.032-0.042 mm (0.0013-0.0017 in.)
Piston rings	
End gap	0.15-0.65 mm (0.006-0.026 in.)
Crankshaft and connecting rod	
Crankpin to rod clearance, standard	0.034 mm (0.0013 in.)
Service limit	0.08 mm (0.003 in.)

(continued)

4

Table 13 ENGINE SPECIFICATIONS (continued)

Crankshaft and connecting rod (continued)	
Big end side play, standard	0.40 mm (0.016 in.)
Service limit	0.60 mm (0.024 in.)
Oil pump output/3 minutes @ 2000 rpm	
1978 & earlier models	2.8 cc (0.095 oz.)
1979 & later (A8 on)	3.6-4.1 cc (0.122-0.139 oz.)
Port timing (degrees, minutes)	
Rotary valve intake, open-close	120 BTDC-55 ATDC
Transfer ports	
1978 & earlier models	58, 35 from BDC
1979 & later (A8 on)	59 from BDC
Exhaust port	
1978 & earlier models	84, 16 from BDC
1979 & later (A8 on)	84, 30 from BDC
Rotary valve thickness	
1978 & earlier models, standard	3.1 mm (0.12 in.)
Service limit	2.8 mm (0.11 in.)
1979 & later (A8 on), standard	0.7 mm (0.028in.)
Service limit	0.5 mm (0.02 in.)
Rotary valve cover depth	
1978 & earlier models, standard	3.4 mm (0.13 in.)
Service limit	4.0 mm (0.16 in.)
1979 & later (A8 on), standard	0.85 mm (0.033 in.)
Service limit	1.5 mm (0.06 in.)
Clutch type	3
Transmission speeds	5 speeds (Type 1)***
KH100	
General	
Bore and stroke (mm)	49.5 × 51.8
Displacement (cc)	99
Cylinder	
Standard bore diameter	49.508-49.523 mm (1.9491-1.9497 in.)
Service limit	49.61 mm (1.9531 in.)
Piston to cylinder clearance	0.032-0.042 mm (0.0013-0.0017 in.)
Piston rings	
End gap	0.15-0.65 mm (0.006-0.026 in.)
Crankshaft and connecting rod	
Crankpin to rod clearance, standard	0.034 mm (0.0013 in.)
Service limit	0.08 mm (0.003 in.)
Big end side play, standard	0.40 mm (0.016 in.)
Service limit	0.60 mm (0.024 in.)
Oil pump output/3 minutes @ 2000 rpm	2.8 cc (0.095 oz.)
Port timing (degrees, minutes)	
Rotary valve intake, open-close	120 BTDC-55 ATDC
Transfer ports	58, 35 from BDC
Exhaust port	84, 16 from BDC
Rotary valve thickness, standard	3.1 mm (0.12 in.)
Service limit	2.8 mm (0.11 in.)
Rotary valve cover depth, standard	3.4 mm (0.13 in.)
Service limit	4.0 mm (0.16 in.)
Clutch type	3
Transmission speeds	5 speeds (Type 1)
KM100	
General	
Bore and stroke (mm)	49.5 × 51.8
Displacement (cc)	99
Cylinder	
Standard bore diameter	
KM100-A1, A2, A3 & A4	49.5 mm (1.949 in.)

(continued)

Table 13 ENGINE SPECIFICATIONS (continued)

Standard bore diameter (continued)	
KM100-A6 & A7	49.518 mm (1.950 in.)
Service limit	49.58 mm (1.952 in.)
Piston to cylinder clearance	0.032-0.042 mm (0.0013-0.0017 in.)
Piston rings	
End gap	0.15-0.65 mm (0.006-0.026 in.)
Crankshaft and connecting rod	
Crankpin to rod clearance, standard	0.034 mm (0.0013 in.)
Service limit	0.08 mm (0.003 in.)
Big end side play, standard	0.40 mm (0.016 in.)
Service limit	0.60 mm (0.024 in.)
Oil pump output/3 minutes @ 2000 rpm	2.8 cc (0.095 oz.)
Port timing (degrees, minutes)	
Rotary valve intake, open-close	120 BTDC-55 ATDC
Transfer ports	58, 35 from BDC
Exhaust port	84, 16 from BDC
Rotary valve thickness	
KM100-A1, A2, A3 & A4, standard	3.1 mm (0.12 in.)
Service limit	2.8 mm (0.11 in.)
KM100-A6 & A7	0.7 mm (0.028in.)
Rotary valve cover depth	
KM100-A1, A2, A3 & A4, standard	3.4 mm (0.13 in.)
Service limit	4.0 mm (0.16 in.)
KM100-A6 & A7, standard	1.15 mm (0.045 in.)
Service limit	1.5 mm (0.06 in.)
Clutch type	3
Transmission speeds	5 speeds (Type 1)
KV100	
General	
Bore and stroke (mm)	49.5 × 51.8
Displacement (cc)	99
Cylinder	
Standard bore diameter	49.508-49.523 mm (1.9491-1.9497 in.)
Service limit	49.61 mm (1.9531 in.)
Piston to cylinder clearance	0.032-0.042 mm (0.0013-0.0017 in.)
Piston rings	
End gap	0.15-0.65 mm (0.006-0.026 in.)
Crankshaft and connecting rod	
Crankpin to rod clearance	0.034 mm (0.0013 in.)
Big end side play, standard	0.40 mm (0.016 in.)
Service limit	0.60 mm (0.024 in.)
Oil pump output/3 minutes @ 2000 rpm	2.8 cc (0.095 oz.)
Port timing (degrees, minutes)	
Rotary valve intake, open-close	120 BTDC-55 ATDC
Transfer ports	58, 35 from BDC
Exhaust port	84, 16 from BDC
Rotary valve thickness, standard	3.1 mm (0.12 in.)
Service limit	2.8 mm (0.11 in.)
Rotary valve cover depth, standard	3.4 mm (0.13 in.)
Service limit	4.0 mm (0.16 in.)
Clutch type	3
Transmission speeds	5 speeds 2 Ranges (Type 2)
115-125 cc models	
C2SS & C2TR	
General	
Bore and stroke (mm)	53 × 52.5
Displacement (cc)	115
Cylinder	
Standard bore diameter	53.0 mm (2.087 in.)
	(continued)

4

Table 13 ENGINE SPECIFICATIONS (continued)

Piston to cylinder clearance	0.004-0.040 mm (0.00016-0.0016 in.)
Piston rings	
End gap	0.15-0.30 mm (0.006-0.012 in.)
Crankshaft and connecting rod	
Crankpin to rod clearance, standard	0.021 mm (0.0009 in.)
Service limit	0.20 mm (0.008 in.)
Big end side play, standard	0.28 mm (0.011 in.)
Service limit	0.45 mm (0.018 in.)
Oil pump output/3 minutes @ 2000 rpm	3.1 cc (0.11 oz)
Port timing (degrees, minutes)	
Rotary valve intake, open-close	
Early models	110 BTDC-45 ATDC
Later models	110 BTDC-55 ATDC
Transfer ports	
Early models	57, 30 from BDC
Later models	60 from BDC
Exhaust port	
Early models	78, 30 from BDC
Later models	82 from BDC
Rotary valve thickness, standard	3.1 mm (0.12 in.)
Service limit	2.8 mm (0.11 in.)
Rotary valve cover depth, standard	3.5 mm (0.14 in.)
Service limit	4.0 mm (0.16 in.)
Clutch type	4
Transmission speeds	
C2SS & C2TR (except 1969 C2TR)	4 speeds (Type 4)
C2TR (1969)	4 speeds 2 ranges (Type 4)****
F6	
General	
Bore and stroke (mm)	52 × 58.8
Displacement (cc)	124
Cylinder	
Standard bore diameter	52.0 mm (2.047 in.)
Piston to cylinder clearance	0.072 mm (0.0028 in.)
Piston rings	
End gap	0.15-0.65 mm (0.006-0.026 in.)
Crankshaft and connecting rod	
Crankpin to rod clearance, standard	0.014 mm (0.0006 in.)
Service limit	0.06 mm (0.0023 in.)
Big end side play, standard	0.38 mm (0.015 in.)
Service limit	0.60 mm (0.024 in.)
Oil pump output/3 minutes @ 2000 rpm	4.1 cc (0.14 oz.)
Port timing (degrees, minutes)	
Rotary valve intake, open-close	115 BTDC-55 ATDC
Transfer ports	57, 30 from BDC
Exhaust port	87 from BDC
Rotary valve thickness, standard	3.1 mm (0.12 in.)
Service limit	2.8 mm (0.11 in.)
Rotary valve cover depth, standard	3.5 mm (0.14 in.)
Service limit	4.0 mm (0.16 in.)
Clutch type	1
Transmission speeds	5 speeds (Type 3)
KD125	
General	
Bore and stroke (mm)	56.0 × 50.6
Displacement (cc)	124
Cylinder	
Standard bore diameter	56.0 mm (2.205 in.)
Piston to cylinder clearance	0.069 mm (0.0027 in.)

(continued)

Table 13 ENGINE SPECIFICATIONS (continued)

Piston rings	
End gap	0.15-0.65 mm (0.006-0.026 in.)
Crankshaft and connecting rod	
Crankpin to rod clearance, standard	0.024 mm (0.0009 in.)
Service limit	0.08 mm (0.003 in.)
Big end side play, standard	0.375 mm (0.015 in.)
Service limit	0.60 mm (0.024 in.)
Oil pump output/3 minutes @ 2000 rpm	3.4 cc (0.115 oz.)
Port timing (degrees, minutes)	
Rotary valve intake, open-close	115 BTDC-55 ATDC
Transfer ports	56 from BDC
Exhaust port	83 from BDC
Rotary valve thickness, standard	0.4 mm (0.016 in.)
Service limit	0.25 mm (0.01 in.)
Rotary valve cover depth, standard	0.85 mm (0.003 in.)
Service limit	1.2 mm (0.047 in.)
Clutch type	5
Transmission speeds	6 speeds (Type 5)
KE125	
General	
Bore and stroke (mm)	56.0 × 50.6
Displacement (cc)	124
Cylinder	
Standard bore diameter	
KE125-A3, A4 & A5	56.0 mm (2.205 in.)
1979 & later (A6 on), standard	56.007 mm (2.205 in.)
Service limit	56.08 mm (2.208 in.)
Piston to cylinder clearance	
KE125-A3, A4 & A5	0.069 mm (0.0027 in.)
1979 & later (A6 on)	0.066 mm (0.0026 in.)
Piston rings	
End gap	0.15-0.65 mm (0.006-0.026 in.)
Crankshaft and connecting rod	
Crankpin to rod clearance, standard	0.024 mm (0.0009 in.)
Service limit	0.08 mm (0.003 in.)
Big end side play, standard	0.375 mm (0.015 in.)
Service limit	0.60 mm (0.024 in.)
Oil pump output/3 minutes @ 2000 rpm	3.4 cc (0.115 oz.)
Port timing (degrees, minutes)	
Rotary valve intake, open-close	115 BTDC-55 ATDC
Transfer ports	56 from BDC
Exhaust port	
KE125-A3, A4 & A5	83 from BDC
1979 & later (A6 on)	80 from BDC
Rotary valve thickness	
KE125-A3, A4 & A5, standard	0.4 mm (0.016 in.)
Service limit	0.25 mm (0.01 in.)
1979 & later (A6 on), standard	0.7 mm (0.028 in.)
Service limit	0.5 mm (0.02 in.)
Rotary valve cover depth	
KE125-A3, A4 & A5, standard	0.85 mm (0.033 in.)
Service limit	1.2 mm (0.047 in.)
1979 & later (A6 on), standard	0.85 mm (0.033 in.)
Service limit	1.5 mm (0.06 in.)
Clutch type	5
Transmission speeds	6 speeds (Type 5)
KS125	
General	
Bore and stroke (mm)	56.0 × 50.6
Displacement (cc)	124

(continued)

4

Table 13 ENGINE SPECIFICATIONS (continued)

Cylinder	
Standard bore diameter	56.0 mm (2.205 in.)
Piston to cylinder clearance	0.069 mm (0.0027 in.)
Piston rings	
End gap	0.15-0.65 mm (0.006-0.026 in.)
Crankshaft and connecting rod	
Crankpin to rod clearance, standard	0.024 mm (0.0009 in.)
Service limit	0.08 mm (0.003 in.)
Big end side play, standard	0.375 mm (0.015 in.)
Service limit	0.60 mm (0.024 in.)
Oil pump output/3 minutes @ 2000 rpm	3.4 cc (0.115 oz.)
Port timing (degrees, minutes)	
Rotary valve intake, open-close	115 BTDC-55 ATDC
Transfer ports	56 from BDC
Exhaust port	83 from BDC
Rotary valve thickness, standard	0.4 mm (0.016 in.)
Service limit	0.25 mm (0.01 in.)
Rotary valve cover depth, standard	0.85 mm (0.033 in.)
Service limit	1.2 mm (0.047 in.)
Clutch type	5
Transmission speeds	6 speeds (Type 5)
KX125 (1974-1976)	
General	
Bore and stroke (mm)	56.0 × 50.6
Displacement (cc)	124
Cylinder	
Standard bore diameter	56.01 mm (2.205 in.)
Piston to cylinder clearance	0.046 mm (0.0018 in.)
Piston rings	
End gap	0.15-0.65 mm (0.006-0.026 in.)
Crankshaft and connecting rod	
Crankpin to rod clearance, standard	0.024 mm (0.0009 in.)
Service limit	0.08 mm (0.003 in.)
Big end side play, standard	0.375 mm (0.015 in.)
Service limit	0.60 mm (0.024 in.)
Oil mix ratio	1 part oil to 20 parts gasoline
Port timing (degrees, minutes)	
Rotary valve intake, open-close	135 BTDC-65 ATDC
Transfer ports	64 from BDC
Exhaust port	92 from BDC
Rotary valve thickness, standard	0.4 mm (0.016 in.)
Service limit	0.25 mm (0.01 in.)
Rotary valve cover depth, standard	0.85 mm (0.033 in.)
Service limit	1.2 mm (0.047 in.)
Clutch type	5
Transmission speeds	6 speeds (Type 5)

169-175 cc models	
F2 & F2TR	
General	
Bore and stroke (mm)	62 × 56
Displacement (cc)	169
Cylinder	
Standard bore diameter	62.0 mm (2.441 in.)
Piston to cylinder clearance	0.072 mm (0.0028 in.)
Piston rings	
End gap	0.20-0.65 mm (0.008-0.026 in.)
Crankshaft and connecting rod	
Crankpin to rod clearance, standard	0.014 mm (0.0006 in.)
Service limit	0.06 mm (0.0023 in.)

(continued)

Table 13 ENGINE SPECIFICATIONS (continued)

Crankshaft and connecting rod (continued)	
Big end side play, standard	0.38 mm (0.015 in.)
Service limit	0.60 mm (0.024 in.)
Oil pump output/3 minutes @ 2000 rpm	5.5 cc (0.19 oz.)
Port timing (degrees, minutes)	
Rotary valve intake, open-close	110 BTDC-45 ATDC
Transfer ports	60 from BDC
Exhaust port	86 from BDC
Rotary valve thickness, standard	3.1 mm (0.12 in.)
Service limit	2.8 mm (0.11 in.)
Rotary valve cover depth, standard	3.5 mm (0.14 in.)
Service limit	4.0 mm (0.16 in.)
Clutch type	4
Transmission speeds	4 speeds (Type 4)
F3	
General	
Bore and stroke (mm)	62 × 56
Displacement (cc)	169
Cylinder	
Standard bore diameter	62.0 mm (2.441 in.)
Piston to cylinder clearance	0.072 mm (0.0028 in.)
Piston rings	
End gap	0.20-0.65 mm (0.008-0.026 in.)
Crankshaft and connecting rod	
Crankpin to rod clearance, standard	0.014 mm (0.0006 in.)
Service limit	0.06 mm (0.0023 in.)
Big end side play, standard	0.38 mm (0.015 in.)
Service limit	0.60 mm (0.024 in.)
Oil pump output/3 minutes @ 2000 rpm	5.5 cc (0.19 oz.)
Port timing (degrees, minutes)	
Rotary valve intake, open-close	110 BTDC-60 ATDC
Transfer ports	57, 46 from BDC
Exhaust port	86, 50 from BDC
Rotary valve thickness, standard	3.1 mm (0.12 in.)
Service limit	2.8 mm (0.11 in.)
Rotary valve cover depth, standard	3.5 mm (0.14 in.)
Service limit	4.0 mm (0.16 in.)
Clutch type	4
Transmission speeds	4 speeds (Type 4)
F7	
General	
Bore and stroke (mm)	61.5 × 58.8
Displacement (cc)	174
Cylinder	
Standard bore diameter	61.5 mm (2.421 in.)
Piston to cylinder clearance	0.064 mm (0.0025 in.)
Piston rings	
End gap	0.20-0.65 mm (0.008-0.026 in.)
Crankshaft and connecting rod	
Crankpin to rod clearance, standard	0.014 mm (0.0006 in.)
Service limit	0.06 mm (0.0023 in.)
Big end side play, standard	0.38 mm (0.015 in.)
Service limit	0.60 mm (0.024 in.)
Oil pump output/3 minutes @ 2000 rpm	5.5 cc (0.19 oz.)
Port timing (degrees, minutes)	
Rotary valve intake, open-close	115 BTDC-55 ATDC
Transfer ports	55, 30 from BDC
Exhaust port	82 from BDC

4

(continued)

Table 13 ENGINE SPECIFICATIONS (continued)

Rotary valve thickness, standard	3.1 mm (0.12 in.)
Service limit	2.8 mm (0.11 in.)
Rotary valve cover depth, standard	3.5 mm (0.14 in.)
Service limit	4.0 mm (0.16 in.)
Clutch type	1
Transmission speeds	5 speeds (Type 3)
KD175 (1976-1979) & KE175 (1976-1982)	
General	
Bore and stroke (mm)	61.5 × 58.8
Displacement (cc)	174
Cylinder	
Standard bore diameter	61.5 mm (2.421 in.)
Piston to cylinder clearance	0.040 mm (0.0016 in.)
Piston rings	
End gap	0.20-0.65 mm (0.008-0.026 in.)
Crankshaft and connecting rod	
Crankpin to rod clearance, standard	0.019 mm (0.0007 in.)
Service limit	0.07 mm (0.0028 in.)
Big end side play, standard	0.375 mm (0.015 in.)
Service limit	0.60 mm (0.024 in.)
Oil pump output/3 minutes @ 2000 rpm	4.1 cc (0.14 oz.)
Port timing (degrees, minutes)	
Rotary valve intake, open-close	115 BTDC-55 ATDC
Transfer ports	55 from BDC
Exhaust port	83 from BDC
Rotary valve thickness, standard	0.7 mm (0.028 in.)
Service limit	0.5 mm (0.02 in.)
Rotary valve cover depth, standard	1.15 mm (0.045 in.)
Service limit	1.5 mm (0.060 in.)
Clutch type	5
Transmission speeds	5 speeds (Type 3)
238-350 cc models	
F4	
General	
Bore and stroke (mm)	70 × 62
Displacement (cc)	238
Cylinder	
Standard bore diameter	70.0 mm (2.756 in.)
Piston to cylinder clearance	0.082 mm (0.003 in.)
Piston rings	
End gap	0.20-0.65 mm (0.008-0.026 in.)
Crankshaft and connecting rod	
Crankpin to rod clearance, standard	0.014 mm (0.0006 in.)
Service limit	0.06 mm (0.0023 in.)
Big end side play, standard	0.43 mm (0.017 in.)
Service limit	0.60 mm (0.024 in.)
Oil pump output/3 minutes @ 2000 rpm	6.0 cc (0.20 oz.)
Port timing (degrees, minutes)	
Rotary valve intake, open-close	110 BTDC-45 ATDC
Transfer ports	57, 30 from BDC
Exhaust port	78, 30 from BDC
Rotary valve thickness, standard	3.1 mm (0.12 in.)
Service limit	2.8 mm (0.11 in.)
Rotary valve cover depth, standard	3.5 mm (0.14 in.)
Service limit	4.0 mm (0.16 in.)
Clutch type	4
Transmission speeds	4 speeds (Type 4)

(continued)

Table 13 ENGINE SPECIFICATIONS (continued)

F21M

General	
Bore and stroke (mm)	70×62
Displacement (cc)	238
Cylinder	
Standard bore diameter	70.0 mm (2.756 in.)
Piston to cylinder clearance	0.127 mm (0.005 in.)
Piston rings	
End gap	0.20-0.65 mm (0.008-0.026 in.)
Crankshaft and connecting rod	
Crankpin to rod clearance, standard	0.014 mm (0.0006 in.)
Service limit	0.06 mm (0.0023 in.)
Big end side play, standard	0.43 mm (0.017 in.)
Service limit	0.60 mm (0.024 in.)
Oil mix ratio	1 part oil to 20 parts gasoline
Port timing (degrees, minutes)	
Rotary valve intake, open-close	120 BTDC-60 ATDC
Transfer ports	62 from BDC
Exhaust port	85 from BDC
Rotary valve thickness, standard	3.1 mm (0.12 in.)
Service limit	2.8 mm (0.11 in.)
Rotary valve cover depth, standard	3.5 mm (0.14 in.)
Service limit	4.0 mm (0.16 in.)
Clutch type	4
Transmission speeds	4 speeds (Type 4)

F8

General	
Bore and stroke (mm)	68×68
Displacement (cc)	246.8
Cylinder	
Standard bore diameter	68.0 mm (2.667 in.)
Piston to cylinder clearance	0.157 mm (0.006 in.)
Piston rings	
End gap	0.20-0.65 mm (0.008-0.026 in.)
Crankshaft and connecting rod	
Crankpin to rod clearance, standard	0.05 mm (0.0019 in.)
Service limit	0.06 mm (0.0023 in.)
Big end side play, standard	0.43 mm (0.017 in.)
Service limit	0.60 mm (0.024 in.)
Oil pump output/3 minutes @ 2000 rpm	6.0 cc (0.20 oz.)
Port timing (degrees, minutes)	
Rotary valve intake, open-close	110 BTDC-50 ATDC
Transfer ports	59 from BDC
Exhaust port	83 from BDC
Rotary valve thickness, standard	0.5 mm (0.02 in.)
Service limit	0.4 mm (0.01 in.)
Rotary valve cover depth, standard	0.8 mm (0.03 in.)
Clutch type	1
Transmission speeds	5 speed (Type 6)

F81M

General	
Bore and stroke (mm)	68×68
Displacement (cc)	246.8
Cylinder	
Standard bore diameter	68.0 mm (2.667 in.)
Piston to cylinder clearance	0.082 mm (0.003 in.)
Piston rings	
End gap	0.20-0.65 mm (0.008-0.026 in.)

4

(continued)

Table 13 ENGINE SPECIFICATIONS (continued)

Crankshaft and connecting rod	
Crankpin to rod clearance, standard	0.05 mm (0.0019 in.)
Service limit	0.06 mm (0.0023 in.)
Big end side play, standard	0.43 mm (0.017 in.)
Service limit	0.60 mm (0.024 in.)
Oil mix ratio	1 part oil to 20 parts gasoline
Port timing (degrees, minutes)	
Rotary valve intake, open-close	130 BTDC-65 ATDC
Transfer ports	59 from BDC
Exhaust port	87, 40 from BDC
Rotary valve thickness, standard	0.5 mm (0.02 in.)
Service limit	0.4 mm (0.01 in.)
Rotary valve cover depth, standard	0.8 mm (0.03 in.)
Clutch type	1
Transmission speeds	5 speed (Type 6)
F5	
General	
Bore and stroke (mm)	80.5 × 68
Displacement (cc)	346
Cylinder	
Standard bore diameter	80.5 mm (3.169 in.)
Piston to cylinder clearance	0.20 mm (0.0078 in.)
Piston rings	
End gap	0.25-0.65 mm (0.010-0.026 in.)
Crankshaft and connecting rod	
Crankpin to rod clearance, standard	0.05 mm (0.0019 in.)
Service limit	0.06 mm (0.0023 in.)
Big end side play, standard	0.43 mm (0.017 in.)
Service limit	0.60 mm (0.024 in.)
Oil pump output/3 minutes @ 2000 rpm	10.0 cc (0.34 oz.)
Port timing (degrees, minutes)	
Rotary valve intake, open-close	110 BTDC-50 ATDC
Transfer ports	57 from BDC
Exhaust port	82 from BDC
Rotary valve thickness, standard	0.5 mm (0.02 in.)
Service limit	0.4 mm (0.01 in.)
Rotary valve cover depth, standard	0.8 mm (0.03 in.)
Clutch type	1
Transmission speeds	5 speed (Type 6)
F9	
General	
Bore and stroke (mm)	80.5 × 68
Displacement (cc)	346
Cylinder	
Standard bore diameter	80.5 mm (3.169 in.)
Piston to cylinder clearance	0.10 mm (0.004 in.)
Piston rings	
End gap	0.25-0.65 mm (0.010-0.026 in.)
Crankshaft and connecting rod	
Crankpin to rod clearance, standard	0.05 mm (0.0019 in.)
Service limit	0.06 mm (0.0023 in.)
Big end side play, standard	0.43 mm (0.017 in.)
Service limit	0.60 mm (0.024 in.)
Oil pump output/3 minutes @ 2000 rpm	10.0 cc (0.34 oz.)
Port timing (degrees, minutes)	
Rotary valve intake, open-close	120 BTDC-60 ATDC
Transfer ports	57 from BDC
Exhaust port	82 from BDC

(continued)

Table 13 ENGINE SPECIFICATIONS (continued)

Rotary valve thickness, standard	0.5 mm (0.02 in.)
Service limit	0.4 mm (0.01 in.)
Rotary valve cover depth, standard	0.8 mm (0.03 in.)
Clutch type	1
Transmission speeds	5 speed (Type 6)

* The 4 speed transmission of J Series motorcycles is similar to Type 1.

** Exhaust port timing for G3SS-C, G3SS-D, G3TR-C & G3TR-D models is 83° from BDC.

*** The transmission shift forks of 1980 and later KE100 (A9 B13) models are located by shift rails similar to Type 5.

**** The transmission of 1969 C2TR motorcycles is four speed (Type 4), but with a two speed range similar to that used on G4TR models (Type 2).

4

CHAPTER FIVE

FUEL SYSTEM

For proper operation, a gasoline engine must be supplied with fuel and air, mixed in the proper proportions by weight. A mixture in which there is an excess of fuel is said to be rich. A lean mixture is one which contains insufficient fuel. It is the function of the carburetors to supply the proper mixture to the engine under all operating conditions.

Kawasaki machines are equipped with Mikuni carburetors. Service procedures are similar for the various carburetors. Differences are pointed out where they exist. Carburetors may be of either independent float or twin float type.

Tables 1-5 are found at the end of the chapter.

CARBURETION OPERATION

The essential functional parts of Kawasaki carburetors are a float and a float valve mechanism for maintaining a constant fuel level in the float bowl, a pilot system for supplying fuel at low speeds, a main fuel system which supplies the engine at medium and high speeds and a starter system, which supplies the very rich mixture needed to start a cold engine. The operation of each system is discussed in the following paragraphs.

Float Mechanism

Figure 1 illustrates a typical float mechanism. Proper operation of the carburetor is dependent on maintaining a constant fuel level in the carburetor bowl. As fuel is drawn from the float bowl, the float level drops. When the float drops, the float needle valve moves away from its seat and allows fuel to

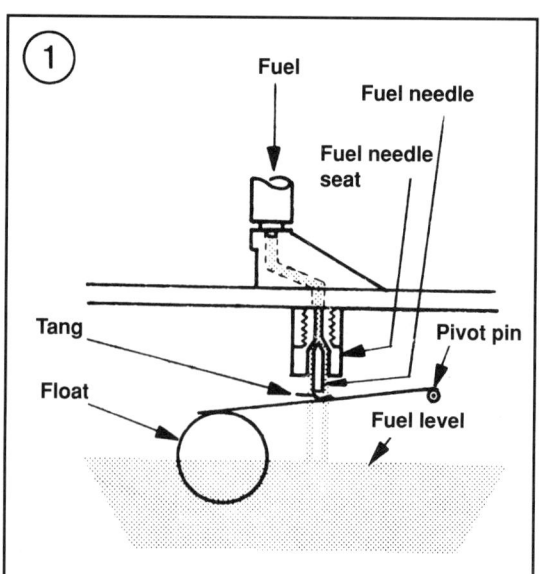

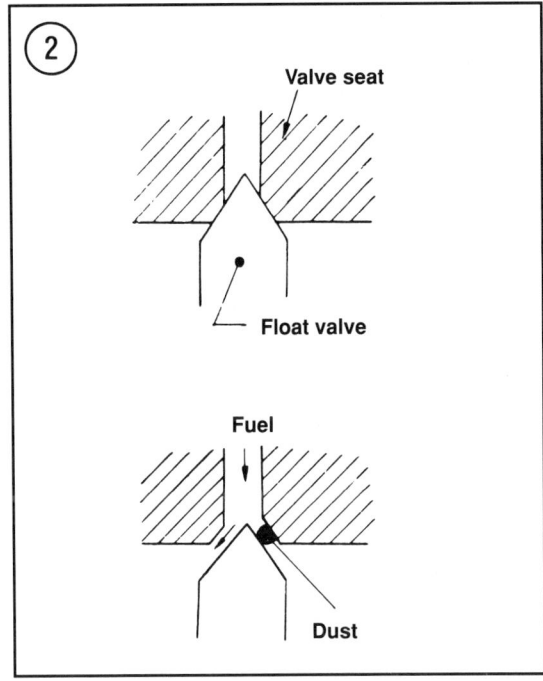

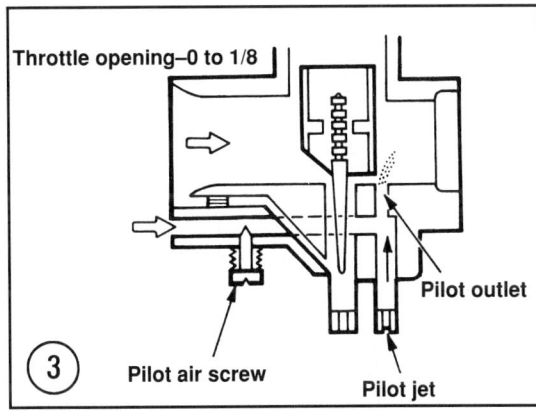

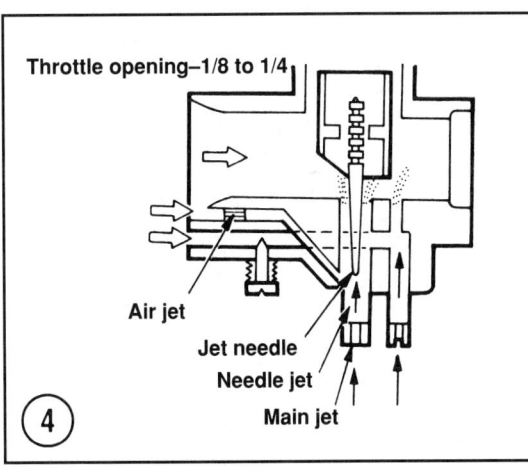

flow past the valve and seat into the float bowl. As this occurs, the float is then raised, pressing the needle valve against its seat, thereby shutting off fuel flow. It can be seen from this discussion that a small piece of dirt can be trapped between the valve and seat, preventing the valve from closing and allowing fuel to rise beyond the normal level, resulting in flooding. **Figure 2** illustrates this condition.

Pilot System

Under idle or low speed conditions, at less than 1/8 throttle, the engine doesn't require much fuel or air and the throttle valve is almost closed. A separate pilot system is required for operation under such conditions. **Figure 3** illustrates the operation of the pilot system. Air is drawn through the pilot air inlet and controlled by the pilot air screw. This air is then mixed with fuel drawn through the pilot jet. The air/fuel mixture then travels from the pilot outlet into the main air passage, where it is further mixed with air prior to being drawn into the engine. The pilot air screw controls the idle mixture.

If proper idle and low speed mixture cannot be obtained within the normal adjustment range of the idle mixture screw, refer to **Table 1**.

Main Fuel System

As the throttle is opened still more, up to about 1/4 open, the pilot circuit begins to supply less of the mixture to the engine, as the main fuel system, illustrated in **Figure 4**, begins to function. The main jet, the needle jet, the jet needle and the air jet make up the main fuel circuit. As the throttle valve opens more than about 1/8 of its travel, air is drawn through the main port and passes under the throttle valve in the main bore. The velocity of the air stream results in reduced pressure around the jet needle. Fuel then passes through the main jet, past the needle jet and jet needle and into the air stream where it is atomized and sent to the carburetor. As the throttle valve opens, more air flows through the carburetor and the jet needle, which is attached to the throttle slide, rises to permit more fuel to flow.

A portion of the air bled past the air jet passes through the needle jet bleed air inlet into the needle jet, where the air is mixed with the main air stream and atomized.

Airflow at small throttle openings is controlled primarily by the cutaway on the throttle slide. As the throttle is opened wider, up to about 3/4 open, the circuit draws air from 2 sources, as shown in **Figure 5**. The first source is air passing through the venturi; the second source is through the air jet. Air passing through the venturi draws fuel through the needle jet. The jet needle is tapered and therefore allows more fuel to pass. Air passing through the air jet passes to the needle jet to aid atomization of the fuel there.

Figure 6 illustrates the circuit at high speeds. The jet needle is withdrawn almost completely from the needle jet. Fuel flow is then controlled by the main jet. Air passing through the air jet continues to aid atomization of the fuel as described in the previous paragraphs.

Any dirt which collects in the main jet or in the needle jet obstructs fuel flow and causes a lean mixture. Any clogged air passage, such as the air bleed opening or air jet, may result in an overrich mixture. Other causes of a rich mixture are a worn needle jet, loose needle jet, or loose main jet. If the jet needle is worn, it should be replaced, however it may be possible to effect a temporary repair by placing the needle jet clip in a higher groove.

Starter System

A cold engine requires a mixture which is far richer than normal. **Figure 7** illustrates the starter system. When the rider operates the lever, the starter plunger (13) is pulled upward. As the engine is cranked, suction from the engine draws fuel through the starter jet (10). This fuel is then mixed with air from the bleed air port (11) in the float chamber (12). This mixture is further mixed with primary air coming through the air passage (14) and is the delivered to the engine through the port (15) behind the throttle valve. Note that the mixture from the starter system is mixed with that from the pilot system.

CARBURETOR OVERHAUL

There is no set rule regarding frequency of carburetor overhaul. A carburetor used on a machine used primarily for street riding may go 5,000 miles without attention. If the machine is used in dirt, the carburetor might need an overhaul in less than 1,000 miles. Poor engine performance, hesitation and little response to idle mixture adjustment are all symptoms of possible carburetor malfunctions. As a general rule, it is good practice to overhaul the carburetor each time you perform a routine decarbonization of the engine.

Disassembly, Independent Float Carburetors

Figure 8 is an exploded view of a typical independent float carburetor. Refer to this illustration during disassembly.

1. Remove the mixing chamber cap (**Figure 9**), if this step was not done previously.

2. Remove the spring, then pull out the throttle slide (**Figure 10**).

3. Remove both vent tubes (**Figure 11**).

4. Remove 4 retaining screws, then pull off the float bowl (**Figure 12**). Note carefully how each float is installed (**Figure 13**).

5. Pull out the float lever pivot pin (**Figure 14**). Note carefully how the float lever is installed; it is possible to put it back in upside-down.

6. Pull out the float needle valve (**Figure 15**), then its seat (**Figure 16**). Note the location of each fiber washer as it is removed.

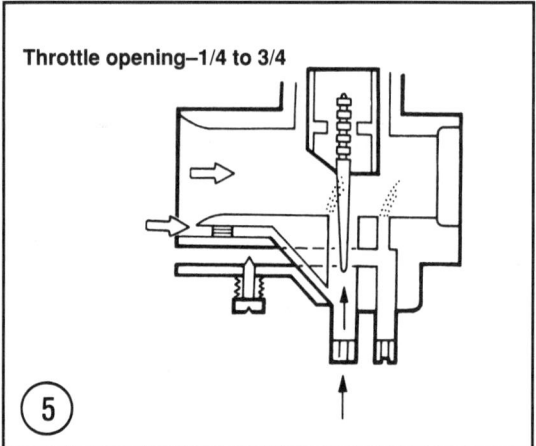

Throttle opening–1/4 to 3/4

⑤

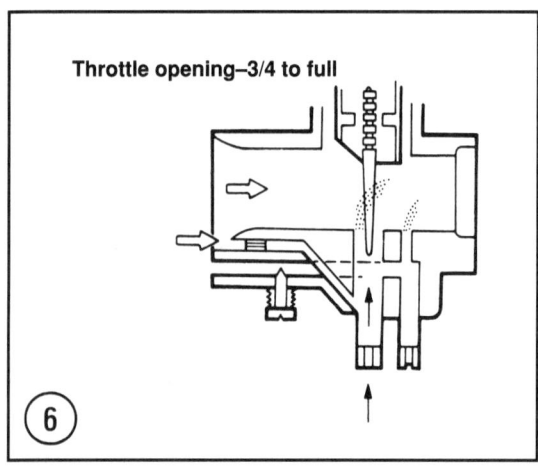

Throttle opening–3/4 to full

⑥

7. Remove the main jet (**Figure 17**) and with it, the needle jet retaining washer. Note which side of the washer goes up.

8. Turn the carburetor so that the needle jet falls out (**Figure 18**). Be sure to catch it as it falls; it is of soft brass and may be damaged otherwise. Note that there is a locating groove on the needle jet.

9. Remove the pilot jet (**Figure 19**).

10. Flatten the lock tab, then remove the retaining nut (**Figure 20**) to remove the starter plunger assembly.

11. Remove the idle mixture (pilot air) screw (**Figure 21**).

12. Remove the idle speed screw (**Figure 22**)

13. Reverse Steps 1 through 12 for reassembly.

NOTE
*1978 and later models have a floating, spring loaded jet needle (**Figure 23**). Proper installation of the jet needle in the throttle slide is necessary for proper operation. Insert the parts in the throttle valve in this order: needle spring, thin spacer, jet needle with clip in proper groove, thick spacer, throttle spring seat with its projection facing down.*

Twin Float Carburetor Disassembly

Figure 24 is an exploded view of a typical twin float carburetor. Refer to this illustration during disassembly.

1. Remove the ring nut from the mixing chamber (**Figure 25**) if this step was not done previously.

2. Remove the throttle slide (**Figure 26**).

3. Remove 4 retaining screws, then pull off the float bowl (**Figure 27**).

4. Pull out the float pivot shaft (**Figure 28**) to remove the float assembly. Handle this float gently to prevent bending.

5. Remove the main jet and needle jet as a unit (**Figure 29**), by unscrewing the needle jet from the carburetor body.

6. Separate the main jet from the needle jet (**Figure 30**).

7. Remove the pilot jet (**Figure 31**).

8. Remove the starter plunger assembly by loosening its spring cover (**Figure 32**). Be careful, since the spring is under compression.

9. Remove the pilot air screw (**Figure 33**).

10. Remove the float needle valve assembly (**Figure 34**).

11. To disassemble the throttle slide assembly, remove the cotter pin (**Figure 35**).

12. Push the jet needle out from the throttle slide (**Figure 36**).

13. Reverse Steps 1 through 12 for reassembly.

NOTE
*1978 and later models have a floating, spring loaded jet needle (**Figure 37**). Proper installation of the jet needle in the throttle slide is necessary for proper*

5

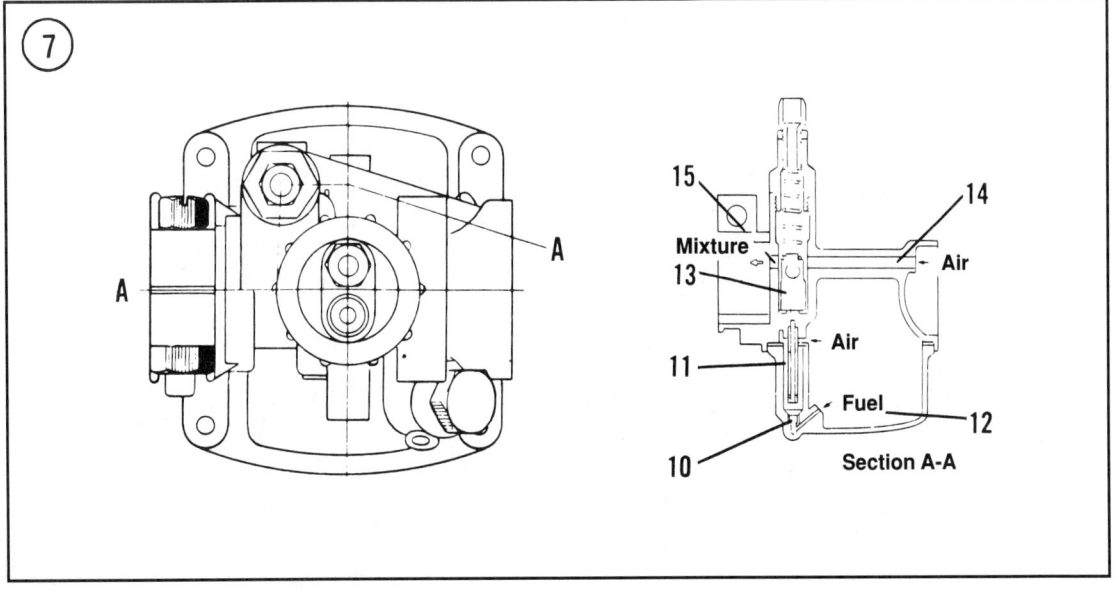

TYPICAL INDEPENDENT FLOAT CARBURETOR

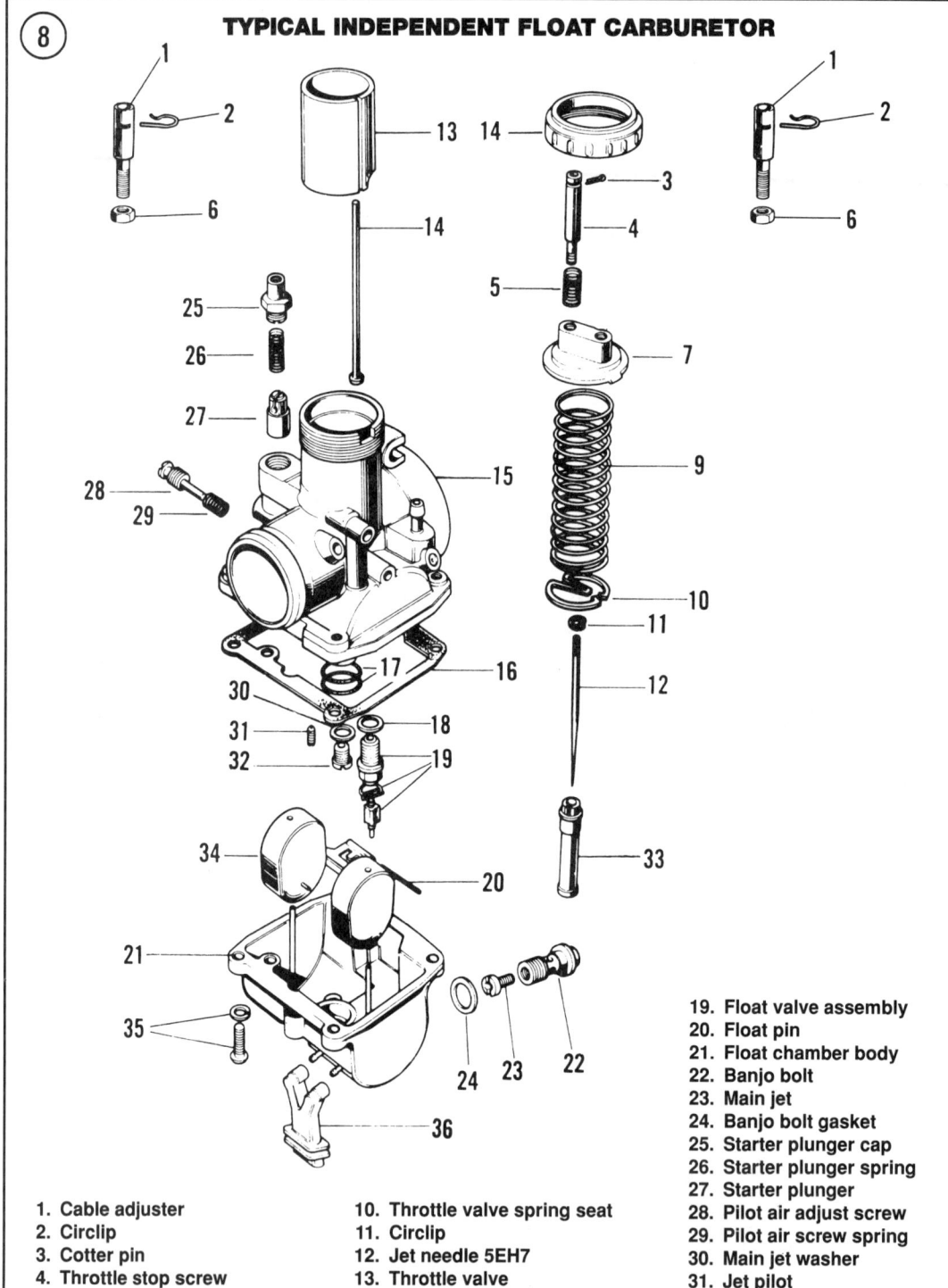

1. Cable adjuster
2. Circlip
3. Cotter pin
4. Throttle stop screw
5. Throttle stop screw spring
6. Cable adjuster locknut
7. Mixing chamber top
8. Mixing chamber cap
9. Throttle valve spring
10. Throttle valve spring seat
11. Circlip
12. Jet needle 5EH7
13. Throttle valve
14. Throttle valve stop rod
15. Mixing chamber body
16. Float chamber gasket
17. V-ring
18. Float valve seat washer
19. Float valve assembly
20. Float pin
21. Float chamber body
22. Banjo bolt
23. Main jet
24. Banjo bolt gasket
25. Starter plunger cap
26. Starter plunger spring
27. Starter plunger
28. Pilot air adjust screw
29. Pilot air screw spring
30. Main jet washer
31. Jet pilot
32. Main jet
33. Needle jet
34. Float
35. Float chamber screw
36. Overflow pipe grommet

operation. Insert the parts in the throttle valve in this order: needle spring, thin spacer, jet needle with clip in proper groove, thick spacer, throttle spring seat with its projection facing down.

Inspection

Shake the float to check for gasoline inside (**Figure 38**). If fuel leaks into the float, the float chamber fuel level will rise, resulting in an overrich mixture. Replace the float if it is deformed or leaking.

Replace the float valve if its seating end is scratched or worn. Depress the float valve gently with your finger and make sure that the valve seats properly. If the float valve spring is weak, fuel will overflow, causing an overrich mixture and flooding the float chamber whenever the fuel petcock is open.

Clean all parts in carburetor cleaning solvent. Dry the parts with compressed air. Clean the jets and other delicate parts with compressed air after the float bowl has been removed. Use new gaskets upon reassembly.

Single Float Carburetor

The procedures for removing and servicing the single float carburetors (**Figure 39** and **Figure 40**)

used on some models are similar to other carburetors previously described.

CARBURETOR ADJUSTMENT

Carburetor adjustment is not normally required except for occasional adjustment of idling speed (see Chapter Three), or at time of carburetor overhaul. The adjustments described here should only be undertaken if the rider has definite reason to believe they are required.

Float/Arm Height Adjustment

The fuel level in the carburetor float bowl is critical to proper performance. The fuel flow rate from the bowl up to the carburetor bore depends not only on the vacuum in the throttle bore and the size of the jets, but also upon the fuel level. Kawasaki gives a specification of actual *fuel level, measured* from the lower lip of the carb body (**Figure 41**).

This measurement is more useful than a simple float height measurement because actual fuel level can vary from bike to bike, even when their floats are set at the same height. However, fuel level inspection requires a special fitting that screws into the bottom of the carburetor. You can get the proper

5

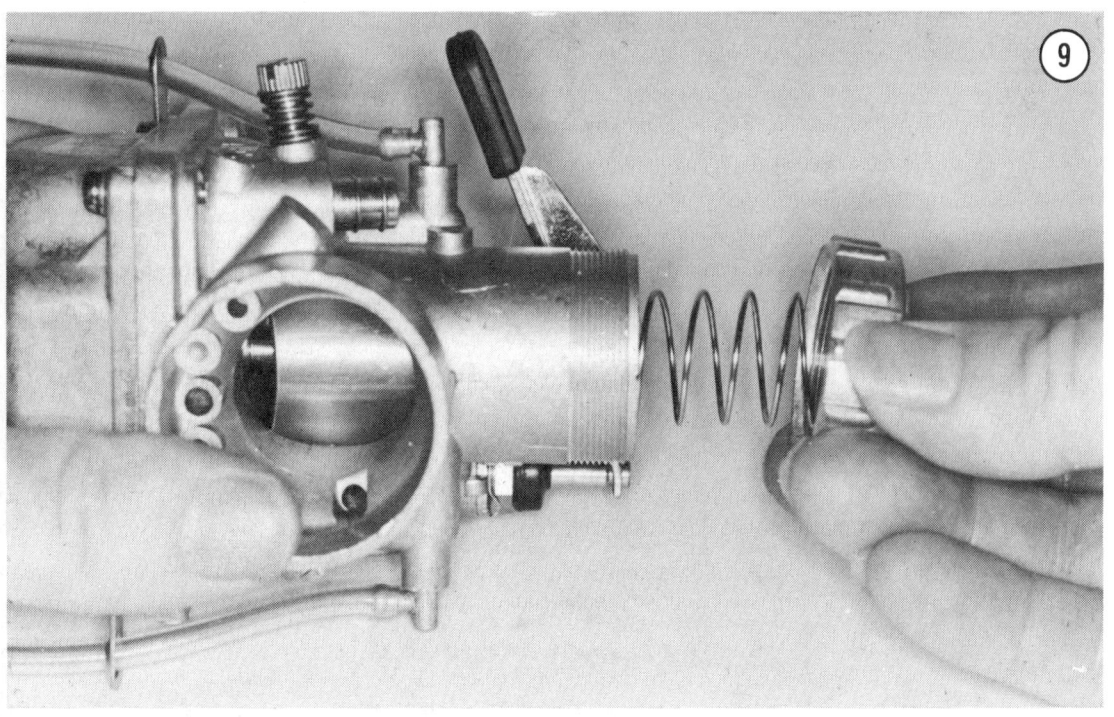

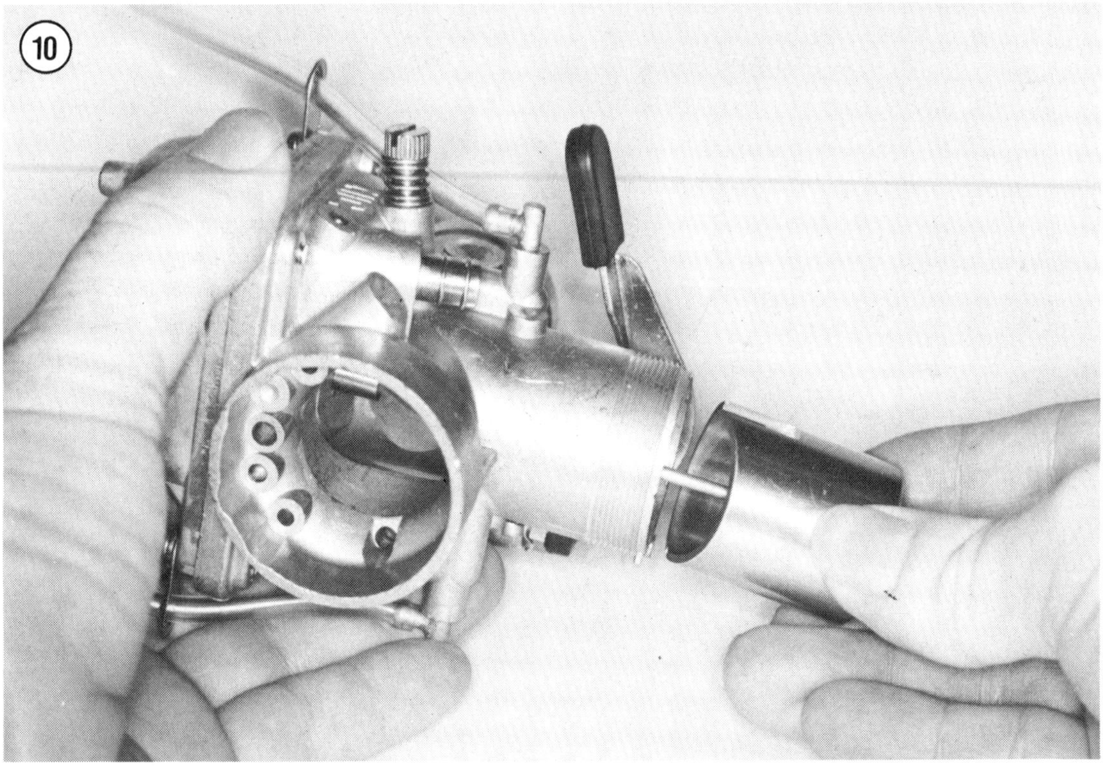

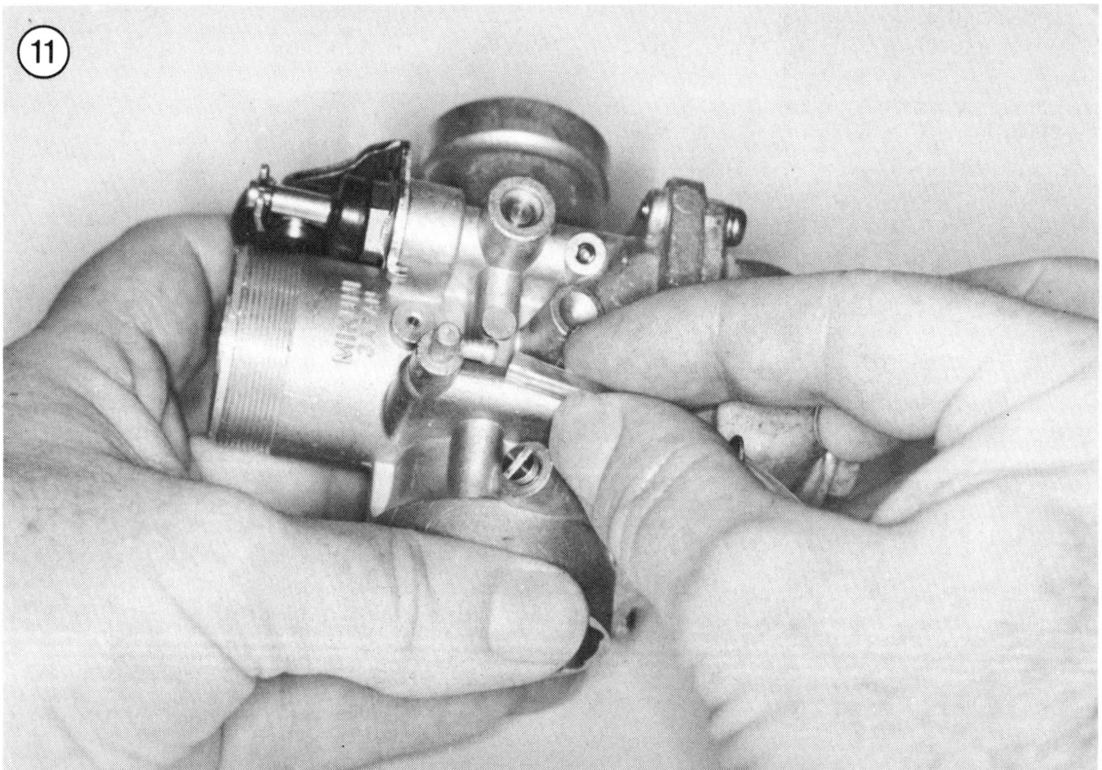

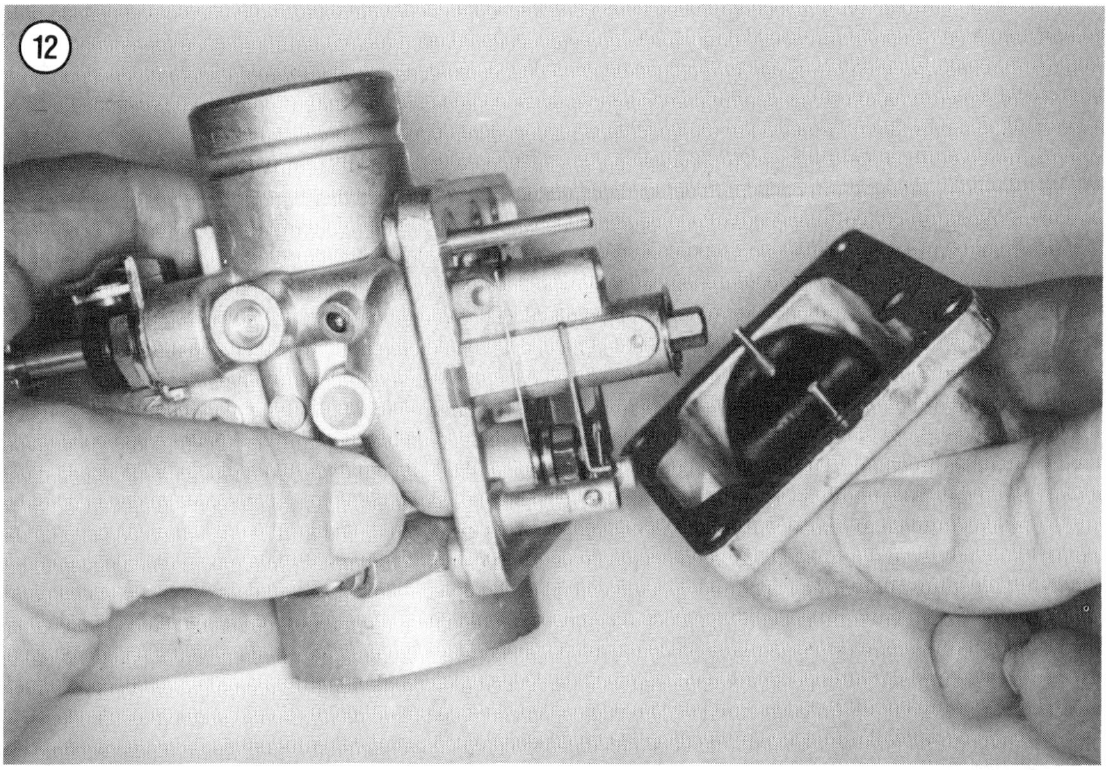
12

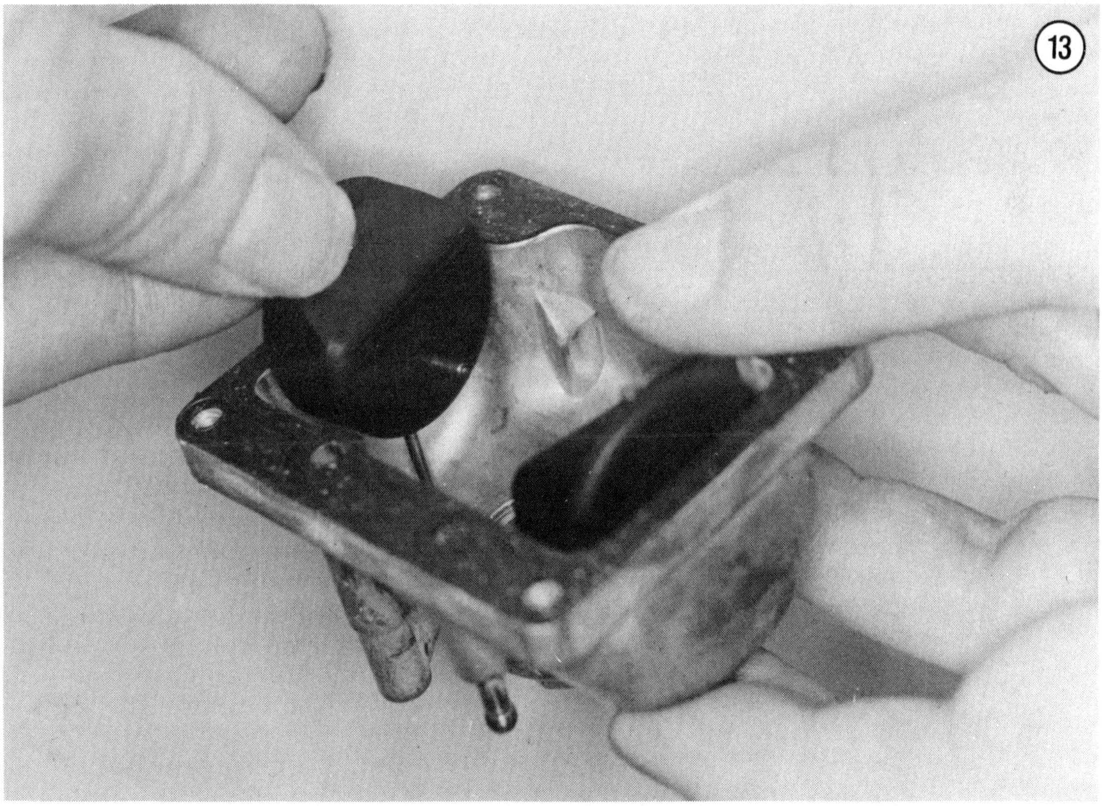
13

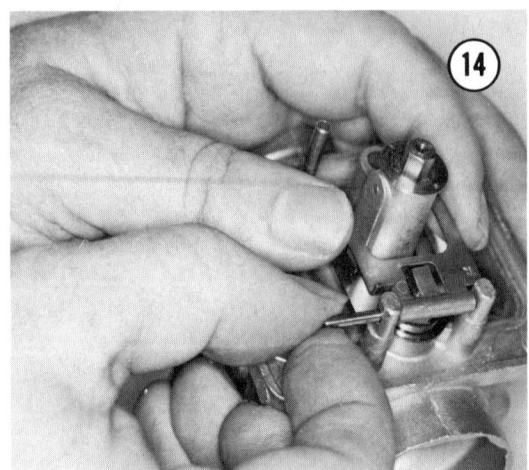

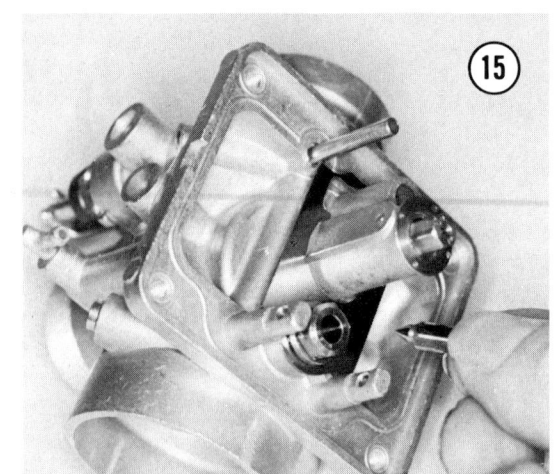

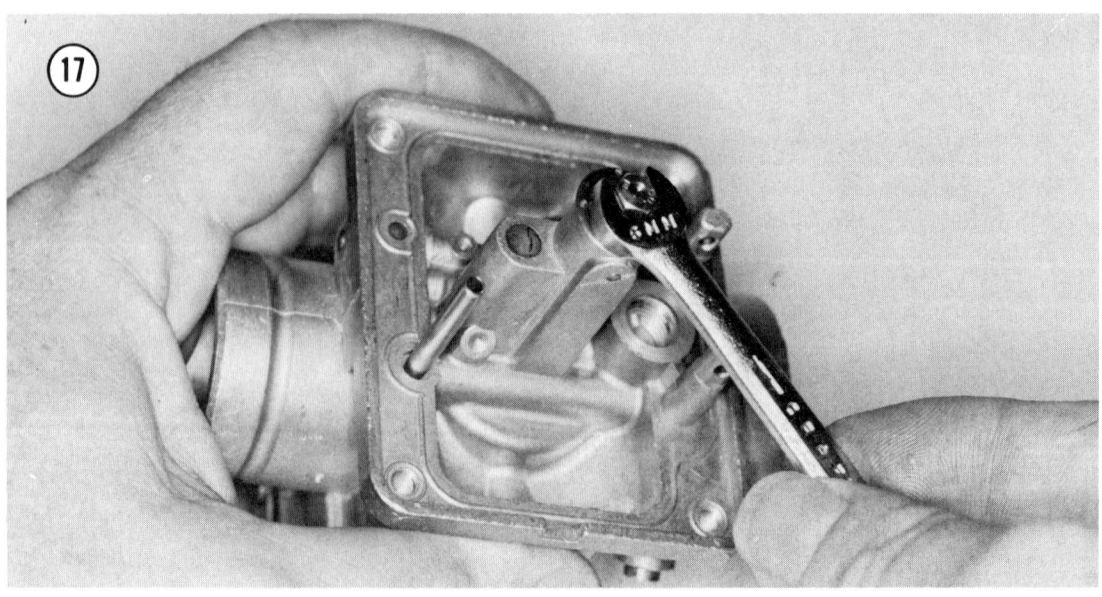

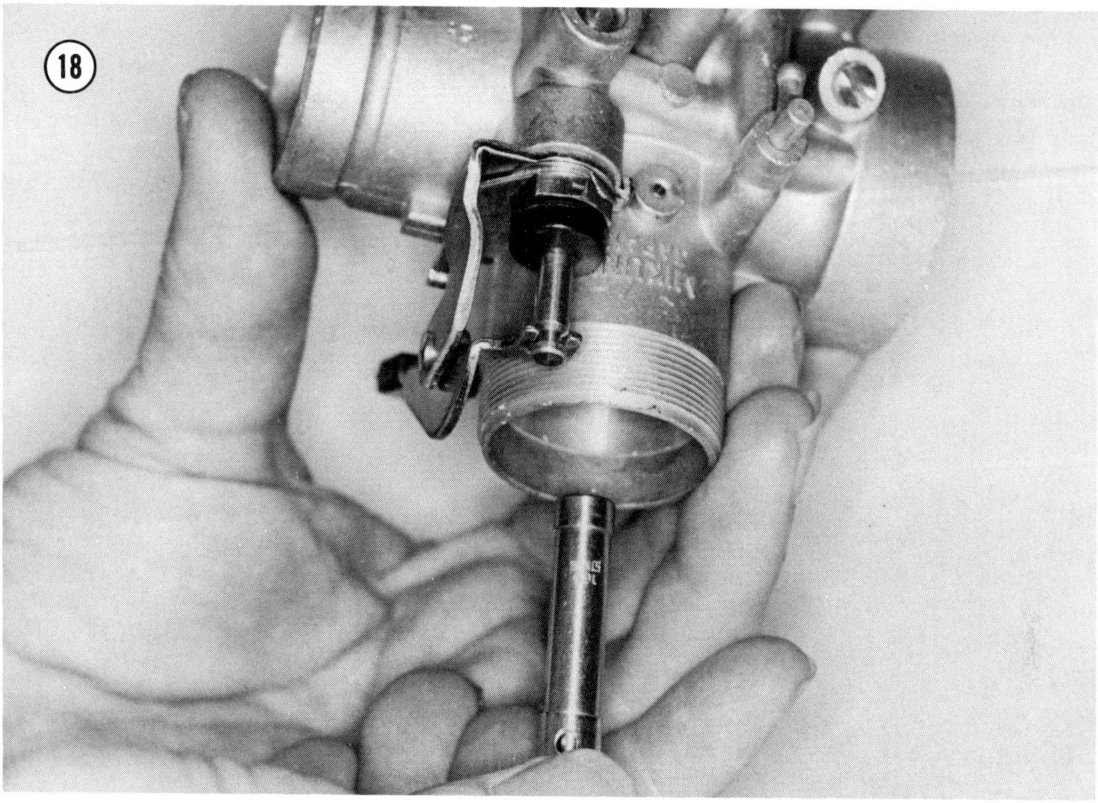
18

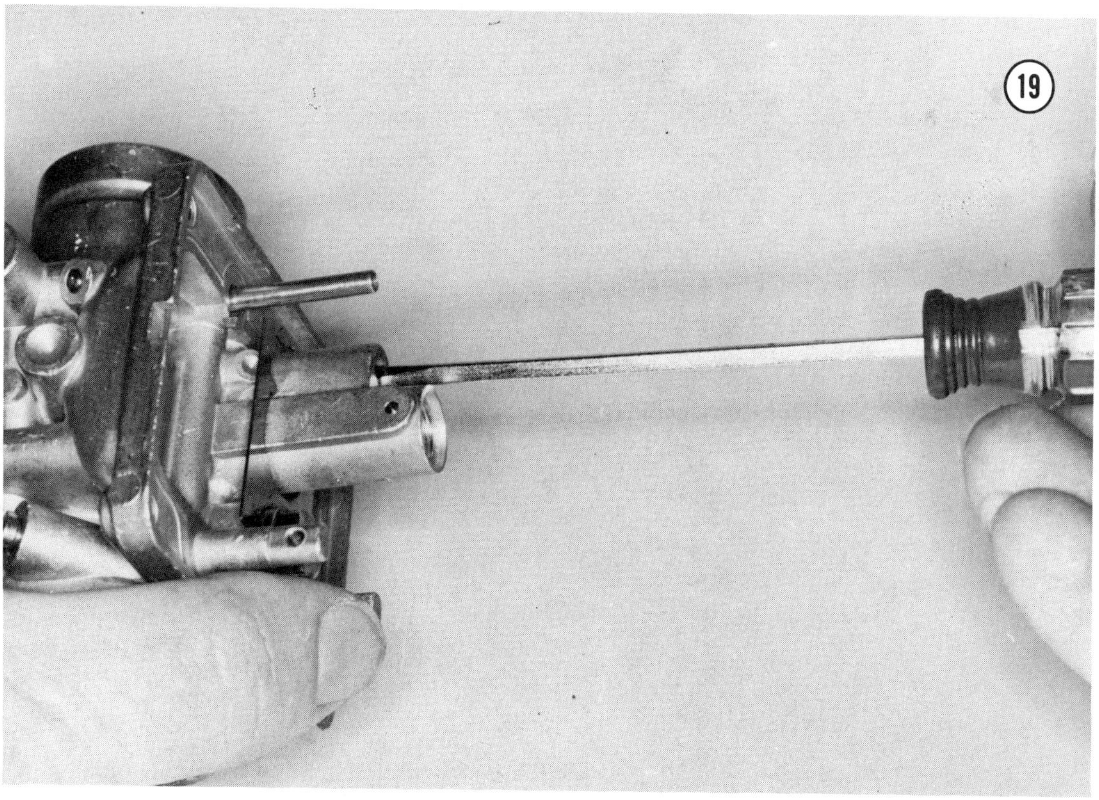
19

fitting at your Kawasaki dealer, or you can make one out of a cork and a piece of plastic tubing (**Figure 42**).

The fuel level is adjusted by bending the float arm tang and you can approximate the proper fuel level by setting the initial float/arm height.

Initial float/arm height setting

1. Remove the float bowl from the carburetor.

2. *On models with a one-piece float:* Hold the carburetor on its side so the float assembly doesn't compress the spring-loaded float needle and meas-

ure the distance from the metal float bowl gasket surface to the top of float (**Figure 43**). The float arm tang should be just touching the float needle.

3. *On models with separate floats:* Hold the carb upside-down and gently push the float arm down until the float arm tang just touches the float needle without compressing its spring. Measure the distance from the end of the float arm to the needle jet holder boss (**Figure 44**).

4. If the measurement differs from that specified in **Table 2**, bend the float tang as required to get the right float height.

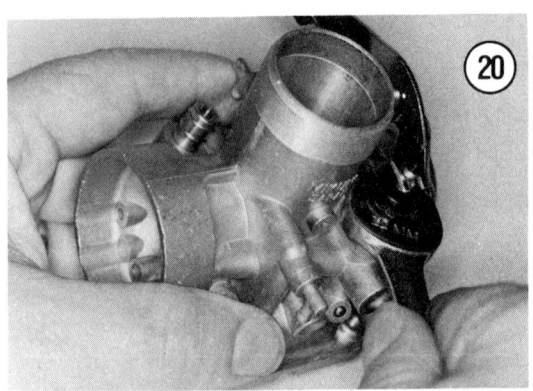

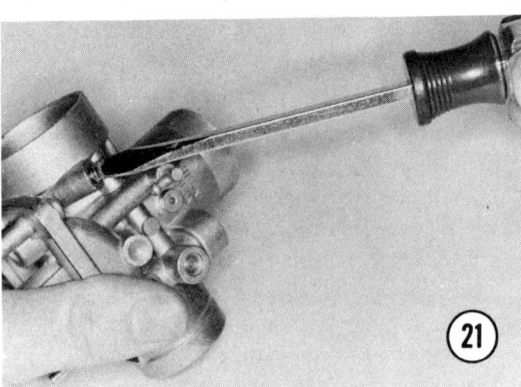

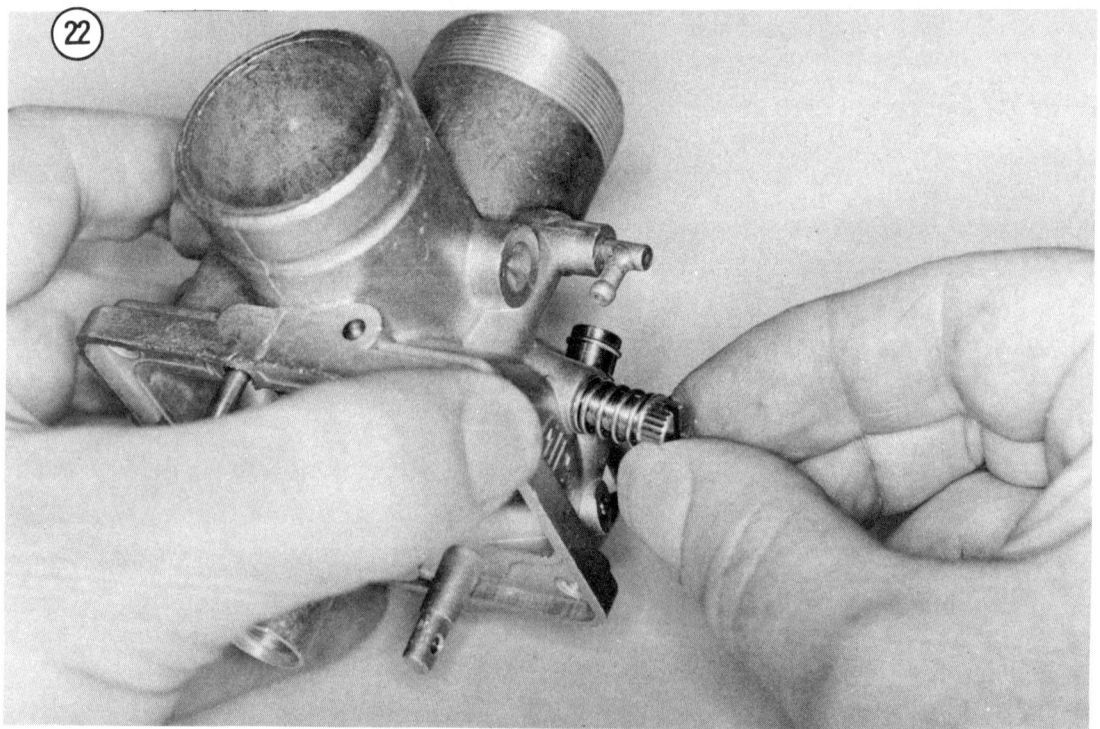

5. Install the float bowl.

Fuel level inspection

The fuel level in the carburetor bowl (float chamber) is critical to proper performance. The flow rate of fuel from the bowl up to the carburetor bore depends not only on the vacuum in the throttle bore and the size of the jets, but also on the height of the fuel. Kawasaki specifies the correct fuel level as the distance between the top edge of the float bowl and the level of the fuel in the float bowl (A, **Figure 41**). This check of the actual fuel level is more accurate than measuring float height and should be used whenever the correct fuel level is known.

To check fuel level, shut fuel off or remove the carburetor. Remove the main jet holder (22, **Figure 39**) or the drain plug (30, **Figure 40**) from the bottom of the float bowl and attach a suitable fuel level gauge (**Figure 42**). Hold the carburetor level and raise the clear plastic tube (B, **Figure 41**) of the gauge up against the side of the carburetor. If the carburetor is removed, temporarily attach the hose from the fuel tank and hold the carburetor level. Turn the fuel ON and wait for the level in the gauge tube to raise, then stabilize. Measure the distance (A, **Figure 41**) between the level of the fuel in the gauge tube and the top edge of the float bowl.

Check the specifications listed in **Table 2** and compare with the measured distance. If fuel level is too high, the inlet needle may be leaking or the float may need to be adjusted. If the fuel level is too low, the inlet needle may be stuck shut, the fuel tank may

be out of gasoline or the float may need to be adjusted.

If the fuel height is incorrect, turn fuel off and remove the float bowl from the carburetor. If the inlet needle is suspected of leaking or sticking, remove the float and correct the problem, then recheck fuel level. Bend the tang (**Figure 44**) up to lower the fuel level or down to raise the fuel level. Assemble the carburetor and recheck fuel level after any change.

> *NOTE*
> *Increasing the **float** height increases the fuel level measurement. Increasing the **float arm** measurement decreases the fuel level measurement.*

Speed Range Adjustments

The carburetor on your machine was designed to provide the proper mixture under all operating conditions. Little or no benefit will result from experimenting. However, unusual operating conditions such as sustained operation at high altitudes or unusually high or low temperatures may make modifications to the standard specifications desirable. The adjustments described in the following paragraphs should only be undertaken if the rider has definite reason to believe they are required. Make the tests and adjustments in the order specified.

Figure 46 illustrates typical carburetor components which may be changed to meet individual operating conditions. Shown left to right are the main jet, needle jet, jet needle and clip and throttle valve.

Make a road test at full throttle for final determination of main jet size. To make such a test, operate the motorcycle at full throttle for at least 2 minutes, then shut the engine off, release the clutch and bring the machine to a stop. If at full throttle, the engine runs "heavily," the main jet is too large. If the engine runs better by closing the throttle slightly, the main jet is too small. The engine will run at full throttle evenly and regularly if the main jet is the correct size.

After each such test, remove and examine the spark plug. The insulator should have a light tan color. If the insulator has black sooty deposits, the mixture is too rich. If there are signs of intense heat, such as a blistered white appearance, the mixture is too lean.

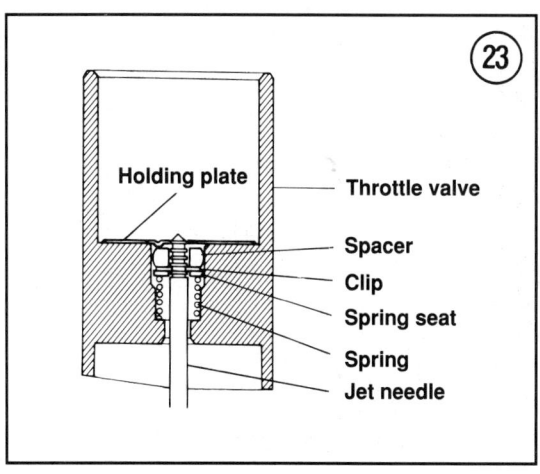

(23)

Holding plate — Throttle valve

— Spacer

— Clip

— Spring seat

— Spring

— Jet needle

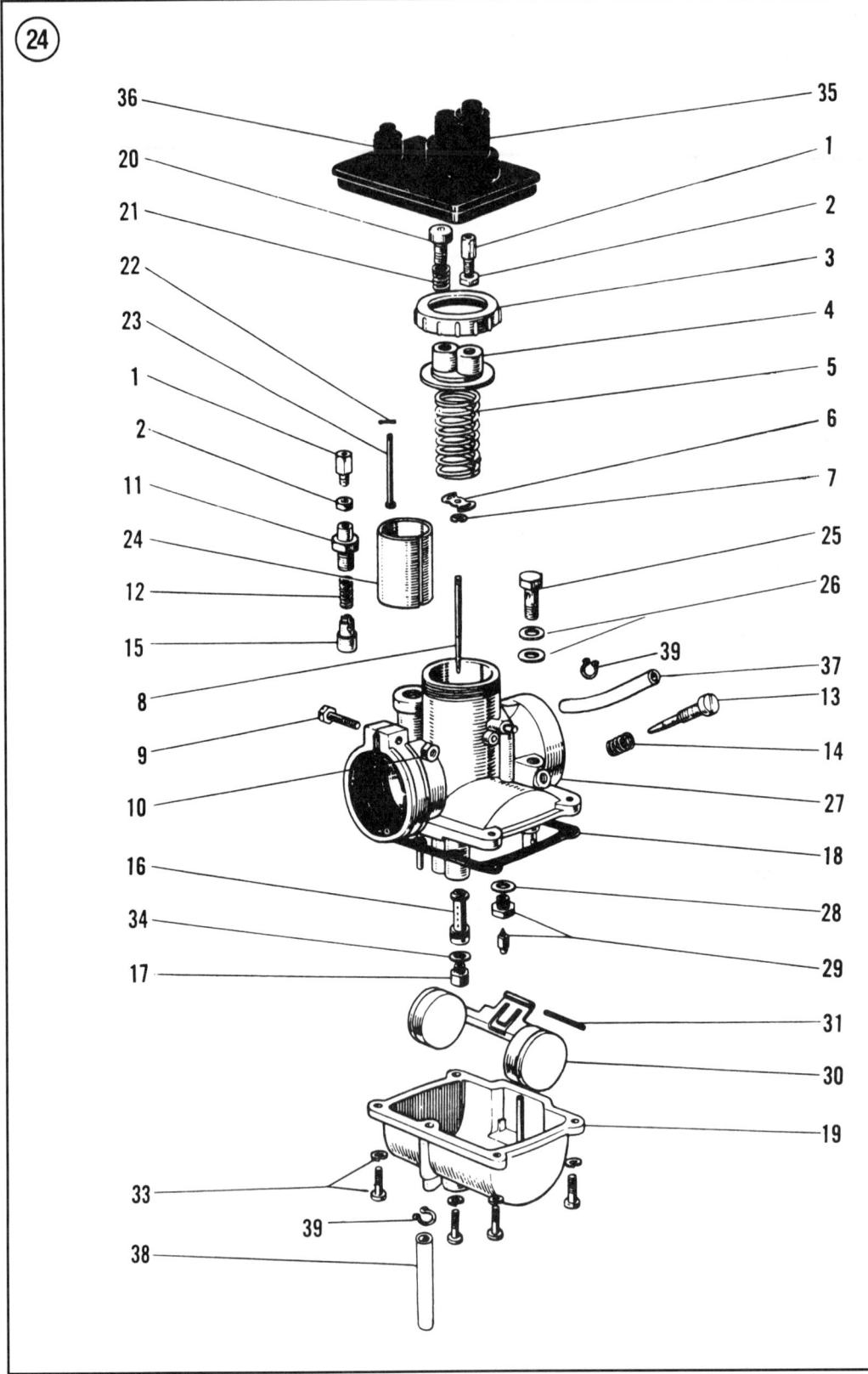

TYPICAL TWIN FLOAT CARBURETOR

1. Cable adjuster
2. Cable adjuster locknut
3. Mixing chamber cap
4. Mixing chamber top
5. Throttle valve spring
6. Throttle valve spring seat
7. Needle clip
8. Jet needle
9. Carburetor mounting clamp screw
10. Nut
11. Starter plunger cap
12. Starter plunger spring
13. Pilot air adjusting screw
14. Pilot air adjusting screw spring
15. Starter plunger
16. Needle jet
17. Main jet
18. Float chamber gasket
19. Float chamber body
20. Throttle adjuster
21. Throttle adjuster spring
22. Cotter pin
23. Throttle valve stop rod
24. Throttle valve
25. Banjo bolt
26. Gasket
27. Mixing chamber body
28. Float valve seat washer
29. Float valve complete
30. Float
31. Float pin
33. Float chamber fitting screw
34. Main jet washer
35. Carburetor cap grommet
36. Carburetor cap
37. Fuel overflow pipe
38. Air vent pipe
39. Circlip

5

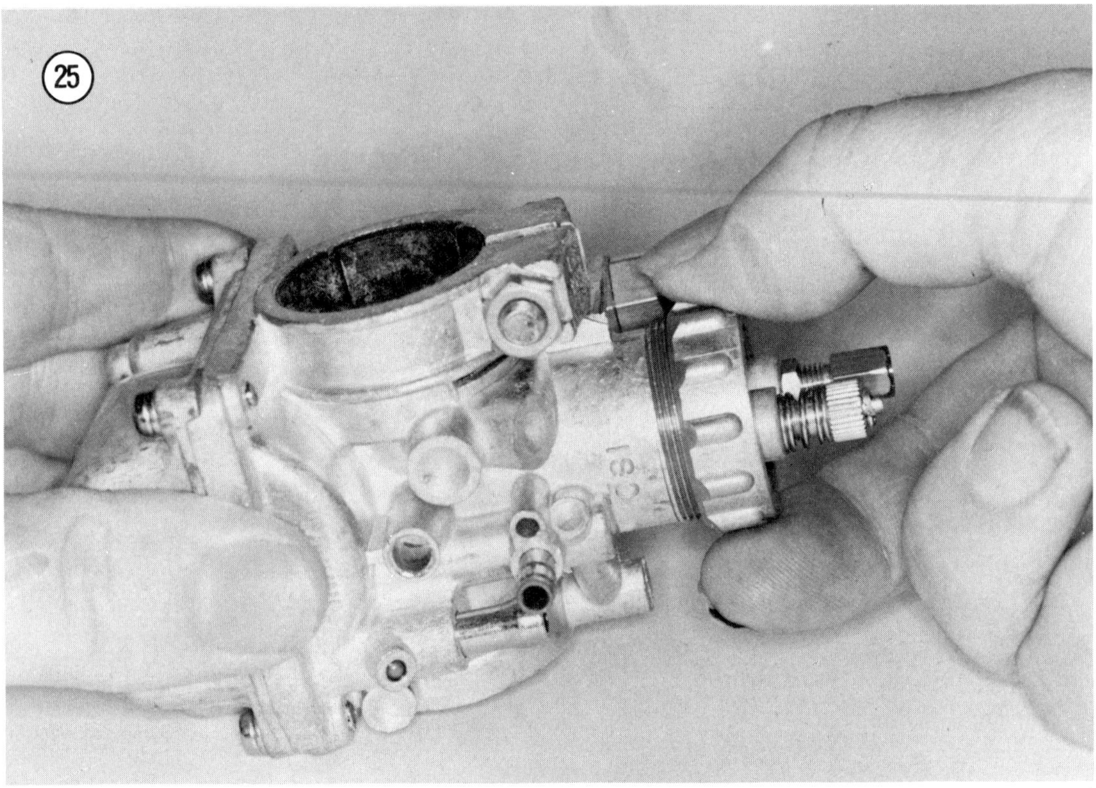

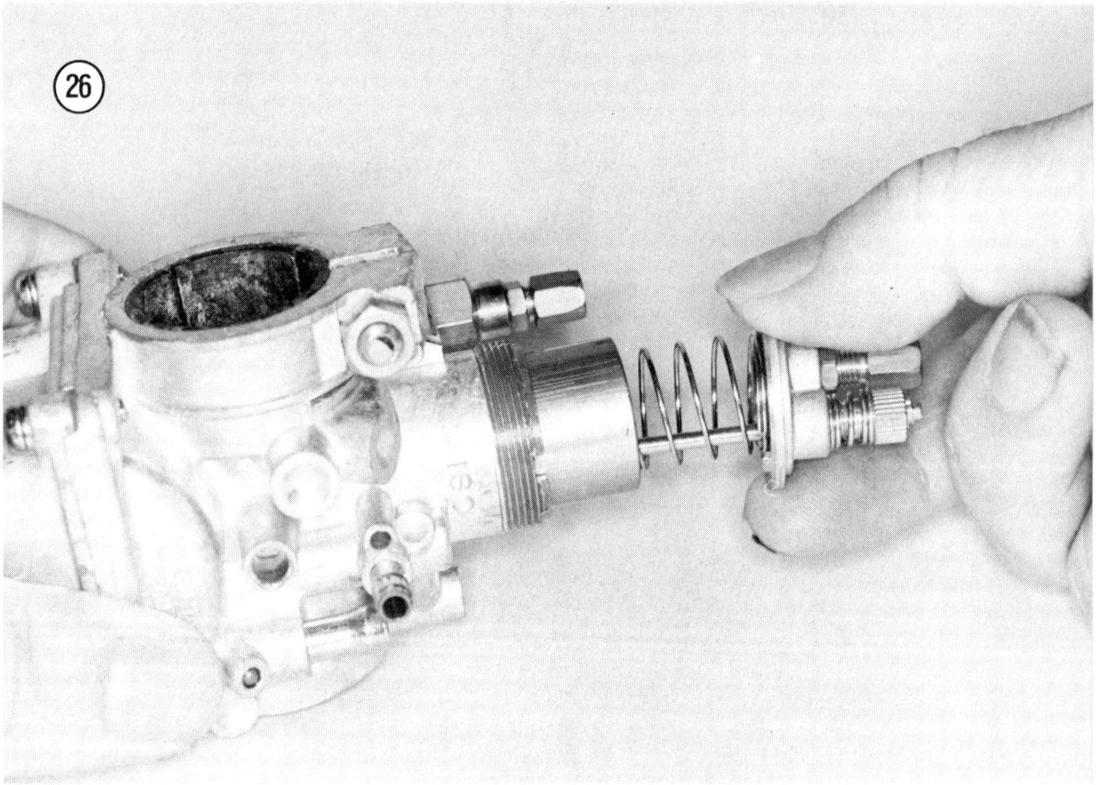

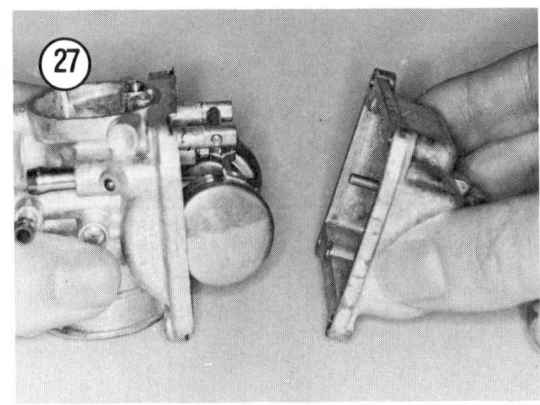

As a general rule, main jet size should be reduced approximately 5% for each 3,000 feet (1,000 meters) above sea level.

Table 3 lists symptoms caused by rich and lean mixtures.

Adjust the pilot air screw as follows.

The idle fuel/air mixture affects low speed emissions, as well as idling stability and smooth transition to partial throttle openings. The idle mixture should *not* be adjusted on emission-controlled bikes (street or dual purpose bikes made after January 1, 1978) unless the factory setting has been altered.

1. Turn in the idle mixture screw until it seats lightly, then back it out 1 to 1-3/4 turns. See **Table 2** for your motorcycle's standard idle mixture screw setting.

2. Start the engine, then ride the bike long enough to warm it thoroughly.

3. Turn the idle speed adjuster until the engine runs slower and begins to falter.

4. *Non-emission controlled bikes only:* Turn the idle mixture screw as required to make the engine run smoothly. Repeat Steps 3 and 4 to achieve the lowest stable idle speed.

5. *Emission controlled bikes (1978-1/2 on):* Turn the idle speed adjuster to achieve the lowest stable idle speed.

5

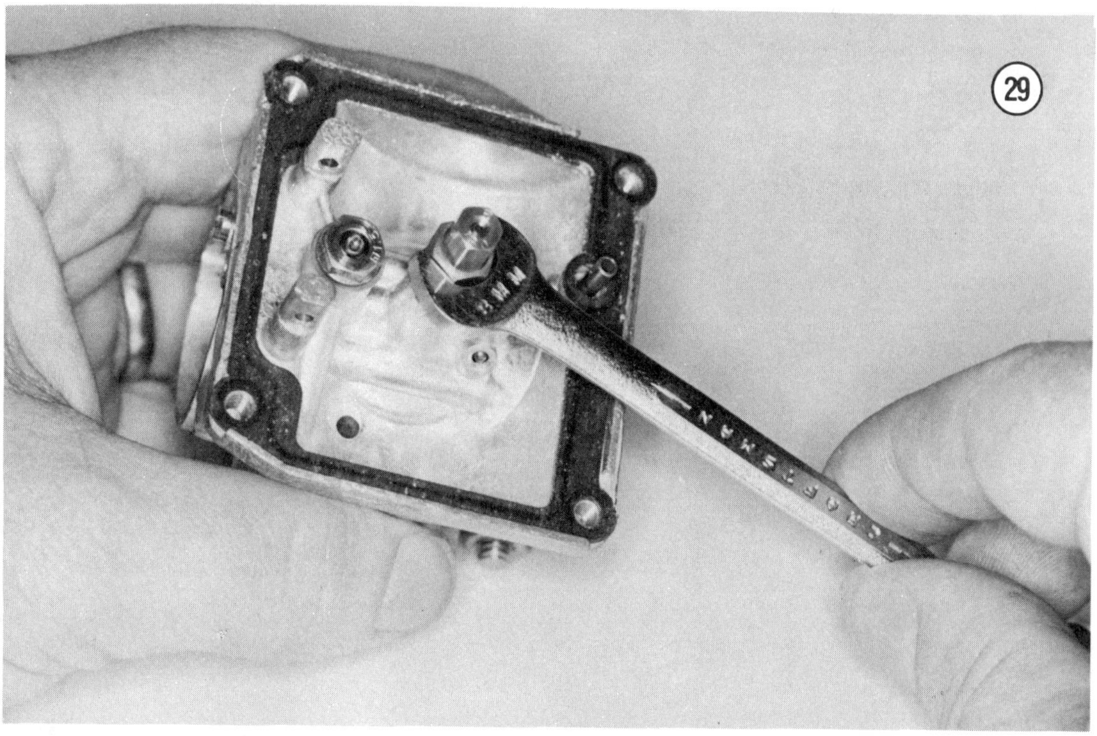

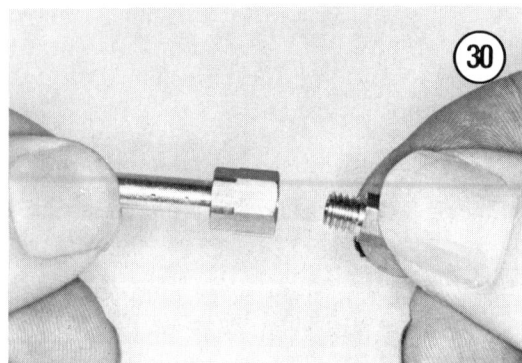

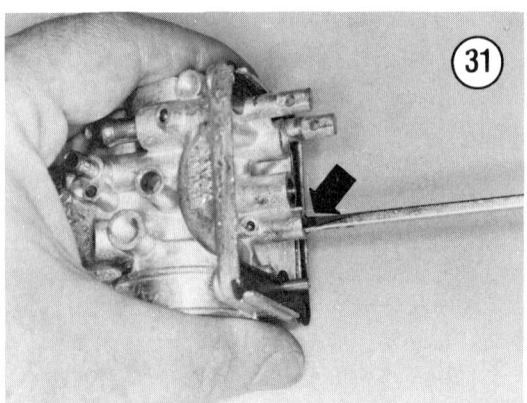

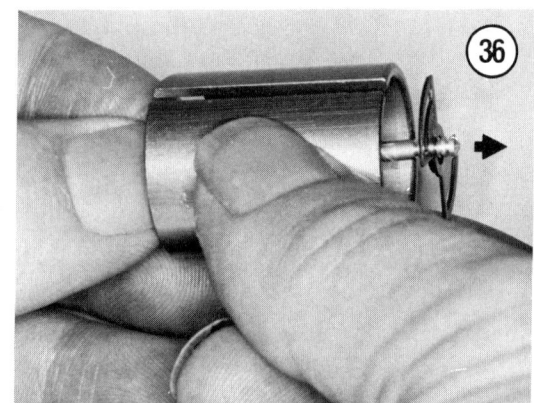

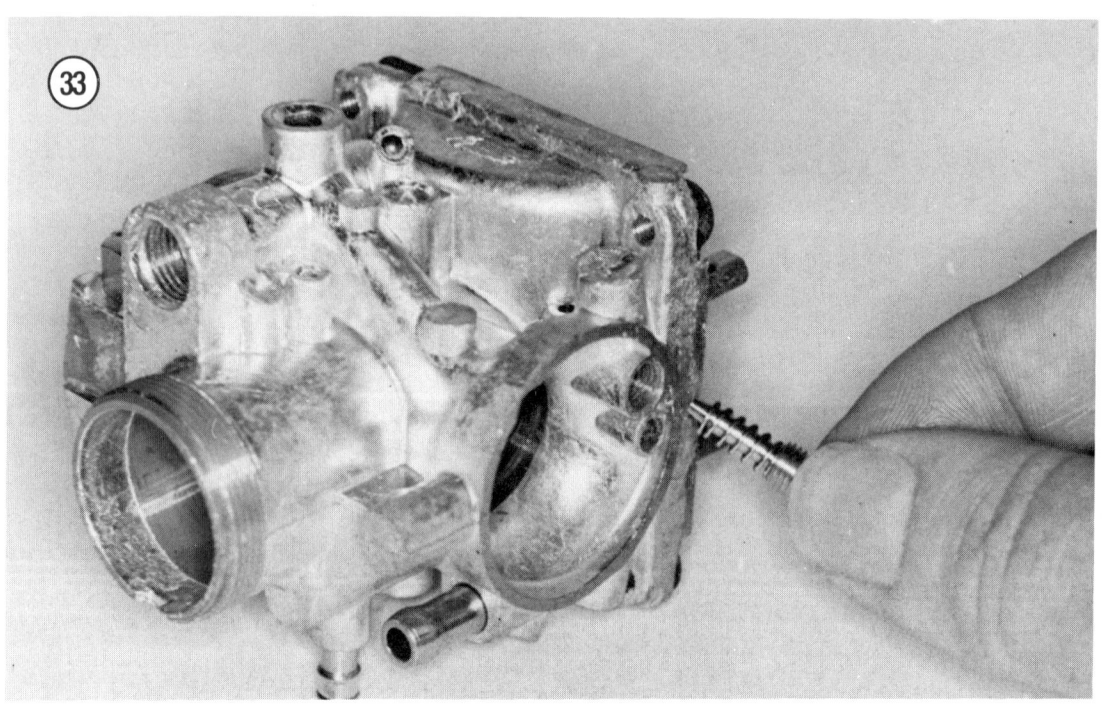

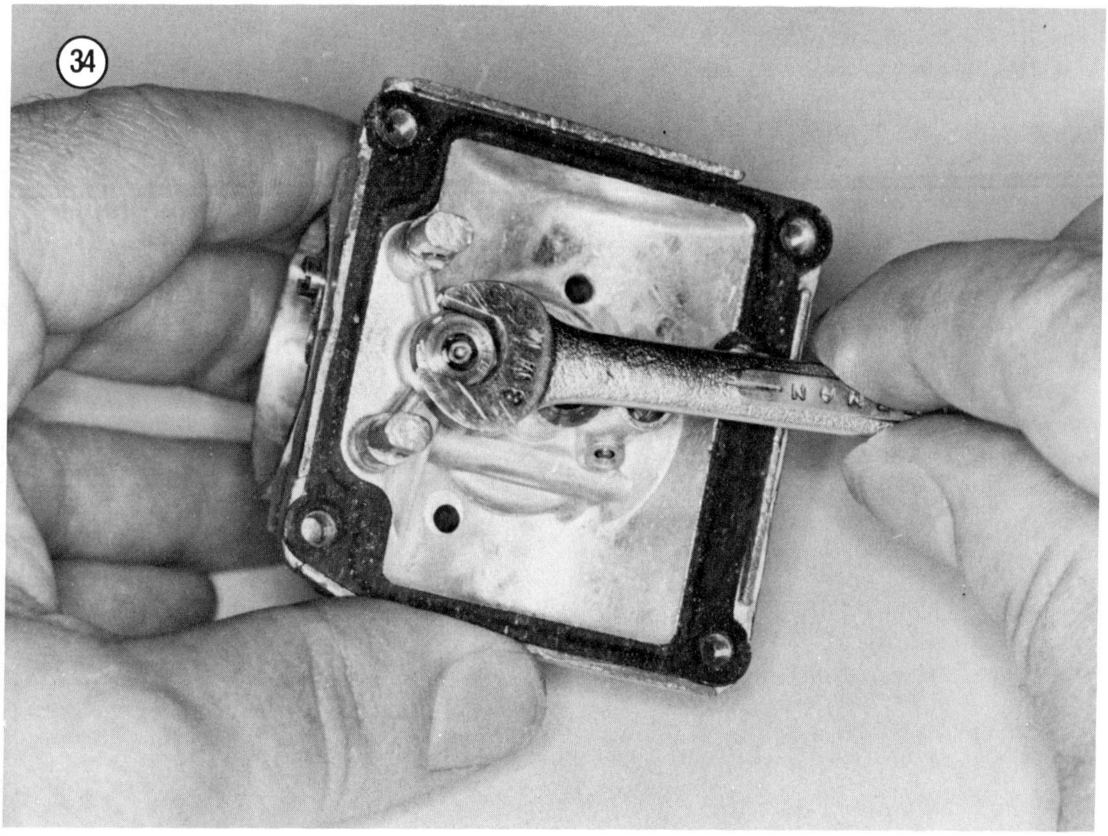

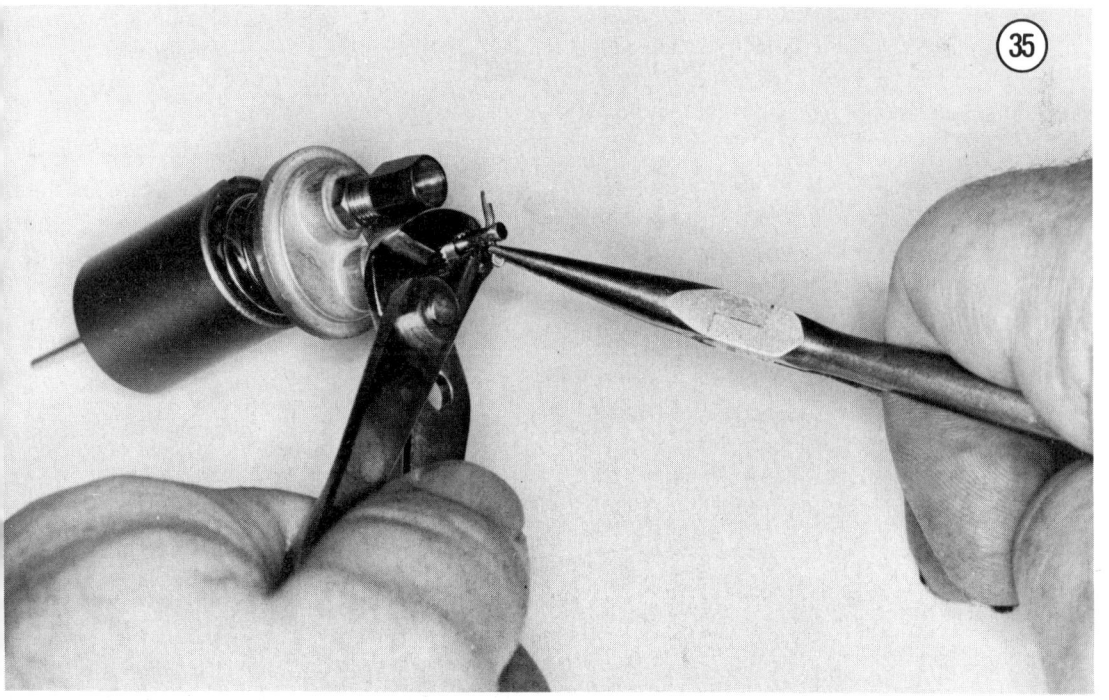

5

Next, determine the proper throttle valve cutaway size. With the engine running at idle, open the throttle. If the engine does not accelerate smoothly from idle, turn the pilot air screw in (clockwise) slightly to enrich the mixture. If the condition still exists, return the air screw to its original position and replace the throttle valve with one which has a smaller cutaway. If engine operation is made worse by turning the air screw, replace the throttle valve with one which has a larger cutaway. For operation at 1 to 3/4 throttle opening, adjustment is made with the jet needle. Operate the engine at half throttle in a manner similar to that for full throttle tests described earlier. To enrich the mixture, place the jet needle clip in a lower groove. Conversely, placing the clip in a higher groove leans the mixture.

A summary of carburetor adjustments is given in **Table 4**.

CARBURETOR COMPONENTS

The following paragraphs describe the various components of the carburetor which may be changed to vary the performance characteristics.

Throttle Valve

The throttle valve cutaway controls airflow at small throttle openings. Cutaway sizes are numbered. Larger numbers permit more air to flow at a given throttle opening and result in a leaner mixture. Conversely, smaller numbers result in a richer mixture.

Jet Needle

The jet needle, together with the needle jet, controls the mixture at medium speeds. As the throttle valve rises to increase airflow through the carburetor, the jet needle rises with it. The tapered portion of the jet needle rises from the needle jet and allows more fuel to flow, thereby providing the engine with the proper mixture at up to about 3/4 throttle opening. The grooves at the top of the jet needle permit adjustment of the mixture ratio in the medium speed range.

Needle Jet

The needle jet operates with the jet needle. Several holes are drilled through the side of the needle jet. These holes meter the airflow from the air jet. Air from the air jet is bled into the needle jet to assist in atomization of the fuel.

Main Jet

The main jet controls the mixture at full throttle and has some effect at lesser throttle openings. Each main jet is stamped with a number. Fuel flow is approximately proportional to the number. Larger numbers provide a richer mixture.

MISCELLANEOUS CARBURETOR PROBLEMS

Water in the carburetor float bowl and sticking carburetor slide valves can result from careless washing of the motorcycle. To remedy the problem,

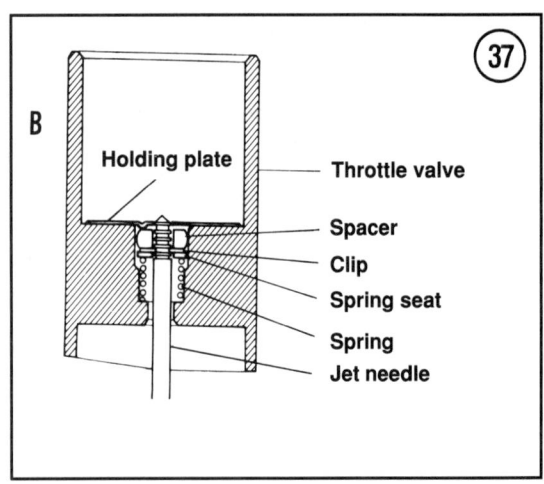

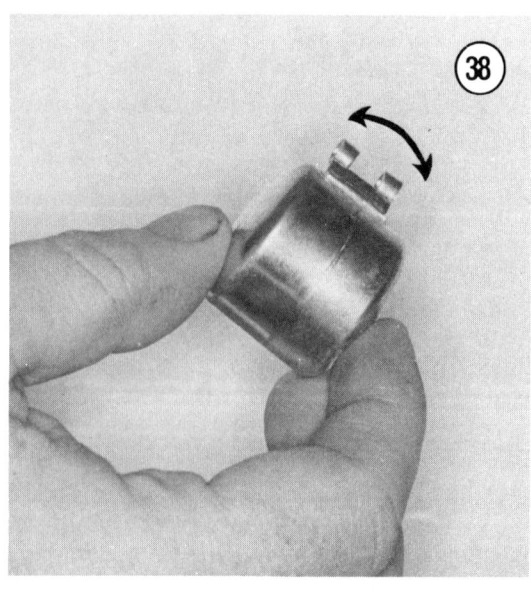

remove and clean the carburetor bowl, main jet and any other affected parts. Be sure to cover the air intake when washing the machine.

Be sure that the ring nut on the top of the carburetor is secure. Also be sure that the carburetor mounting bolts are tight.

If gasoline leaks past the float bowl gasket, high speed fuel starvation may occur. Varnish deposits on the outside of the float bowl are evident of this condition.

Dirt in the fuel may lodge in the float valve and cause an overrich mixture. As a temporary measure, tap the carburetor lightly with any convenient tool to dislodge the dirt. Clean the fuel tank, petcock, fuel line and carburetor at the first opportunity, should this occur.

Figures 39-46 and Tables 1-5 are on the following pages.

5

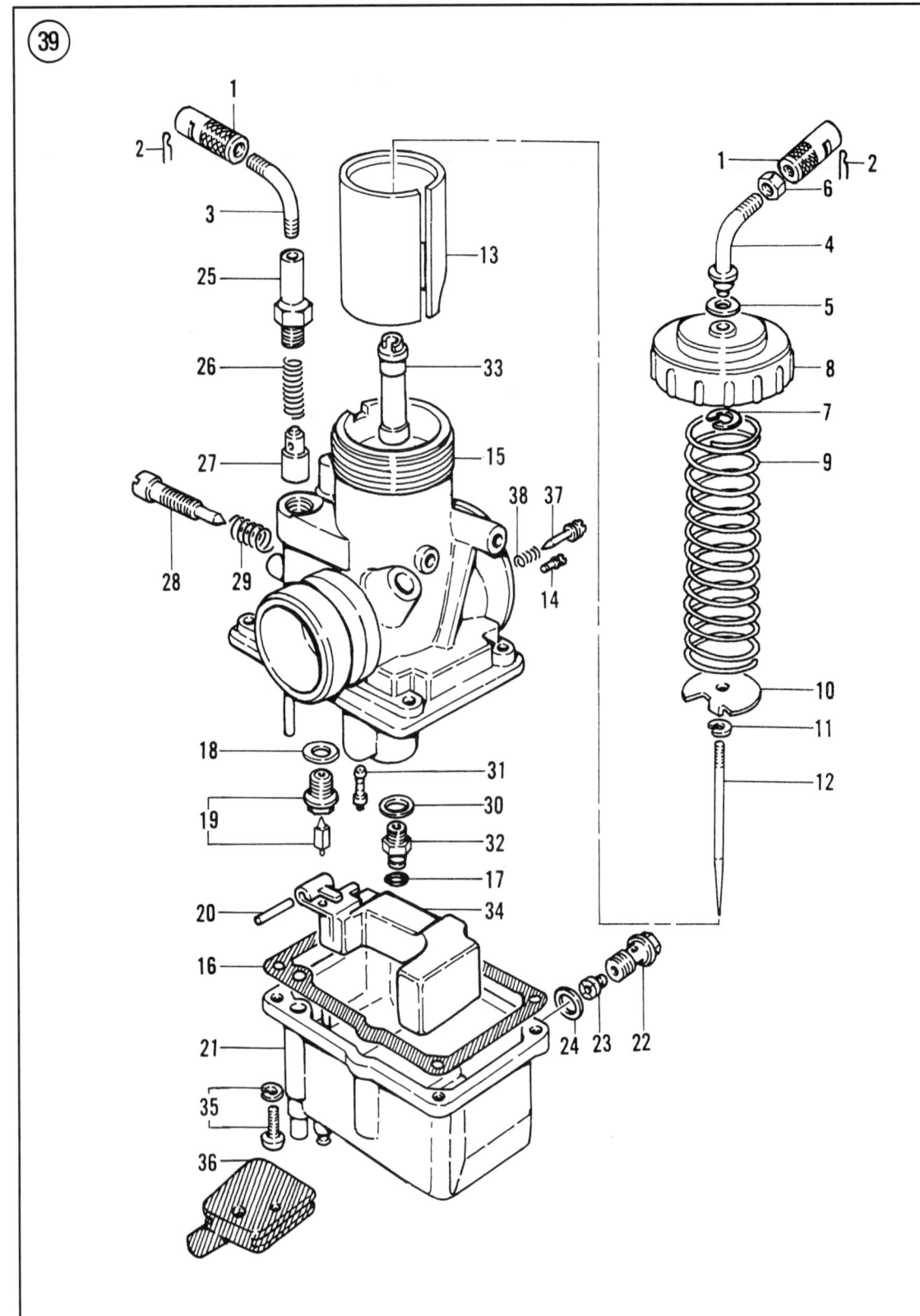

TYPE 1 SINGLE FLOAT CARBURETOR

1. Cable adjusters
2. Circlips
3. Starter (choke) cable guide
4. Throttle cable guide
5. Gasket
6. Cable adjuster locknuts
7. Circlip
8. Mixing chamber top
9. Throttle valve spring
10. Throttle valve spring seat
11. Circlip
12. Jet needle
13. Throttle valve
14. Air jet
15. Mixing chamber body
16. Float chamber gasket
17. Sealing ring
18. Sealing washer
19. Inlet (float) valve assembly
20. Float pin
21. Float bowl
22. Main jet holder
23. Main jet
24. Gasket
25. Starter (choke) cable cap
26. Starting valve spring
27. Starting valve plunger
28. Idle speed stop screw
29. Spring
30. Sealing washer
31. Pilot jet
32. Needle jet holder
33. Needle jet
34. Float
35. Float chamber screw
36. Overflow pipe grommet
37. Pilot air (idle mixture) screw
38. Spring

5

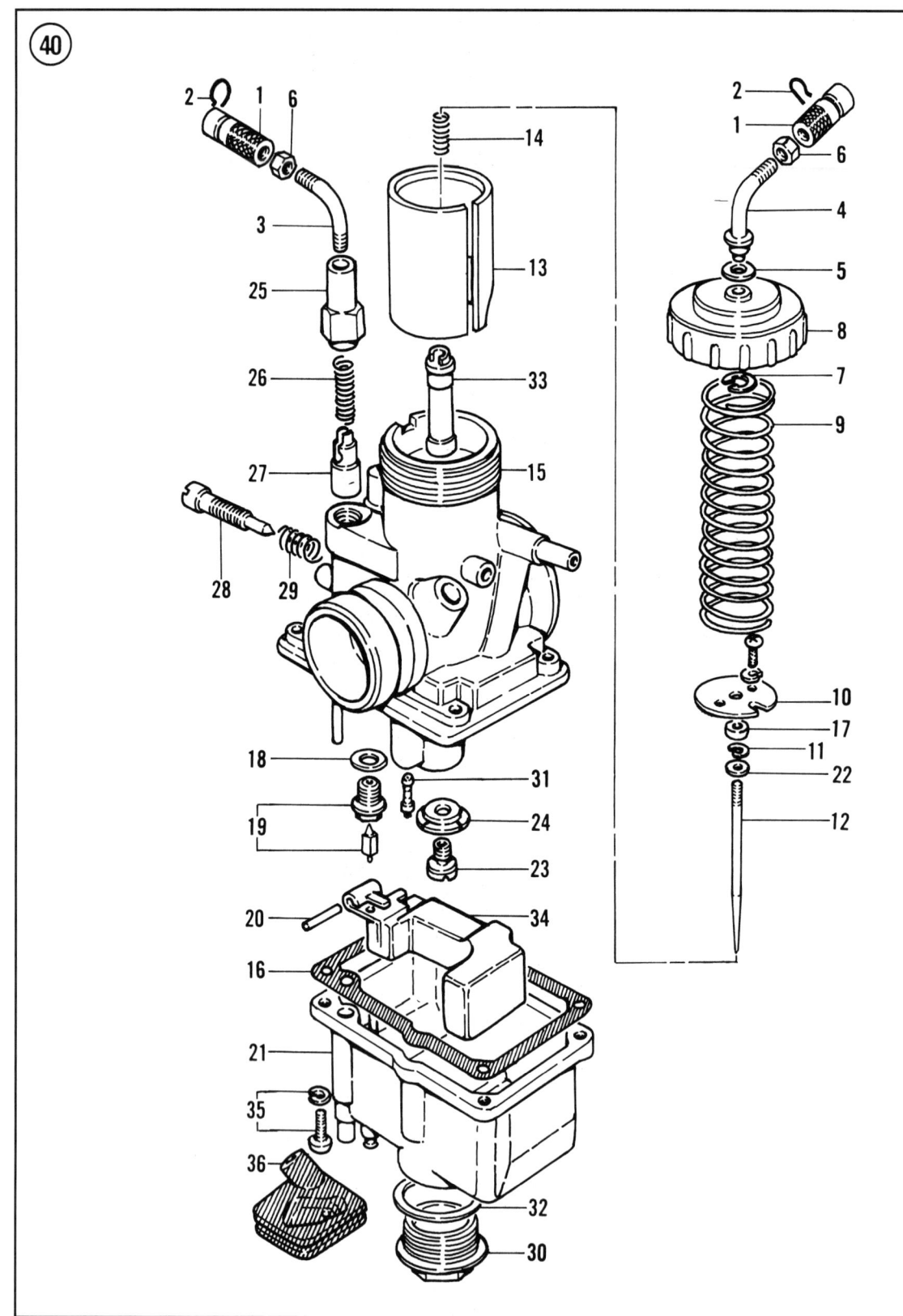

TYPE 2 SINGLE FLOAT CARBURETOR

1. Cable adjusters
2. Circlips
3. Starter (choke) cable guide
4. Throttle cable guide
5. Gasket
6. Cable adjuster locknuts
7. Circlip
8. Mixing chamber top
9. Throttle valve spring
10. Throttle valve spring seat
11. Circlip
12. Jet needle
13. Throttle valve
14. Spring
15. Mixing chamber body
16. Float chamber gasket
17. Spacer
18. Sealing washer
19. Inlet (float) valve assembly
20. Float pin
21. Float bowl
22. Spring seat
23. Main jet
24. Baffle plate
25. Starter (choke) cable cap
26. Starting valve spring
27. Starting valve plunger
28. Idle speed stop screw
29. Spring
30. Drain plug
31. Pilot jet
32. Gasket
33. Needle jet
34. Float
35. Float chamber screw
36. Overflow pipe grommet

5

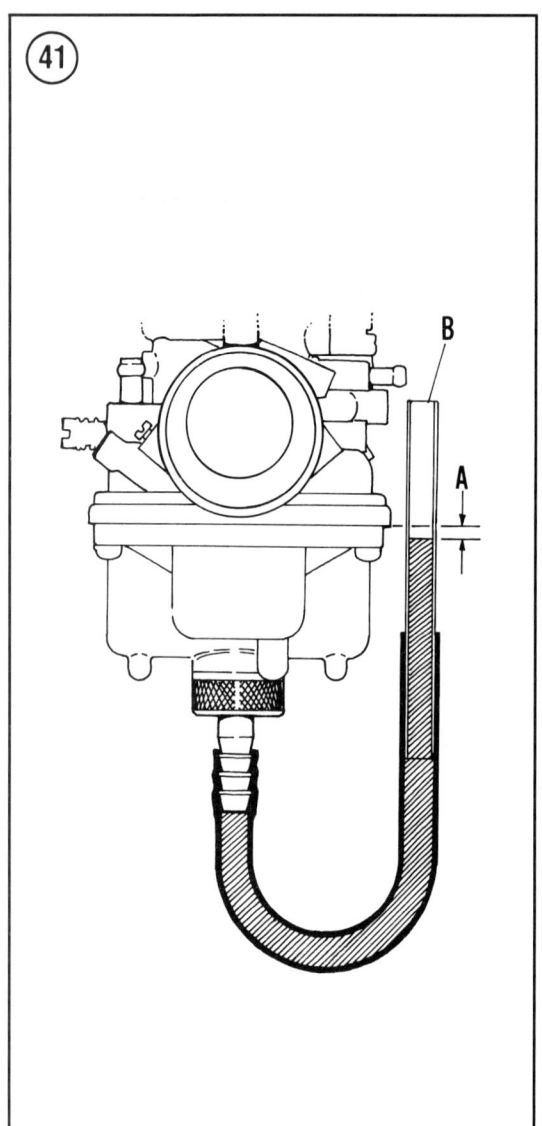

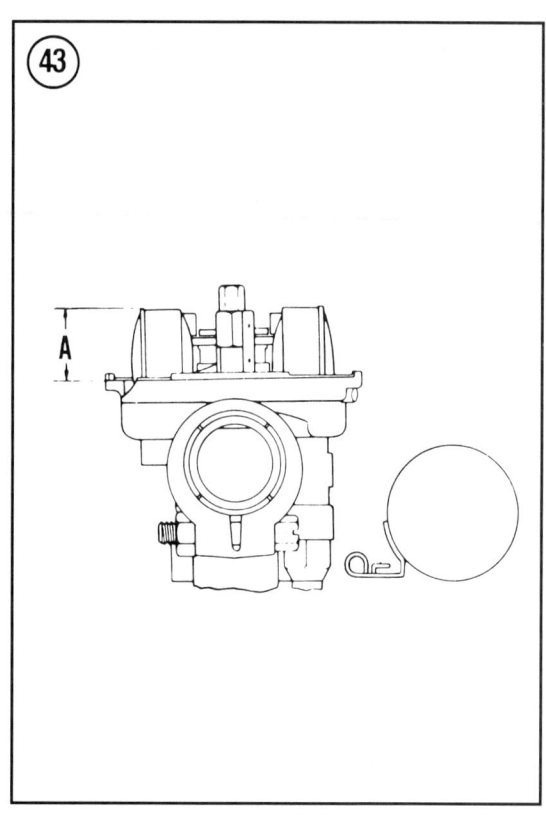

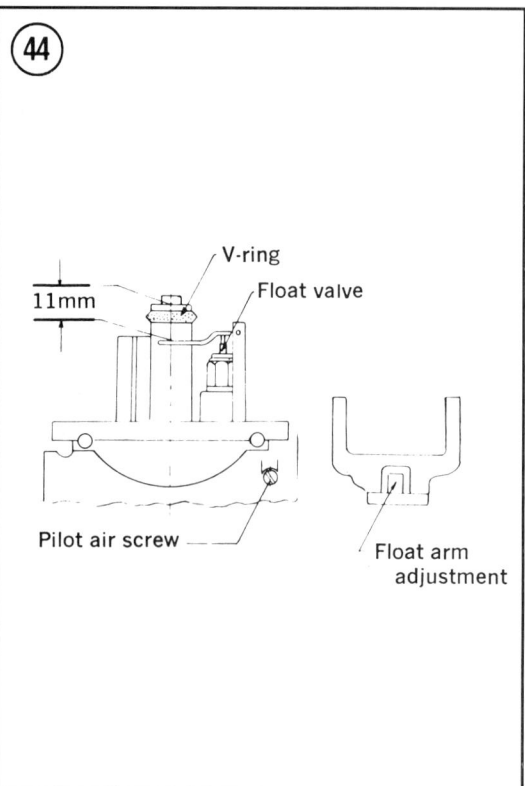

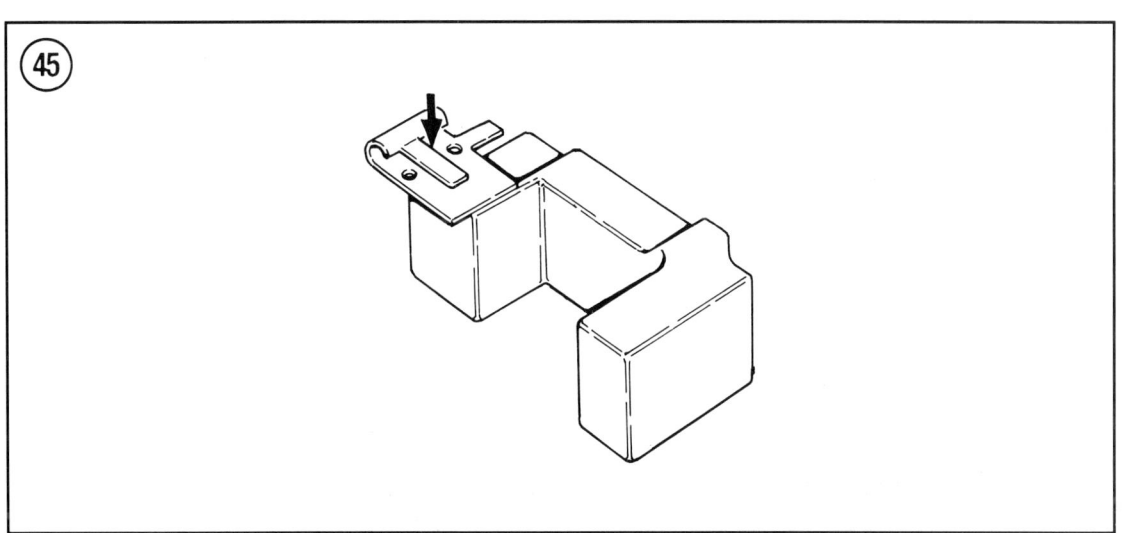

5

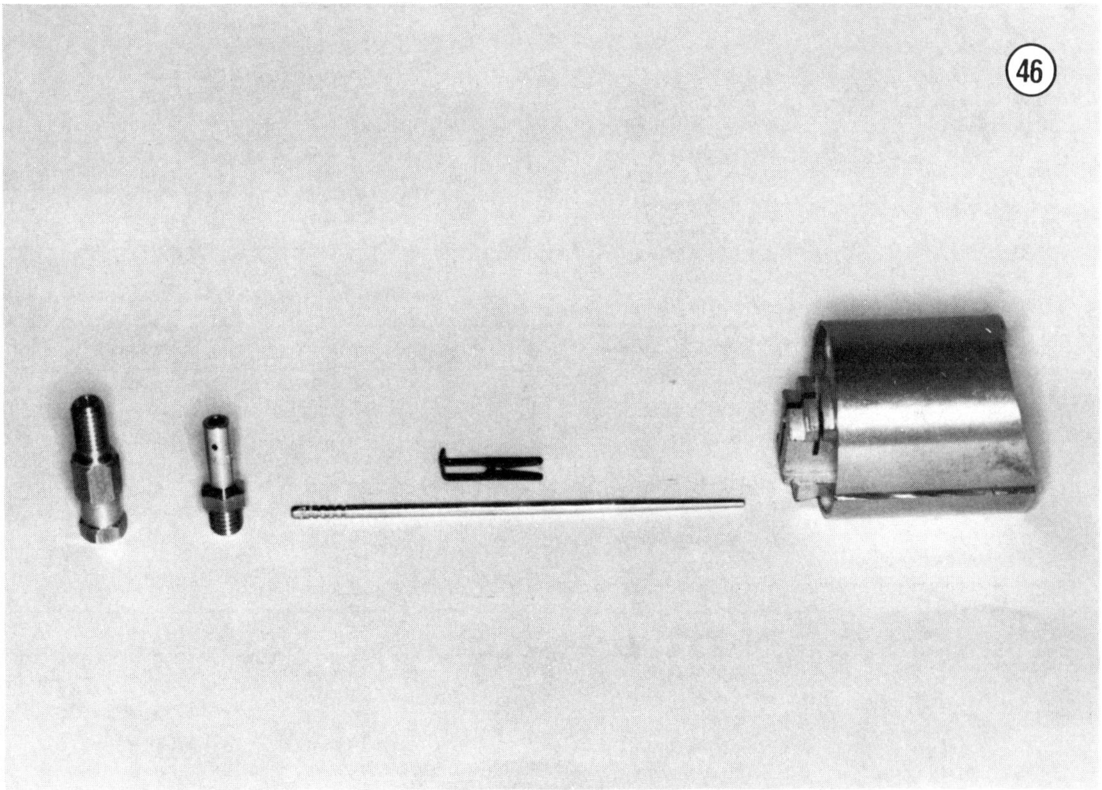

Table 1 IDLE MIXTURE

Too rich	Too lean
Clogged pilot air intake	Obstructed pilot jet
Clogged air passage	Obstructed jet outlet
Clogged air bleed opening	Worn throttle valve
Pilot jet loose	Carburetor mounting loose

Table 2 CARBURETOR ADJUSTMENTS

79-100 cc models	*Idle mixture screw	Idle speed	Float level	Fuel level
KD80 (1975, 1976 & 1980-1987)	1 1/2 turns open	**	24 mm	4 mm
J Series	1 1/2 turns open	**	18 mm	4 mm
MC1-A, MC1-B & MC1M	1 1/2 turns open	**	24 mm	4 mm
G3SS & G3TR	1 1/4-1 1/2 turns open	**	24 mm	4-4.5 mm
D1	1 3/4 turns open	**	18 mm	—
G4TR	1 1/4-1 1/2 turns open	**	24 mm	4 mm
G5	1 1/2 turns open	**	24 mm	4 mm
G31M	1 1/2 turns open	**	23 mm	—
KD100	1 1/4 turns open	**	24 mm	4 mm
KE100	1 1/2 turns open	**	24 mm	4 mm
KH100, KM100 & KV100	1 1/4 turns open	**	24 mm	4 mm

115-125 cc models	*Idle mixture screw	Idle speed	Float level	Fuel level
C2SS & C2TR	1 1/2 turns open	**	18 mm	—
F6	1 3/4 turns open	**	19 mm	5 mm
KD125	1 1/2 turns open	**	24 mm	4 mm
KE125-A3, A4 & A5 (1976-1978)	1 1/2 turns open	**	19 mm	4 mm
KE125-A6 -A12 (1979-1985)	1 1/4 turns open	**	19 mm	4 mm
KS125	1 1/2 turns open	**	19 mm	4 mm
KX125 (1974-1976)	1 1/2 turns open	**	19 mm	4 mm

169-175 cc models	*Idle mixture screw	Idle speed	Float level	Fuel level
F2 & F2TR	1 3/4 turns open	**	22-24 mm	—
F3	1 3/4 turns open	**	24-26 mm	—
F7	1 1/2 turns open	**	18 mm	5 mm
KD175 (1976-1979)	1 1/4 turns open	**	18 mm	3.5 mm
KE175 (1976-1982)	1 1/4 turns open	**	18 mm	3.5 mm

238-350 cc models	*Idle mixture screw	Idle speed	Float level	Fuel level
F4	1 1/4 turns open	**	24-26 mm	—
F21M	1 1/4 turns open	**	24-26 mm	—
F8	1 3/4 turns open	**	28 mm	7 mm
F81M	1 1/4 turns open	**	28 mm	7 mm
F5	1 13/4 turns open	**	18 mm	5.5 mm
F9	1 1/2 turns open	**	18 mm	5.5 mm

* Idle mixture (pilot screw) settings are approximate and should be set for optimum running.
** Engine idle speed should be adjusted as slow as possible while maintaining smooth running without stalling.

Table 3 IDLE MIXTURE TROUBLESHOOTING

Condition	Symptom	Condition	Symptoms
Rich mixture	Rough idle Black exhaust smoke Hard starting, especially when hot "Blubbering" under acceleration Black deposits in exhaust pipe Gas-fouled spark plug Poor gas mileage Engine performs worse as it warms up	Lean mixture	Backfiring Rough idle Overheating Hesitation upon acceleration Engine speed varies at fixed throttle Loss of power White color on spark plug insulator Poor acceleration

Table 4 CARBURETOR ADJUSTMENTS

Throttle opening	Adjustment	If too rich	If too lean
0-1/8	Air screw	Turn out	Turn in
1/8-1/4	Throttle valve cutaway	Use larger cutaway	Use smaller cutaway
1/4-3/4	Jet needle	Raise clip	Lower clip
3/4-full	Main jet	Use smaller number	Use larger number

Table 5 CARBURETOR SPECIFICATIONS

79-100 cc models	
KD80 (1975, 1976 & 1980-1987)	
Size	19 mm
Main jet	80
Needle jet	O-6/2
Jet needle	4EJ7
Clip position	3
Slide cut-away	2.0
Pilot jet	17.5
Float level	24 mm
Fuel level	4 mm
Pilot screw	1 1/2 turns open
J Series	
Manufacturer	Mikuni
Size	17 mm
I.D. mark	
Main jet	110
Needle jet	E-2
Jet needle	4L4
Clip position	3
Slide cut-away	1.5
Float level	18 mm
Fuel level	4 mm
Pilot screw	1 1/2 turns open
MC1-A, MC1-B & MC1M	
Manufacturer	Mikuni
Model	VM19SC
Main jet	75
Needle jet	O-2/2
Jet needle	4EJ7
Clip position	3
Slide cut-away	2.0
Pilot jet	17.5
Float level	24 mm
Fuel level	4 mm
Pilot screw	1 1/2 turns open
(continued)	

5

Table 5 CARBURETOR SPECIFICATIONS (continued)

79-100 cc models (continued)	
G3SS, A, B	
Manufacturer	Mikuni
Model	VM19SC
Main jet	160
Needle jet	E-4/1
Jet needle	5I2
Clip position	3
Slide cut-away	2.0
Pilot jet	17.5
Float level	24 mm
Fuel level	4 mm
Pilot screw	1 1/4 turns open
G3SS-C, D & E	
Manufacturer	Mikuni
Model	VM19SC
Main jet	77.5
Needle jet	4EJ7
Jet needle	O-2
Clip position	3
Slide cut-away	2.0
Float level	24 mm
Fuel level	4 mm
Pilot screw	1 1/2 turns open
G3TR (90cc)	
Manufacturer	Mikuni
Model	VM19SC
Main jet	160
Needle jet	E-4/1
Jet needle	5I2
Clip position	3
Slide cut-away	2.0
Pilot jet	17.5
Float level	24 mm
Pilot screw	1 1/4 turns open
G3TR-A & B (100cc)	
Manufacturer	Mikuni
Model	VM19SC
Main jet	180
Needle jet	E-6/1
Jet needle	5I1
Clip position	3
Slide cut-away	2.0
Pilot jet	17.5
Float level	24 mm
Fuel level	4.5 mm
Pilot screw	1 1/4 turns open
G3TR-C (100cc)	
Manufacturer	Mikuni
Model	VM19SC
Main jet	107.5
Needle jet	E-6/1
Jet needle	5I1
Clip position	3
Slide cut-away	2.0
Pilot jet	17.5
Float level	24 mm
Fuel level	4.5 mm
Pilot screw	1 1/4 turns open
(continued)	

Table 5 CARBURETOR SPECIFICATIONS (continued)

79-100 cc models (continued)	
D1	
Manufacturer	Mikuni
Model	VM17SC
Main jet	150
Needle jet	E-2
Jet needle	4L4
Clip position	3
Slide cut-away	1.5
Pilot jet	15
Float level	18 mm
Pilot screw	1 3/4 turns open
G4TR, A & B	
Manufacturer	Mikuni
Model	VM19SC
Main jet	180
Needle jet	E-6/1
Jet needle	5I1
Clip position	3
Slide cut-away	2.5
Pilot jet	17.5
Float level	24 mm
Fuel level	4 mm
Pilot screw	1 1/4 turns open
G4TR-C	
Manufacturer	Mikuni
Model	VM19SC
Main jet	107.5
Needle jet	E-6/1
Jet needle	5I1
Clip position	3
Slide cut-away	2.5
Float level	24 mm
Fuel level	4 mm
Pilot screw	1 1/4 turns open
G4TR-D & E	
Manufacturer	Mikuni
Model	VM19SC
Main jet	75
Needle jet	4EJ7
Jet needle	O-4/2
Clip position	2
Slide cut-away	2.0
Float level	24 mm
Fuel level	4 mm
Pilot screw	1 1/2 turns open
G5 & -A	
Manufacturer	Mikuni
Model	VM19SC
Main jet	102.5
Needle jet	E-4/2
Jet needle	5I1
Clip position	3-4
Slide cut-away	2.0
Pilot jet	17.5
Float level	24 mm
Fuel level	4 mm
Pilot screw	1 1/2 turns open
(continued)	

5

Table 5 CARBURETOR SPECIFICATIONS (continued)

79-100 cc models (continued)	
G5-B & C	
Manufacturer	Mikuni
Model	VM19SC
Main jet	75
Needle jet	O-2/2
Jet needle	4EJ7
Clip position	3
Slide cut-away2.0	
Pilot jet	17.5
Float level	24 mm
Fuel level	4 mm
Pilot screw	1 1/2 turns open
G31M	
Manufacturer	Mikuni
Model	VM24SC
Main jet	170-180
Needle jet	O-6
Jet needle	4DG6
Clip position	3
Slide cut-away	3.0
Pilot jet	35
Float level	23 mm
Pilot screw	1 1/2 turns open
KD100	
Size	19 mm
Main jet	77.5
Needle jet	O-2
Jet needle	4EJ7
Clip position	3
Slide cut-away	2.0
Float level	24 mm
Fuel level	4 mm
Pilot screw	1 1/4 turns open
KE100-A5, A6 & A7 (1976-1978)	
Manufacturer	Mikuni
Model	VM19SC
Main jet	75
Needle jet	O-2/2
Jet needle	4EJ7
Slide cut-away2.0	
Clip position	3
Pilot jet	17.5
Float level	24 mm
Fuel level	4 mm
Pilot screw	1 1/2 turns open
KE100-A8-on (1979-on)	
Model	VM19SC
Main jet	77.5
Needle jet	O-2
Jet needle	4EJ12
Clip position	3
Slide cut-away2.0	
Pilot jet	15
Fuel level	3-5 mm
Pilot screw	1 1/2 turns open
KH100	
Size	19 mm
Main jet	77.5
	(continued)

Table 5 CARBURETOR SPECIFICATIONS (continued)

79-100 cc models (continued)	
Needle jet	O-2/2
Jet needle	4EJ7
Clip position	3
Slide cut-away	2.0
Float level	24 mm
Fuel level	4 mm
Pilot screw	1 1/4 turns open
KM100	
Size	19 mm
Main jet	77.5
Needle jet	0-2/2
Jet needle	4EJ7
Clip position	3
Slide cut-away	2.0
Float level	24 mm
Fuel level	4 mm
Pilot screw	1 1/4 turns open
KV100	
Size	19 mm
Main jet	75
Needle jet	4EJ7
Jet needle	O-4/2
Clip position	2
Slide cut-away	2.0
Float level	24 mm
Fuel level	4 mm
Pilot screw	1 1/4 turns open
115-125 cc models	
C2SS (early)	
Manufacturer	Mikuni
Model	VM18SC
Main jet	140-170
Needle jet	E-6
Jet needle	4J9
Clip position	3
Slide cut-away	2.5
Pilot jet	17.5
Float level	18 mm
Pilot screw	1 1/2 turns open
C2SS (late) & C2TR	
Manufacturer	Mikuni
Model	VM18SC
Main jet	160
Needle jet	E-4
Jet needle	4J9
Clip position	3
Slide cut-away	2.5
Float level	18 mm
Pilot screw	1 1/2 turns open
F6	
Manufacturer	Mikuni
Model	VM24SC
Main jet	125
Needle jet	O-2/4
Jet needle	4J13
Clip position	3
Slide cut-away	2.5
(continued)	

5

Table 5 CARBURETOR SPECIFICATIONS (continued)

115-125 cc models (continued)

Pilot jet	30
Float level	19 mm
Fuel level	5 mm
Pilot screw	1 3/4 turns open
KD125	
Size	24 mm
Main jet	100
Needle jet	O-4/2
Jet needle	4EJ3
Clip position	4
Slide cut-away	2.5
Float level	19 mm
Fuel level	4 mm
Pilot screw	1 1/2 turns open
KE125-A3, A4 & A5 (1976-1978)	
Size	24 mm
Main jet	100
Needle jet	O-4/2
Jet needle	4EJ3
Clip position	4
Slide cut-away	2.5
Fuel level	19 mm
Fuel level	4 mm
Pilot screw	1 1/2 turns open
KE125-A6 (1979)	
Manufacturer	Mikuni
Model	VM24SS
Main jet	100
Needle jet	O-4/2
Jet needle	4EJ3
Clip position	4
Slide cut-away	2.5
Pilot jet	30
Float level	19 mm
Service fuel level	3.0-5.0 mm
Pilot screw	1 1/4 turns open
KE125-A7 - A12 (1980-1985)	
Manufacturer	Mikuni
Model	VM24SS
Main jet	87.5
Needle jet	O-2
Jet needle	4EJ20
Clip position	3
Slide cut-away	2.5
Pilot jet	30
Float level	19 mm
Service fuel level	3.5-5.5 mm
Pilot screw	1 1/4 turns open
KS125	
Size	24 mm
Main jet	100
Needle jet	O-4/2
Jet needle	4EJ3
Clip position	4
Slide cut-away	2.5
Float level	19 mm
Fuel level	4 mm
Pilot screw	1 1/2 turns open

(continued)

Table 5 CARBURETOR SPECIFICATIONS (continued)

115-125 cc models (continued)	
KX125 (1974-1976)	
Model	VM26SC
Main jet	107.5
Needle jet	O-2/8
Jet needle	4EJ3
Clip position	3
Slide cut-away	2.5
Pilot jet	40
Float level	19 mm
Fuel level	4 mm
Pilot screw	1 1/2 turns open
169-175 cc models	
F2 & F2TR	
Manufacturer	Mikuni
Model	22 mm
Main jet	230
Needle jet	N-8
Jet needle	4J13
Clip position	2
Slide cut-away	
Float level	22-24 mm
Pilot screw	1 3/4 turns open
F3	
Manufacturer	Mikuni
Size	26 mm
Main jet	190
Needle jet	N-6
Jet needle	4J13
Clip position	3
Slide cut-away	2.0
Float level	24-26 mm
Pilot screw	1 3/4 turns open
F7, A & B (1971-1973)	
Manufacturer	Mikuni
Model	VM26SC
Main jet	105
Needle jet	O-2/2
Jet needle	4EJ3
Clip position	3
Slide cut-away	2.5
Pilot jet	30
Float level	18 mm
Fuel level	5 mm
Pilot screw	1 1/4 turns open
F7C & D (1974-1975)	
Manufacturer	Mikuni
Model	VM26SC
Main jet	105
Needle jet	O-6/2
Jet needle	4EJ3
Clip position	3
Slide cut-away	3.0
Pilot jet	30
Float level	18 mm
Fuel level	5 mm
Pilot screw	1 1/4 turns open

5

(continued)

Table 5 CARBURETOR SPECIFICATIONS (continued)

169-175 cc models (continued)	
KD175 (1976-1979)	
Size	26 mm
Main jet	102.5
Needle jet	O-8/2
Jet needle	4EJ3
Clip position	3
Slide cut-away	2.5
Float level	18 mm
Fuel level	3.5 mm
Pilot screw	1 1/4 turns open
KE175 (1976-1982)	
Size	26 mm
Main jet	102.5
Needle jet	O-8/2
Jet needle	4EJ3
Clip position	3
Slide cut-away	2.5
Float level	18 mm
Fuel level	3.5 mm
Pilot screw	1 1/4 turns open

238-350 cc models	
F4	
Manufacturer	Mikuni
Size	28 mm
Main jet	150-170
Needle jet	O-2
Jet needle	5DP7
Clip position	3
Slide cut-away	2.5
Float level	24-26 mm
Pilot screw	1 1/4 turns open
F21M (early)	
Manufacturer	Mikuni
Size	28 mm
Main jet	170
Needle jet	O-0
Jet needle	4L6
Clip position	2
Slide cut-away	1.5
Float level	24-26 mm
Pilot screw	1 1/4 turns open
F21M (late)	
Manufacturer	Mikuni
Size	28 mm
Main jet	170
Needle jet	P-0
Jet needle	5D1
Clip position	2
Slide cut-away	2.5
Float level	24-26 mm
Pilot screw	1 1/4 turns open
F8	
Manufacturer	Mikuni
Model	VM30SC
Main jet	117.5
Needle jet	O-8
Jet needle	5EL9

(continued)

Table 5 CARBURETOR SPECIFICATIONS (continued)

238-350 cc models (continued)	
Clip position	2
Slide cut-away	2.5
Pilot jet	30
Float level	28 mm
Fuel level	7 mm
Pilot screw	1 3/4 turns open
F81M	
Manufacturer	Mikuni
Model	VM30SC
Main jet	130
Needle jet	O-6/2
Jet needle	5EH7
Clip position	3
Slide cut-away	2.5
Pilot jet	
Float level	28 mm
Fuel level	7 mm
Pilot screw	1 3/4 turns open
F5 (early)	
Manufacturer	Mikuni
Model	VM32SC
I.D. mark	F5-3
Main jet	132.5
Needle jet	O-8
Jet needle	5FL11
Clip position	2
Slide cut-away	2.5
Float level	18 mm
Fuel level	5.5 mm
Pilot screw	1 1/4 turns open
F5 (late)	
Manufacturer	Mikuni
Model	VM32SC
I.D. mark	F5-4
Main jet	132.5
Needle jet	O-8/2
Jet needle	5EJ11
Clip position	3
Slide cut-away	1.0
Float level	18 mm
Fuel level	5.5 mm
Pilot screw	1 1/4 turns open
F9	
Manufacturer	Mikuni
Model	VM32SC
Main jet	120
Needle jet	O-6
Jet needle	5EJ13
Clip position	3
Slide cut-away	1.5
Pilot jet	10
Float level	18 mm
Fuel level	5.5 mm
Pilot screw	1 1/2 turns open
F9-A, B & C	
Manufacturer	Mikuni
Model	VM32SC
Main jet	120
(continued)	

5

Table 5 CARBURETOR SPECIFICATIONS (continued)

238-350 cc models (continued)	
Needle jet	O-6/2
Jet needle	5EJ13
Clip position	3
Slide cut-away	2.5
Pilot jet	17.5
Float level	18 mm
Fuel level	5.5 mm
Pilot screw	1 1/2 turns open

CHAPTER SIX

ELECTRICAL SYSTEM

This chapter discusses operating principles and maintenance of the ignition, lighting and charging systems.

Tables 1-5 are at the end of the chapter.

FLYWHEEL MAGNETO

A flywheel magneto provides electrical power for the ignition and electrical systems of most of the machines covered by this manual. Separate coils within the magneto supply current for ignition, daytime and nighttime operation and battery charging. Alternating current produced by the magneto is used for ignition and lights, except for stoplights and turn signals. A rectifier converts this alternating current into direct current for charging the battery and operating the horn and turn signals. **Figure 1** illustrates a typical magneto.

1979 and later 100cc and 125cc models are equipped with a combined solid state regulator/rectifier for true voltage regulation. The system functions much the same as earlier magneto systems, but there is no distinction between daytime and nighttime operation. Refer to *Solid State Regulator/Rectifier,* later in this chapter.

Figure 2 is a circuit diagram of a typical magneto which operates the ignition, charging and lighting systems. As the flywheel rotates, permanent magnets attached to the flywheel revolve past the various windings in the magneto, thereby inducing current in the windings.

When the contact breaker points are closed, the current (approximately 4 amperes) developed in the ignition coil is grounded and no current is delivered to the ignition coil. When the points open, this current is delivered to the primary winding of the ignition coil. The 200 or 300 volts across the coil primary winding is stepped up to a very high voltage of 10,000 to 15,000 volts required to jump the spark plug gap. A capacitor (condenser) is connected across the ignition points to prevent them from arcing as they open.

Nighttime riding imposes an additional load on the magneto because of the use of lights. To accommodate the different current requirements, the lighting coil is tapped for both day and night loads.

The rectifier serves 2 purposes. It converts alternating current generated by the magneto into direct current for charging the battery and it also prevents the battery from discharging through the magneto when the magneto output voltage is too low to charge the battery.

Magnetos on some models have 3 charging taps. The pink wire is used during night operation. The blue or yellow/green wires are used for day operation. In cases where the battery is chronically undercharged, connect the blue wire from the magneto to the blue wire at the main switch. Connect the yellow/green wire to the blue wire at the main switch when the battery is overcharged.

Figure 3 is a simplified diagram of the system on F5 and F9 models. The silicon voltage regulator

6

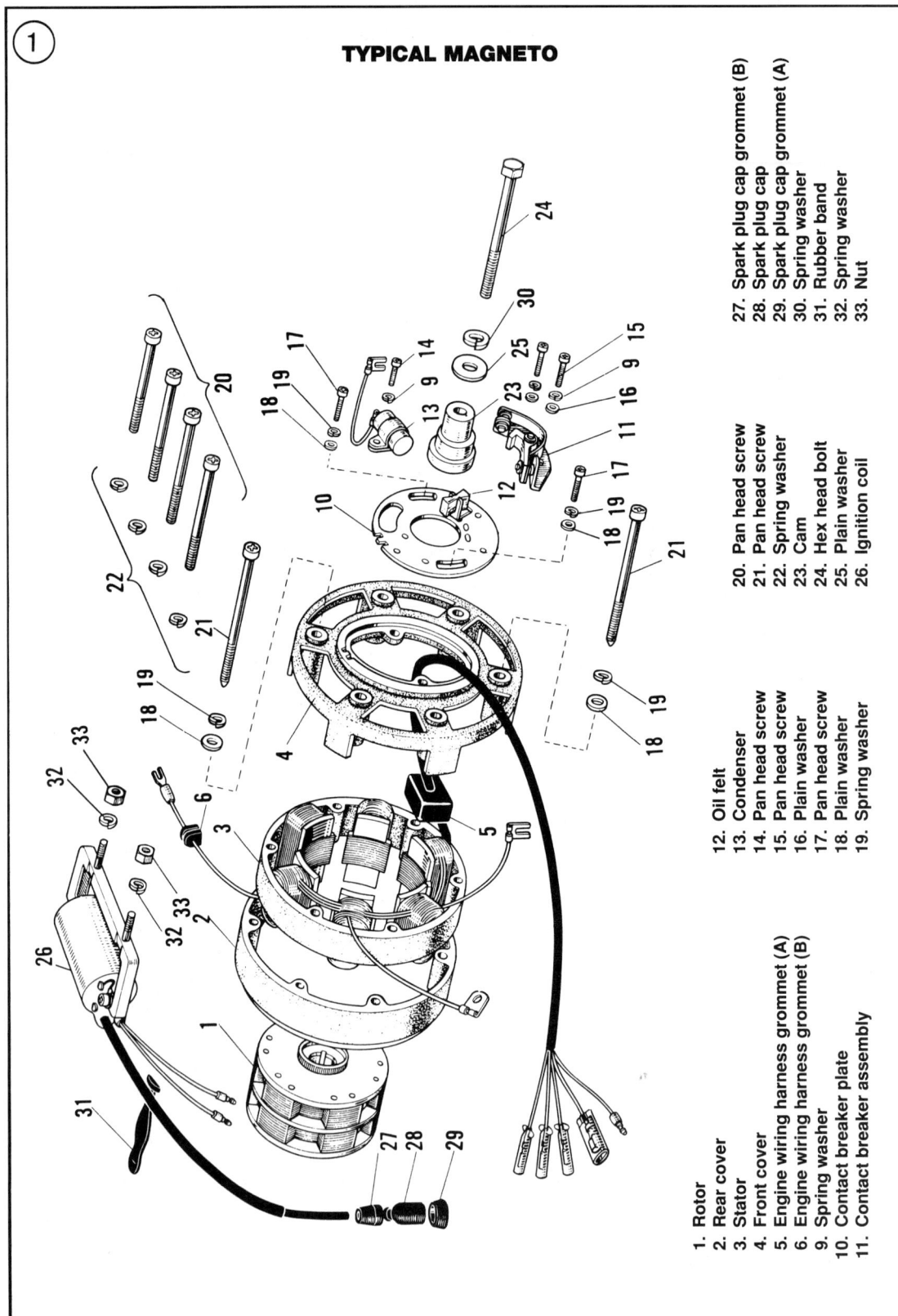

① TYPICAL MAGNETO

1. Rotor
2. Rear cover
3. Stator
4. Front cover
5. Engine wiring harness grommet (A)
6. Engine wiring harness grommet (B)
9. Spring washer
10. Contact breaker plate
11. Contact breaker assembly

12. Oil felt
13. Condenser
14. Pan head screw
15. Pan head screw
16. Plain washer
17. Pan head screw
18. Plain washer
19. Spring washer

20. Pan head screw
21. Pan head screw
22. Spring washer
23. Cam
24. Hex head bolt
25. Plain washer
26. Ignition coil

27. Spark plug cap grommet (B)
28. Spark plug cap
29. Spark plug cap grommet (A)
30. Spring washer
31. Rubber band
32. Spring washer
33. Nut

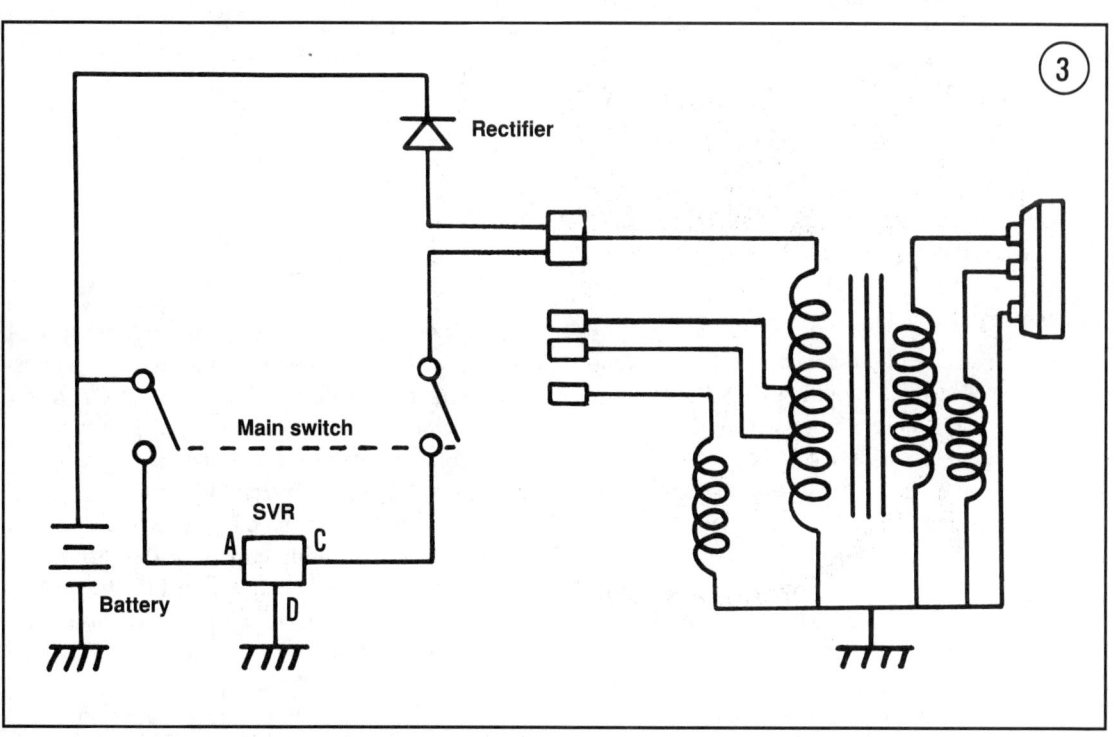

TYPICAL MAGNETO CIRCUIT

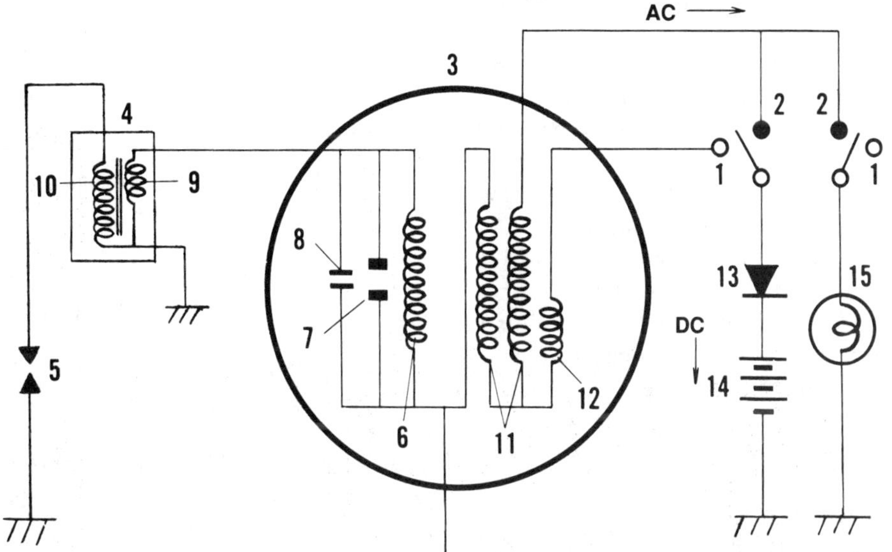

1. Daytime running
2. Nighttime running
3. Flywheel magneto
4. Ignition coil
5. Spark plug
6. Ignition primary coil
7. Contact breaker
8. Capacitor
9. Ignition primary coil
10. Ignition secondary coil
11. Lighting coil
12. Differential winding coil
13. Rectifier
14. Battery
15. AC lamp load
 (headlight and taillight)

(SVR) serves to control charging voltage in the day riding condition. Note that the SVR is not in the circuit during night riding conditions. If the DC load is reduced, as in the case of a burned-out brake light, the battery may be overcharged.

Note that the lighting coil serves mainly to operate the headlight, but it also furnishes power to the speedometer, tachometer and high beam indicator bulbs. If the headlight burns out, the other bulbs will burn out also because of excess voltage.

Magnetos on models F5, F7 and F9 (**Figure 4**) are basically similar to those on conventional magneto-ignition models except that the ignition coil is replaced with an exciter coil and a signal coil to meet requirements of the capacitor discharge system.

MAGNETO TROUBLESHOOTING

In the event that an ignition malfunction is believed to be caused by a defective magneto on models with breaker points, check the coils, condenser and breaker points as described in the following paragraphs.

Magneto Ignition Coil

With the magneto wiring disconnected, block the breaker points open with a piece of paper such as a business card. Measure the resistance between the black wire and ground with a low-range ohmmeter. If resistance is approximately 0.5 ohm, the coil is good.

Disconnect the ground wire between the ignition coil and the magneto base. Measure insulation resistance between the iron core and the coil. Insulation resistance should be at least 5 megohms.

Condenser

Measure capacity of the condenser, using a condenser tester. The value should be 0.18-0.25 microfarad. With the condenser ground wire disconnected, measure insulation resistance between the outer case and the positive terminal. Insulation resistance should be over 5 megohms.

In the event that no test equipment is available, a quick test of the condenser may be made by connecting the negative lead or case to the negative terminal of a 6-volt battery and the positive lead to the positive terminal. Allow the condenser to charge for a few seconds, then quickly disconnect the battery and touch the condenser leads together. If you observe a spark as the leads touch, you can assume that the condenser is good.

Arcing between the breaker points is a common symptom of a defective condenser.

Breaker Points

Refer to Chapter Three for details of breaker point service and ignition timing.

STARTER-GENERATOR

The F2 and F3 models are equipped with a combination starter-generator instead of a magneto. **Figure 5** is an exploded view of this unit. The armature rotates with the engine crankshaft. Attached to the end of the armature shaft is the breaker cam. This unit operates as a generator when the engine is running and as a starting motor when the engine is stopped. Associated with the starter-generator is a cut-out relay, voltage regulator and starter relay. **Figure 6** is a schematic diagram of the associated circuitry. Refer to this diagram during the following discussion.

Starter Relay

The starter relay is enclosed within the voltage regulator unit. **Figure 7** illustrates the relay circuit. Pressing the starter switch energizes the relay coil and closes the relay contact. Current then flows from the battery, through the relay contact and finally through the series field winding (M) of the starter-generator.

Cut-Out Relay

When the engine is off or running at low speed, the battery must be disconnected from the generator to prevent it from discharging. The cut-out relay performs this function. As engine speed increases, output voltage of the generator increases to a value sufficient to charge the battery. When this occurs, a voltage sensing coil in the cut-out relay closes the relay contacts, permitting current to flow from the generator to the battery and external loads. As the engine slows down, generator output decreases and current tends to flow from the battery to the generator. A second coil in the cut-out relay senses this reverse current and allows the contacts to open

F5, F7 AND F9 MAGNETO CIRCUITRY

④

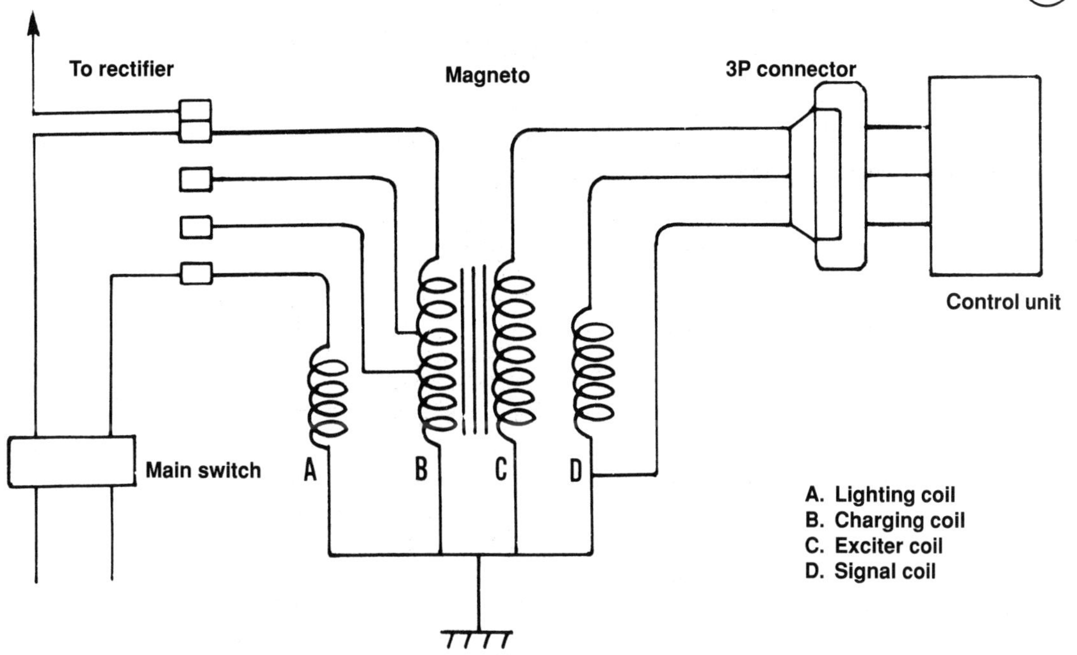

To rectifier

Magneto

3P connector

Control unit

Main switch

A B C D

A. Lighting coil
B. Charging coil
C. Exciter coil
D. Signal coil

⑤

STARTER-GENERATOR
(F2, F3)

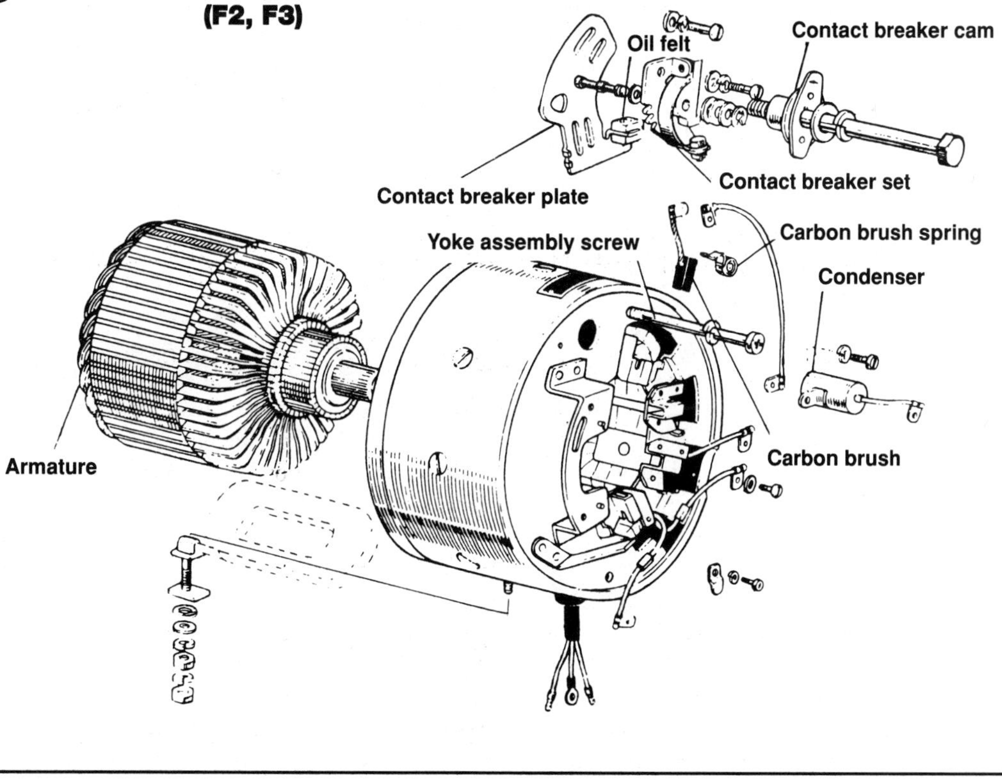

6

Oil felt

Contact breaker cam

Contact breaker plate

Contact breaker set

Yoke assembly screw

Carbon brush spring

Condenser

Carbon brush

Armature

⑥

STARTER-GENERATOR CIRCUITRY
(F2, F3)

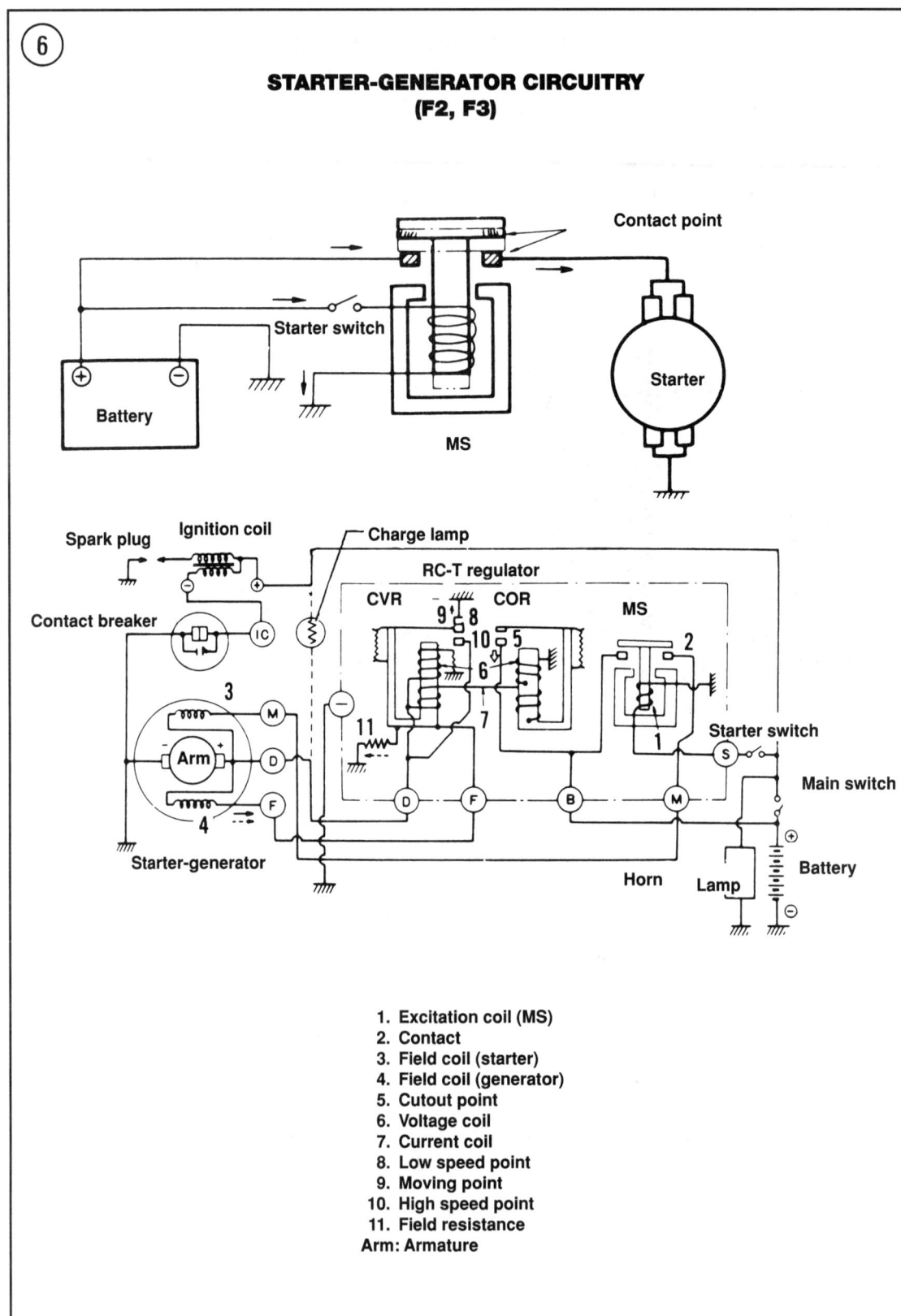

1. Excitation coil (MS)
2. Contact
3. Field coil (starter)
4. Field coil (generator)
5. Cutout point
6. Voltage coil
7. Current coil
8. Low speed point
9. Moving point
10. High speed point
11. Field resistance
Arm: Armature

again, thereby disconnecting the battery and generator.

Voltage Regulator

Varying engine speeds and electrical loads affect the generator output. The voltage regulator maintains the output voltage at a constant level by controlling the field current in the generator. **Figure 7** illustrates its operation.

With contacts (8) and (9) closed, the field is grounded and the generator produces its maximum

output. As the output rises, voltage regulator coil (6) pulls contacts (8) and (9) apart, thereby inserting resistance (10) into the field circuit. The resistance decreases generator field current, which results in less output from the generator. As output from the generator decreases, contacts (8) and (9) close again and the cycle repeats. The cycling action tends to maintain constant generator output. At high engine speeds and light electrical loads, the action of contacts (8) and (9) may not be sufficient to limit generator output. If output voltage tends to go very high, coil (6) pulls contact (9) all the way to contact (10), thus short-circuiting the field and causing generator output to decrease almost to zero. Voltage regulation is then effected by cycling of contact (9) between midposition and contact (10).

Starter-Generator
Removal/Installation

1. Remove shift pedal.

2. Remove left crankcase cover.

3. Remove breaker cam (**Figure 8**).

4. Remove yoke retaining screws, then pull yoke from engine (**Figure 9**).

5. Using a suitable puller, remove armature (**Figure 10**).

6. Remove Woodruff key from crankshaft.

6

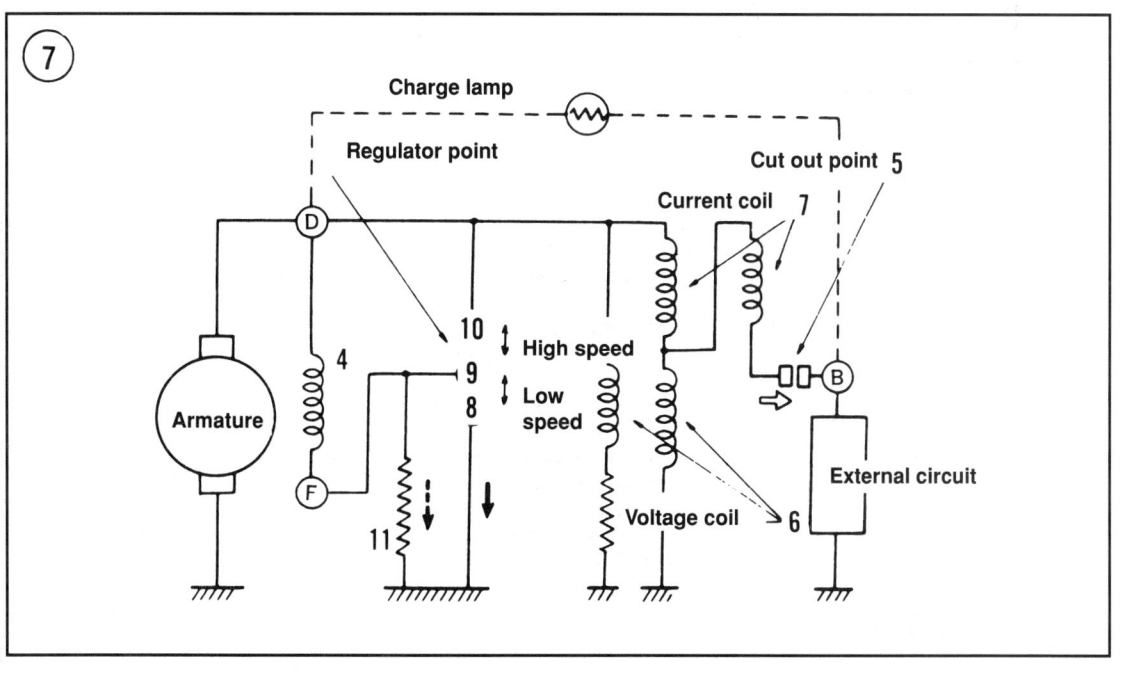

Reverse the removal procedure to install the starter-generator. If brushes were removed, don't install them until after the yoke assembly is in position. If the brushes were not removed, it will be necessary to position them as shown in **Figure 11** before the yoke can be installed. Use brush spring to hold brush in position for installation (1). Be sure to snap them into position before starting the engine. Brush (2) should ride on commutator with applied force from brush spring if correctly positioned.

STARTER-GENERATOR TROUBLESHOOTING

Malfunctions within the starter-generator system can be divided into 3 main categories:

  a. Starter does not work properly.
  b. Generator output is too low, resulting in an undercharged battery.
  c. Generator output is too high, resulting in an overcharged battery.

Starter Troubleshooting

Table 1 lists symptoms, probable causes and remedies for starter malfunctions.

Generator Troubleshooting

In the case of charging system malfunctions, it is necessary to determine whether the generator or the regulator is at fault. To determine which, refer to **Figure 12**, then proceed as follows.

1. Disconnect the wires from terminal (D) and (F) of the regulator.

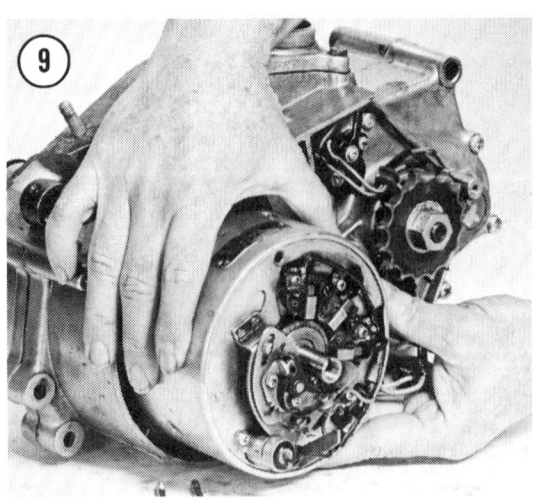

2. Connect the wire which was removed from terminal (F) to a good ground. Connect an accurate voltmeter (0-20 VDC) between the wire removed from terminal (D) and ground.

3. Start the engine and run it at 2,200 rpm. If the meter indicates more than 13 volts, it can be assumed that the generator is OK.

If the meter indications are not as specified, the starter generator is faulty.

Checking the Yoke

Clean the yoke assembly of all foreign material and remove it from the machine.

1. Use an ohmmeter to measure insulation resistance between positive brush and ground. If the meter indicates continuity, check for a short circuit at the brush holder or terminal (D). Note that the negative brush holder is not insulated.

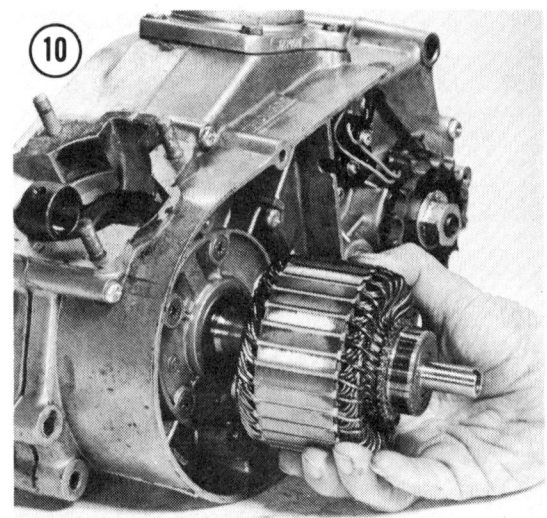

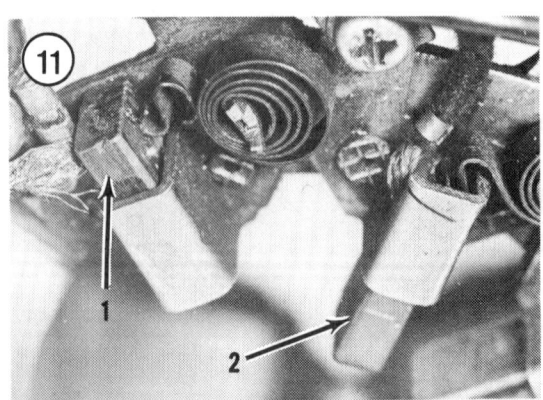

2. Measure field coil resistance between terminals (F) and (D). Field coil resistance should be between 5-8 ohms.

3. Set the ohmmeter to its highest range. Measure insulation resistance between terminal (F) and a good ground. Insulation resistance should be essentially infinite.

If the measurements obtained in Step 2 or Step 3 are not as specified, replace the yoke. If the yoke assembly is good, check the brushes and the armature.

Checking the Brushes

Poor brush condition is one of the most frequent causes of low generator output. Remove the brushes and examine them carefully. Each brush must contact the commutator with at least 3/4 of its contact surface. If either brush is worn excessively, replace both brushes.

If the brushes and the commutator are rough, misalignment of the armature and crankshaft may be the cause. Check the tapered bore of the armature and smooth it if there are any burrs.

When replacing brushes, be sure that the positive brush lead doesn't touch the brush holder or the edge of the breaker plate. Also be sure that the negative brush lead doesn't touch the positive brush spring.

Checking the Armature

1. Clean the commutator of oil, dust and foreign material.

2. If the commutator is rough or covered with carbon dust, polish it with a fine emery paper. If a light polishing does not clean up the surface, remove the armature and turn the commutator in a lathe. Do not reduce the commutator diameter by more than 0.08 in. (2.0 mm).

3. Undercut the mica segments between the commutator segments with a hacksaw blade to a depth of 0.02-0.04 in. (0.05-1.0 mm). Remove the dust between the segments.

4. Use an ohmmeter or armature growler to determine that no commutator segment is shorted to the shaft. If any short exists, replace the armature.

Checking the Regulator

Varying engine speeds and electrical loads affect output of the generator. The regulator controls generator output and also disconnects the battery from the generator whenever generator output voltage is less than that of the battery, thereby preventing battery discharge through the generator.

Disconnect the wire from terminal (B) at the regulator. Be careful that this wire doesn't become grounded. Connect the voltmeter between terminal (B) of the regulator and ground, as shown in **Figure 13**. Start the engine and run it at 2,500 rpm. The voltmeter should indicate 14.7-15.7 volts.

Observe the contacts on the cut-out relay as you slowly increase engine speed. The contacts should close when voltmeter indicates 12.5-13.5 volts.

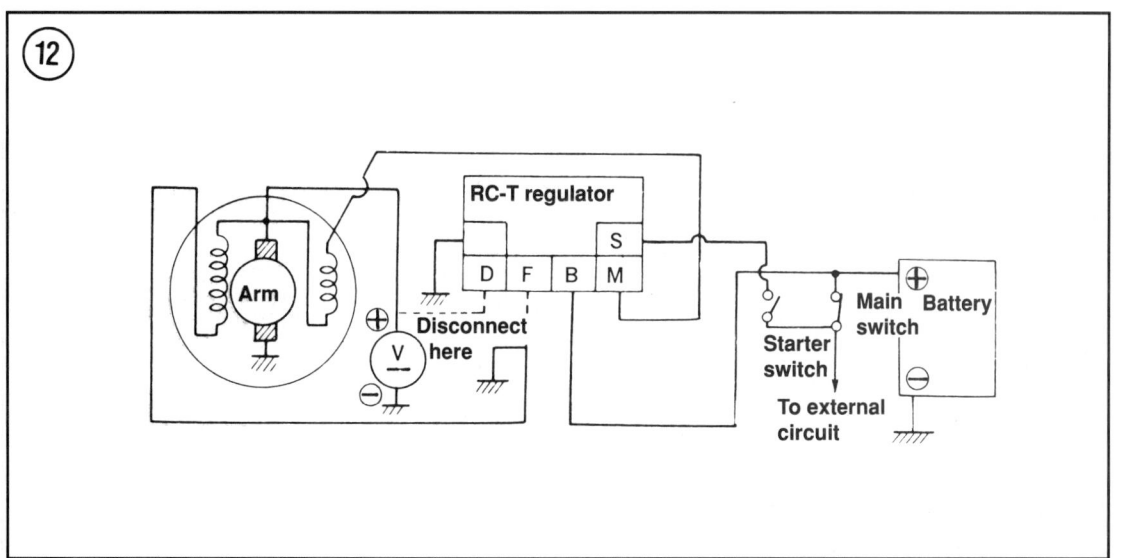

Adjusting the Voltage Regulator

CAUTION
Disconnect the battery before removing the regulator cover. Do not make any adjustments with the battery in place.

Remove the regulator cover and adjust the regulator by bending the adjustment spring. Bending the spring downward raises the voltage setting. The voltage regulator can be identified by its 2 contact points.

The cut-out relay can be identified by a single set of contacts which are normally open. The relay rarely, if ever, needs adjustment. Usually all that is required is to dress the contacts lightly to remove any corrosion or light pitting. Should adjustment be required, bend the spring retainer up or down as required. Lowering the spring retainer raises the voltage setting.

Ignition Coil

The ignition coil is a form of transformer which develops the high voltage required to jump the spark plug gap. The only maintenance required is keeping the electrical connections clean and tight and making sure the coil is mounted securely. If coil condition is doubtful, there are several checks which should be made.

1. Measure resistance with an ohmmeter between the positive and negative primary terminals. Resistance should indicate approximately 5 ohms for most coils on these machines. Some coils, however, have a primary resistance less than 2 ohms.

2. Measure resistance between either primary terminal and the secondary high voltage terminal. Resistance should be in the range of 5,000-11,000 ohms. If the bike is operated for extended periods with the battery disconnected or with the battery circuit fuse blown, rectifier damage may result. Avoid such operation and check the fuse from time to time.

3. Scrape the paint from the coil housing down to bare metal. Measure the resistance between this bare spot and the high voltage terminal. Insulation resistance must be at least 3 megohms (2 million ohms).

4. If these checks don't reveal any defects, but coil condition is still doubtful, replace the coil with one known to be good.

Be sure that you connect the primary wires correctly.

RECTIFIER

The rectifier serves 2 purposes. First, it converts alternating current generated by the magneto into direct current for battery charging. Second, it prevents the battery from discharging through the charging coil in the magneto when the engine isn't turning fast enough to charge the battery.

To test the rectifier, refer to **Figure 14**. Connect the negative terminal of a 6-volt battery to the blue/white lead on the rectifier. Connect a small

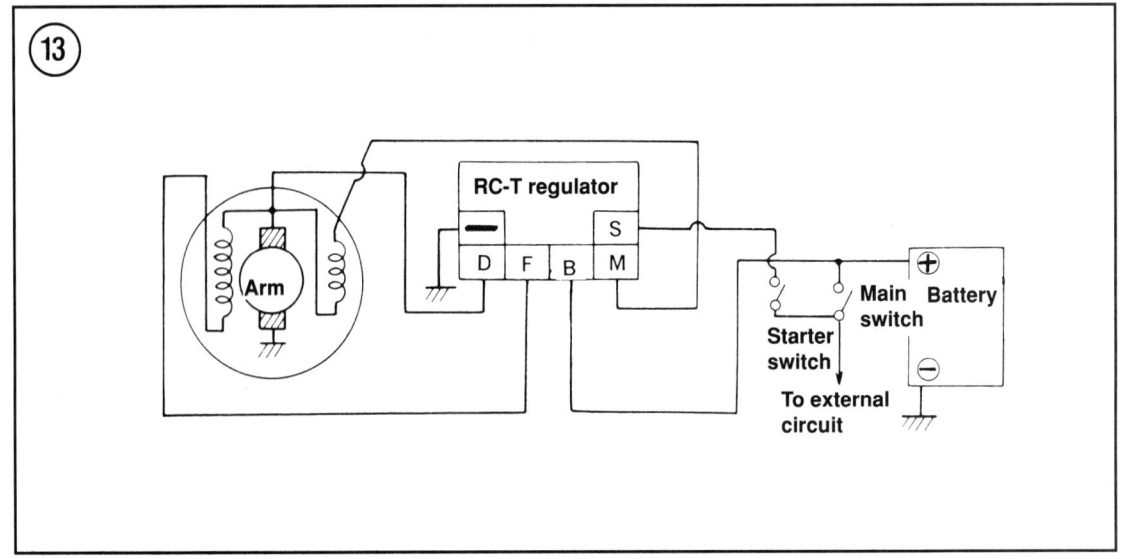

6-volt bulb, such as a taillight bulb, in series with positive battery lead, then connect the other terminal of the bulb to the brown wire on the rectifier. If the bulb lights, the rectifier is defective and must be replaced. Reverse the rectifier leads so that the negative battery lead is connected to the brown rectifier lead and the positive lead and lamp are connected to the blue/ white lead. The lamp should now light. If not, replace the rectifier.

HIGH VOLTAGE CABLE

This cable carries the current from the ignition coil to the spark plug. If it becomes sharply bent or is allowed to chafe against the frame, damage and eventual destruction will occur. Pay particular attention to the routing of this cable.

CAPACITOR DISCHARGE
IGNITION SYSTEM OPERATION

Some models are equipped with a capacitor discharge (CD) ignition system. This solid state system, unlike conventional ignition systems, uses no breaker points or other moving parts. **Figure 15** illustrates the capacitor discharge system. Alternating current from the exciter coil is rectified and used to charge the capacitor. As the piston approaches firing position, a pulse from the signal coil is rectified, shaped and then used to trigger the silicon controlled rectifier (SCR) which in turn allows the capacitor to discharge quickly into the primary circuit of the ignition coil, where the voltage is stepped up to fire the spark plug.

Refer to Chapter Three for details of ignition timing.

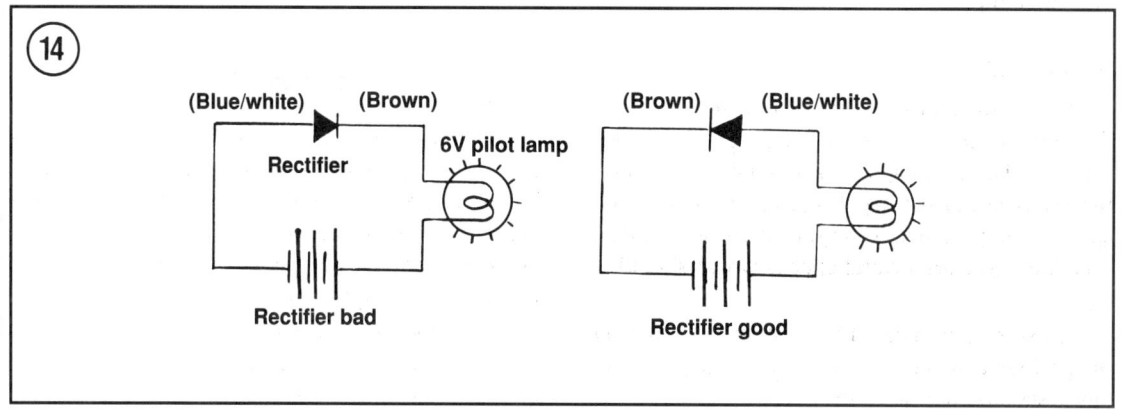

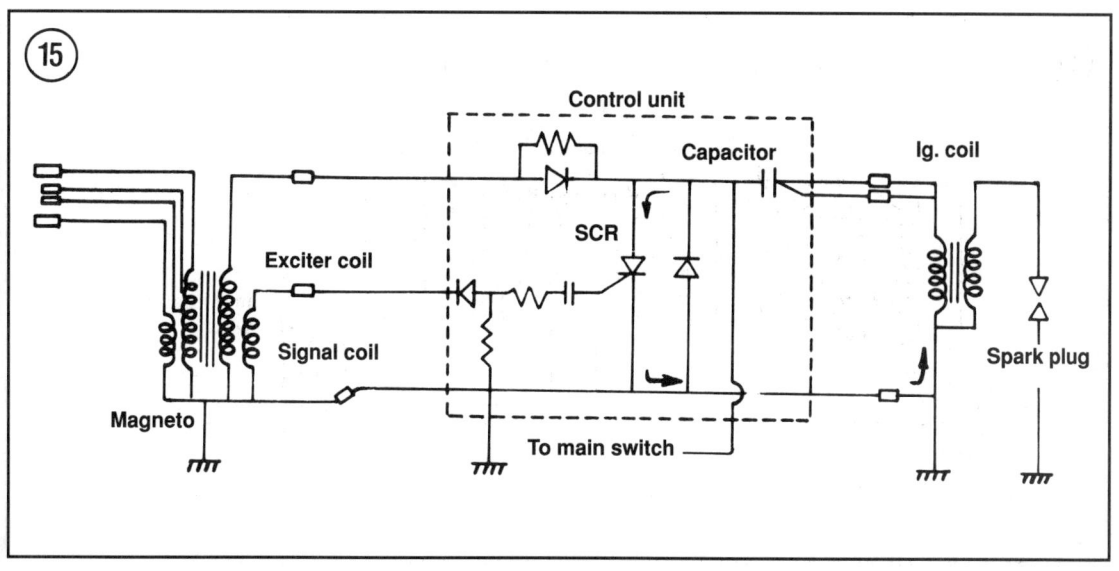

Magneto

To check the magneto, disconnect the wires from the main switch, the rectifier and the control unit. Measure resistance between each listed lead and the black lead with an ohmmeter. A schematic diagram of the magneto is shown in **Figure 16**. Resistance of each coil should be approximately as specified in **Table 2**.

> *NOTE*
> *When installing a new pulser coil on a KD175 or KE175, make sure the red lead connects to the top of the pulser coil and the blue lead to the bottom of the pulser coil. Improper lead connection can retard ignition timing by about 15°.*

Ignition Coil

Check the ignition coil with an ohmmeter. Resistance between the green/white terminal and the black terminal should be approximately 0.21 ohm. Resistance between the black terminal and the output terminal should be approximately 1,800 ohms. If after these checks, coil condition is still doubtful, substitute a coil known to be good.

Ignition Coil and Control Unit Tests

The control unit tester shown in **Figure 17** is required to test these units. To check the ignition coil with the tester, proceed as follows.

1. Insert power cord (K) into receptacle (B) on the tester. Connect the power cord into a standard 110-volt outlet. Be sure power switch (D) is OFF.
2. Insert the connector of accessory cord (H) into receptacle (A) on the tester.
3. Insert the high voltage cable of the ignition coil into receptacle (E). Connect the 2-pole connector on cord (H) to the ignition coil.
4. Set switch (L) to COIL.
5. Press rocker switch (D) to ON.
6. Press push-button (C). If there is no spark at gap (M), the coil is defective.

After you test the coil, remove it from the tester, then test the control unit.

1. Perform Step 2 and Step 3 above.
2. Connect the 3-pole connector on cord (H) to the receptacle on the control unit.
3. Set switch (L) to UNIT.
4. Press switch (D) to ON.
5. Press push-button (C). Pilot lamp (G) will light and there will be a strong spark discharge in the 3 needle spark gap if the control is good. If there is no spark, replace the control unit.

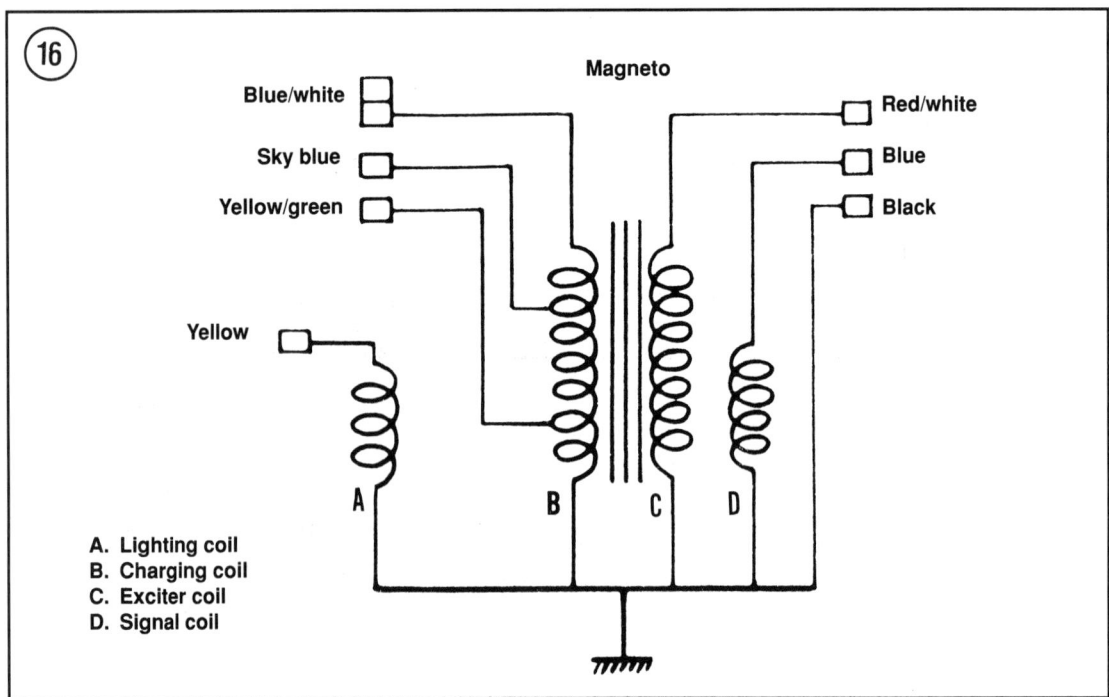

(16)

Magneto

Blue/white

Sky blue

Yellow/green

Yellow

Red/white

Blue

Black

A. Lighting coil
B. Charging coil
C. Exciter coil
D. Signal coil

It is also possible to test the control unit and ignition coil together.

1. Perform Step 1 and Step 2 of the coil test.
2. Connect both the coil and the control unit to the tester using the terminals on cable (H).
3. Connect the high voltage cable from the coil to receptacle (E) on the tester.
4. Set switch (L) to UNIT.
5. Set switch (D) to ON.
6. Press push-button (C).
7. If there is a spark discharge at spark gap (M) and pilot lamp (G) lights, both the ignition coil and the control unit are good. If there is no spark, each unit must be tested separately.

SOLID STATE VOLTAGE REGULATOR

Some machines are equipped with a solid state unit which is used as a voltage regulator (SVR in **Figure 18**). This consists of a zener diode (ZD), a silicon controlled rectifier (SCR) and 2 resistors, as shown in **Figure 19**. Refer to this illustration during the following discussion.

Assume that the main switch is closed. As engine speed increases, output voltage from the magneto tends to increase. If the battery is fully charged, the voltage at point (A) will tend to rise. If it reaches the zener voltage (7.0 ±0.5 volts), the zener diode conducts in the reverse direction, thereby triggering the silicon controlled rectifier. When the silicon controlled rectifier conducts, magneto output is grounded, thereby reducing its output voltage to near zero. As the voltage at junction (A) drips, the zener diode ceases to conduct and removes the trigger signal to the silicon controlled rectifier.

Checking the SVR

Connect a test lamp in series with a 6-volt battery, or use an ohmmeter to determine whether there is continuity between points (C) and (D). The continuity test lamp should not light or the ohmmeter should show no continuity. Reverse the continuity test connections to the SVR. If the lamp lights or the ohmmeter indicates continuity, the unit is defective. Also be sure that terminal (C) is not shorted to case.

If the facilities are available, connect the test circuit shown in **Figure 20**. Slowly increase the voltage from the power supply and observe the lamp. The lamp must light when the voltmeter indicates 6.5-7.5 volts. If not, the unit must be replaced. Reduce the power supply voltage to 1.0 volt below the point where the lamp became lit. Disconnect the battery momentarily, then reconnect it. If the test lamp lights, replace the SVR.

SOLID STATE REGULATOR/RECTIFIER (1979 AND LATER)

1979 and later 100cc and 125cc models are equipped with a combined solid state regulator/rectifier for true voltage regulation. **Figure 21** is a typical schematic diagram of the regulator/rectifier

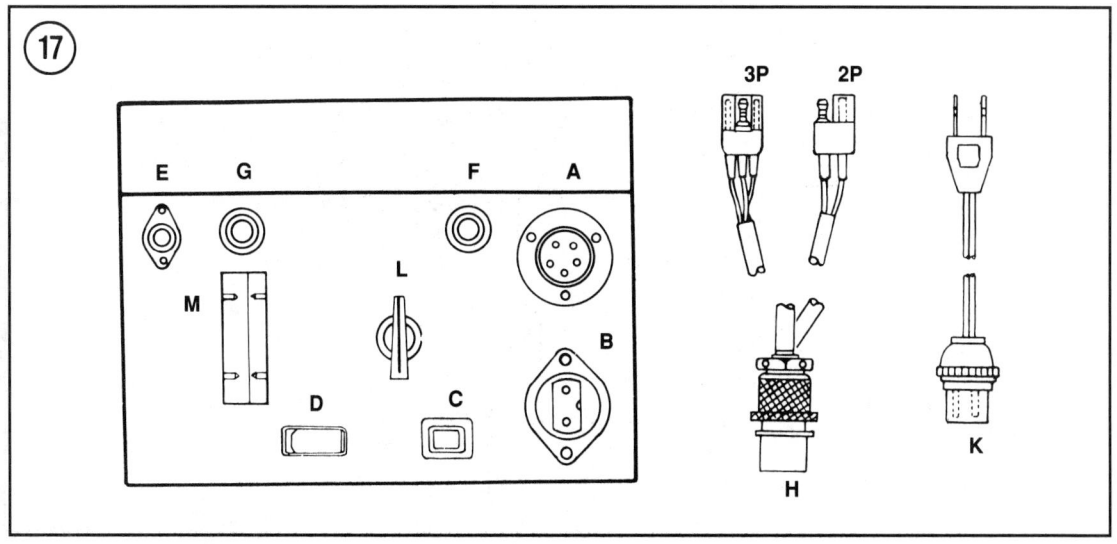

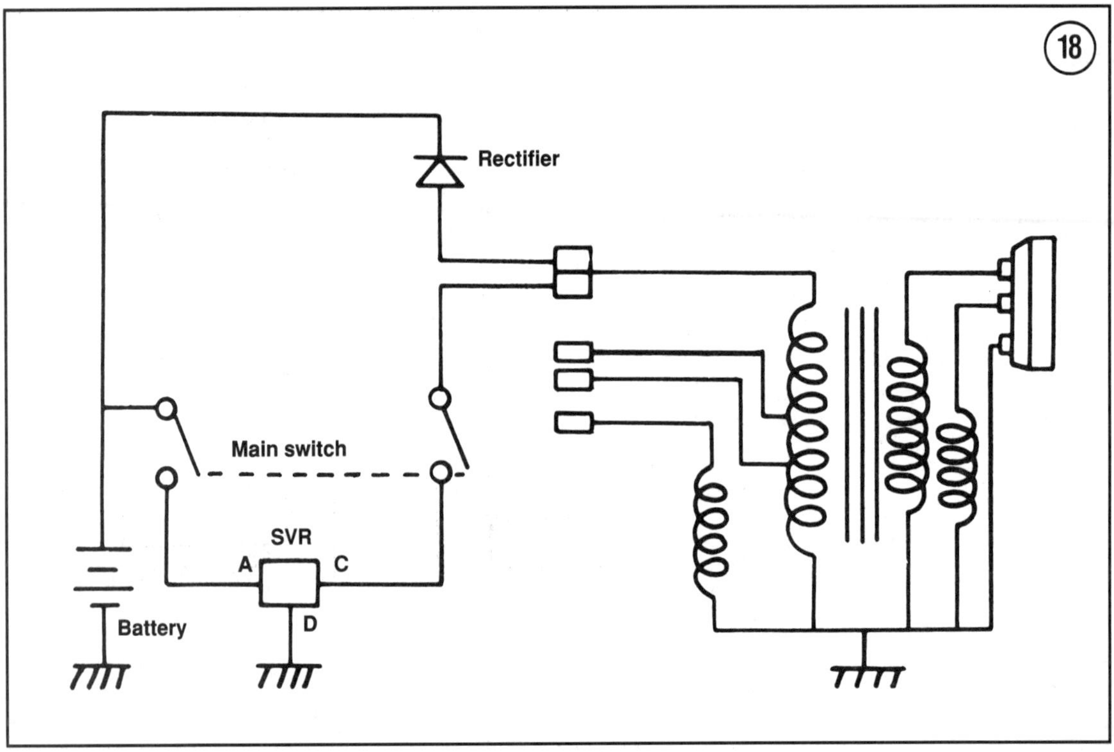
18
Rectifier
Main switch
SVR
A
C
D
Battery

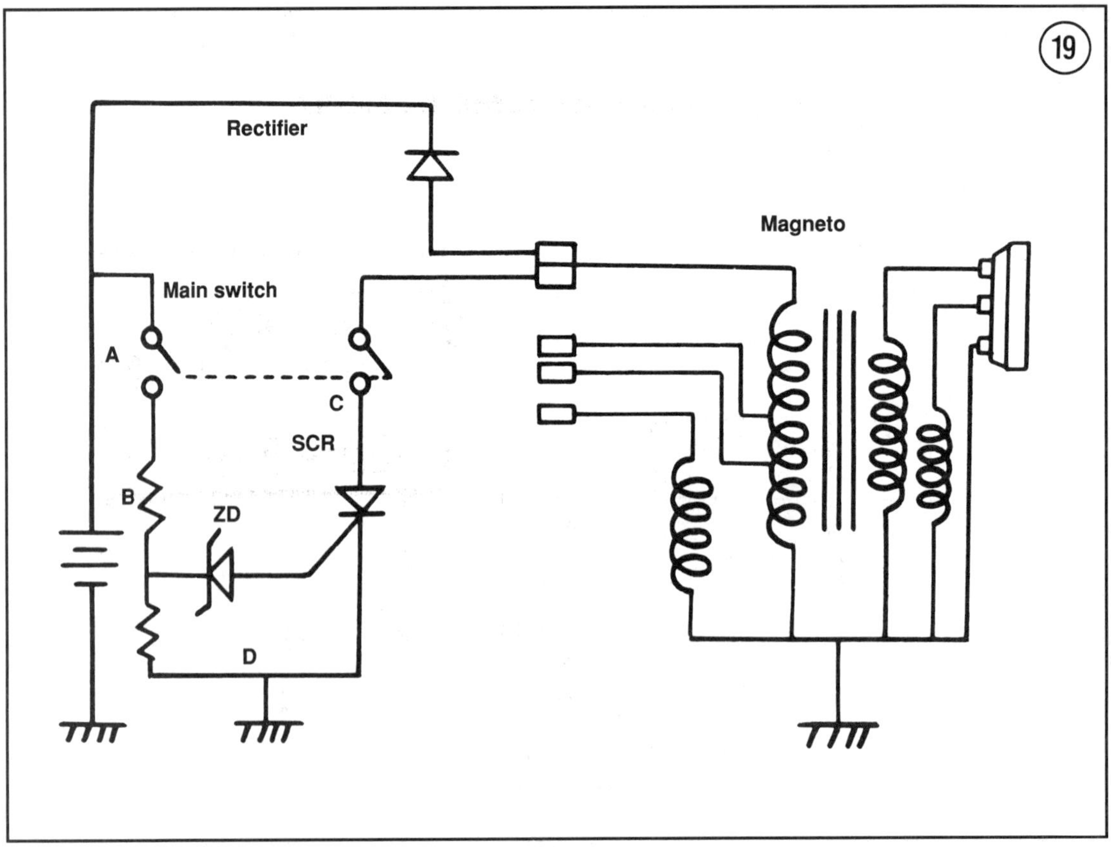
19
Rectifier
Magneto
Main switch
A
C
SCR
B
ZD
D

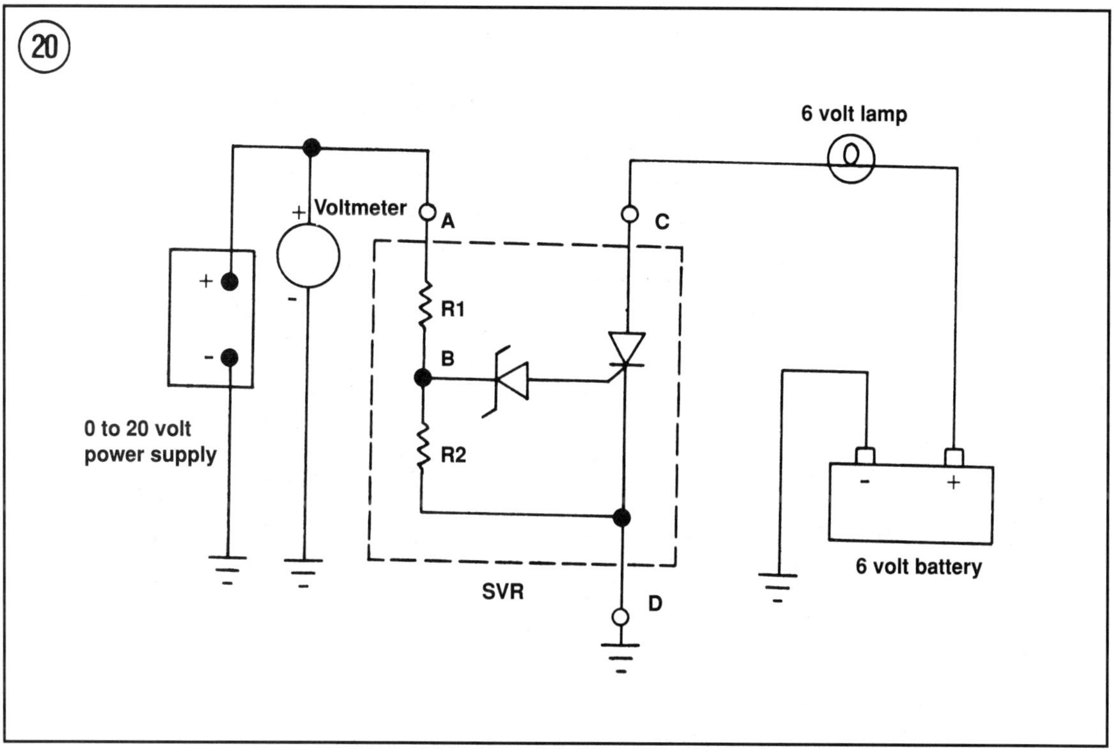

20

+ Voltmeter

A

R1

B

R2

SVR

D

0 to 20 volt
power supply

6 volt lamp

C

6 volt battery

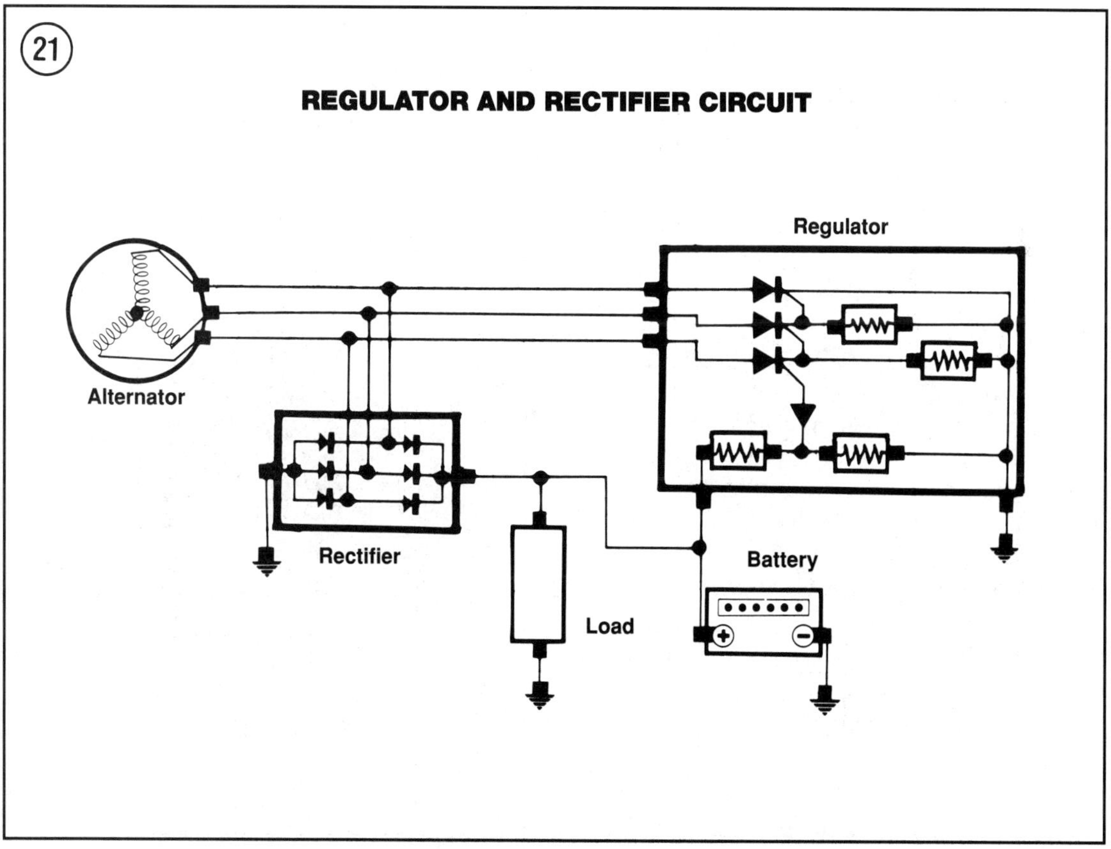

21

REGULATOR AND RECTIFIER CIRCUIT

6

Regulator

Alternator

Rectifier

Load

Battery

circuit. The combined unit is not adjustable and must be replaced if defective.

CHARGING SYSTEM TEST
(1979 AND LATER)

Whenever you suspect charging system trouble, make sure the battery is in good condition before checking the rest of the charging system. Check the specific gravity. If the battery is not fully charged, have it charged before proceeding with these tests.

Charging System Test

1. Start the engine and let it reach normal operating temperature.
2. Connect a 0-15 DC voltmeter to the battery as shown in **Figure 22**.
3. Bring the engine speed from idle to 4,000 rpm, observing the voltage as you go. The voltage should be at or near battery voltage at idle and it should increase gradually with engine speed, up to about 8 volts.
4. If the reading is higher than about 8 volts, the regulator/rectifier or its brown lead is faulty and should be replaced. If the reading is less than 8 volts or does not increase with engine speed, check the magneto output and lighting/charge coil resistance.

Magneto Output Voltage

1. Remove the fuel tank and disconnect the 2-pole connector on the yellow magneto leads.
2. Connect a 0-250 AC voltmeter to each of the yellow magneto leads.
3. Start the engine and observe the magneto output voltage. It should be about 25 volts at 4,000 rpm. If the voltage is within specification, any charging problems are due to a faulty regulator/rectifier. If the voltage is much lower, the magneto is faulty. Check lighting/charging coil resistance.

Lighting/Charging Coil Resistance

1. With the engine OFF and an ohmmeter set on the 1 ohm scale, check resistance between the pair of yellow leads as described in *Magneto Output Voltage*. The resistance should be about 0.20 ohms.
2. Set the ohmmeter on the highest scale and check resistance between each yellow lead and ground. The resistance should be infinite.

3. If the coil resistance is OK, but magneto output is low, the rotor may have become demagnetized. Replace the rotor.

LIGHTS

Machines designed to be ridden on public streets are equipped with lights. Check them periodically to be sure that they are working properly.

Headlight

The headlight unit consists primarily of a lamp body, a dual-filament bulb, a lens and reflection unit, a rim and a socket. To adjust the headlight, loosen the mounting bolts and move the assembly as required.

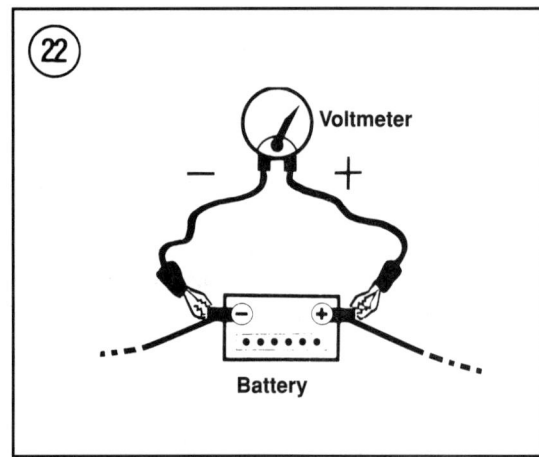

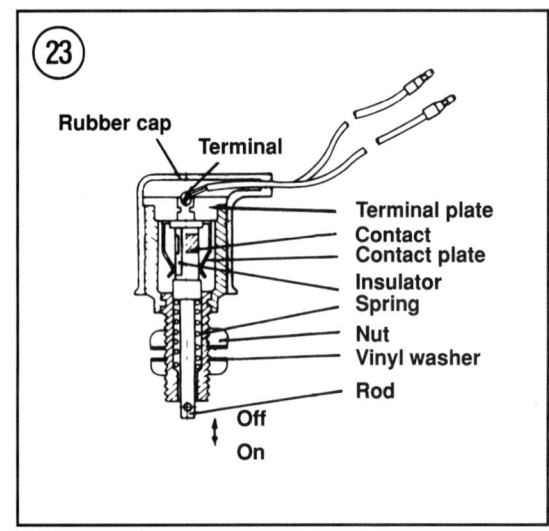

Brake Light

Figure 23 illustrates the brake light switch. The switch is actuated by the brake pedal. Adjust the switch so that the stoplight goes on just before braking action occurs. Move the switch body up or down as required for adjustment. Tighten the clamp nut after adjustment.

Turn Signals

Kawasaki bikes are equipped with 2 different types of turn signal flasher relays. Most F series models use one type; the G series uses another. If replacement becomes necessary, be sure you replace with the proper type.

If any turn signal bulb burns out, be sure to replace it with the same type. Improper action of the flasher relay, or even failure to operate may result from the use of the wrong bulbs.

HORN

Current for the horn is supplied by the battery. One horn terminal is connected to the battery through the main switch. The other terminal is connected to the horn button. When the rider presses the button, current flows through the horn. **Figure 24** illustrates horn construction. As current flows through the coil, the core becomes magnetized and attracts the armature. As the armature moves, it opens the contacts, cutting off the current. The diaphragm spring then returns the armature to its original position. This process repeats rapidly until the rider releases the horn button. The action of the armature striking the end of the core produces the sound which is amplified by the resonator.

MAIN SWITCH

Service on the main switch is limited to checking continuity between the various circuits.

BATTERY

Most Kawasaki bikes are equipped with lead-acid storage batteries, smaller in size but similar in construction to those found in automobiles.

WARNING
Read and thoroughly understand the section on safety precautions before doing any battery service.

Safety Precautions

When working with batteries, use extreme care to avoid spilling or splashing electrolyte. This electrolyte is sulfuric acid, which can destroy clothing and cause serious chemical burns. If any electrolyte is spilled or splashed on clothing or body, it should be immediately neutralized with a solution of baking

6

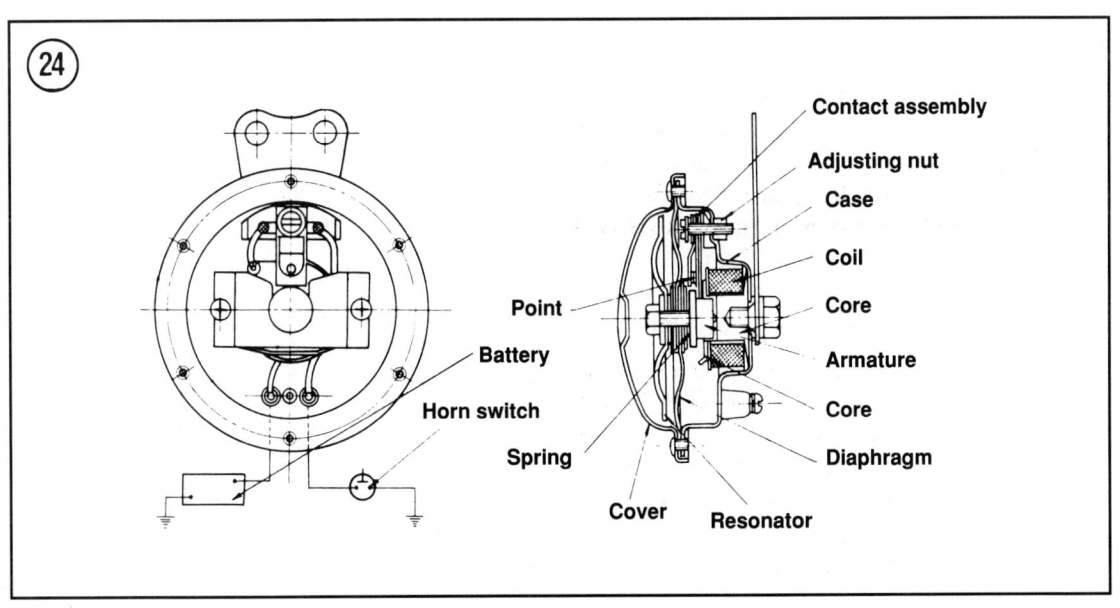

Contact assembly
Adjusting nut
Case
Coil
Core
Point
Battery
Armature
Horn switch
Core
Spring
Diaphragm
Cover   Resonator

soda and water, then flushed with plenty of clean water.

Electrolyte splashed into the eyes is extremely dangerous. Safety glasses should always be worn when working with batteries. If electrolyte is splashed into the eye, force the eye open, flood with cool clean water for about 5 minutes and call a physician immediately.

If electrolyte is spilled or splashed onto painted or unpainted surfaces, it should be neutralized immediately with baking soda solution and then rinsed with clean water.

When batteries are being charged, highly explosive hydrogen gas forms in each cell. Some of this gas escapes through the filler openings and may form an explosive atmosphere around the battery. *This explosive atmosphere may exist for hours.* Sparks, open flames or a lighted cigarette can ignite this gas causing an internal explosion and possible serious personal injury. The following precautions should be taken to prevent an explosion.

1. Do not smoke or permit any open flame near any battery being charged or which has been recently charged.

2. Do not disconnect live circuits at battery terminals, because a spark usually occurs where a live circuit is broken. Care must always be taken when connecting or disconnecting any battery charger; be sure its power switch is OFF before making or breaking any connections. Poor connections are a common cause of electrical arcs which cause explosions.

Electrolyte Level

Battery electrolyte level should be checked regularly, particularly during hot weather. Most batteries are marked with electrolyte level limit lines (**Figure 25**). Always maintain the fluid level between the 2 lines, using distilled water as required for replenishment. Distilled water is available at most supermarkets. It is sold for use in steam irons and is quite inexpensive.

Overfilling leads to loss of electrolyte, resulting in poor battery performance, short life and excessive corrosion. Never allow the electrolyte level to drop below the top of the plates. That portion of the plates exposed to air may be permanently damaged, resulting in the loss of battery performance and shortened life.

Excessive use of water is an indication that the battery is being overcharged. The two most common causes of overcharging are high battery temperature or high voltage regulator setting. It is advisable to check the voltage regulator, on machines so equipped, if this situation exits.

Cleaning

Check the battery occasionally for presence of dirt or corrosion. The top of the battery, in particular, should be kept clean. Acid film and dirt permit

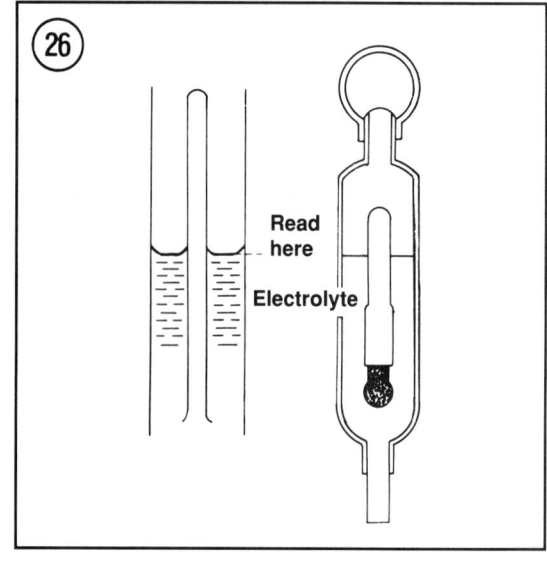

current to flow between terminals, which will slowly discharge the battery.

For best results when cleaning, wash first with dilute ammonia or baking soda solution, then flush with plenty of clean water. Take care to keep filler plugs tight so that no cleaning solution enters the cells.

Battery Cables

To ensure good electrical contact, cables must be clean and tight on battery terminals. If the battery or cable terminals are corroded, the cables should be disconnected and cleaned separately with a wire brush and baking soda solution. After cleaning, apply a very thin coating of petroleum jelly to the battery terminals before installing the cables. After connecting the cables, apply a light coating to the connection. This procedure will help to prevent future corrosion.

Battery Charging

WARNING
Do not smoke or permit any open flame in any area where batteries are being charged or immediately after charging. Highly explosive hydrogen gas is formed during the charging process. Be sure to reread Safety Precautions in the beginning of this section.

Motorcycle batteries are not designed for high charge or discharge rates. For this reason, it is recommended that a motorcycle battery be charged at a rate not exceeding 10% of its ampere-hour capacity. That is, do not exceed 0.5-ampere charging rate for a 5 ampere-hour battery. This charge rate should continue for 10 hours if the battery is completely discharged, or until specific gravity of each cell is up to 1.260-1.280, corrected for temperature. If after prolonged charging, specific gravity of one or more cells does not come up to at least 1.230, the battery will not perform as well as it should, but it may continue to provide satisfactory service for a time.

Some temperature rise is normal as a battery is being charged. Do not allow the electrolyte temperature to exceed 110° F. Should temperature reach that figure, discontinue charging until the battery cools, then resume charging at a lower rate.

Testing State of Charge

Although sophisticated battery testing devices are on the market, they are not available to the average motorcycle owner and their use is beyond the scope of this book. A hydrometer, however, is an inexpensive tool and will tell much about battery condition.

To use a hydrometer, place the suction tube into the filler opening and draw in just enough electrolyte to life the float. Hold the instrument in a vertical position and read specific gravity on the scale, where the float stem emerges from the electrolyte (**Figure 26**).

Specific gravity of the electrolyte varies with temperature, so it is necessary to apply a temperature correction to the reading so obtained. For each 10° that battery temperature exceeds 80° F, add 0.004 to the indicated specific gravity. Likewise, subtract 0.004 from the indicate value for each 10° that battery temperature is below 80° F.

Repeat this measurement for each battery cell. If there is more than 0.050 difference (50 points) between cells, battery condition is questionable.

State of charge may be determined from **Table 3**.

Dont measure specific gravity immediately after adding water. Ride the machine a few miles to ensure thorough mixing of the electrolyte.

It is most important to maintain batteries fully charged during cold weather. A fully charged battery freezes at a much lower temperature than does one which is partially discharged. Freezing temperature depends on specific gravity (see **Table 4**).

6

Table 1 STARTER TROUBLESHOOTING

Symptom	Probable cause	Remedy
Starter does not work	Low battery	Recharge battery
	Worn brushes	Replace brushes
	Internal short	Repair or replace defective component
	Relay inoperative	Replace votage regulator
	Defective wiring or connections	Repair wire or clean and tighten
	Defective switch	Replace switch
Starter action is weak	Low battery	Recharge battery
	Pitted relay contacts	Clean contacts or replace voltage regulator
	Brushes worn	Replace brushes
	Defective wiring or connections	Repair wire or clean and tighten connections
	Short in commutator	Replace armature
Starter runs continuously	Stuck relay	Dress contacts or replace voltage regulator

Table 2 MAGNETO COIL RESISTANCE*

Coil	Connection	Resistance (ohms)
External ignition coil	Primary to coil ground	1.2-2.5
	Secondary (spark plug lead) to coil ground	6.5k-12.0k
Standard ignition exciter (under flywheel)	Primary to coil ground	220
Lighting coil (under flywheel)	Yellow lead to ground	0.15-0.23
Signal coil (CDI models)	Signal wire to ground	75

*Resistance tests will detect an open (inoperable) circuit, but are intended as a guide only. Production and service coils may be manufactured to different specifications. It is important to know that coil windings may test slightly outside the ranges listed, but still operate satisfactorily.

Table 3 STATE OF CHARGE

Specific gravity	State of charge
1.110-1.130	Discharged
1.140-1.160	Almost discharged
1.170-1.190	One-quarter charged
1.200-1.220	One-half charged
1.230-1.250	Three-quarters charged
1.260-1.280	Fully charged

Table 4 BATTERY FREEZING TEMPERATURE

Specific gravity	Freezing temperature (°F)
1.110	18
1.120	13
1.140	8
1.160	1
1.180	−6

(continued)

Table 4 BATTERY FREEZING TEMPERATURE (continued)

Specific gravity	Freezing temperature (°F)
1.200	−17
1.220	−31
1.240	−50
1.260	−75
1.280	−92

Table 5 BATTERY APPLICATION

Model	Battery
80-100cc	
D1	6N4-2A
J1	6N4-2A or 12N9-4B
G3TRA, G4TR, G5	6N4-2A-3
G3SS, G3TRD/E, G5B/C, MC1	6N4-2A-5
KE/KH/KM/KV100	6N4-2A-5
KE100 (1979-on), KM100 (1978-on)	6N6-1D-2
125-175cc	
C2SS, C2TR, F6	6N4-2A
KE/KS125, KE175	6N6-1D-2
F2, F3	12N12-3B
F7	6N4-2A-5
250-350cc	
F4	12N6-4A
F8, F5, F9	6N2-2A
F9A/B/C	6N4B-2A-2

Table 6 IGNITION SPECIFICATIONS*

79-100 cc models	
KD80 (1975, 1976 & 1980-1987)	
Spark plug	
NGK	B7HS
ND	W22FS
Gap	0.6-0.7 mm (0.024-0.028 in.)
Ignition timing	
Piston position	1.86 mm (0.073 in.)
° BTDC	20
Breaker point gap	Set to correct timing
J Series	
Spark plug	
NGK	B6H
ND	W17F
Gap	0.6-0.7 mm (0.024-0.028 in.)
Ignition timing	
Piston position	1.58 mm (0.062 in.)
° BTDC	19
Breaker point gap	0.30-0.40 mm (0.012-0.016 in.)
MC1-A, MC1-B & MC1M	
Spark plug	
NGK	B7HS
ND	W25FN
Gap	0.6-0.7 mm (0.024-0.028 in.)

(continued)

6

Table 6 IGNITION SPECIFICATIONS (continued)

Ignition timing	
Piston position	1.96 mm (0.077 in.)
° BTDC	20
Breaker point gap	Set to correct timing
G3SS	
Spark plug	
NGK	B8HS
ND	W24FS
Gap	0.6-0.7 mm (0.024-0.028 in.)
Ignition timing	
Piston position	1.96 mm (0.077 in.)
° BTDC	20
Breaker point gap	0.30-0.40 mm (0.012-0.016 in.)
G3TR	
Spark plug	
NGK	B7HS
ND	W25FS
Gap	0.6-0.7 mm (0.024-0.028 in.)
Ignition timing	
Piston position	1.96 mm (0.077 in.)
° BTDC	20
Breaker point gap	0.30-0.40 mm (0.012-0.016 in.)
D1	
Spark plug	
NGK	B7H
ND	W22F
Gap	0.6-0.7 mm (0.024-0.028 in.)
Ignition timing	
Piston position	1.58 mm (0.062 in.)
° BTDC	19
Breaker point gap	0.30-0.40 mm (0.012-0.016 in.)
G4TR	
Spark plug	
NGK	B7HS
ND	W25FN
Gap	0.6-0.7 mm (0.024-0.028 in.)
Ignition timing	
Piston position	1.96 mm (0.077 in.)
° BTDC	20
Breaker point gap	0.30-0.40 mm (0.012-0.016 in.)
G5	
Spark plug	
NGK	B8HS
ND	W24FS
Gap	0.6-0.7 mm (0.024-0.028 in.)
Ignition timing	
Piston position	1.96 mm (0.077 in.)
° BTDC	20
Breaker point gap	0.30-0.40 mm (0.012-0.016 in.)
G31M	
Spark plug	
NGK	B8HN
ND	W25FN
Gap	0.6-0.7 mm (0.024-0.028 in.)
Ignition timing	
Piston position	2.58 mm (0.099 in.)
° BTDC	23
Breaker point gap	0.30-0.40 mm (0.012-0.016 in.)

(continued)

Table 6 IGNITION SPECIFICATIONS (continued)

KD100
  Spark plug
    NGK   B7HS
    ND   W22FS
    Gap   0.6-0.7 mm (0.024-0.028 in.)
  Ignition timing
    Piston position   1.96 mm (0.077 in.)
    ° BTDC   20
  Breaker point gap   Set to correct timing
KE100 1978 & earlier
  Spark plug
    NGK   B8HS
    ND   W24FS
    Gap   0.6-0.7 mm (0.024-0.028 in.)
  Ignition timing
    ° BTDC   20
    Piston position   1.96 mm (0.077 in.)
  Breaker point gap   Set to correct timing
KE100 1979 & later (A8 on)
  Spark plug
    NGK   B8ES
    ND   W24ES
    Gap   0.7-0.8 mm (0.028-0.032 in.)
  Ignition timing
    ° BTDC   23 @ 1,300 rpm
    Piston position   2.58 mm (0.099 in.)
  Breaker point gap   Set to correct timing
KH100
  Spark plug
    NGK   B8HS
    ND   W24FS
    Gap   0.6-0.7 mm (0.024-0.028 in.)
  Ignition timing
    Piston position   1.96 mm (0.077 in.)
    ° BTDC   20
  Breaker point gap   Set to correct timing
KM100 & KV100
  Spark plug
    NGK   B7HS
    ND   W22FS
    Gap   0.6-0.7 mm (0.024-0.028 in.)
  Ignition timing
    Piston position   1.96 mm (0.077 in.)
    ° BTDC   20
  Breaker point gap   Set to correct timing

115-125 cc models

C2SS & C2TR
  Spark plug
    NGK   B7HS
    ND   W22FS
    Gap   0.6-0.7 mm (0.024-0.028 in.)
  Ignition timing
    Piston position   1.78 mm (0.070 in.)
    ° BTDC   19
  Breaker point gap   0.30-0.40 mm (0.012-0.016 in.)

6

(continued)

Table 6 IGNITION SPECIFICATIONS (continued)

F6	
Spark plug	
NGK	B8HS
ND	W24FS
Gap	0.6-0.7 mm (0.024-0.028 in.)
Ignition timing	
Piston position	2.94 mm (0.116 in.)
° BTDC	23
Breaker point gap	0.30-0.40 mm (0.012-0.016 in.)
KD125	
Spark plug	
NGK	B8HS
ND	W24FS
Gap	0.6-0.7 mm (0.024-0.028 in.)
Ignition timing	
Piston position	1.96 mm (0.077 in.)
° BTDC	20
Breaker point gap	Set to correct timing
KE125 1979 & earlier	
Spark plug	
NGK	B8HS
ND	W24FS
Gap	0.6-0.7 mm (0.024-0.028 in.)
Ignition timing	
° BTDC	23 @1,300 rpm
Piston position	2.52 mm (0.099 in.)
Breaker point gap	Set to correct timing
KE125-A7 1980	
Spark plug	
NGK	B9ES
ND	—
Gap	0.7-0.8 mm (0.028-0.032 in.)
Ignition timing	
° BTDC	23 @1,300 rpm
Piston position	2.52 mm (0.099 in.)
Breaker point gap	Set to correct timing
KE125 1981 & later (A8 on)	
Spark plug	
NGK	B9ES
ND	—
Gap	0.7-0.8 mm (0.028-0.032 in.)
Ignition timing	
° BTDC	21 @ 1,300 rpm
Piston position	2.52 mm (0.099 in.)
Breaker point gap	Set to correct timing
KS125	
Spark plug	
NGK	B8HS
ND	W24FS
Gap	0.6-0.7 mm (0.024-0.028 in.)
Ignition timing	
° BTDC	21 @ 1,300 rpm
Piston position	2.52 mm (0.099 in.)
Breaker point gap	Set to correct timing
KX125 (1974-1976)	
Spark plug	
NGK	B9EV
ND	W27ESG
Gap	0.6 mm (0.024 in.)

(continued)

Table 6 IGNITION SPECIFICATIONS (continued)

Ignition timing	
° BTDC	20 @ 6,000 rpm
Piston position	1.91 mm (0.075 in.)
Breaker point gap	Breakerless CDI

169-175 cc models

F2 & F2TR	
Spark plug	
NGK	B7HS
ND	W22FS
Gap	0.6-0.7 mm (0.024-0.028 in.)
Ignition timing	
Piston position	2.09 mm (0.082 in.)
° BTDC	20
Breaker point gap	0.30-0.40 mm (0.012-0.016 in.)
F3	
Spark plug	
NGK	B8HS
ND	W24FS
Gap	0.6-0.7 mm (0.024-0.028 in.)
Ignition timing	
Piston position	2.75 mm (0.108 in.)
° BTDC	23
Breaker point gap	0.30-0.40 mm (0.012-0.016 in.)
F7	
Spark plug	
NGK	B9HS
ND	W27FS
Gap	0.6-0.7 mm (0.024-0.028 in.)
Ignition timing	
° BTDC	23 @ 6,000 rpm
Piston position	2.94 mm (0.116 in.)
Breaker point gap	Breakerless CDI
KD175 & KE175 (1976-1979)	
Spark plug	
NGK	B9HS
ND	W27FS
Gap	0.6-0.7 mm (0.024-0.028 in.)
Ignition timing	
° BTDC	22 @ 4,000 rpm
Piston position	2.69 mm (0.102 in.)
Breaker point gap	Breakerless CDI

238-350 cc models

F4	
Spark plug	
NGK	B9HS
ND	W27FS
Gap	0.6-0.7 mm (0.024-0.028 in.)
Ignition timing	
Piston position	3.09 mm (0.121 in.)
° BTDC	23
Breaker point gap	0.30-0.40 mm (0.012-0.016 in.)
F21M	
Spark plug	
NGK	B8HN
ND	W25FN
Gap	0.6-0.7 mm (0.024-0.028 in.)

6

(continued)

Table 6 IGNITION SPECIFICATIONS (continued)

Ignition timing	
Piston position	3.09 mm (0.121 in.)
° BTDC	23
Breaker point gap	0.30-0.40 mm (0.012-0.016 in.)
F8	
Spark plug	
NGK	B8HS
ND	W24FS
Gap	0.6-0.7 mm (0.024-0.028 in.)
Ignition timing	
Piston position	2.59 mm (0.101 in.)
° BTDC	20
Breaker point gap	0.30-0.40 mm (0.012-0.016 in.)
F81M	
Spark plug	
NGK	B9HS
ND	W27FS
Gap	0.6-0.7 mm (0.024-0.028 in.)
Ignition timing	
Piston position	2.34 mm (0.092 in.)
° BTDC	19
Breaker point gap	0.30-0.40 mm (0.012-0.016 in.)
F5 & F9	
Spark plug	
NGK	B10H
ND	W31FS
Gap	0.9-1.0 mm (0.035-0.039 in.)
Ignition timing	
° BTDC	23 @ 6,000 rpm
Piston position	3.41 mm (0.134 in.)
Breaker point gap	Breakerless CDI

*Make sure that the spark plug has the correct thread length (reach) for the application as well as the correct heat range. Occasionally a motorcycle may be equipped with a cylinder head which requires a spark plug with a different length of thread than the one listed in the following table, so it is important to check the actual thread length in the cylinder head as well as the following table. Spark plug threads and the threads in the cylinder head should be the same length.

CHAPTER SEVEN

FRAME, SUSPENSION AND STEERING

Tables 1-6 are at the end of the chapter.

HANDLEBARS

The handlebar is made from solid drawn steel tubing. Most of the manual controls (**Figure 1**) are mounted on the handlebar assembly. Wiring from the switches on the handlebar assembly is routed to the headlight assembly, where it is connected to the main wiring harness.

Disassembly

1. Loosen the clutch cable locknut (**Figure 2**), then rotate the adjustment nut to provide the inner clutch cable with sufficient slack to remove the clutch cable from the lever.
2. Loosen the front brake adjustment (**Figure 3**), then remove the brake cable (**Figure 4**) from the brake lever on the handlebar. On early models, the front brake stop lamp switch is built into the front brake cable. Disconnect the switch lead (**Figure 5**) from the main wire harness before you remove the cable.
3. Disassemble the throttle grip assembly (**Figure 6**), then remove the control cable.

4. Disassemble the starter lever (**Figure 7**), then remove the starter cable. On F series and G4TR models, the throttle and starter cables are built into the throttle grip assembly.
5. Remove the horn, turn signal and headlight leads from the wire harness inside the headlight assembly, then disassemble the left-hand grip assembly (**Figure 8**).
6. Remove the clamp bolts (**Figure 9**), then remove the handlebar from the bracket.

Inspection

Examine the handlebar for cracking or bending. Minor bends may be straightened. Replace the handlebar if any cracks exist or in the event of major bending.

Installation

Reverse the removal procedure to install the handlebar. Pass the wiring through the handlebar tubing and through the cord protector in the headlight. After installation, adjust the play in the throttle, clutch and starter lever cables. Adjust the play in the front brake lever to 0.8-1.2 in. (20-30 mm) by means of the brake adjusting nut on the brake.

7

HANDLEBAR AND CONTROLS

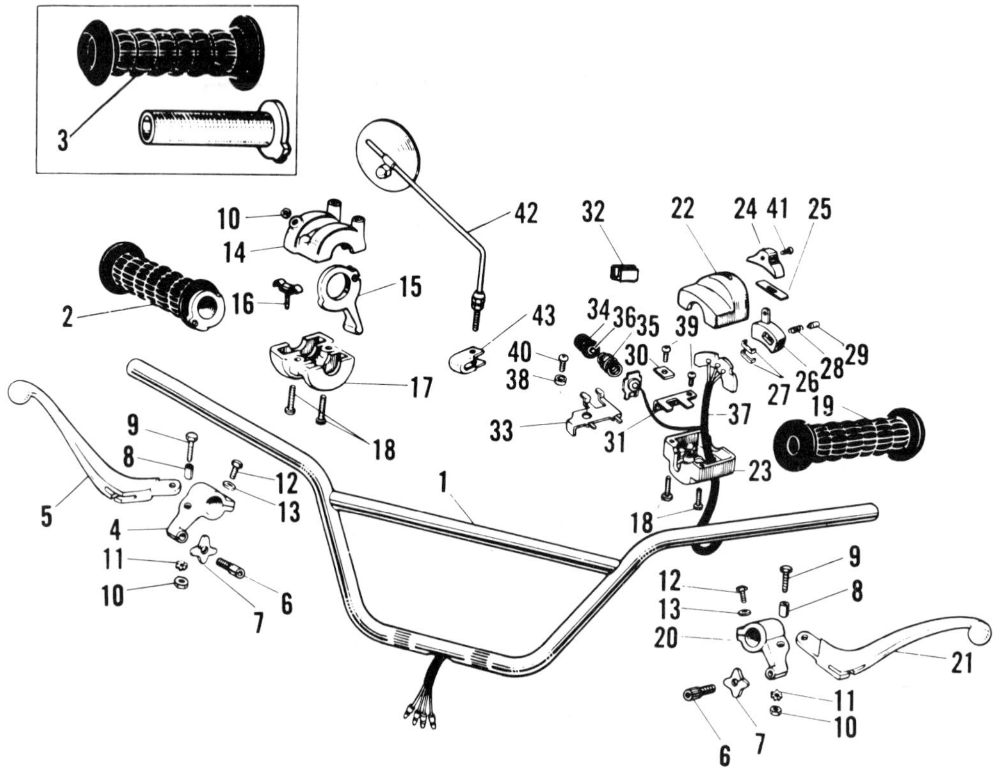

1. Handlebar
2. Throttle grip
3. Grip rubber
4. Brake lever holder
5. Lever
6. Screw
7. Nut
8. Collar
9. Bolt
10. Nut
11. Lockwasher
12. Bolt
13. Washer
14. Upper case
15. Lever
16. Spring
17. Lower case
18. Screw
19. Grip rubber
20. Lever holder
21. Lever
22. Upper case
23. Lower case
24. Knob
25. Spring
26. Switch
27. Contact plate
28. Spring
29. Contact
30. Switch holder
31. Switch holder
32. Cap
33. Switch holder
34. Horn button
35. Spring
36. Contact
37. Wiring harness
38. Washer
39. Screw
40. Screw
41. Screw
42. Mirror
43. Bracket

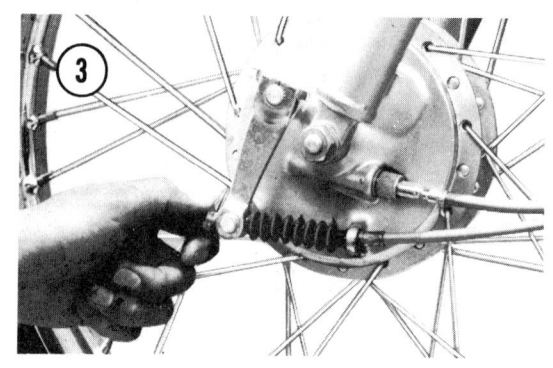

WHEELS AND TIRES

Tires

Figure 10 is a cutaway view of a typical wheel and the tire assembly. **Figure 11** is a sectional view of a tire mounted on its rim. Various tire sizes are fitted to Kawasaki machines. Refer to the specifications for tire sizes for your machine. Tires are available in different tread types to suit the different requirements of the rider. **Table 1** lists the normal tire pressures for the various models, measured with the tires cold. It is normal for tire pressure to increase after prolonged operation. Do not bleed air from a hot tire to decrease the pressure.

Check the tires periodically for wear, bruises, cuts or other damage. Remove any small stones which may lodge in the tread with a small screwdriver or similar tool.

Rims

The rim supports the tire and provides rigidity to the wheel assembly. A rim band protects the inner tube from abrasion. Rims on model F5 are of aluminum for light weight.

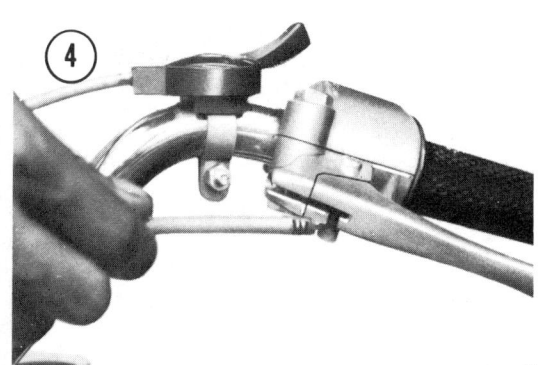

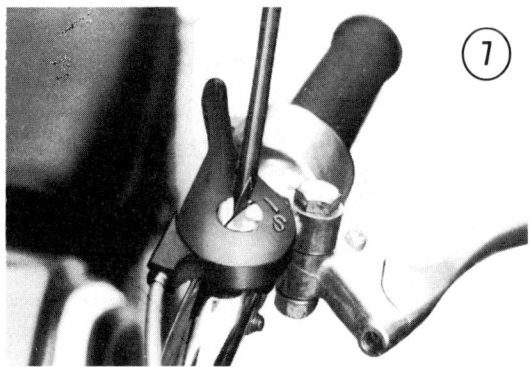

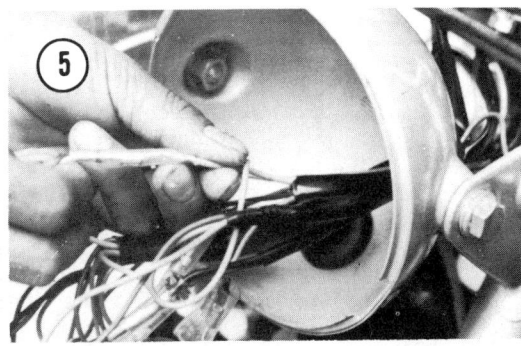

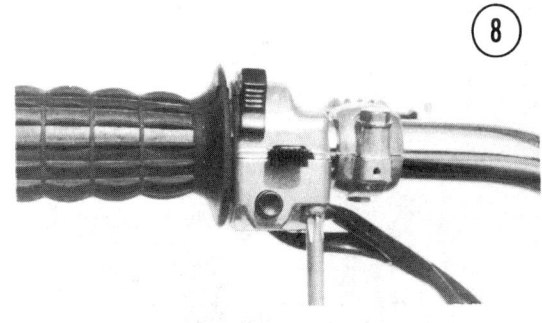

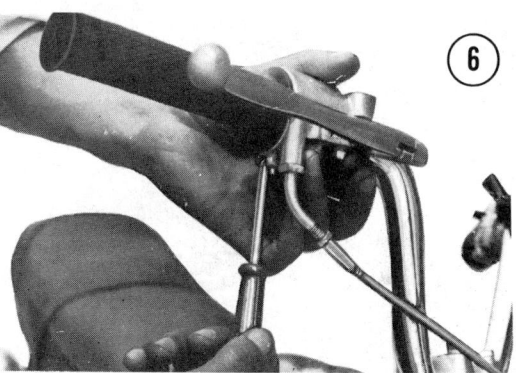

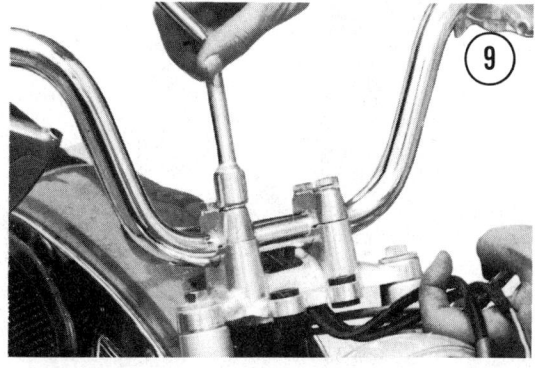

Spokes

The spokes support the weight of the motorcycle and rider and transmit tractive and braking forces, as shown in **Figure 12**. Diagram A illustrates action of the braking forces, as shown in **Figure 12**. Diagram A illustrates action of the spokes as they support the machine. Tractive forces are shown in diagram B. Braking forces are shown in diagram C.

Check the spokes periodically for looseness or bending. A bent or otherwise faulty spoke will adversely affect neighboring spokes and should therefore be replaced immediately. To remove the spoke, completely unscrew the threaded portion, then remove the bend end from the hub.

Spokes tend to loosen as the machine is used. Retighten each spoke one turn, beginning with those on one side of the hub, then those on the other side. Tighten the spokes on a new machine after the first 50 miles of operation, then at 50-mile intervals until they no longer loosen.

If the machine is subjected to particularly sever service, as in off-road or competition riding, check the spokes frequently.

Bead protector

Some F series models are equipped with bead protectors (**Figure 13**) on each wheel. The bead protector prevents the tire from slipping on the rim, especially during maximum effort braking at high speeds and thereby prevents damage to the valve stem.

Wheel Balance

An unbalanced wheel results in unsafe riding conditions. Depending on the degree of unbalance and the speed of the motorcycle, the rider may experience anything from a mild vibration to a violent shimmy which may even result in loss of control. Balance weights (**Figure 14**) are applied to the

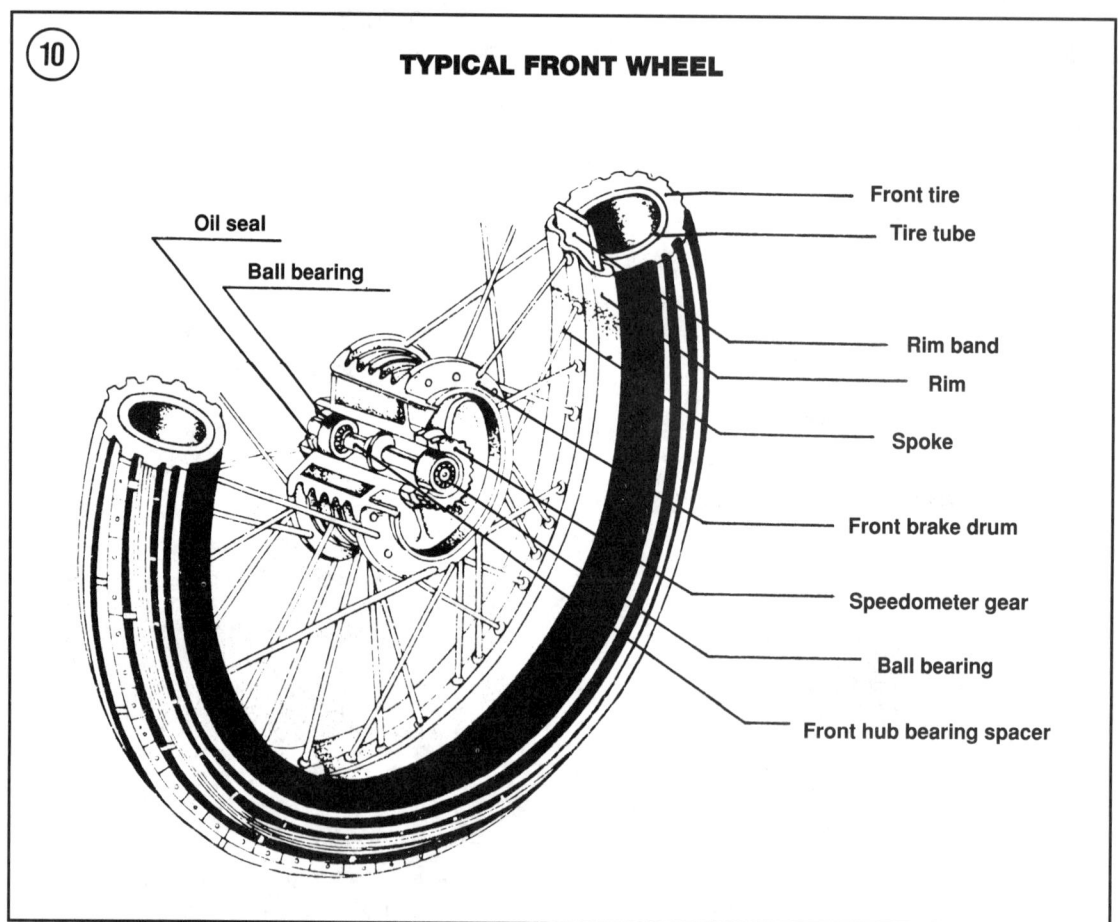

(10) TYPICAL FRONT WHEEL

Oil seal

Ball bearing

Front tire

Tire tube

Rim band

Rim

Spoke

Front brake drum

Speedometer gear

Ball bearing

Front hub bearing spacer

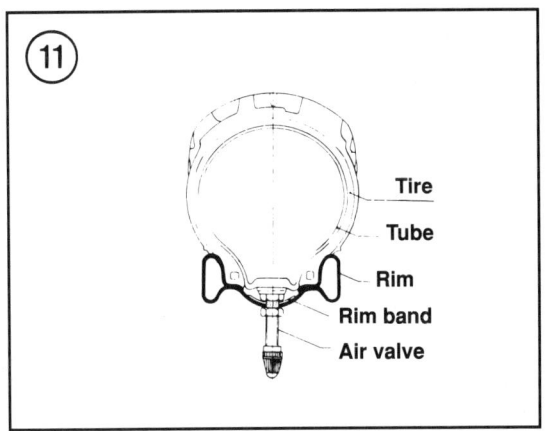

spokes on the light side of the wheel to correct this condition.

Before you attempt to balance the wheel, check to be sure that the wheel bearings are in good condition and properly lubricated. Also make sure that the brakes don't drag, so that the wheel rotates freely. With the wheel free of the ground, spin it slowly and allow it to come to rest by itself. Add balance weights to the spokes on the light side as required, so that the wheel comes to rest at a different position each time it is spun. Balance weights are available in weights of 10, 20 and 30 grams. Remove the drive chain when you balance the rear wheel.

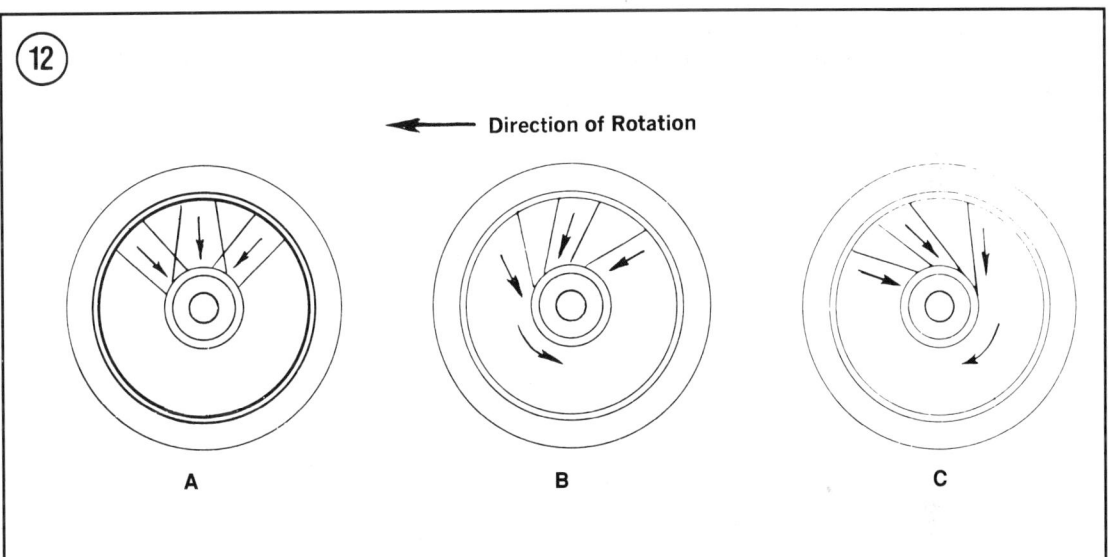

Direction of Rotation

A   B   C

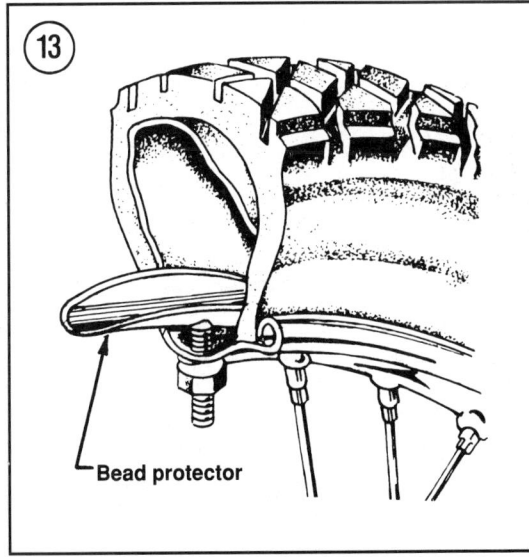

Bead protector

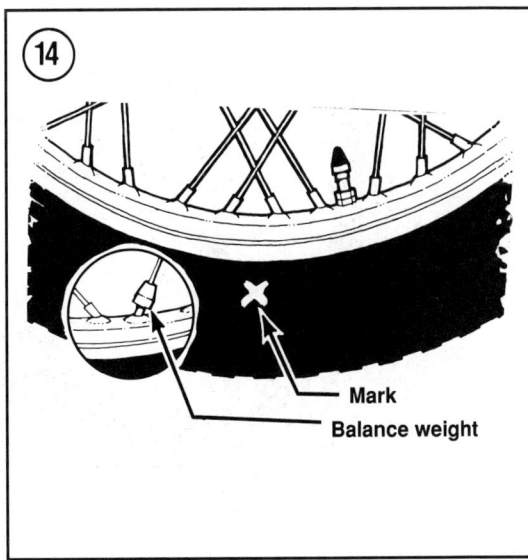

Mark
Balance weight

7

Front Hub

Figure 15 is an exploded view of a typical front hub. The entire hub assembly rotates on 2 ball bearings. The speedometer gears transmit the front wheel rotation to the speedometer. The brake panel supports the brake mechanism.

Rear Hub

An exploded view of the rear hub on most models is shown in **Figure 16**. The rear hub consists of 4 major parts: brake drum, brake panel, sprocket coupling and rear sprocket. The rear wheel bearings are mounted in the brake drum. The brake panel sup-

ports the brake mechanism, except for the brake drum. The sprocket coupling absorbs shocks throughout the entire drive train. The sprocket transmits engine power to the rear wheel through the sprocket coupling.

On some models, the sprocket is bolted directly to the hub; no shock damper is used. Such an undamped hub is shown in **Figure 17**. The rear sprocket on model F5 is made from aluminum to further reduce weight.

Front Wheel Removal

Front wheel removal is similar for all models. Proceed as follows:

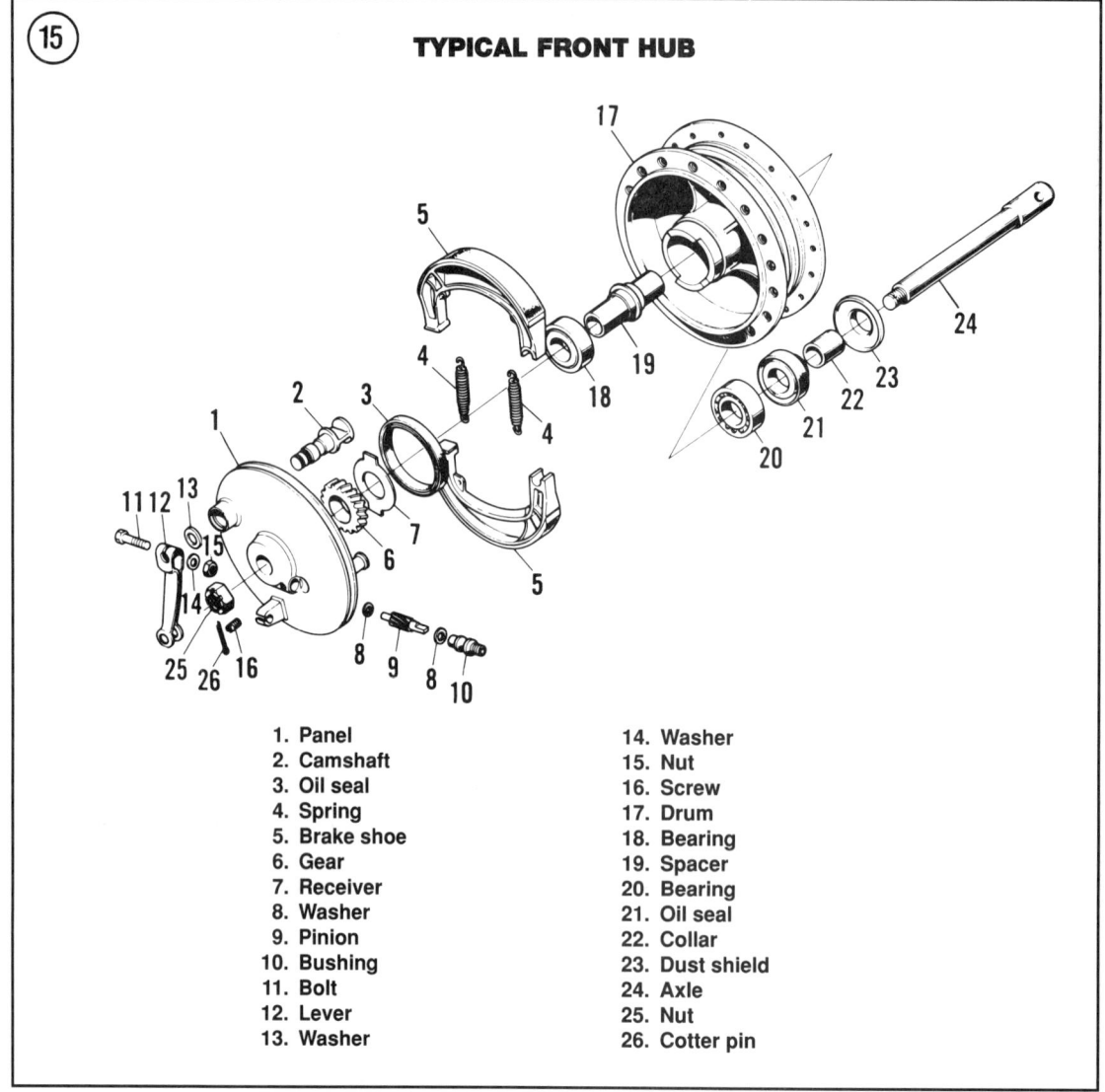

TYPICAL FRONT HUB

1. Panel
2. Camshaft
3. Oil seal
4. Spring
5. Brake shoe
6. Gear
7. Receiver
8. Washer
9. Pinion
10. Bushing
11. Bolt
12. Lever
13. Washer
14. Washer
15. Nut
16. Screw
17. Drum
18. Bearing
19. Spacer
20. Bearing
21. Oil seal
22. Collar
23. Dust shield
24. Axle
25. Nut
26. Cotter pin

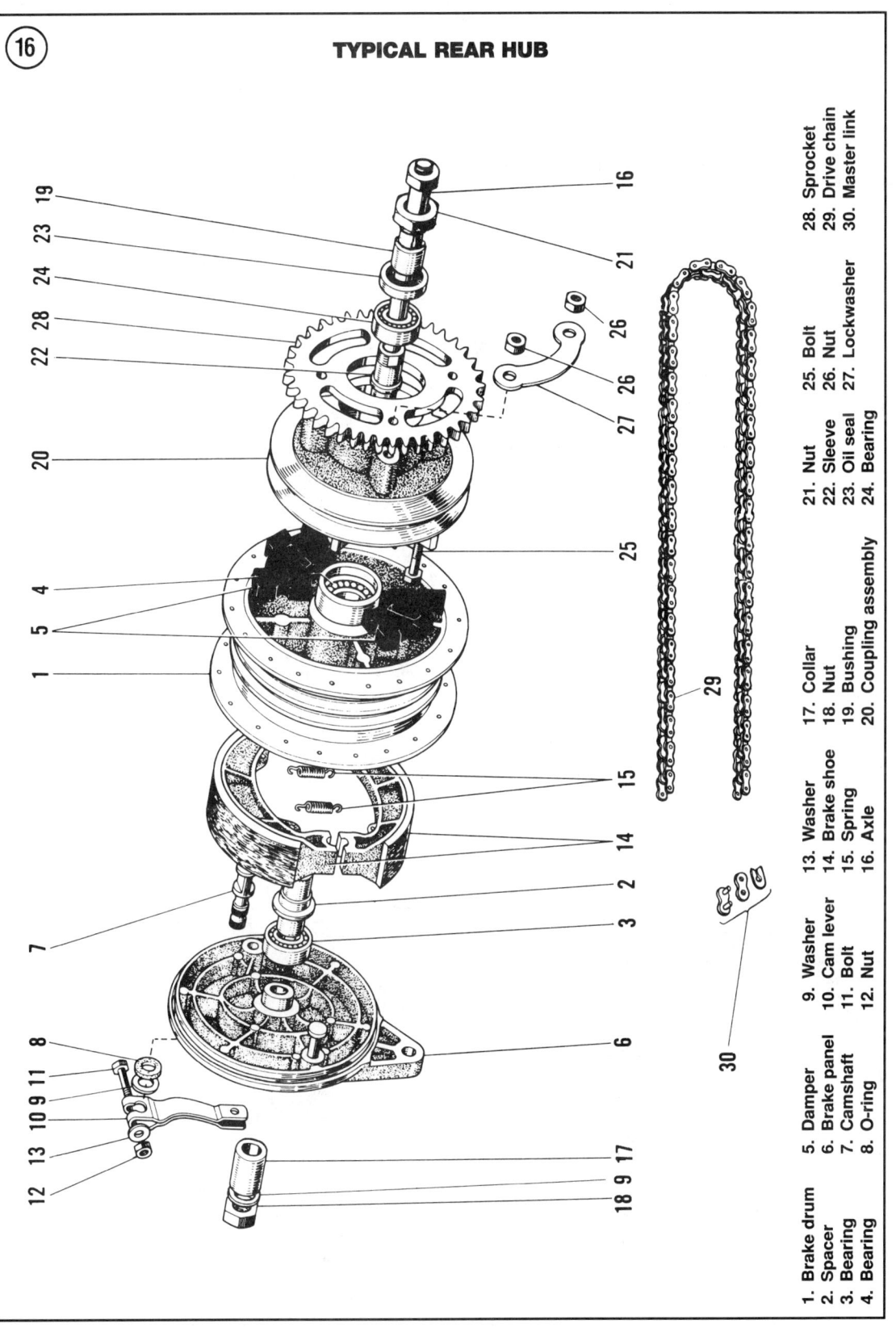

TYPICAL REAR HUB

16

1. Brake drum
2. Spacer
3. Bearing
4. Bearing
5. Damper
6. Brake panel
7. Camshaft
8. O-ring
9. Washer
10. Cam lever
11. Bolt
12. Nut
13. Washer
14. Brake shoe
15. Spring
16. Axle
17. Collar
18. Nut
19. Bushing
20. Coupling assembly
21. Nut
22. Sleeve
23. Oil seal
24. Bearing
25. Bolt
26. Nut
27. Lockwasher
28. Sprocket
29. Drive chain
30. Master link

7

(17)

REAR HUB
(UNDAMPED TYPE)

1. Panel
2. Brake shoe
3. Spring
4. Camshaft
5. Bolt
6. Washer
7. Nut
8. O-ring
9. Lever
10. Drum
11. Bearing
12. Spacer
13. Bearing
14. Oil seal
15. Axle
16. Collar
17. Pivot
18. Nut
19. Cotter pin
20. Sprocket
21. Bolt
22. Washer

(18)

(19)

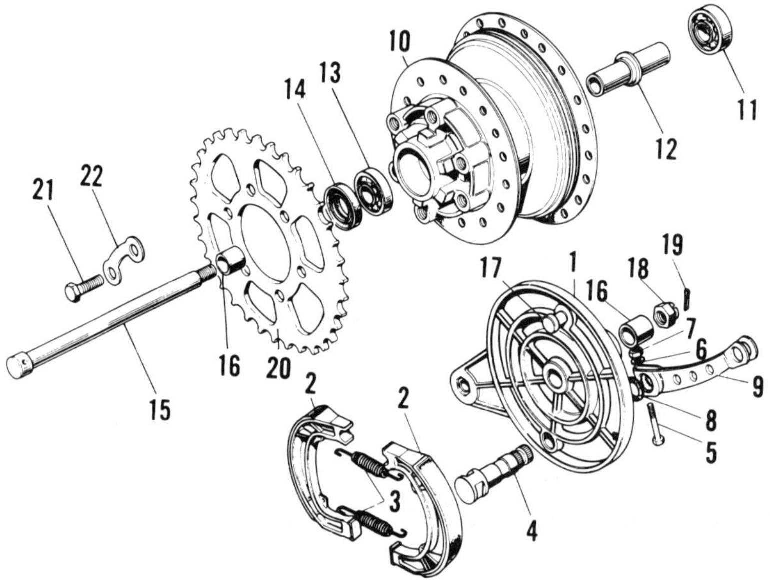

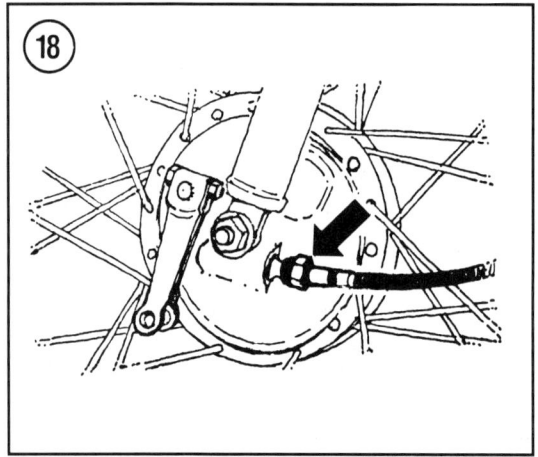

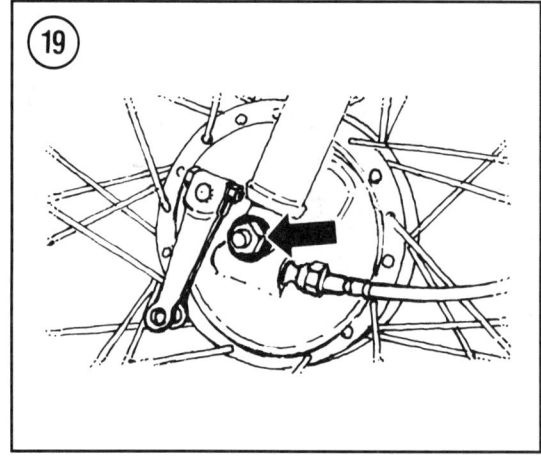

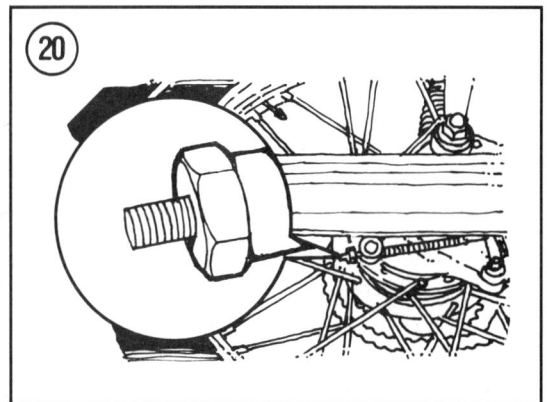

1. Loosen the front brake adjustment nut, then remove the brake cable at the front hub.

2. Loosen speedometer cable nut (**Figure 18**), then remove the speedometer cable.

3. Raise the front of the motorcycle and support it on a box or stand placed under the engine.

4. Remove the front hub shaft nut (**Figure 19**) on the side of the front brake panel.

CAUTION
Do not attempt to loosen the nut on the other end of the shaft.

5. On Models F5, F8, F9 and F81M, separate the brake torque link from the front fork.

6. Pull out the shaft and remove the wheel from the motorcycle.

Rear Wheel Removal

1. Remove the rear brake adjustment nut (**Figure 20**), then remove the inner brake cable from the brake lever. Apply pressure to the brake pedal when you remove the brake cable.

2. Remove the torque link.

3. Remove the chain cover. (**Figure 21**).

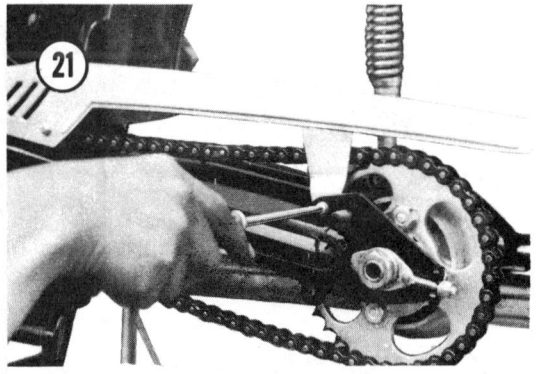

4. Remove the clip from the master link (**Figure 22**), then remove the chain. It may be necessary to rotate the rear wheel to position the master link for convenient removal. Then remove the drive chain.

5. Remove the axle shaft nut on the sprocket side (**Figure 23**).

CAUTION
Do not attempt to remove the nut on the other end of the shaft.

6. Pull out the shaft.

7. Remove the spacer, then lean the machine to one side and remove the wheel and brake mechanism together.

Wheel Disassembly

1. Pry each brake shoe from the brake panel (**Figure 24**), using a large screwdriver or similar tool.

2. Insert a long drift punch from the inner side of the brake drum, with its end against the inner race of the wheel bearing on the opposite side. Drive out the bearing and oil seal together. Be sure to re-position the drift punch after each hammer blow so that the bearing is not cocked in its bore.

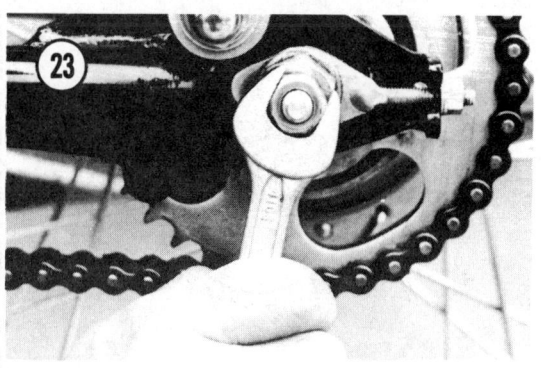

7

3. Insert the drift punch from the other side of the brake drum, then repeat Step 2 to drive out the other bearing.

Inspection

1. Support each wheel shaft in a lathe, V-blocks or other suitable centering device. Rotate the shaft through a complete revolution. Straighten or replace the shaft if it is bent more than 0.016 in. (0.4 mm).

2. Check the inner and outer races of the wheel bearings for cracks, galling or pitting. Rotate the bearings by hand and check for roughness. Measure the bearings for wear as shown in **Figure 25**. Replace the bearings if wear exceeds the limits shown.

3. Inspect the main and auxiliary lips of the oil seal (**Figure 26**) for wear or damage. Replace oil seal if there is any doubt about its condition.

4. On machines so equipped, inspect the rubber shock dampers in the rear hub (**Figure 27**). Replace the dampers if worn or damaged.

Wheel Reassembly

Reverse the disassembly procedure to reassemble the wheel. Observe the following notes as you reassemble the wheel.

1. Clean the wheel bearings carefully, then lubricate them before installation.

2. Use an arbor press to install the bearings and oil seals. Be sure that the bearings and seals are seated squarely in their bores.

3. Be sure that there are no scratches, oil or grease on the inner surface of the brake drum or on the friction surfaces of the brake shoes. Clean the contact surfaces thoroughly with lacquer thinner before assembly.

4. Torque the shaft and torque link nuts as given in **Table 2**.

5. Secure the axle and torque link nuts with cotter pins (**Figure 28**) after the nuts are tightened.

6. Check the wheels for runout after assembly.

Checking Wheel Runout

To measure runout of the wheel rim, support the wheel so it is free to rotate. Position a dial indicator as shown in **Figure 29**. Observe the dial indicator as you rotate the wheel through a complete revolution. The runout limit for all models is 0.04 in. (1.0 mm).

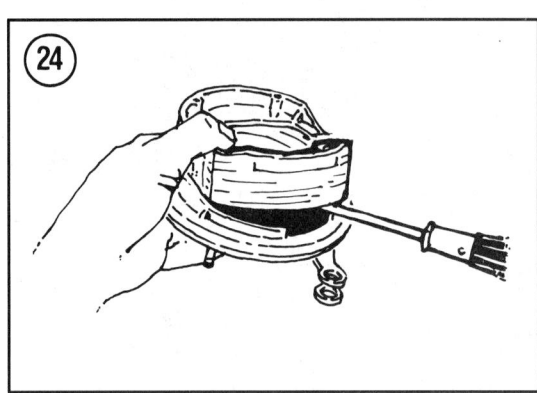

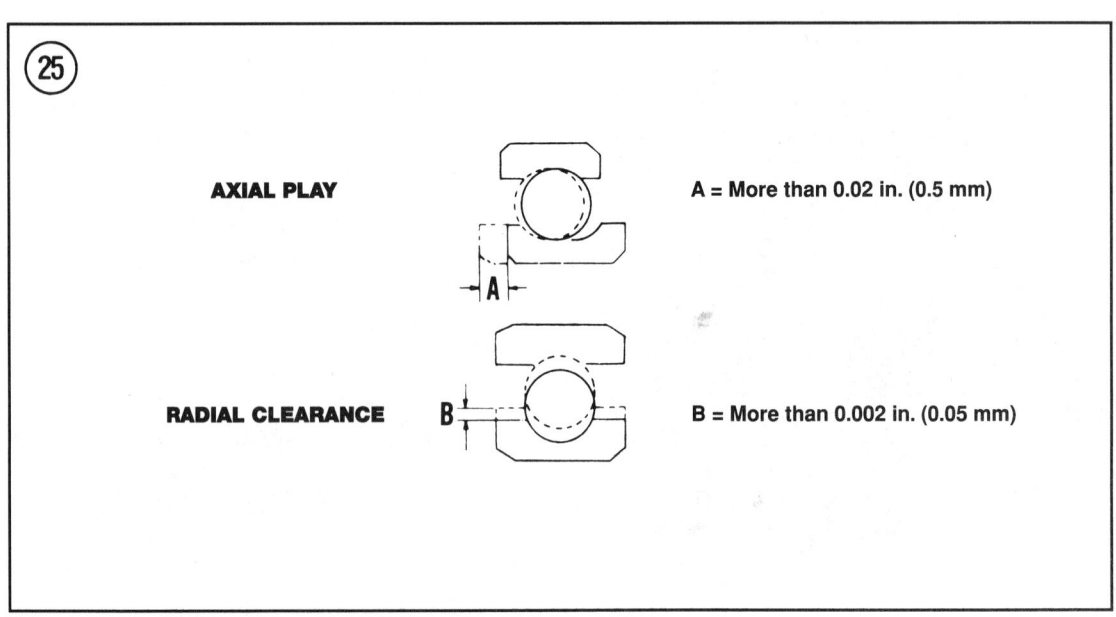

AXIAL PLAY

A = More than 0.02 in. (0.5 mm)

RADIAL CLEARANCE B

B = More than 0.002 in. (0.05 mm)

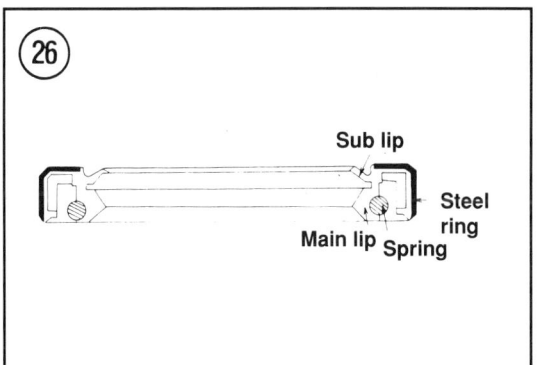

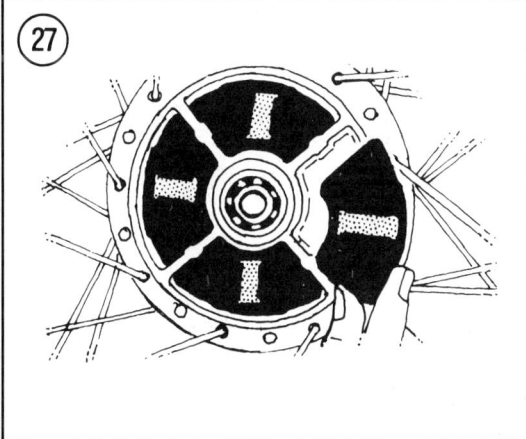

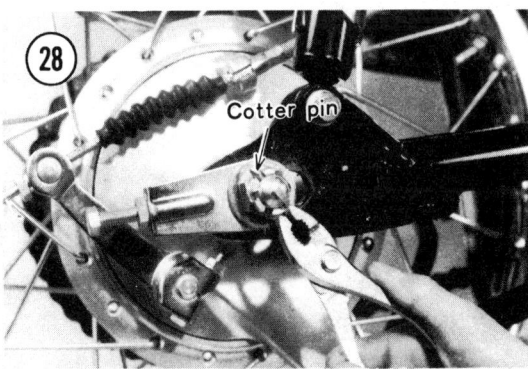

Excessive runout may be caused by a bent rim or loose spokes. Repair or replace as required.

BRAKES

Figure 30 illustrates the major parts of the brakes. Operation of the brake pedal or lever rotates a camshaft, which in turn forces the brake shoes into contact with the brake drum.

Brake Inspection

Periodically check the brakes for wear and the presence of foreign matter. Grooves in the drum, deep enough to snag a fingernail, are an indication that the drum should be turned down on a lathe and new shoes fitted. This type of wear can be avoided to a great extent if the brakes are disassembled and thoroughly cleaned after the motorcycle has been ridden in mud or deep sand.

Use vernier calipers and check brake drums for out-of-round or excessive wear (**Figure 31**). Standard brake drum diameter is either 100, 120, 130, 140 or 150 mm. If the drum is worn to a diameter larger than 0.75 mm bigger than the standard diameter, the wheel hub must be replaced for safety.

Examine the brake linings for oil, grease or dirt. Oil-soaked linings cannot be satisfactorily rejuvenated; they should be replaced. Dirt imbedded in the lining may be removed with a wire brush.

7

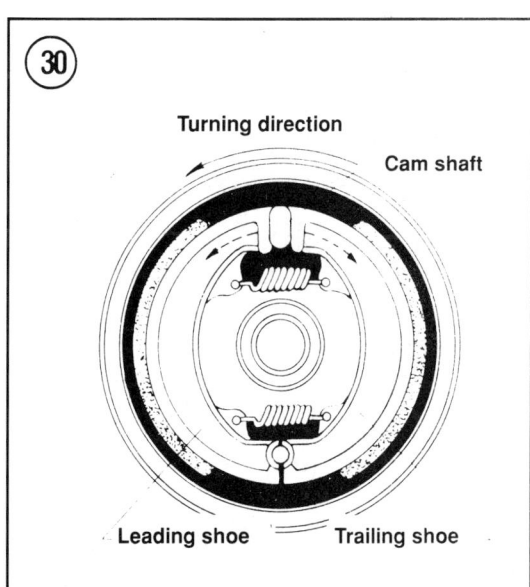

Measure the thickness of the lining at its thinnest part (**Figure 32**). Replace both shoes when any portion of the lining is worn to about 1/16 in. (1.5 mm).

Check the brake shoe return springs free length (**Figure 33**). If the springs are stretched and weak, they wont fully retract the shoes from the drum, resulting in a power robbing drag on the drums and premature wear of the lining. Replace the springs if they are longer than the limit given in **Table 3**.

Measure the clearance between the brake camshaft and the bushing in the brake panel. Standard clearance for all models is 0.0008-0.0028 in. (0.02-0.07 mm). Replace the camshaft and/or the brake panel if the clearance exceeds 0.02 in. (0.5 mm). To reassemble the brake mechanism, reverse the disassembly procedure. Be sure that the front brake cable is approximately perpendicular to the brake cam lever (**Figure 34**). Grease the brake pedal bearing, brake lever and brake cam bearings in the brake panel.

Brake Adjustment

Adjust the front brake by turning the adjustment nut at the front brake cam lever. The adjustment is correct if braking action begins when the front brake lever (**Figure 35**) is pulled approximately one inch (25 mm). Since the front brake stop lamp switch is built into the cable, no adjustment on it is required.

Adjust the rear brake by turning the adjustment nut until braking action begins at 3/4 to 1-1/4 in. (20-30 mm) travel of the brake pedal (**Figure 36**). Adjust the rear brake stop lamp switch (**Figure 37**) so that the stop lamp lights when the brake pedal has traveled 0.6-0.8 in. (15-20 mm).

FRONT FORKS

Two basic types of front forks are used on these machines. Early model machines are equipped with forks identified by a large tube nut securing the fork assembly (3, **Figure 38** and 13, **Figure 39**). There are 2 categories of early model forks, one for smaller models (**Figure 38**) and one for larger models (**Figure 39**).

Forks on later model machines can be identified by the Allen bolt in the bottom of each fork leg (31, **Figure 55**).

CAUTION
Be sure that you correctly identify your forks and use the right procedures or serious damage may result.

Some F5, F7, F8 and F9 models feature Hatta forks which allow the rider to adjust trail, caster and stroke to suit various riding conditions.

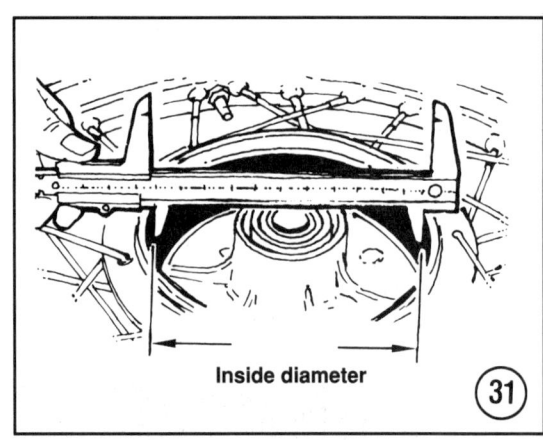
Inside diameter (31)

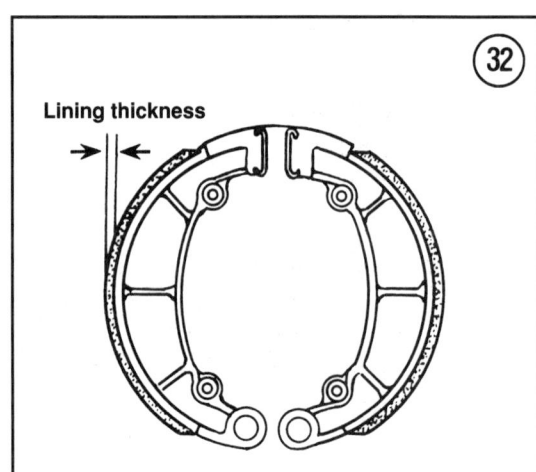
Lining thickness (32)

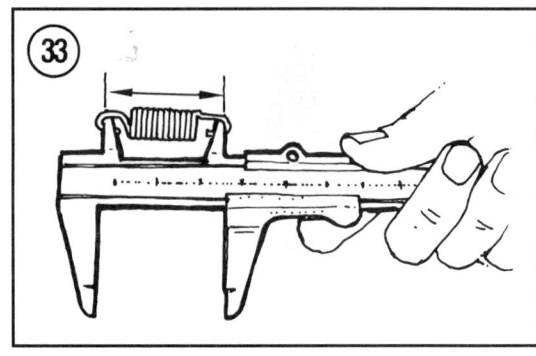
(33)

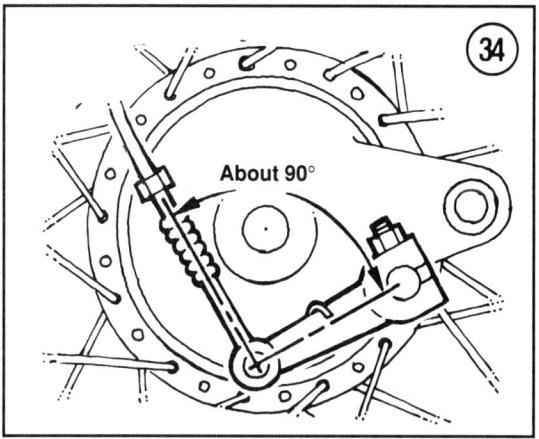

About 90°

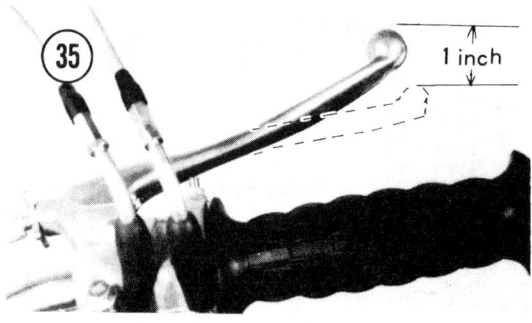

1 inch

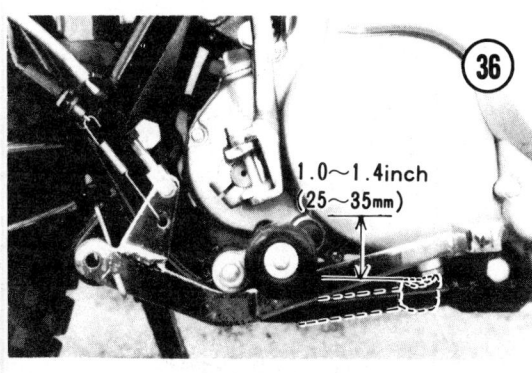

1.0~1.4inch
(25~35mm)

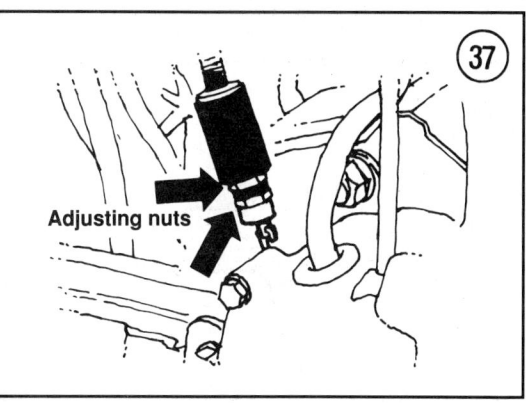

Adjusting nuts

Removal (Early Models)

The initial steps for fork removal are similar for all models. Proceed as follows.

1. Remove all connectors in the headlight assembly from the main wire harness, as shown in **Figure 40**.

2. Remove the headlight assembly (**Figure 41**).

3. Remove the speedometer and tachometer, as shown in **Figure 42** and **Figure 43**.

On all but F series models, remove the forks from the machine as follows.

1. Remove the upper bolts (**Figure 44**).

2. Remove the lower bolts from the underbracket (**Figure 45**).

3. Pull the fork tubes downward to remove them.

F series models require that the oil be drained from the forks, as shown in **Figure 46**, before removal.

Disassembly/Assembly (Early Models)

1. Remove the dust seal, spring, dust boots and spring guide.

2. Invert the fork and drain the oil.

3. Wrap a piece of rubber sheeting or a section of inner tube around the outer tube nut and clamp the nut in a vise (**Figure 47**). Be careful that you do not deform the tube by clamping the vise too tightly.

4. Turn the outer tube counterclockwise to separate the tubes. The outer tube may be turned easily by using the front axle shaft as a lever, as shown in **Figure 48**.

5. Assembly is the reveres of these steps. Replace oil seal and O-ring attached to outer tube.

Inspection

1. Assemble inner and out tubes (**Figure 49**), then slide them together. Check for looseness, noise or binding. Replace defective parts.

2. Any scratches or roughness on the inner tube in the area where it passes through the oil seal will damage the oil seal. Examine this area carefully.

3. Inspect the dust seal carefully. If this seal is damaged, foreign material will enter the fork.

4. Measure the free length of each fork spring. Replace any spring which is shorter than the repair limit. See **Table 4**.

Installation (Early Models)

Fork installation varies according to model. On smaller models, proceed as follows.

7

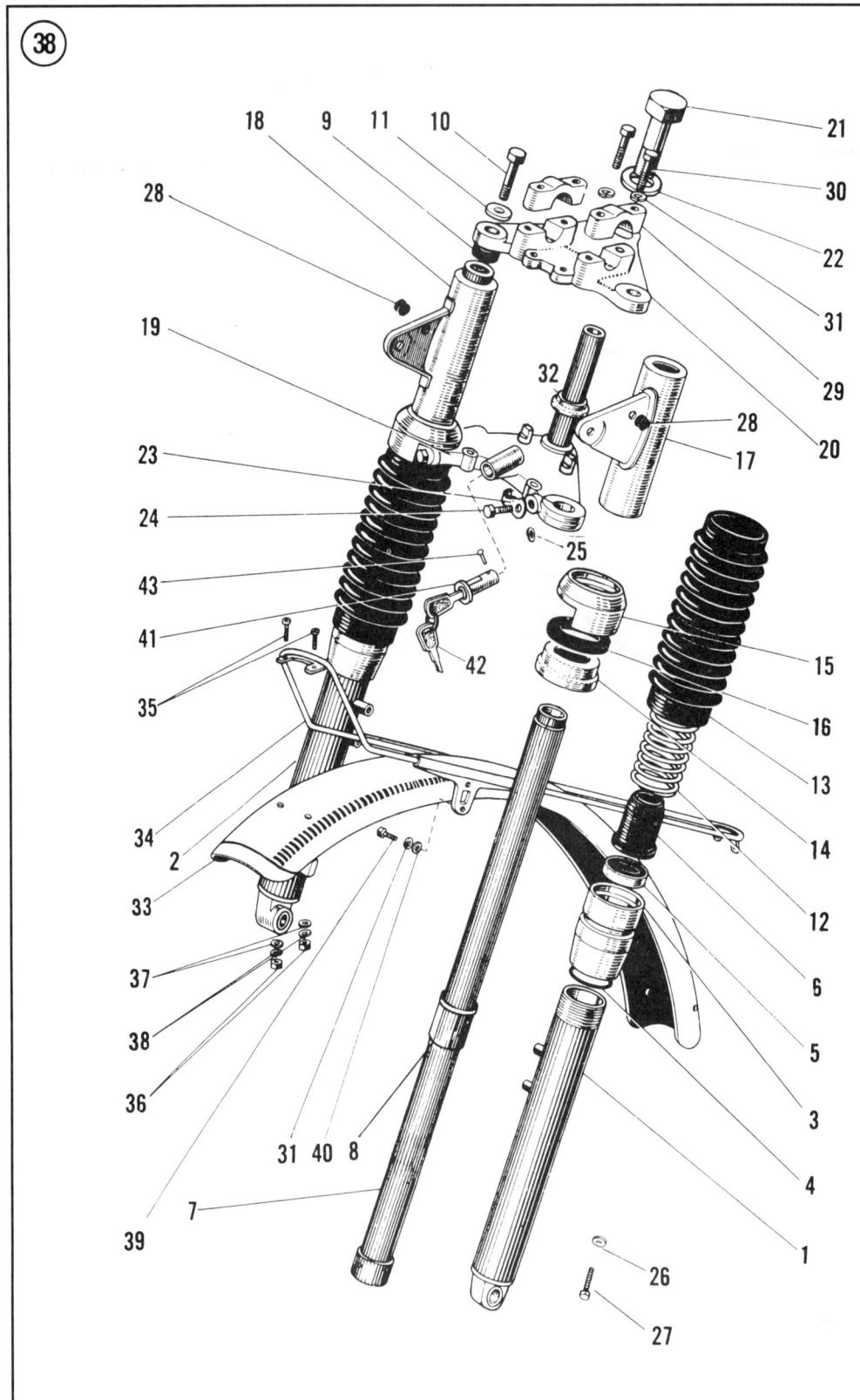

FRONT FORK
(EARLY, SMALLER MODELS)

1. Tube
2. Tube
3. Tube nut
4. O-ring
5. Seal
6. Dust shield
7. Tube
8. Guide
9. Gasket
10. Bolt
11. Washer
12. Spring
13. Dust cover
14. Guide
15. Ring
16. Gasket
17. Cover
18. Cover
19. Steering stem
20. Steering stem head
21. Bolt
22. Washer
23. Clamp
24. Bolt
25. Washer
26. Gasket
27. Screw
28. Cap
29. Handlebar holder
30. Bolt
31. Washer
32. Bearing cone
33. Fender
34. Fender stay
35. Screw
36. Nut
37. Washer
38. Lockwasher
39. Bolt
40. Washer
41. Steering lock
42. Key set
43. Rivet

7

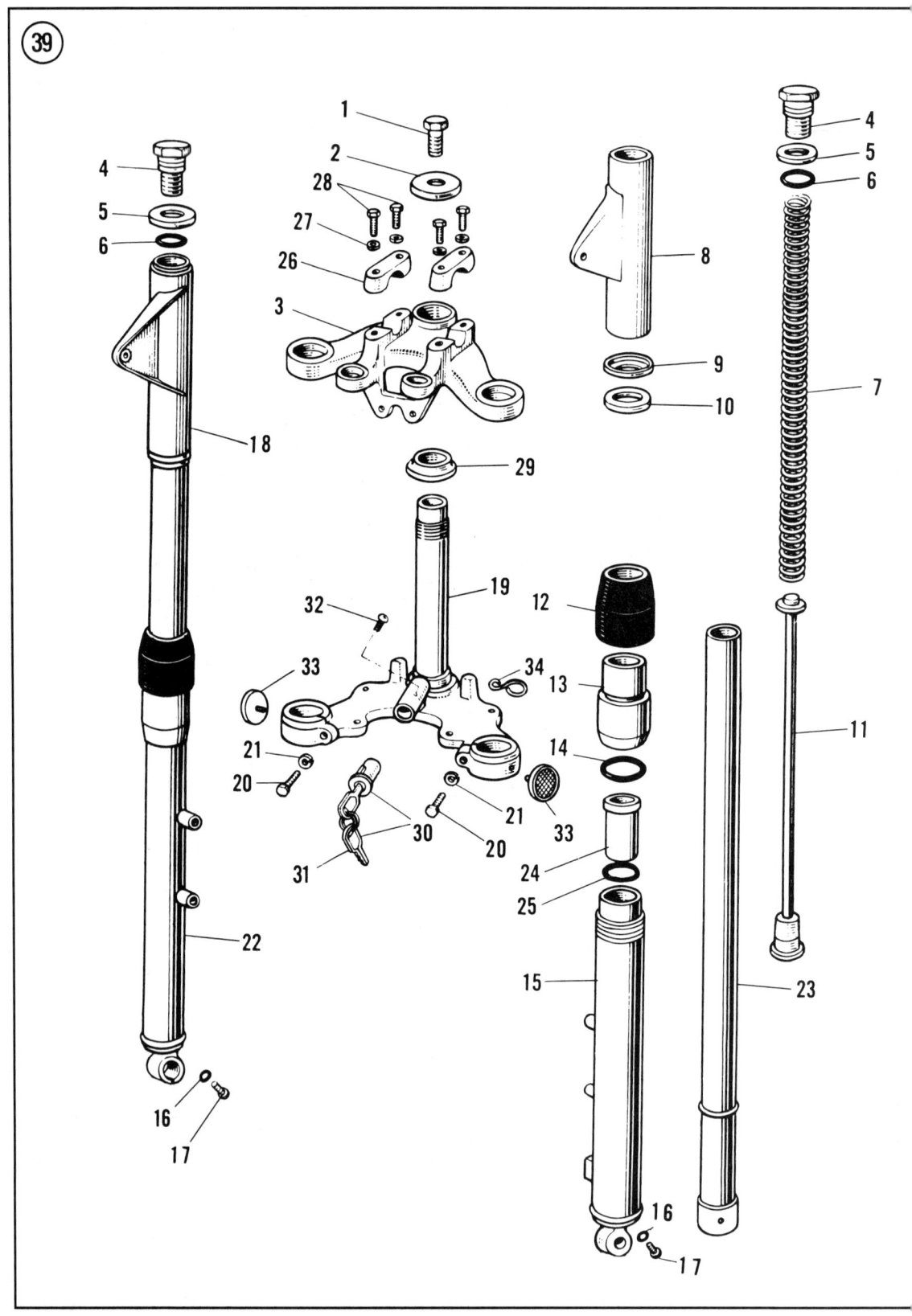

FRONT FORK
(EARLY, LARGER MODELS)

1. Bolt
2. Washer
3. Steering stem head
4. Bolt
5. Washer
6. O-ring
7. Spring
8. Cover
9. Guide
10. Gasket
11. Spring holder
12. Dust shield
13. Nut
14. O-ring
15. Tube
16. Gasket
17. Screw
18. Cover
19. Steering stem
20. Bolt
21. Lockwasher
22. Tube
23. Tube
24. Guide
25. Oil seal
26. Handlebar holder
27. Lockwasher
28. Bolt
29. Lower bearing cone
30. Steering lock
31. Key set
32. Rivet
33. Reflector
34. Clamp

7

1. Install the fork cover gasket, fork cover ring and fork cover to the underbracket.

2. Insert the front fork from underneath the underbracket, then pull the fork fully upward.

If you cannot push or pull the fork all the way up until it seats against the steering stem head, use a long threaded rod to screw into the forks inner tube and pull it up (**Figure 50**). The threads should be the same as used on the fork top bolt.

3. Hold the fork in position by clamping the inner tube clamp bolt.

4. Partially tighten the top bolt.

5. Temporarily loosen inner tube clamp bolt.

6. Tighten the top bolt fully.

7. Tighten the inner tube clamp bolt fully.

On model G4TR, insert the front fork from the bottom of the steering stem. Push the inner tube upward until the end of the inner tube reaches the stepped portion of the steering stem head, then secure it with the upper bolt. Finally, tighten the steering stem bolt.

8. On larger models, place the left and right lamp bracket and the rubber damper in position between the upper and lower brackets. Insert the fork from below, then tighten the bolts. Adjust the fork as

desired after installation as outlined in the following steps.

  a. Refer to **Figure 51** and **Figure 52**. (A) is the standard position, (B) is the off-road position and (C) is the position for high speed riding.

  b. To adjust the position of the steering stem, refer to **Figure 53**. (D) is the standard riding position. Positions (E) and (F) are used as desired for high speed riding. Loosen the 4 clamp bolts on the steering stem, slide the tubes into the desired position, then tighten the 4 clamp bolts.

  c. Refer to **Figure 54** for fork spring adjustment. The spring tension is varied by removing the

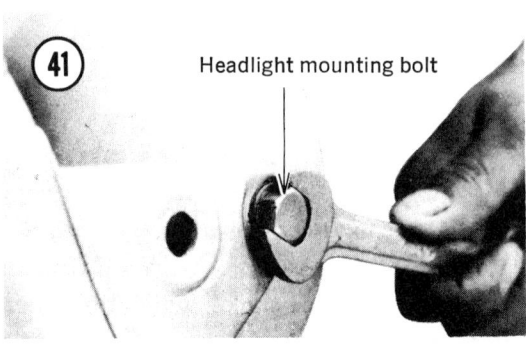

Headlight mounting bolt

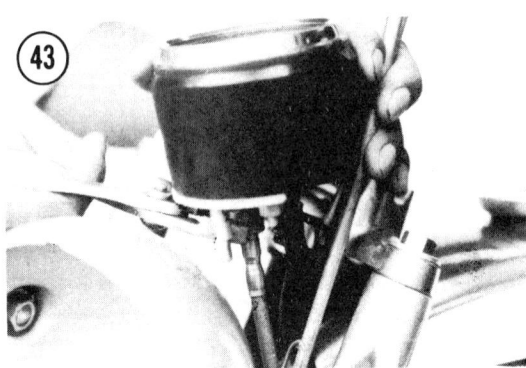

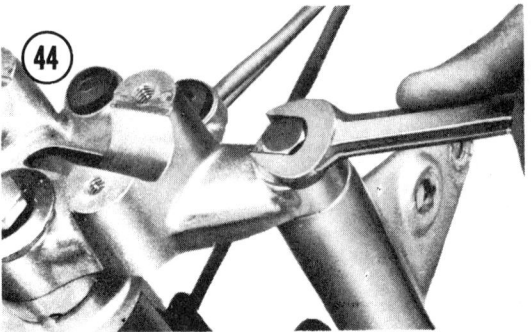

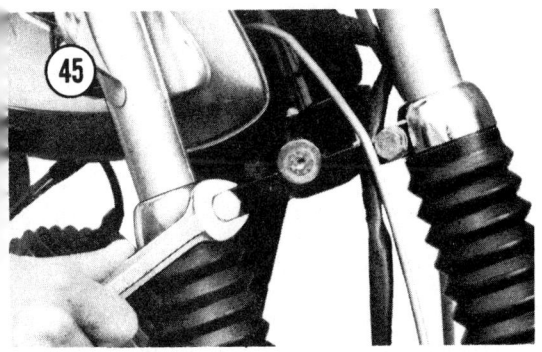

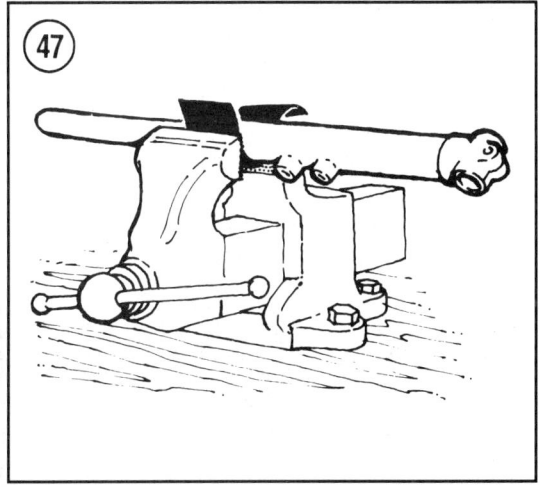

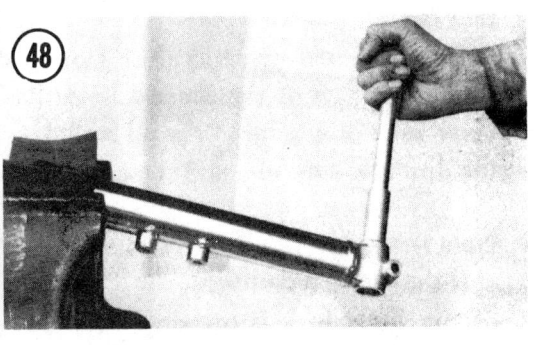

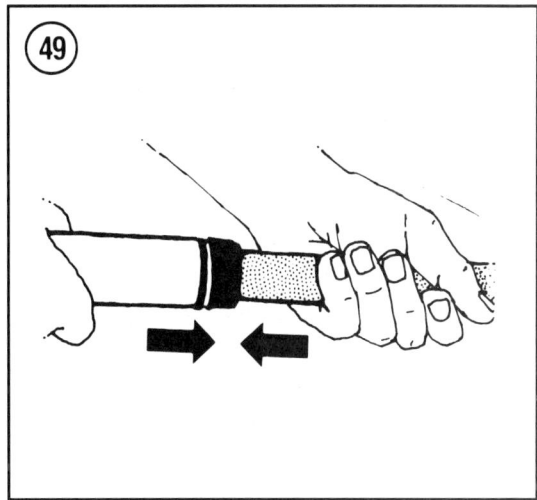

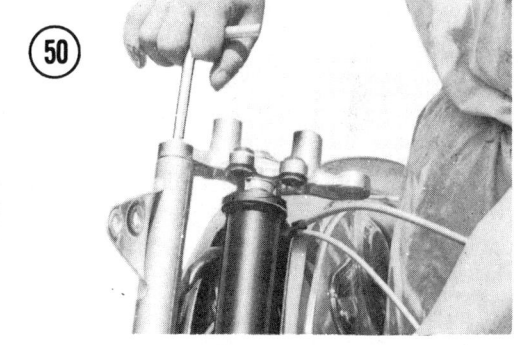

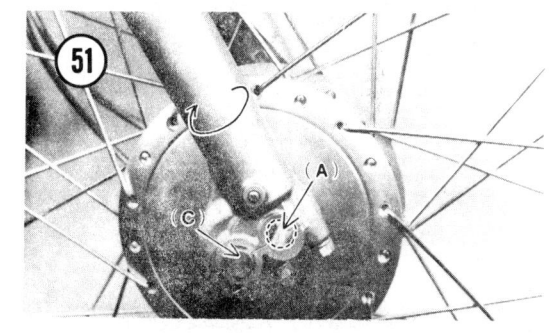

7

rubber cap, then turning the rod to position (A), (B) or (C), as required.

Removal/Installation (Late Models)

Refer to **Figure 55** for this procedure.

1. Remove front wheel. If fork tube is to be disassembled, loosen top bolt (**Figure 56**).

2. Using an Allen wrench, loosen upper and lower clamp bolts (**Figure 57**). Using a twisting motion, work fork tube down and out.

> *NOTE*
> *If fork tube cannot be removed by twisting, remove fork cover and damper rubbers (Figure 58).*

3. Installation is the reverse of these steps. Keep the following points in mind:
   a. Smear a small amount of oil on inside of damper rubbers at the end of fork covers.
   b. Slide fork tube up through lower and upper clamps until upper surface of top bolt flange is even with upper edge of stem head.
   c. Torque upper and lower clamp bolts to 11-16.5 ft.-lb. (1.5-2.3 mkg).
   d. Torque top bolt to 11-14.5 ft.-lb. (1.5-2.0 mkg).

Disassembly (Later Models)

Refer to **Figure 55** for this procedure.

1. Remove top bolt and remove spring (**Figure 59**).

2. Pour out oil. Pump fork if necessary to remove all oil.

3. Slide dust seal off inner tube.

4. Using special tools and Allen wrench, remove Allen bolt from bottom of outer tube (**Figure 60**) and pull inner tube from outer tube.

> *NOTE*
> *If special tools are unavailable, take the fork tubes to your local Kawasaki dealer. He can disassemble them and replace the seals in much less time than it would take to fabricate the necessary special tools.*

5. Slide cylinder, piston unit and spring out of the top of the inner tube (**Figure 61**).

6. Remove circlip from outer tube and remove oil seal (**Figure 62**). It may be necessary to heat outer tube around the oil seal to facilitate seal removal.

7. Remove cylinder base from top of outer tube.

Inspection

Refer to inspection procedure for early model forks.

Assembly (Later Models)

Refer to **Figure 55** for this procedure.

1. Install cylinder base into outer tube.

2. Install oil seal into outer tube using oil seal driver (**Figure 63**). Install circlip.

3. Install cylinder and piston unit with spring into inner tube. Fit bottom of cylinder into cylinder base and push inner tube fully into outer tube.

4. Apply a non-permanent locking compound (such as Loctite) to Allen bolt. Install and tighten Allen bolt.

5. Slide dust seal into place.

6. Fill fork tube with proper amount of oil (**Table 5**).

7. Install spring with relatively concentrated end at top and replace top bolt. Torque top bolt to 11-14.5 ft.-lb. (1.5-2.0 mkg).

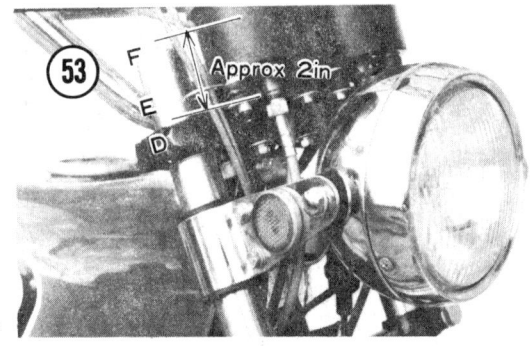

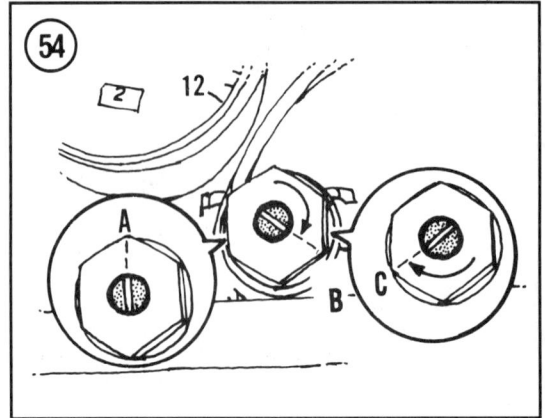

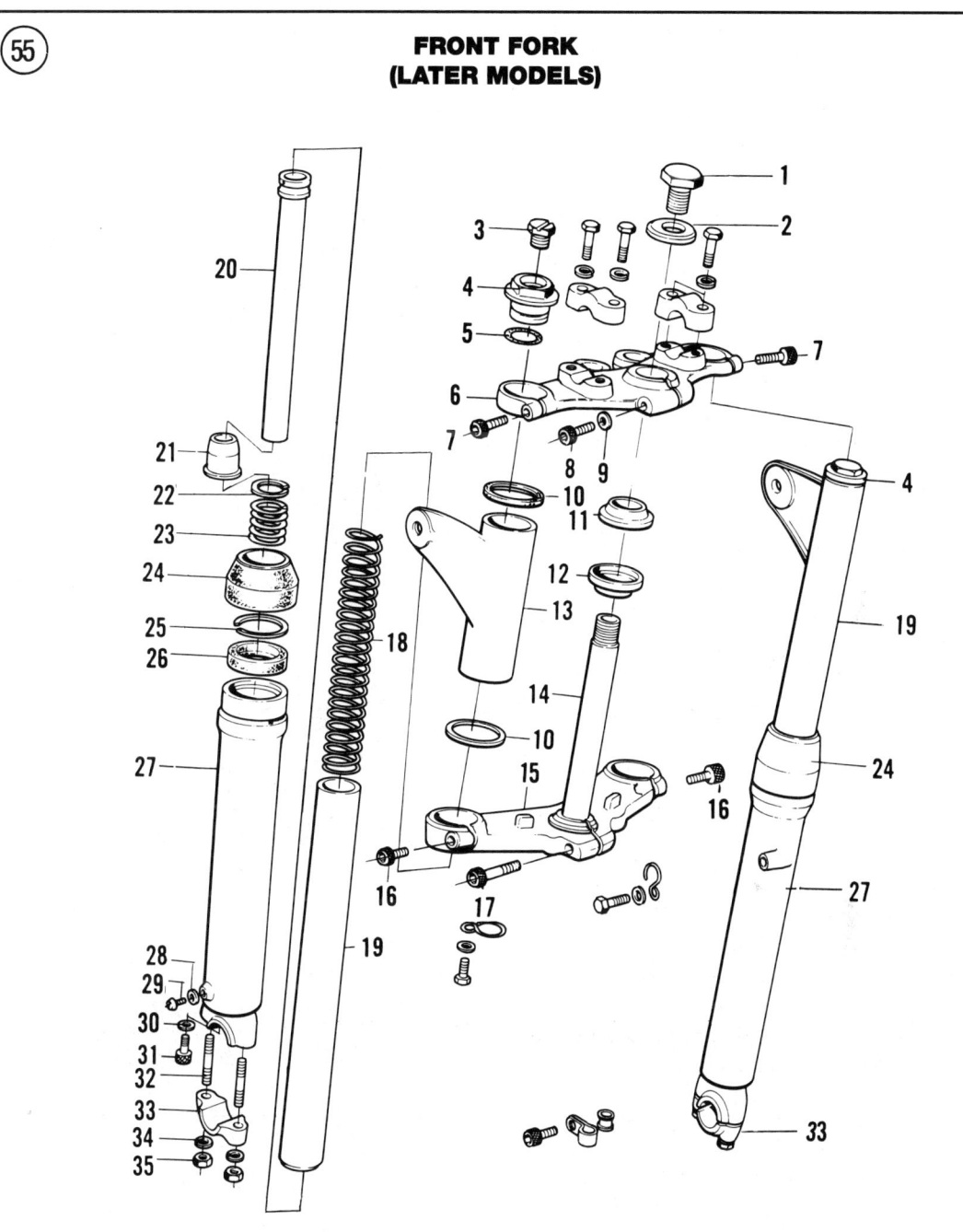

**FRONT FORK
(LATER MODELS)**

1. Stem head bolt	10. Rubber damper	18. Spring	27. Outer tube
2. Washer	11. Outer race	19. Inner tube	28. Gasket
3. Bolt	12. Outer race	20. Cylinder assembly	29. Drain screw
4. Top bolt	13. Fork cover	21. Cylinder base	30. Washer
5. O-ring	14. Steering stem shaft	22. Lockwasher	31. Allen bolt
6. Stem head	15. Steering stem base	23. Spring	32. Stud bolt
7. Clamp bolt	16. Clamp bolt	24. Dust seal	33. Axle clamp
8. Stem head clamp bolt	17. Steering stem base	25. Circlip	34. Lockwasher
9. Washer	clamp bolt	26. Oil seal	35. Nut

7

Fork Oil

Change front fork oil initially at 500 miles (800 km) and every 5,000 miles (8,000 km) thereafter. **Table 5** lists the proper oil quantity for each fork leg.

On some models, the correct quantity of oil in the front forks is given as the distance between the top of the fork tube and the oil contained in the fork tube. To accurately measure this distance, raise the front of the motorcycle and position a block under the engine to hold the front wheel off the ground. It is important to make sure that all weight is removed

Spring

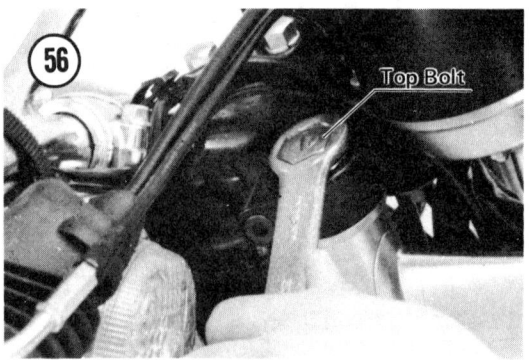

Top Bolt

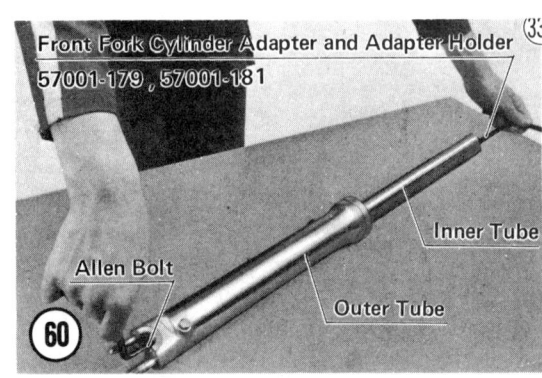

Front Fork Cylinder Adapter and Adapter Holder
57001-179, 57001-181

Allen Bolt

Inner Tube

Outer Tube

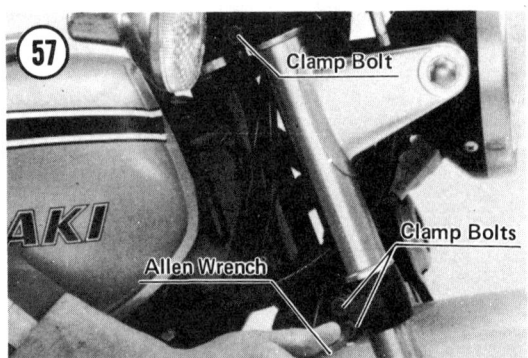

Clamp Bolt

Clamp Bolts

Allen Wrench

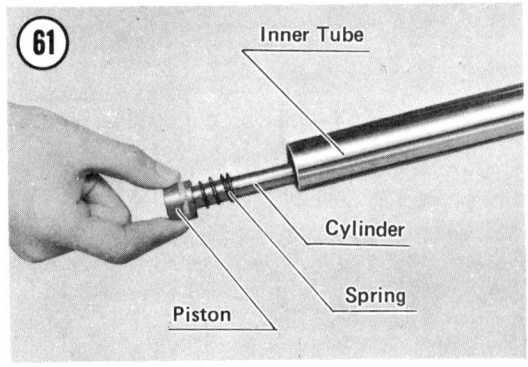

Inner Tube

Cylinder

Spring

Piston

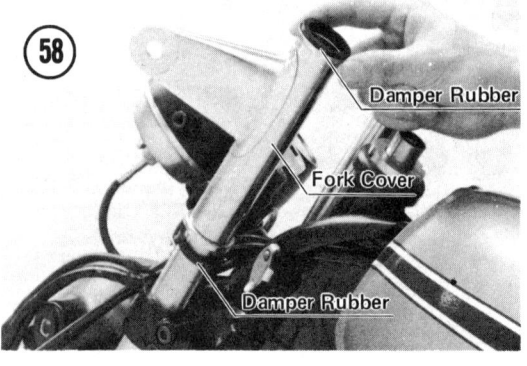

Damper Rubber

Fork Cover

Damper Rubber

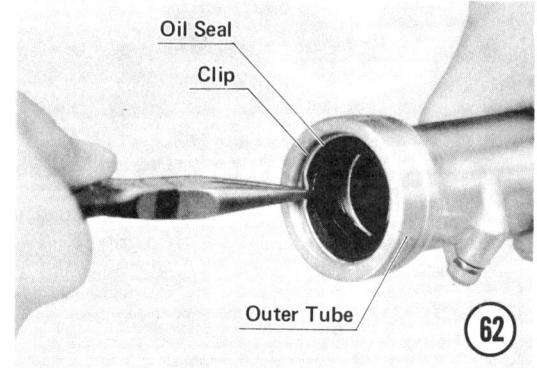

Oil Seal

Clip

Outer Tube

from the front wheel. Remove the top caps from the fork top tubes and use a rod (A, **Figure 64**) to measure the distance (B, **Figure 64**). Refer to **Table 5** for oil level distance specifications for some models.

On some models, the top plug of the fork tubes is a plastic cap pressed into the top opening. A metal spring retaining plug is located further down, inside the fork tube and it is retained by a circlip. The inner plug and its retaining circlip must be removed to check the oil level or to disassemble the fork.

Raise the front of the motorcycle and position a block under the engine to hold the front wheel off the ground.

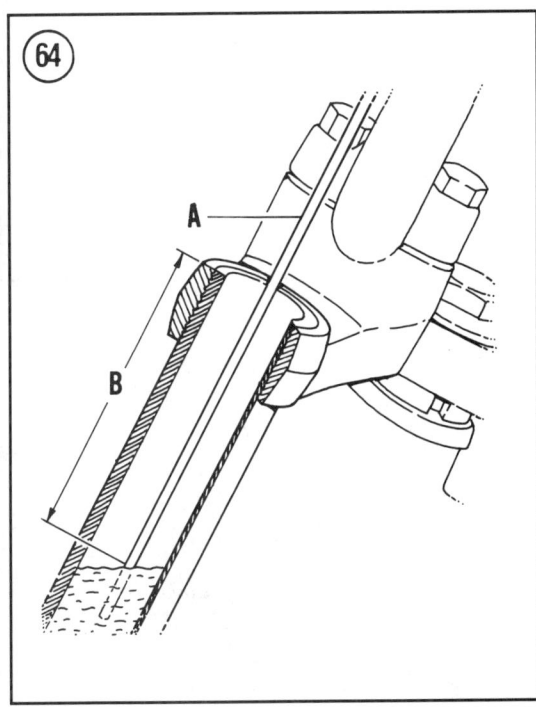

NOTE
It is important to make sure that all weight is removed from the front wheel before disassembling the front fork.

Pry the plastic cap from the top of fork tube and inspect the inner bore of the fork tube. Make sure that inner bore is clean and free of rust. Press the inner plug down with a small diameter rod far enough to dislodge the retaining circlip from the inner groove. Spring pressure should push the inner plug up, out of the fork tube, when circlip is removed. The inner plug is sealed to the fork tube with a sealing ring. The front suspension spring can be withdrawn after plug is removed. It is important to remove the spring before measuring the oil level in the fork.

When assembling forks that have a top plug retained in the fork tubes by a circlip, the smaller diameter of the spring should be down, toward the front wheel axle.

STEERING SYSTEM

Figure 65 is a sectional view of a typical steering stem. The frame head pipe and the underbracket are provided with ball bearings for smooth action.

Disassembly

1. Remove the handlebar, tachometer, speedometer and front fork. Refer to the applicable sections in this chapter.
2. Remove the steering stem head (**Figure 66**).
3. Remove the locknut (**Figure 67**).
4. Pull the underbracket downward to remove it from the machine. Take care that you do not drop the ball bearings during this step.
5. If it is necessary to remove the ball races, tap them out with a hammer and long punch, as shown in **Figure 68**.
6. Remove the lower race from the steering stem with a hammer and chisel (**Figure 69**).

Inspection

Examine the underbracket shaft carefully. Replace it if the shaft is bent. Check the balls and races for cracks, wear or other damage. Do not use a combination of new and used parts in the bearings. Replace the entire bearing assembly if any defects are found.

7

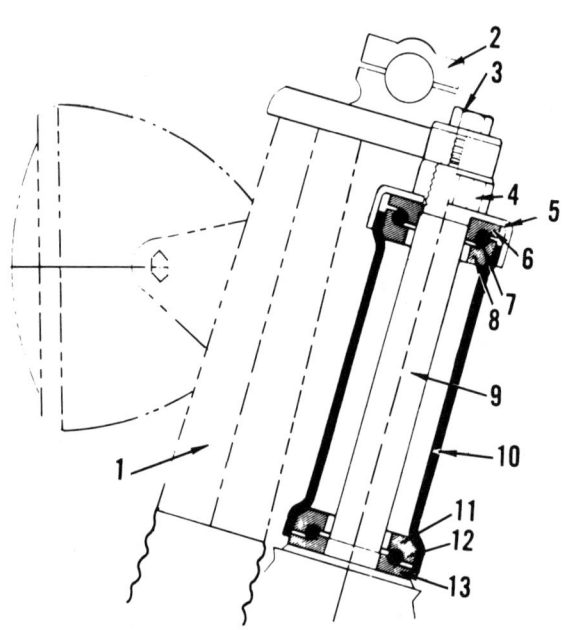

1. Fork cover
2. Handlebar holder
3. Head bolt
4. Locknut
5. Cap
6. Upper bearing
7. Steel ball
8. Bearing race
9. Steering shaft
10. Frame head pipe
11. Bearing race
12. Steel ball
13. Lower bearing cone

Assembly

1. Press in the upper and lower races.

2. Grease balls liberally, then attach them to the upper and lower races, as shown in **Figure 70**.

3. Insert the underbracket shaft from below, install the upper bearing race and temporarily tighten the locknut.

4. Turn the underbracket to the left and right and as you do so, tighten the locknut until the underbracket turns smoothly, with no looseness or binding.

5. Install the steering stem head.

6. Install the front forks.

7. Recheck the adjustment of the locknut by grasping the tips of the forks and checking for any play.

SHOCK ABSORBERS

Figure 71 is a sectional view of a typical rear shock absorber. The major parts of the shock absorber are a spring and a hydraulic damping mechanism encased within the inner and outer shells. The shock absorbers may be adjusted to suit various riding conditions, as shown in **Figure 72**. Adjust both sides equally.

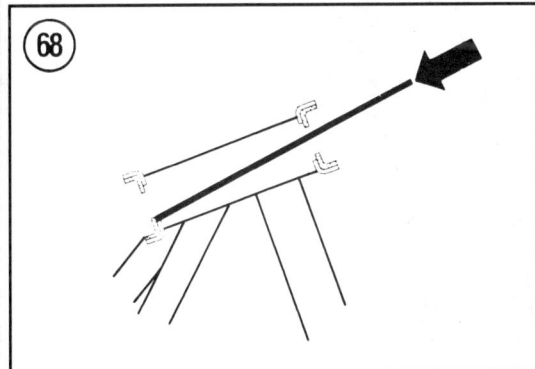

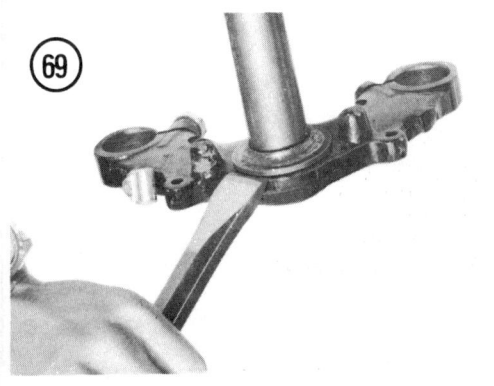

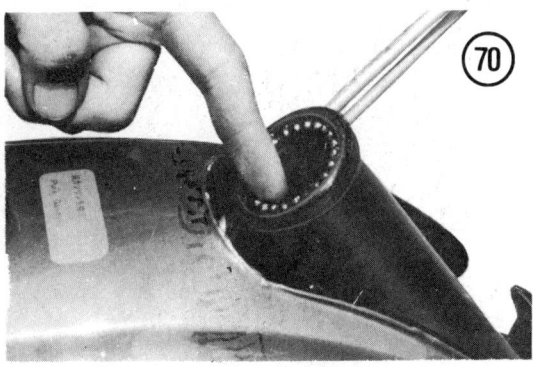

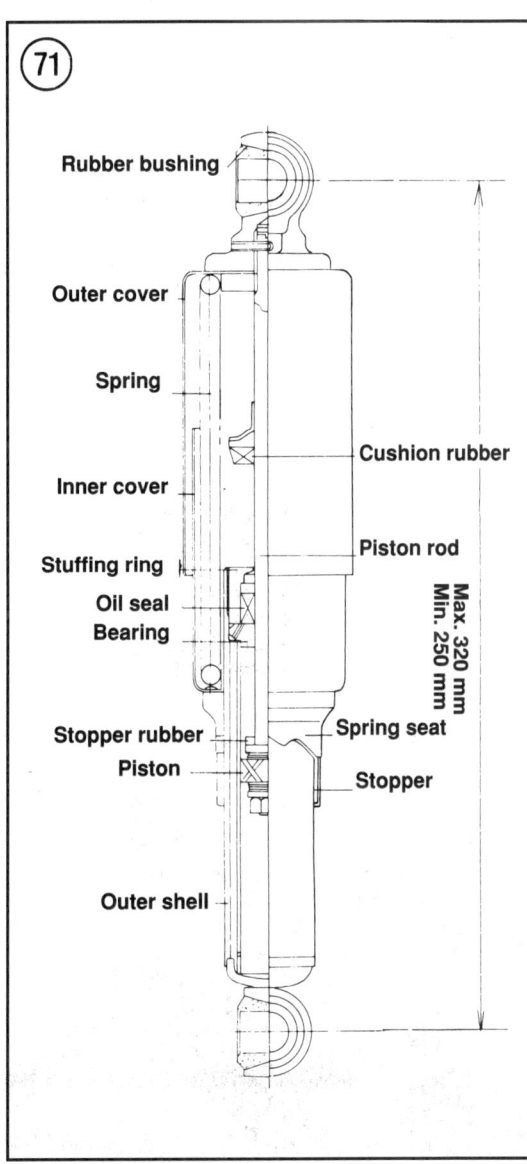

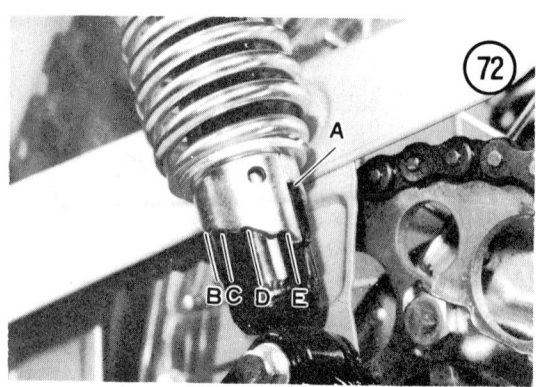

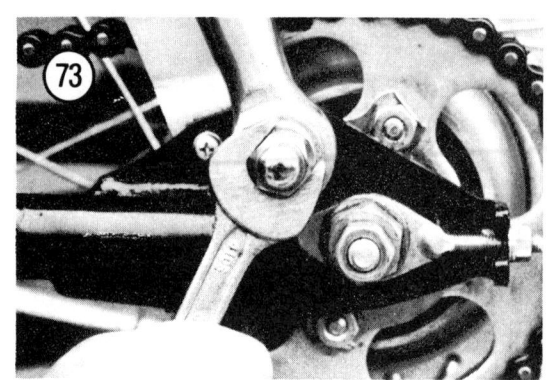

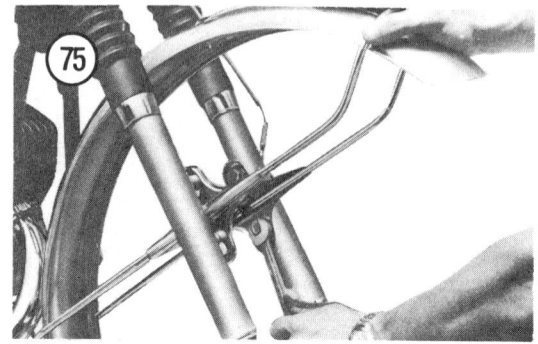

72
A
B
C
D
E

73

74
Brace
Front fender
Rear fender
Supporter
Bracket
Front fender stay

75

76

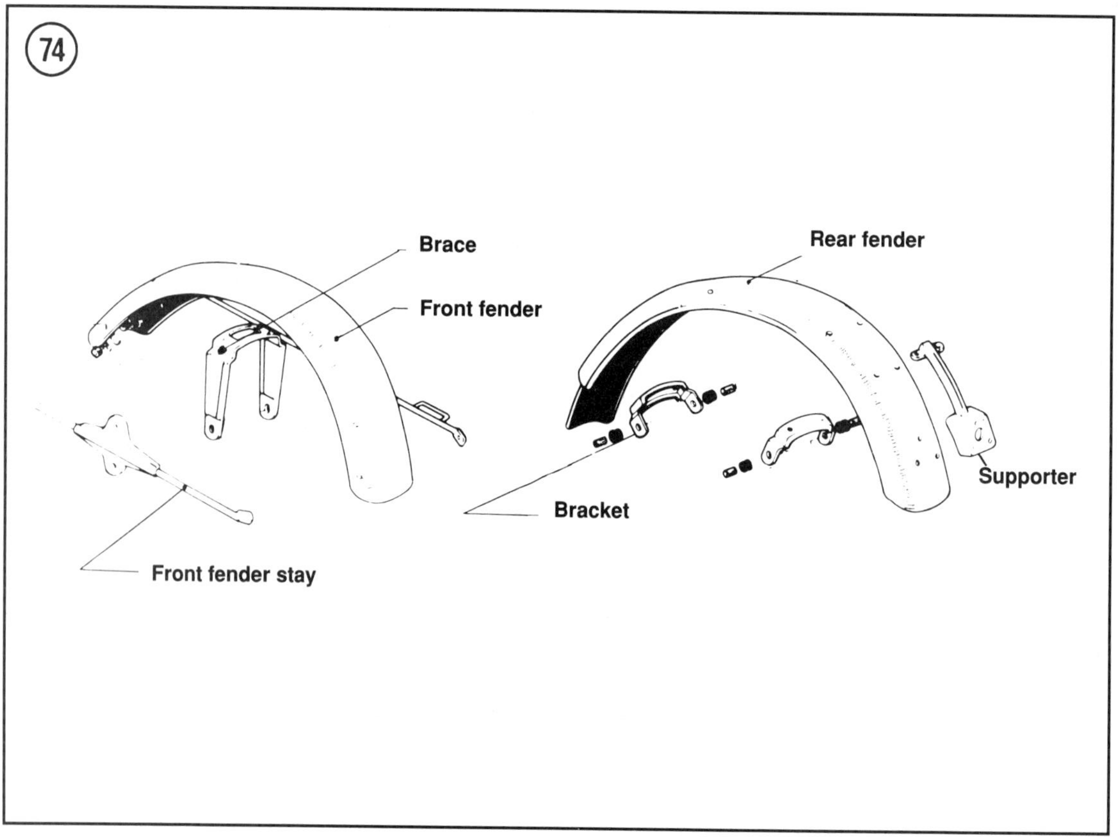

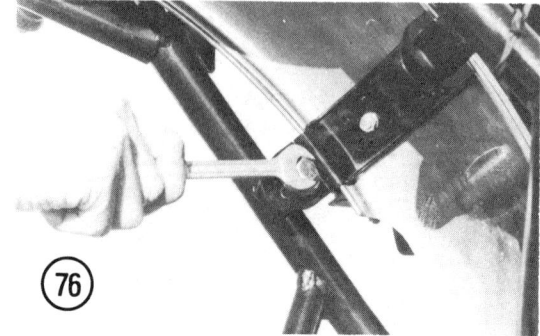

To remove the shock absorbers, remove the mounting bolts. Do not damage the rubber bushings as you remove and replace the bolts. See **Figure 73**.

Check the damping force by attempting to compress and extend the units quickly. If there is no marked difference between the effort required to operate the unit quickly or slowly, or if there are any oil leaks, replace the shock absorber.

FENDERS

Figure 74 illustrates typical fenders and their attaching hardware. Fenders on some models are of aluminum. Front and rear fenders may be taken off easily after the wheels are removed, merely by removing their attaching hardware (**Figure 75** and **Figure 76**).

SWINGING ARM

Figure 77 illustrates a typical swinging arm assembly. The entire assembly pivots up and down on the pivot shaft. The rear part of the swinging arm is attached to the motorcycle frame through the shock absorbers.

Disassembly

1. Remove the drive chain.
2. Remove the rear sprocket (**Figure 78**).
3. Remove the pivot shaft (**Figure 79**).

SWINGING ARM

Pivot shaft

Cap

O-ring

Sleeve

Sleeve

Swinging arm

Bushing

O-ring

Chain adjuster

Adjuster bolt

Torque link

7

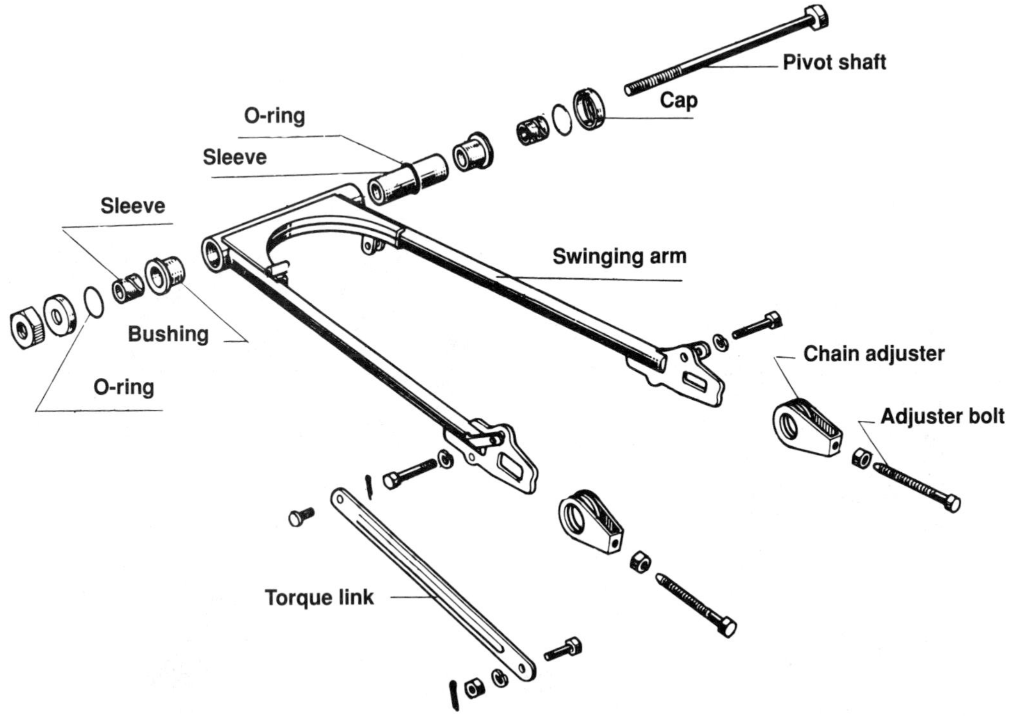

4. Remove the swinging arm (**Figure 80**).

Inspection

The pivot section is susceptible to wear, especially in the bushings and shaft. Examine these parts carefully. Replace the pivot shaft if it is bent more than 0.02 in. (0.5 mm). Replace the bushings and/or the shaft if the clearance between the shaft and the bushings exceeds 0.014 in. (0.35 mm). Shimmy, wander and wheel hop are common symptoms of worn swinging arm bushings. If either of the arms is bent, the rear wheel will be out of alignment. Examine the weld carefully. Replace the entire swinging arm assembly if the weld is cracked.

REAR SPROCKET

To remove the rear sprocket, use a hammer and chisel (**Figure 81**). To remove the lockwashers, then remove the nuts which attach the sprocket to the sprocket coupling.

Any bending of the sprocket will make drive chain adjustment difficult and may result in chain breakage. To check for bending, place the sprocket on a flat surface, then check the gap between the surface and the sprocket. Replace the sprocket if the gap exceeds 0.02 in. (0.5 mm) at any point.

The drive chain may slip from the sprocket if the sprocket is worn noticeably (**Figure 82**).

FUEL AND OIL TANK

Figure 83 illustrates a typical fuel tank. The tank is made from corrosion-resistant steel. A fuel cock is attached to the lower portion of the tank so that the fuel may be shut off when the machine is not running. Some models are equipped with an automatic fuel cock.

Fuel Tank Removal

> *WARNING*
> *These operations, or any other operations which may result in spilled gasoline, are potentially hazardous. Do not smoke or permit any sparks or open flame within 50 feet of work area.*

1. Turn the fuel cock to "O" (STOP). On models F5 and F7, turn the cock to ON or RES.

2. Remove the nut from the front of the tank (**Figure 84**).

3. Remove the strap from the rear of the tank (**Figure 85**).

4. Disconnect the fuel line from the fuel cock.

5. Lift the tank from the machine.

Fuel Cock

Figure 86 is a sectional view of a typical fuel cock. During normal running, fuel is drawn from the main standpipe within the fuel tank, which permits fuel to flow only as long as the fuel level remains about the top of the standpipe. Reserve fuel is supplied from the auxiliary standpipe.

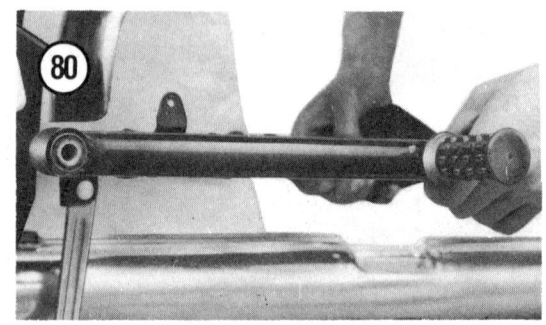

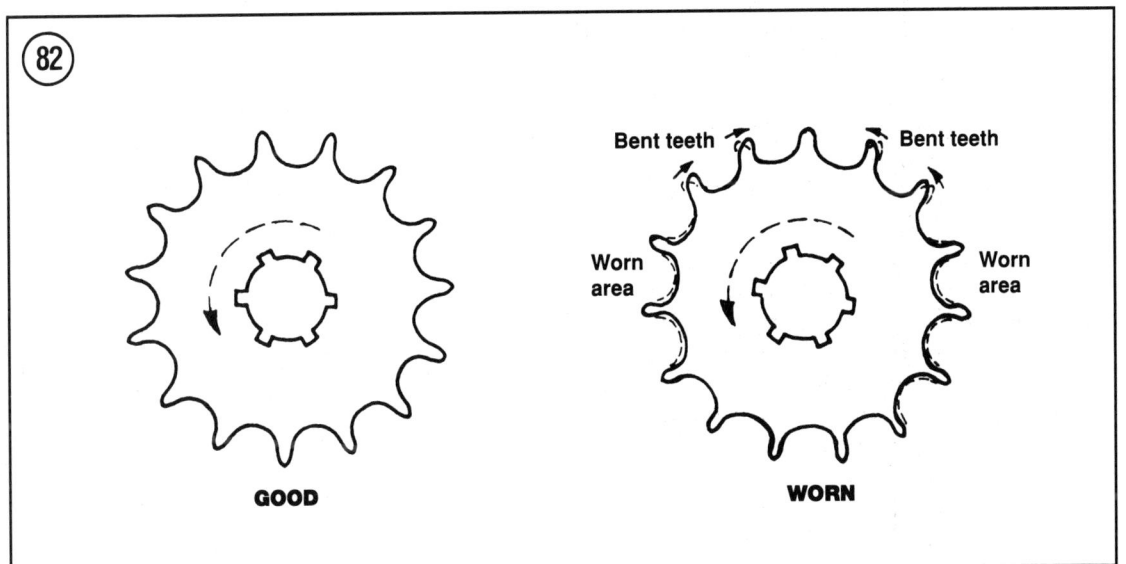

Bent teeth   Bent teeth

Worn
area

Worn
area

GOOD   **WORN**

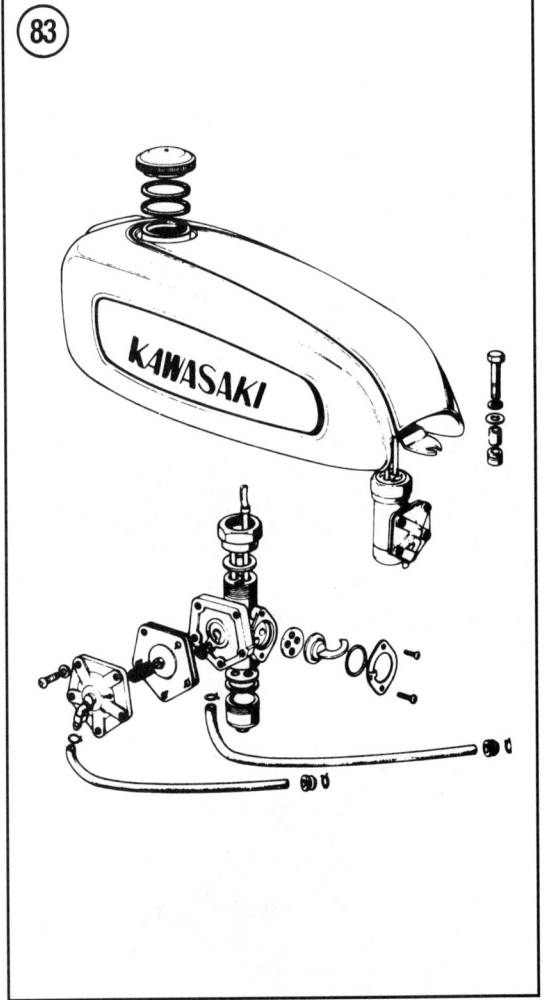

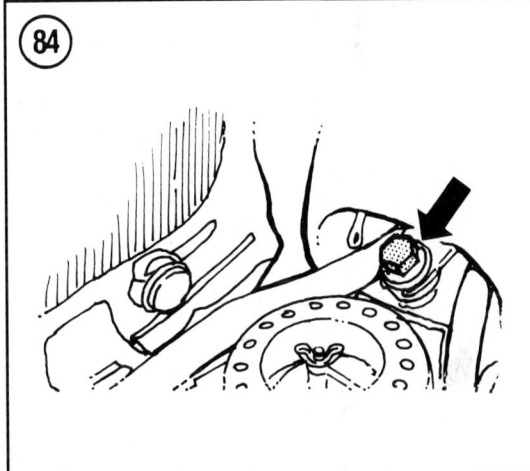

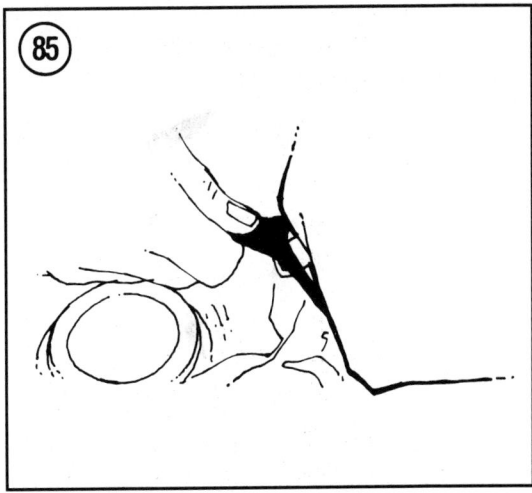

7

Inspect the fuel cock for leakage. Remove and clean the sediment bowl occasionally. Clean the fuel cock by blowing compressed air through it.

Automatic Fuel Cock

Models F5 and F7 are equipped with an automatic fuelcock (**Figure 87**). Negative pressure, developed in the carburetor when the engine is running, is transmitted through a tube to a diaphragm-actuated valve within the assembly.

If the fuel cock leaks, remove the diaphragm cover and diaphragm, then clean the valve and seat. Be sure to assemble the valve correctly (**Figure 88**), with the vent holes aligned. Also, be sure that there are no leaks in the signal tube from the carburetor to the fuel cock. Air leaks will result in poor fuel flow.

Oil Tank

The oil tank (**Figure 89**) is below the seat, on the right side of the machine. Service to the oil tank is limited to occasional cleaning. Remember to bleed oil pump after you clean the tank.

SEAT

Figure 90 illustrates a typical seat and its attaching hardware. To remove the seat, remove the attaching hardware, as shown in **Figure 91** and **Figure 92**

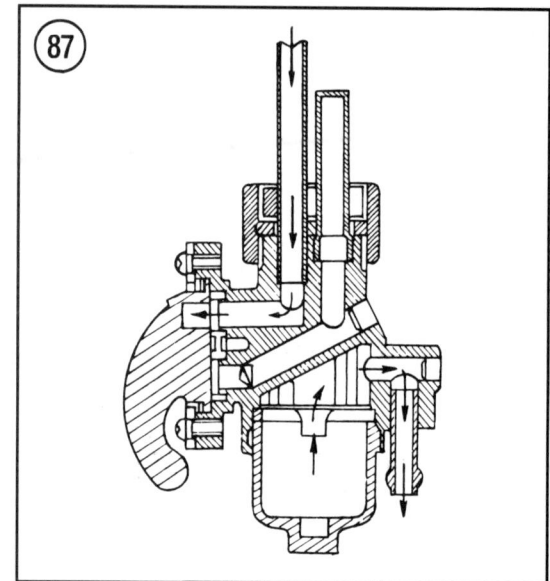

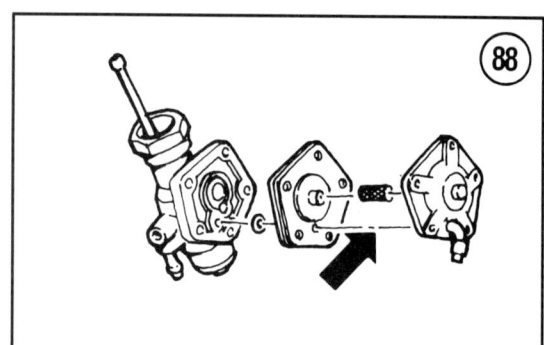

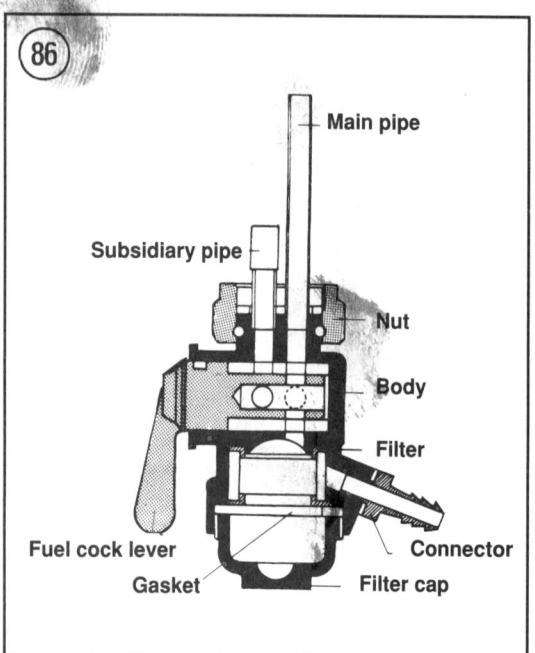

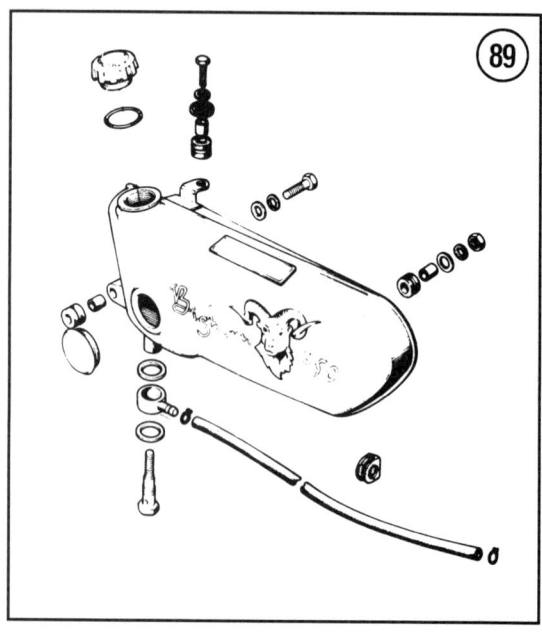

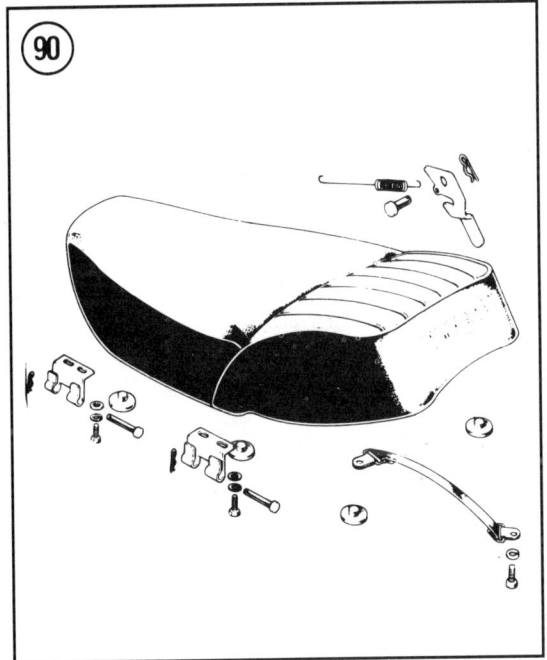

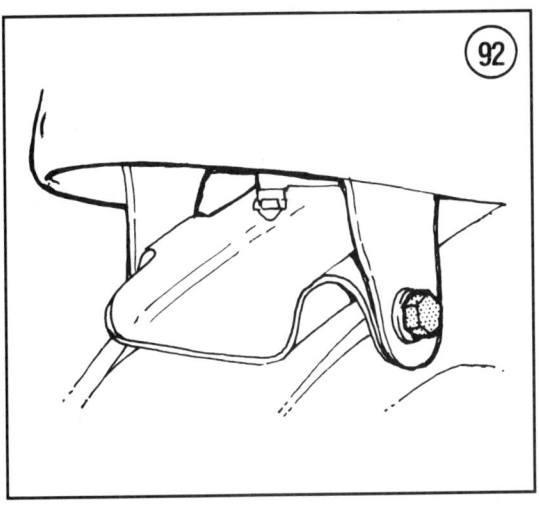

STANDS AND FOOTRESTS

These machines are equipped with various types of stands. Some models have both a center stand and a side, or kickstand (**Figure 93**). Models G4TR, F5, F6, F7 and F8 have only the side stand. Models G31M and F81M are equipped with only a portable stand which is not attached to the frame.

To remove the center stand (**Figure 94**), pull out the cotter pin, pull out the shaft, then remove the spring. To remove the side stand (**Figure 95**), remove the spring, then the attaching bolt.

EXHAUST PIPE AND MUFFLER

Disassembly

On models G31M-A, G4TR and F series, remove the mounting bolts at the rear of the muffler (**Figure 96**), then remove the hook springs (**Figure 97**) which attach the exhaust pipe to the cylinder flange.

Muffler and exhaust pipe removal is accomplished on models G3SS-A and G3TR-A by first removing the cylinder flange (**Figure 98**) and the clamp where the exhaust pipe enters the muffler. Remove the exhaust pipe. The muffler may then be removed by removing the front and rear attaching bolts (**Figure 99**).

To remove the baffle tube, remove the screw at the back of the muffler (**Figure 100**), then pull out the baffle tube (**Figure 101**).

Inspection

Carbon deposits within the exhaust pipe and muffler cause the engine to lose power. Clean carbon from the baffle tube with a wire brush. If the deposits are too heavy to remove with a brush, heat baffle tube with a torch (**Figure 102**) and tap the tube lightly. Clean the carbon from the exhaust pipe by running a used drive chain through the pipe.

As the machine ages, the joint between the exhaust pipe and muffler may leak. Replace the rubber connector if leakage occurs. Always use new gaskets upon reassembly.

DRIVE CHAIN

The drive chain (**Figure 103**) becomes worn after prolonged use. Wear in the pins, bushings and rollers

7

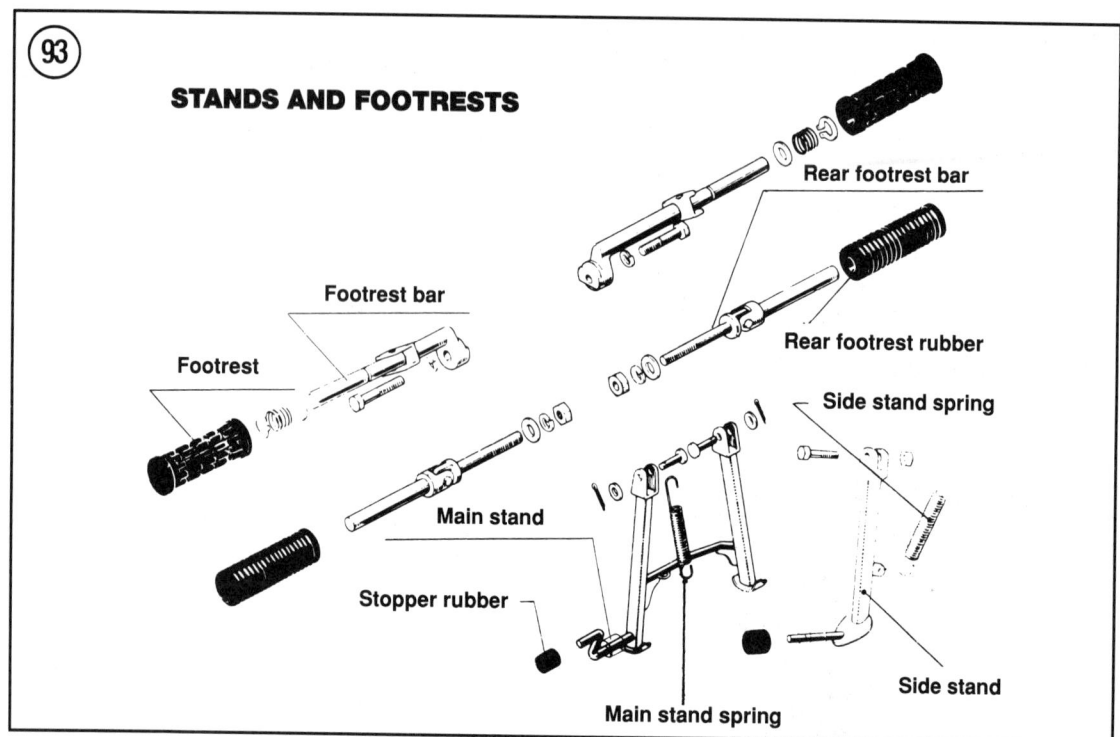

STANDS AND FOOTRESTS

Rear footrest bar

Footrest bar

Footrest

Rear footrest rubber

Side stand spring

Main stand

Stopper rubber

Side stand

Main stand spring

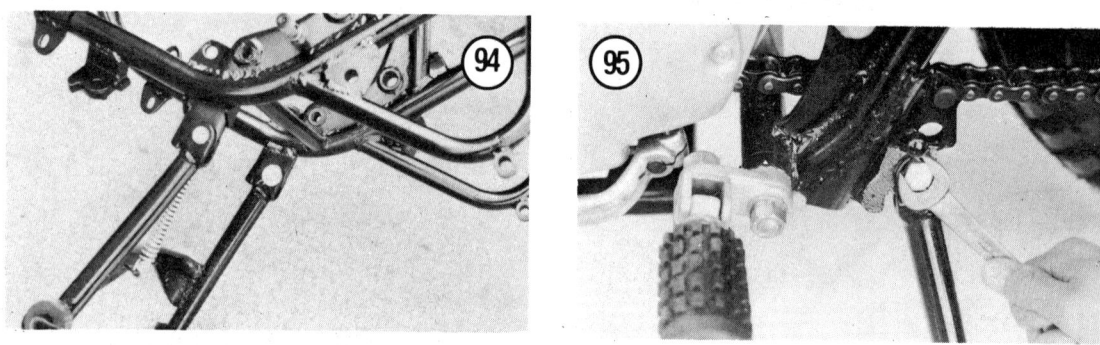

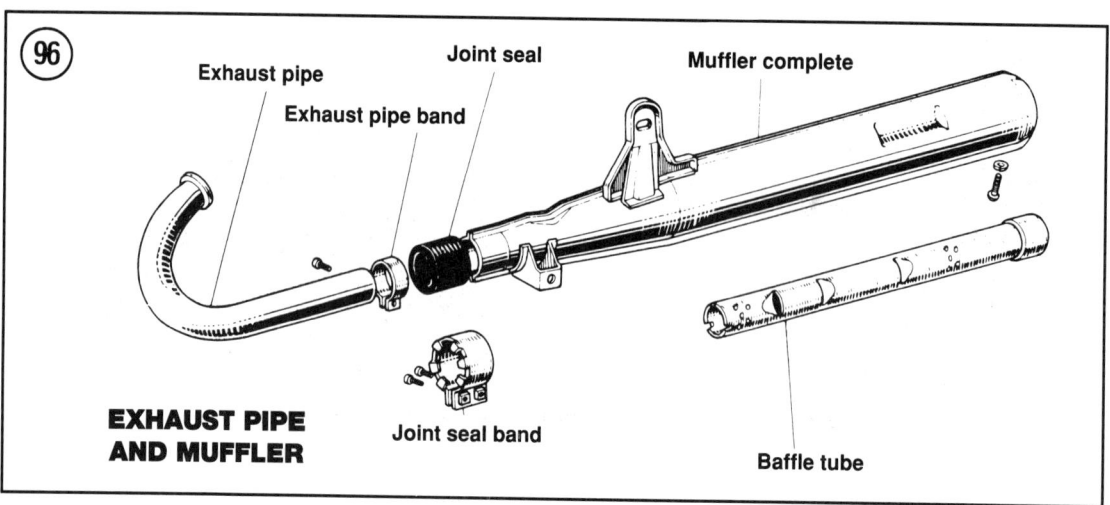

EXHAUST PIPE AND MUFFLER

Exhaust pipe

Joint seal

Muffler complete

Exhaust pipe band

Joint seal band

Baffle tube

causes the chain to stretch. Sliding between the roller surface and sprocket teeth also contributes to wear.

Inspection

Inspect the drive chain periodically. Pay particular attention to cracks in the rollers and link plates and replace the chain if there is any doubt about its condition.

Adjust the free play in the chain so that there is one inch (25 mm) vertical play (**Figure 104**) in the center of the chain run with the machine on the ground. **Figure 105** illustrates the adjustment procedure. Be sure to adjust each side equally. The rear brake is affected by any chain adjustment. Be sure to adjust the rear brake after you adjust the chain (**Figure 106**).

If the chain has become so worn that adjustment is not possible, use a chain breaker (**Figure 107**) or chisel (**Figure 108**) to shorten the chain by one link.

Install the master link so that the clip opening faces opposite to the direction of chain movement (**Figure 109**). Failure to do so may result in loss of the clip and resultant chain breakage.

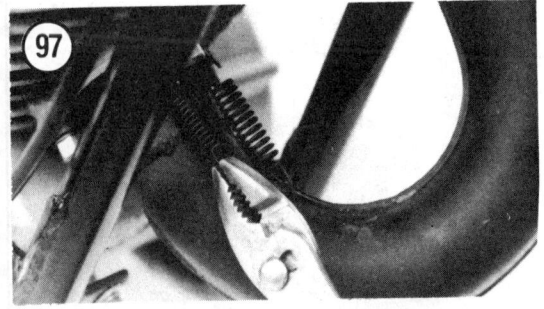

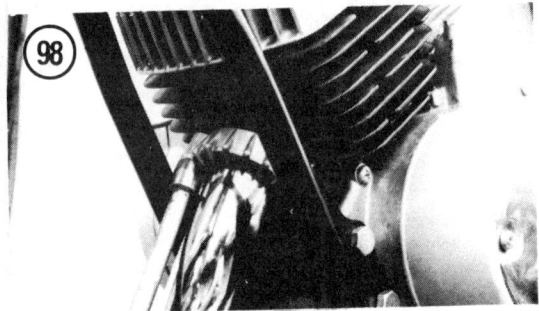

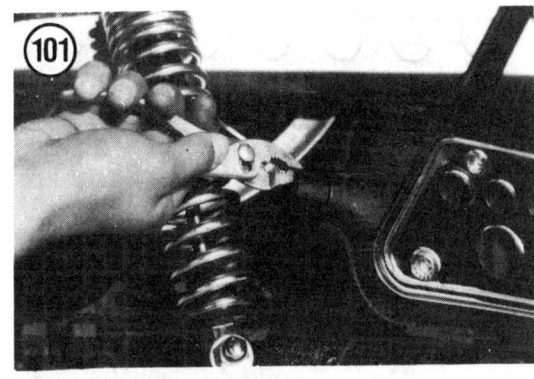

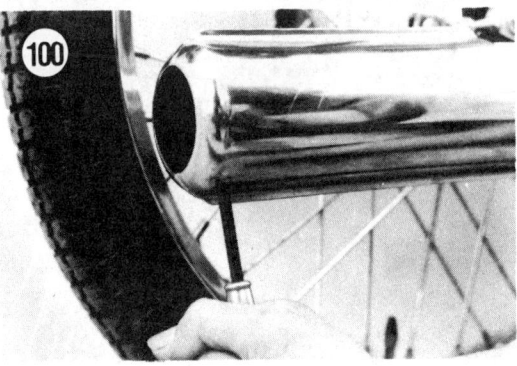

Figures 103-109 and Tables 1-6 are on the following pages.

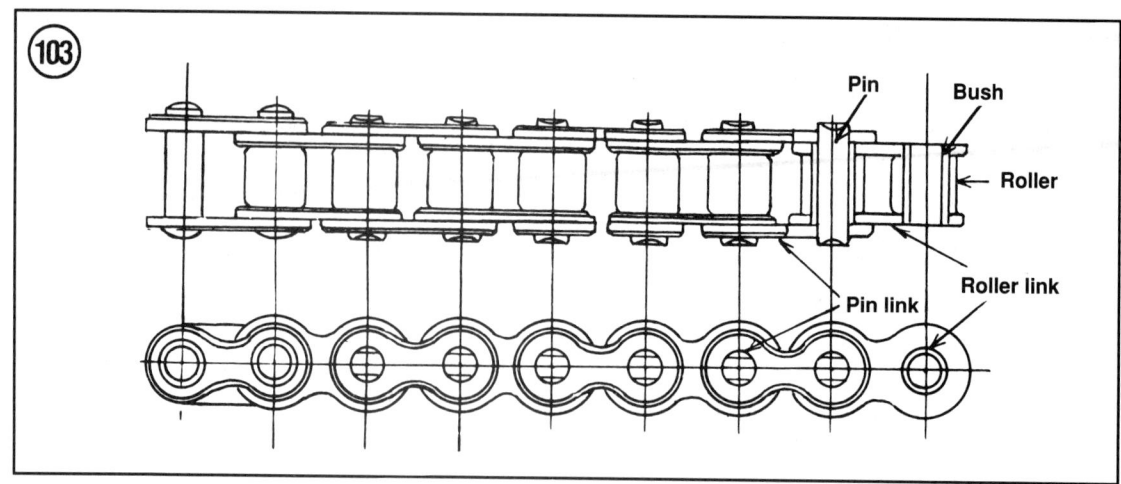

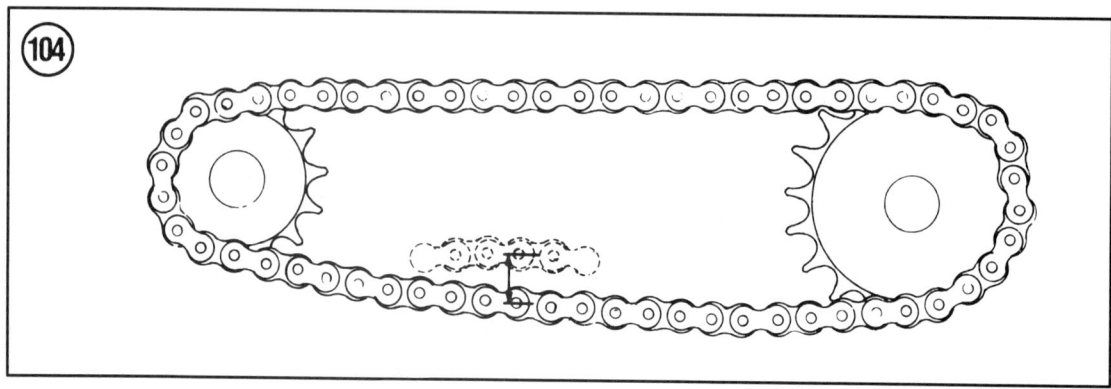

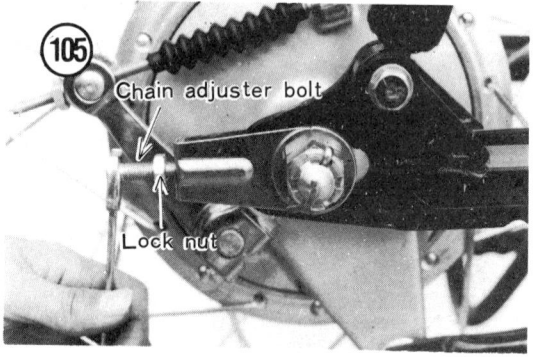

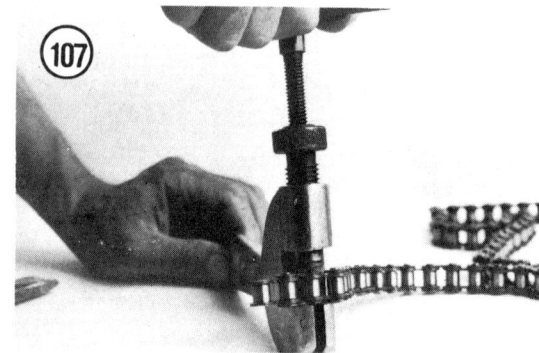

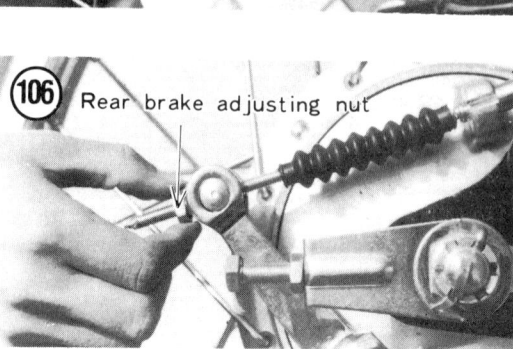

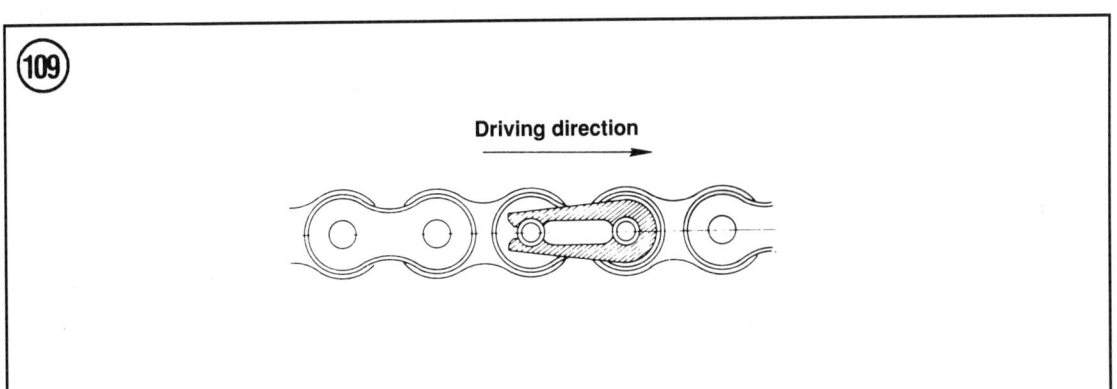

Driving direction

Table 1 TIRE SIZE AND INFLATION PRESSURE

79-100 cc models	Front	psi	Rear	psi
KD80 (1975, 1976 & 1980-1987)	2.50-16	18	2.75-14	18
J Series	2.50-17	22	2.50-17	28
MC1-A & MC1M	2.50-16	23	2.75-14	26
MC1-B	2.50-16	25	3.00-14	28
G3 models	2.50-18	23	2.75-18	28
D1	2.50-17	22	2.50-17	28
G4TR	3.00-18	25	3.00-18	25 (under 215 lb.) 32 (over 215 lb.)
G31M	3.25-18	–	3.25-18	–
G5	*2.75-19	25	3.00-18	25 (under 215 lb.) 32 (over 215 lb.)
KD100	2.25-18	18	2.75-14	18
KE100 (1976-1981)	2.75-19	25	3.00-18	25 (under 215 lb.) 32 (over 215 lb.)
KE100 B2 - B13 (1982-1994)	2.75-19	21	3.00-17	28 (under 215 lb.) 32 (over 215 lb.)
KH100	2.75-18	21	3.00-18	28 (under 215 lb.) 32 (over 215 lb.)
KM100	2.50-16	25	3.00-14	28
KV100	3.00-18	25	3.00-18	25 (under 215 lb.) 32 (over 215 lb.)
115-125 cc models	**Front**	**psi**	**Rear**	**psi**
C2SS	2.75-18	22	3.00-18	28
C2TR	3.00-18	22	3.00-18	28
F6	3.00-18	23	3.25-18	28
KD125	2.75-21	25	3.50-18	25
KE125	2.75-21	25	3.50-18	25
KS125	2.75-21	25	3.50-18	25
KX125 (1974-1976)	3.00-21	–	4.10-18	–
169-175 cc models	**Front**	**psi**	**Rear**	**psi**
F2	2.50-18	22	2.75-18	28
F2TR	2.75-18	22	3.00-18	28
F3	3.00-19	22	3.50-18	28
F7	3.00-19	23	3.50-18	23 (under 215 lb.) 28 (over 215 lb.)
KD175 (1976-1979)	2.75-21	18	3.50-18	18 (under 215 lb.) 21 (over 215 lb.)
KE175 (1976-1982)	2.75-21	25	3.50-18	25 (under 215 lb.) 28 (over 215 lb.)

(continued)

7

Table 1 TIRE SIZE AND INFLATION PRESSURE (continued)

238-350 cc models	Front	psi	Rear	psi
F4	3.25-19	24	4.00-18	31
F21M	3.50-19	–	4.00-18	–
F8	3.25-19	24	4.00-18	31
F81M	3.00-21	–	4.00-18	–
F5	3.00-21	24	4.00-18	28 (under 215 lb.)
				32 (over 215 lb.)
F9	3.00-21	24	4.00-18	28 (under 215 lb.)
				32 (over 215 lb.)

* Some early G5 models are equipped with 2.75-18 front tire.

Table 2 SHAFT AND LINK NUT TORQUES

	Front	Rear
Shaft nut	48-61 ft.-lb. (6.7-8.5 kg-m)	55-68 ft.-lb. (7.7-9.8 kg-m)
Torque link	8.5-11 ft.-lb. (1.2-1.5 kg-m)	16-22 ft.-lb. (2.2-3.1 kg-m)

Table 3 BRAKE RETURN SPRING WEAR LIMIT

Model	in.	mm
C2 Series, D1, J1, G3TR	1.30	33.0
F2, F3, F4	1.97	50.0
F21M		
Front	1.34	34.0
Rear	1.57	50.0
F5, F8, F81M, F9	2.01	51.0
F6, F7, G, M Series	1.34	34.0
KD/KE/KS/KX125		
Short	1.34	34.0
Long	1.89	48.0
KD/KE175		
Short	1.34	34.0
Long	1.89	48.0

Table 4 FORK SPRING MINIMUM FREE LENGTH

79-100 cc models	in.	mm
KD80 (1975, 1976 & 1980-1987)	13.3	338
J Series	5.0	127
MC1-A, MC1-B & MC1M	13.3	338
G3 models	6.1	154
D1	5.0	127
G4TR	11.7	296
G31M		
Short	13.2	336
Long	4.8	121
G5	15.6	395
KD100	13.3	338
KE100		
1976-1979 models	15.6	395
KE100 A9 - B13 (1980-1994)	15.8	402
KH100	15.6	395
KM100 (1976-1977)	13.3	338

(continued)

Table 4 FORK SPRING MINIMUM FREE LENGTH (continued)

KM100 (1978-on)	13.1	334
KV100	15.6	395
115-125 cc models	**in.**	**mm**
C2SS & C2TR	–	–
F6	18.9	480
KD125, KE125 & KS125		
Models with 1 spring	19.3	490
Models with 2 springs (1982 on)		
Upper	2.47	62.8
Lower	16.8	427
KX125 (1974-1976)		
Short	3.1	78
Long	15.9	405
169-175 cc models	**in.**	**mm**
F2 & F2TR	6.9	174
F3	6.7	170
F7		
Short	4.8	121
Long	13.2	336
KD175 (1976-1979)	18.7	475
KE175 (1976-1982)	18.7	475
238-350 cc models	**in.**	**mm**
F4	15.0	380
F21M	14.1	358
F8	18.3	464
F81M	18.3	464
F5	18.3	464
F9	18.3	464

Table 5 APPROXIMATE FORK OIL CAPACITY

79-100 cc models	**SAE Grade**	**oz.**	**cc**
KD80 (1975, 1976 & 1980-1987)	5W/20	3.1	95
J Series	5W/20	4.6	135
MC1-A models	5W/20	3.1	95
G3 models	30	4.4	130
D1	5W/20	4.6	135
G4TR	10W	5.7	174
G31M	20	5.8	170
G5	10W	5.7	174
KD100	5W/20	3.1	95
KE100 (1976-1978)	10W	5.7	174
395 mm from top			
KE100-A8 (1979)	10W	5.3-5.6	158-166
	Maintain oil 395 mm from top		
KE100 A9 - B13 (1980-1994)	10W/20	5.3-5.6	158-166
	Maintain oil 406.5-410.5 mm from top		
KH100	30	4.4	130
KM100	5W/20	3.1	95
KV100	10W	5.7	174

7

(continued)

Table 5 APPROXIMATE FORK OIL CAPACITY (continued)

115-125 cc models	SAE Grade	oz.	cc
C2SS & C2TR			
Early	5W/20	4.0	120
Late	5W/20	5.9	175
F6	10W	5.1	152
KD125	5W/20	5.1	150
KE125 (1976-1979)	5W/20	4.9-5.2	145-155
	Maintain oil 385-415 mm from top		
KE125-A7 & A8 (1980-1981)	5W/20	4.4-4.6	129.5-134.5
	Maintain oil 504-508 mm from top		
KE125-A9 through A12	5W/20	5.5-5.7	162.5-167.5
(1982-1985)	Maintain oil 421-425 mm from top		
KS125	5W/20	5.1	150
	Maintain oil 385-415 mm from top		
KX125 (1974-1976)	5W/20	5.2	153
	Maintain oil 390 mm from top		
169-175 cc models	**SAE Grade**	**oz.**	**cc**
F2 & F2TR	5W/20	5.9	175
F3	5W/20	5.9	175
F7	10W	3.9	115
KD175 (1976-1979)	10W	5.1	150
KE175 (1976-1982)	10W	5.1	150
238-350 cc models	**SAE Grade**	**oz.**	**cc**
F4	10W	6.6	195
F21M	5W/20	6.8	200
F8	10W	5.9	175
F81M	10W	5.9	175
F5	10W	5.9	175
F9	10W	5.9	175

Table 6 DRIVE CHAIN SPECIFICATIONS

79-100 cc models	Chain size	Links (approx.)
KD80 (1975, 1976 & 1980-1987)	428	98
J Series	420	102
MC1 & MC1M	428	96
G3SS	428	104
G3TR	428	106
D1	428	100
G4TR	428	110
G31M	428	–
G5	428	110
KD100	428	96
KE100	428	110
KH100	428	104
KM100-A1 & A2 (1976-1977)	428	96
KM100 A3 - A7 (1978-1981)	428	110
KV100	428	110
115-125 cc models	**Chain size**	**Links (approx.)**
C2SS & C2TR	428	–
F6	428	118
KD125	428	118
KE125	428	118
KS125	428	118
KX125 (1974-1976)	428	124

(continued)

Table 6 DRIVE CHAIN SPECIFICATIONS (continued)

169-175 cc models	Chain size	Links (approx.)
F2 & F2TR	428	–
F3	428	–
F7	428	114
KD175	428	120
KE175	428	120

238-350 cc models	Chain size	Links (approx.)
F4	525	96
F21M	428	118
F8	525	96
F81M	525	96
F5	525	94
F9	525	94

7

INDEX

B

Backfiring 16
Battery 187-189
   service 29
Brakes 207-208
   maintenance 30
   problems 16-17

C

Capacitor discharge ignition system
   operation 181-183
Carburetion operation 134-136
Carburetor
   adjustment 139-152
   components 152
   overhaul 136-139
   problems 152-159
Charging system test (1979 and later) 186
Clutch 53-66
   adjustment 30
Clutch slip or drag 16
Crankcase 69-77
Crankshaft 83-90
Cylinder and cylinder head 44-46

D

Drain pump 96-107
Drive chain 227-231
   maintenance 30

E

Electrical equipment 30
Engine
   cylinder and cylinder head 44-46
   flywheel magneto and starter-generator . . 49-50
   left crankcase cover 49
   lubrication 40-43

(Engine, continued)

Engine, continued
   noises 16
   piston, piston pin and piston rings 46-48
   preparation for disassembly 43
   primary drive gear 52-53
   removal 43-44
   right crankcase cover 51-52
   rotary valve 39-40
   sprocket 50-51
   tune-up 20-29
Exhaust pipe and muffler 227

F

Fenders 223
Flat spots 16
Flywheel magneto 171-174
   and starter-generator 49-50
Fork oil 31
Front forks 208-219
Fuel and oil tank 224-226

G

Gearshift mechanism 68-69

H

Handlebars 197-198
Handling, poor 16
High voltage cable 181
Horn 187

I

Idling, poor 15

K

Kickstarter 77-83

L

Left crankcase cover 49
Lighting problems 17
Lights 186-187

M

Magneto troubleshooting 174
Main switch 187
Maintenance
   battery service 29
   brakes 30
   clutch adjustment 30
   drive chain 30
   electrical equipment 30
   engine tune-up 20-29
   fork oil 31
   racing 19
   regular 19
   steering head bearings 31
   swinging arm 31
   transmission 30
   wheels and tires 31
Mechanic's tips 4-5
Misfiring 16

O

Operating requirements 14-15
Overheating 16

P

Piston, piston pin and piston rings 46-48
Piston seizure 16
Power loss 16
Preparation for engine disassembly 43
Primary drive gear 52-53

R

Rear sprocket 224
Rectifier 180-181
Right crankcase cover 51-52
Rotary valve 66-68
Rotary valve engines 39-40

S

Safety 5-7
Seat 226
Service hints 1-2
Shock absorbers 221-223
Solid state regulator/rectifier
   (1979 and later) 183-186
Solid state voltage regulator 183
Stands and footrests 227
Starter-generator 174-178
   troubleshooting 178-180
Starting difficulties 15
Steering head bearings maintenance 31
Steering system 219-221
Supplies, expendable 4
Swinging arm 223-224
   maintenance 31

T

Tools 3-4
Transmission 90-96
   maintenance 30
Troubleshooting guide 17

V

Vibration, excessive 16

W

Wheels and tires 199-207
   maintenance 31
Wiring diagrams 238-242

8

1982-1992 KE100 (U.K., GENERAL MODELS)

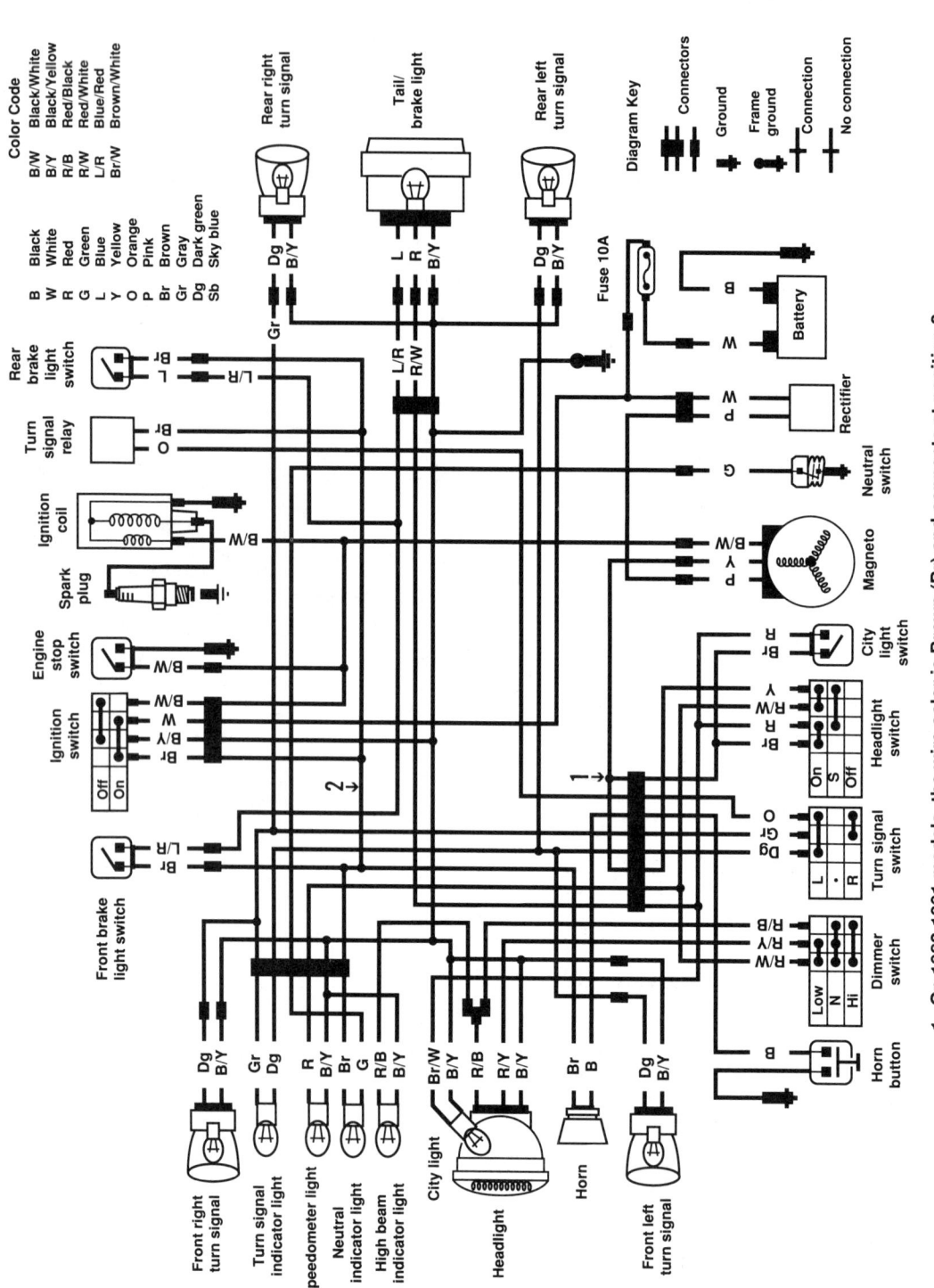

1976-1982 KE125 (U.S. MODEL)

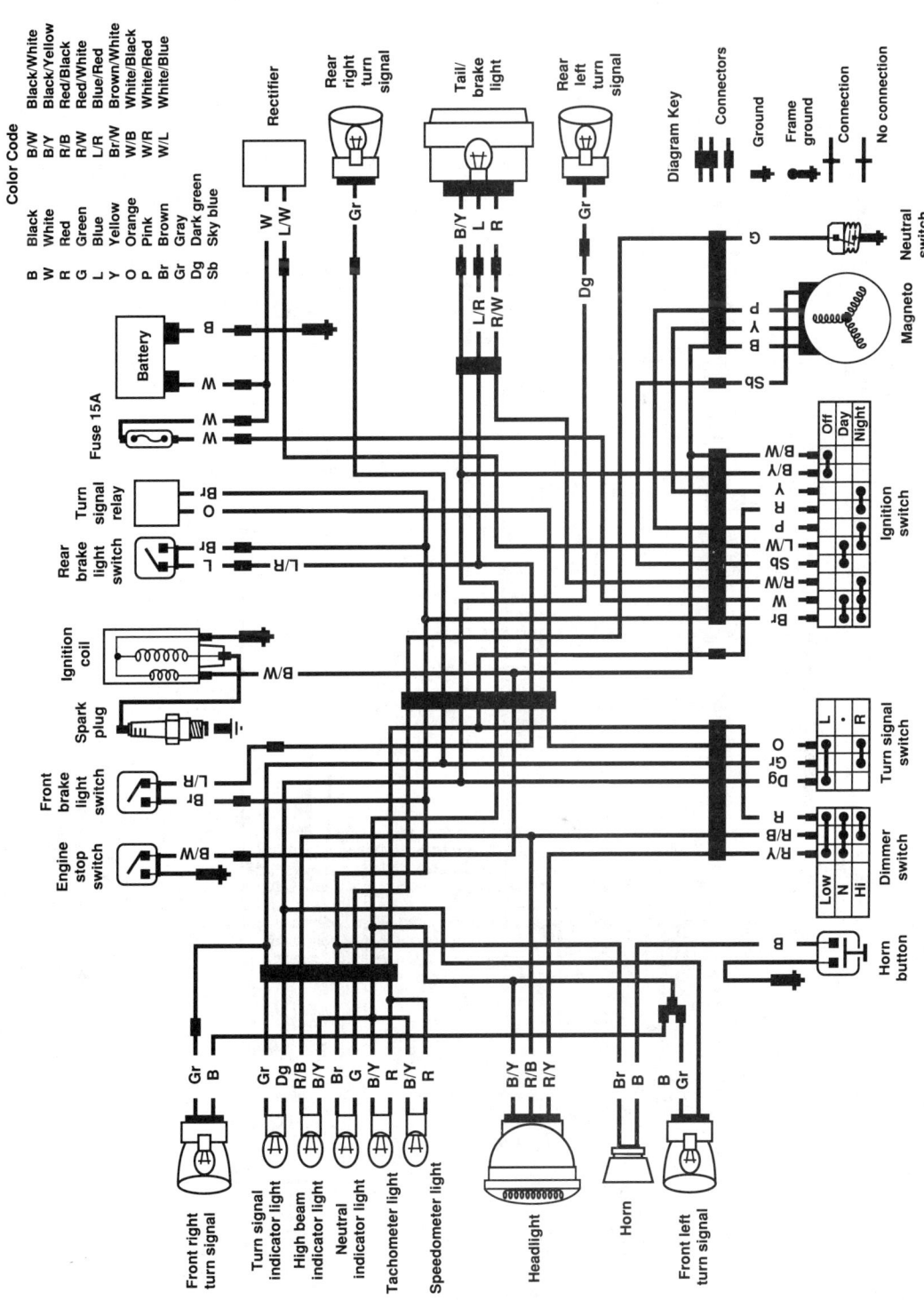

1979-1981 KE100

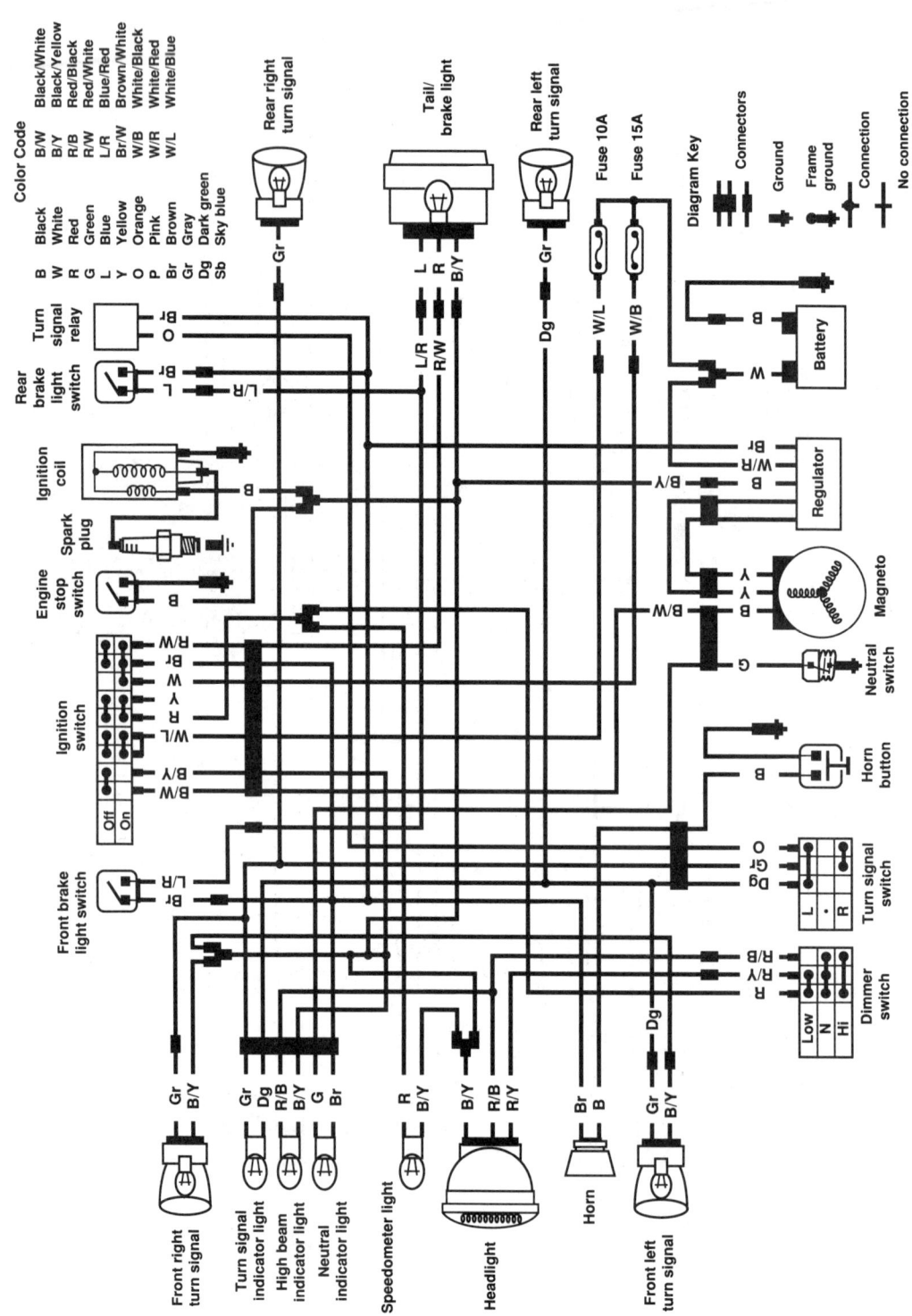

1982-1994 KE100 (U.S. AND CANADIAN MODELS)

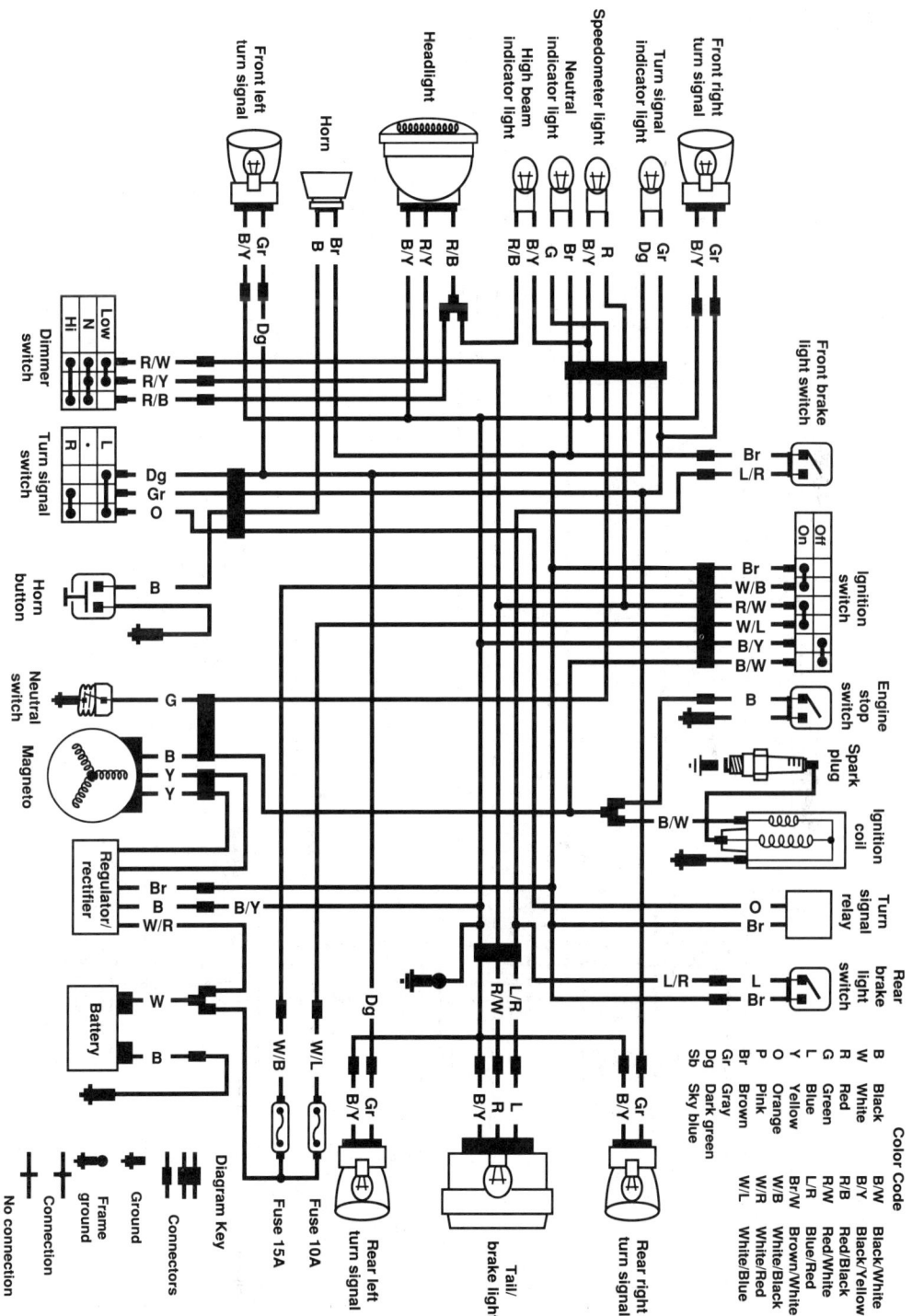

8

MAINTENANCE LOG

Service Performed   **Mileage Reading**

Service Performed	Mileage Reading				
Oil change (example)	2,836	5,782	8,601		
~~10w-30~~ ~~oil change~~					
oil change	2-9-98	10w-30			